DATE DUE

CHINA'S DEMOCRATIC FUTURE

CHINA'S

DEMOCRATIC FUTURE

How It Will Happen and Where It Will Lead

BRUCE GILLEY

Columbia University Press   New York

9325837

Columbia University Press
Publishers Since 1893
New York, Chichester, West Sussex
Copyright © 2004 Columbia University Press
All rights Reserved

Library of Congress Cataloging-in-Publication Data

Gilley, Bruce, 1966–
    China's democratic future : how it will happen and
    where it will lead / Bruce Gilley.
        p. cm.
    Includes bibliographical references and index.
    ISBN 0-231-13084-8 (cloth. : alk. paper)
        1. Democracy—China.   2. China—Politics and
    government—1976–   I. Title.
    JQ1516.G55   2004
    320.951—dc22   2003061124

Columbia University Press books are printed on permanent
and durable acid-free paper
Printed in the United States of America

c 10 9 8 7 6 5 4 3 2 1

References to Internet Web Sites (URLs) were accurate at
the time of writing. Neither the author nor Columbia University Press is responsible for Web sites that may have ex-
pired or changed since the articles were prepared

To the memory of John Rawls,
whose purity of heart inspired this book.

Contents

Introduction

The derrick is positioned just below the rostrum of the Gate of Heavenly Peace in central Beijing. It is a brilliant autumn day. The hydraulic arm and the cables have been secured and checked by the 20-man crew. Crowds stand in awe in the vast Tiananmen Square below, as if they are about to witness a religious event.

At 10 AM sharp, the signal is given and, accompanied by the barking orders of a foreman, a one-ton, 21 foot by 16 foot glass fiber-reinforced plastic painting begins its descent from the rostrum face. It has been quite some years since Mao Zedong stood here before 300,000 people on October 1, 1949 and announced the founding of the People's Republic of China. Now his portrait, hung hastily just a few hours before the founding ceremony, is being removed. China's Communist Party has fallen from power and Mao's portrait is an anachronism.

Mao's face seems to wince with each jerk of the cables as the portrait descends. There is an apprehension in the crowd, as if the profanation of the sacred object might unleash violence from the heavens. But there are no earthquakes, no fireballs. With Mao's enigmatic smile secured in the back of a flatbed truck, the crowd disperses with little fanfare. In a few days time, Mao's tomb in the center of the square will be removed to a museum in his hometown far away in Hunan province. Another dynasty has come and gone.

It has been a month since a group of reformers in the senior ranks of the Chinese Communist Party (CCP) seized power and declared plans to introduce democratic elections, and events have been unfolding quickly. A national constitutional convention is planned for November where more than 5,000 delegates appointed by the interim leadership will attempt to point their country in the direction of a functioning democracy. The Great Hall of the People is buzzing with preparations for the meeting. Across the Avenue of Eternal Peace, the CCP's vacated Zhongnanhai leadership complex has been opened to the public, which throngs through its lakes and villas in fascination.

The end of communist rule and the embrace of democracy in China will be one of the most important events of the twenty-first century. It will mark for the world the virtual end of a remarkable yet tragic experiment in utopianism known as Marxist-Leninism. It will also represent for a fifth of mankind, the largest part of that still not living under democracy, the beginning of the long road to freedom.

Since coming to power in 1949, the CCP has turned China from a poor and benighted nation into a moderately well-off and increasingly influential one. Yet the CCP has failed to keep pace with the changes that have overcome Chinese society since agreeing to step aside from its daily life in the late 1970s. It remains a singular fact that the world's biggest and one of its most dynamic and culturally rich societies continues to be ruled by a corrupt and repressive dictatorship. Yet the balance of power for and against the CCP has shifted. This shift will likely bring an end to its rule in the early decades of this century, and an end to Mao's vigil on the Gate of Heavenly Peace.

This book is an attempt to peer into the future of China's pending constitutional transition. It is not my intention here to make blithe assertions that all is well, or will be, with the democratic project in China. That project, although faultless in appeal, is beset with difficulties in practice. But it is my intention to show that in the early twenty-first century, after nearly a hundred years of frustrating and tragic attempts to create a workable political system following the overthrow of the last dynasty, the Qing, the prospects for the creation and maintenance of a democracy in China are now better than ever. We can already envision how it will happen and where it will lead.

This book, then, offers hope to a nation still reeling from trauma of the 1989 Tiananmen Massacre. It challenges the resignation and disillusion that have gripped public life in China, noting the objective conditions that now favor a democratic transition.

The book is divided into three parts. The first part deals with the crisis of the communist state. After a brief summary of thematic (ch. 1) and historical (ch. 2) issues, we turn to the conditions that, I believe, will lead to the replacement of the CCP regime by a democratic government. We look at the broad outlines of this long-term process, followed by a *tour d'horizon* of the demands for a new system (ch. 3) and the growing ability of Chinese society to bring one about (ch. 4).

I do not, in this forward-looking narrative, attempt to guess which long-term factors will prove singularly decisive. Most scholars writing on China point to the growing pluralization of social interests, political corruption, and international norms as critical. This is a reasonable view. But like all advance looks at history it will no doubt be challenged after the fact by revisionists who point to less well-known issues like historical memory, growing notions of justice, and regional fragmentation. To preempt those debates I adopt an all-inclusive approach here. I am less interested in staking my claim on why democratic transition will happen than on how.

In the second part, I deal with the short-term process of democratic transition, essentially how the CCP will be removed from power and the existing political system replaced by a broadly democratic one. I draw heavily here on comparisons with such transitions during the so-called Third Wave of democratization from the early 1980s to the late 1990s, which included southern and eastern Europe, Latin America, Southeast Asia and, importantly, Taiwan and South Korea. I first examine (ch. 5) the short-term economic and political crisis that I believe will form the backdrop of transition in China. The dangers and implications of this period are considered. I then consider (ch. 6) how the CCP will fall, predicting an elite-led transformation rather than a popular-led overthrow. The key actors in this process and their calculations are examined in detail. Finally (ch. 7), I look at the immediate aftermath of a democratic breakthrough, the response of society and excluded elites, like the military, as well as interested parties such as Taiwan and Tibet.

It is impossible to hazard a guess as to the time when the long-awaited democratic breakthrough will occur in China. It could happen tomorrow or it could take a decade or more. History is replete with examples of nondemocratic regimes that survived well beyond the point where they lacked a minimal degree of legitimacy and where society was in a position to bring about change. The death-bed survival of such regimes owes mainly to contingent factors of happenstance, personality, sudden choices, grave uncertainty, and plain bad luck. In such situations, blithering attempts to allay or repress the forces of political change may appear as signs of the regime's health. Czarist Russia lived on for more than 60 years after its defeat in the Crimean War of 1855 despite having lost both legitimacy and strength. The same goes for the Qing dynasty after its setback in the first Opium War of 1839. Only in retrospect did it become clear how debased those regimes had become.

In our age, in which democratic norms are universally accepted and authoritarian regimes struggle unsuccessfully to disempower societies strengthened by globalization, the time span from delegitimization and disempowerment to replacement is typically shorter. South Africa's racist apartheid regime lasted only a decade from the onset of mass unrest and international economic sanctions in the early 1980s. Communist regimes in Eastern Europe survived only a few years after the withdrawal of Soviet backing in 1988.

In China, the successful military crushing of the Tiananmen Movement in 1989 led many to believe that the factors favoring a democratic transition were hopelessly weak. But the extreme contingency of that event counsels circumspection. Today, there is even less reason to doubt China's democratic potential. Not only has the regime's legitimacy declined, but also society is much stronger than it was in 1989. The balance has shifted decisively against the regime's ability to survive. Even so, the lag between that change and the actual transition may be a decade or more. Large countries in particular—Czarist and then communist Russia, Suharto's Indonesia—have typically suffered longer under debilitated authoritarian regimes. It is entirely possible that the CCP will limp along through the first and even second decades of this century. But in the great sweep of history, that will matter little to its ultimate fate.

The third and final part of the book deals with the building of a workable democracy in China, often called the consolidation phase. Since the democratic project is never finished in any country, this must remain an open-ended analysis. I first (ch. 8) consider the central political issues of constitutional design, elections, the threats to democracy from illiberalism and authoritarianism, secession, and much else. The predictions here include not inconsiderable or infrequent violence, political instability, and violations of democratic norms. However, democratic failure is considered unlikely. I also discuss how democracy in China will be very "Chinese," even though it retains universal fundamental features, just as every democracy is deeply colored by the culture in which it operates.

I then (ch. 9) deal with the competing interests—regional, sectoral, and class—of China's economy and society under democracy, addressing the pressing concerns of world business about that day and considering the important issue of historical reconciliation. Finally (ch. 10), I deal with the range of diplomatic and international issues surrounding the new democracy, especially drawing attention to the implications for Asia and the role of the United States. While China will be able to integrate more fully into the community of nations as a democracy, it will continue to pursue a foreign policy that on important issues of global security, trade policy, and cultural protection will continue to irk many in the West.

I hope that each part of this book fills a useful role in the existing literature on democracy in China. While much has been written on various factors favoring (or discouraging) democracy in China, I intend the first part to serve as a more broad and organic survey than has been written. The second and third parts venture into less familiar terrain. While some broad-brush sketches have been attempted, few if any works present detailed expositions of the likely course of democratic transition and consolidation in China. Overall, I hope this book brings under one roof the various issues relevant to China's democratic future. My aim is to provoke as well as inform, so that my readers will not have to slash their way through dense thickets of statistics or scale daunting walls of theory.

The lack of serious treatment of regime change in China is puzzling given the importance of the country and the evidence of such change elsewhere. One reason is that many scholars and observers simply believe that this scenario is unlikely, that China will be one of the great exceptions to the global trend of democratization. They favor predictions of a maintenance of the present system or a slow transition to some new form of political system. Those who share my belief in the likelihood of a bounded and decisive democratic transition, meanwhile, are understandably reluctant to engage in detailed prediction. For some, it is because such transitions are among the most contingent and therefore unpredictable events in politics. For others, self-censorship may play a role.

Yet this issue is too important to ignore. China is a huge physical, strategic, economic and demographic presence in the world. It will account for 20 percent of world GDP by 2020, and hold steady at a fifth of the world's population. It has 30 long-range nuclear missiles, an arsenal that will rise to 100 by 2015. The fall-out from a botched transition from CCP rule could be catastrophic—recalling former U.S. President Bill Clinton's warning of "a vast region of instability," in Asia caused by China's collapse. Diplomatic vitriol from Beijing and the narrow business and academic interests of those involved in China have exerted a strong influence in curtailing the debate. But doing so is irresponsible and risks leaving the world community unprepared to deal with this major event. It is hoped that by stimulating debate on China's pending transition now—asking the right questions if not providing the right answers—this book will help to ensure that this process is of benefit to the people of China and the world.

In the Great Debate about democracy and China, I find myself at odds with the essentializing drives of both the hostile Manicheans who see China as a hopelessly benighted feudal autocracy and the misty-eyed Orientalists who believe that some utopian synthesis of doctrines will emerge there in future. These are schools of thought which flourish both in China and abroad. China is first and foremost a country of people and a society much like every other. Like every society, and person, it contains the potential for terrible autocracy or wonderful tolerance. And like every society that undergoes a rapid leveling of the playing field between rulers and ruled, it is more and more likely to embrace democracy as the only workable and acceptable solution to a crisis of governance. The laws of social science grind away in China as they do elsewhere, whether people like it or not.

Democracy is not "Western," even if that term could be specified, as anyone who has seen its successful embrace in countries as diverse as India, Thailand, and Japan would admit. Once established, democracy in China will be very "Chinese" (again, whatever that means in light of the vast diversity of Chinese peoples in China and globally) not because China is unique but because democracy is always heavily colored by the culture in which it operates. Like others, I try to walk the fine line between cultural sensitivity and cultural stereotyping, a line that challenges everyone studying China, Chinese included.

I believe that the Chinese are as capable and desirous of democracy as anyone. Orientalists and Manicheans notwithstanding, I do not believe China is cut off from the trends of human history, where the laws of social science are suspended like time in Shangri-La. I therefore take emergent signs of democratic consensus in China as indicative of a future democratic breakthrough.

I do not seek to present all views here, only my own. The hope is that these views are well-supported by evidence from history and the social sciences, as well as events in present-day China. Where useful, I have endeavored to show that the arguments are being made within China, even within the CCP. This may come as a surprise, but the forces of social change work away in China as elsewhere, and it is little surprise that those in positions of responsibility have thought about how to respond to them. I pay less attention to the extensive debates among Chinese intellectuals outside of China to the future ideal form of democracy. While these debates will no doubt color the creation and operation of democracy in China, they are, in light of democratizations elsewhere, only one of a many factors that will influence China's road to a functioning democracy. Social pressures, historical contingency, and political expedience will play an equal role.

I have attempted to retain a descriptive rather than prescriptive point of view throughout this book. My point is that democracy is coming to China and we need to begin thinking about and preparing for that day. This is not to say that I have no ethical bias in favor of democracy. I most assuredly do. But I have sought to keep that at bay here. Readers can judge if the attempt is successful. Still, I note at various points the wide scope for better outcomes in a prescriptive sense. Work begun in the late 1970s on possible future transitions from military rule in Latin America, for example, played an important role in accelerating and shaping those events. For the purposes of those foreign governments, civic groups, and individuals with a stake in democracy in China or wishing to support it, I have sought to draw out the policy implications throughout the narrative. If this book helps actors to accelerate and manage that process wisely, so much the better. My main concern, of course, is a humanistic one, not a strategic one. But the two need not be distinct; an ethical foreign policy should be defined in humanistic terms.

It is worth sounding an early note of humility about the predictions and assertions to follow. By necessity, this book is bound to be "wrong," in many parts. History is at once both enraging and deeply satisfying because it manages to confound most of the people most of the time. No doubt, parts of this book stand a good chance of falling into that wrong-footed majority. Indeed, it may be wrong not just in the details but in the basic premises. As I will have occasion to note frequently, the CCP may survive through contingency, but it may also survive through a deep structure of political organization that I have simply not grasped, bound as I am by the circumstances of my time and unable to perceive the radical implications of the deep social forces that keep the CCP in power. Books about the future can often be wrong, as Marx and his followers famously discovered in 1989. At a certain point every theory of historical change must be open to falsification. If the CCP continues in office for several decades and democracy does not come to China, it must stand as a falsification of this book, not as more evidence of its veracity. If so, I stand merely in the judgement of my times.

So prudence suggests taking what is written on its pages as an informed set of program notes rather than an exact guide to the upcoming performance. Knowing the options, directions, and challenges of China's future may be as valuable as knowing how it will unfold.

For those who vigorously disagree with my augury of a democratic future for China, who see this book as "pure fantasy," I hope it will still retain some use. Obviously, my hope is to persuade them of the premises sketched here. But alternatively, I hope my arguments are sufficiently transparent and my facts sufficiently broad to strengthen their considered dissenting opinions. Whatever your views, the democratic lens is a powerful tool for surveying a nondemocratic state. Through it, light is refracted in surprising and stimulating ways. For China, often-ignored issues like political, economic, and social justice appear most starkly. Things like women's rights, regional identities, historical reconciliation, and the political underrepresentation of central provinces are brought into sudden focus. By contrast, issues like foreign investment, "important speeches" by leaders, great-power ambitions, and highbrow philosophical debates, which dominate much contemporary discussion of China, fade into near-irrelevance. Democracy reminds us of the centrality of the individual, and of the everyday.

Finally, while this book is mainly about China, and the belated arrival of "Mr. Democracy," as he was once called there, to this land, I have sought in the conclusion to suggest how China's transition will improve our understanding of democracy and political systems everywhere. While I broadly endorse the thesis of Francis Fukuyama that liberal democracy has become the only coherent model of political organization in our world—a simple statement of democracy's universal and empirically proven attractions that has often been misrepresented as Western triumphalism—that theory left wide scope, as Fukuyama himself asserted, for diverse forms and modes of democracy, not to mention threats to the stability of democracy itself. It is my contention that China's embrace of democracy, a process that has already begun, will demonstrate the diversity possible within the democratic house. While basic institutions and norms are shared, China's unique democracy will provide the world with a wider understanding of that conception. For a West seeking solutions to a "democratic malaise," China's transition could provide a new source of invigoration.

My own optimism about democracy in China, if the sober conclusions here can be called such, is born of my contacts with China and its people over a decade of traveling in the country as a journalist and writer. It is perhaps no coincidence that, while living for brief spells in China between 1991 and 2002, I usually made by home in neighboring Hong Kong, a free society whose liberal and open Chinese national identity is so vital for democracy in China.

The research and writing for this project began in 1998, and I completed most of the final manuscript during a six-month interlude between the end of my journalism career in Asia and the beginning of my academic career in the United States in 2002. I was kept in bread for those months through the generous support of the International Security and Foreign Policy Program of the Smith Richardson Foundation, which I acknowledge with thanks.

BG
Princeton, New Jersey
July 2003

CHINA'S DEMOCRATIC FUTURE

PART 1
CRISIS

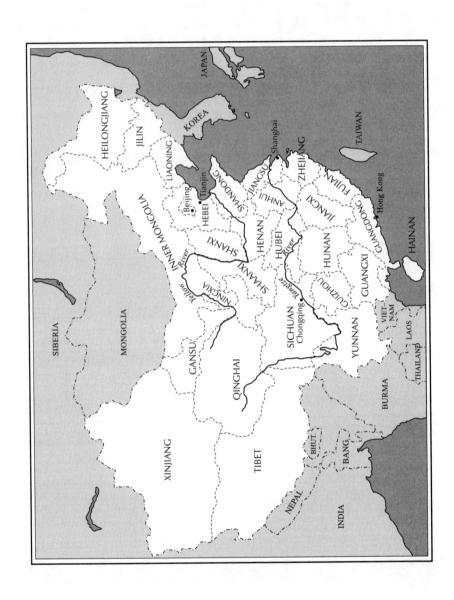

Democracy and China

Democracy's Spread

In late 1912 and early 1913, a unique event occurred in China's history. A year after the abdication of the last emperor, about 20 million citizens walked, bicycled, or rickshawed their way to polling stations across the country to elect a national government.

The franchise was far from universal. It covered only one eighth of the adult population—males over 21 who paid tax, owned property, or held at least an elementary education. Opium-smokers, Buddhist monks, and policemen were among those barred from voting. The men who made it to the poll stations scattered at great distances throughout the vast and poor land represented about half of that select group. There was a vote-fixing controversy in Hunan province. One Shanghai newspaper moaned that parochial and party loyalties were dominating voting: "Just one in a hundred voters is making up their own mind!"[1] Still, the election was generally considered to be fair, free, and a surprising success. In the annals of Chinese history, it remains unique: the first and only popular election of a national government.[2]

China's first national polls did not take place in isolation from world events. By 1918, 33 countries, including the U.S., Britain, and France, had introduced some form of minimal democracy. China might have joined this "first wave" of democratizations, as did Japan. But within a few years, its fledgling democracy failed amidst corruption, violence, and warlordism.

The decades following the end of World War II witnessed a "second wave" of global democratization. These included new democracies in the ex-colonies of Africa and Asia, notably India, as well as a return to democracy by the three Axis powers, including Japan. In China, a spirited government led by the Chinese Communist Party (CCP) took control in 1949 with a liberal constitution and promises of democracy. Thousands of overseas Chinese returned home to build the "new China." Popular elections were held in 1954 for members of local legislatures.

But for a second time, the democratization wave washed past China. In the mid-1950s, having secured control over the country, the CCP's Jacobin leader Mao Zedong veered sharply toward dictatorship, plunging the country into a twenty-year nightmare that killed between 40 and 55 million people.

The third, and most powerful, global democracy wave began in Southern Europe in the 1970s, as the people of Spain, Greece, and Portugal regained the right to choose their leaders. By the 1980s it had swept into Latin America and Asia, carrying the Philippines, South Korea, and Taiwan to democracy. It crested in 1989 and 1991 when the 10 communist regimes of Eastern Europe and Central Asia collapsed, leaving behind 28 new democracies with 400 million newly-free people. Several more countries caught the end of this wave in the 1990s, including Peru, South Africa, Cambodia, and Indonesia.

Again, China made a valiant attempt to join. A massive anti-government uprising gripped the nation for six weeks in the Spring of 1989, spreading to an estimated 341 of China's 400-odd cities. Democracy was one of several demands made against an out-of-touch and corrupt CCP regime. But the pro-democracy forces inside the regime and on the streets proved too weak in the face of a military crackdown. The June Fourth Tiananmen Massacre stands as the last great testament to the frustrated democratic project in China.

In the early twenty-first century, China is increasingly in sparse company as a dictatorship. By 2001, 121 of the world's 192 governments were elected by universal direct votes in reasonably fair and free elections, representing 63 percent of all governments (up from 14 percent in 1950) and 58 percent of the global population. In Asia, 24 of 39 governments were elected.[3] By itself, China comprises about half of that portion of the world's population unable to choose its leaders.

As for the basic freedoms that usually accompany democracy, such as a free press and the right to organize political parties, China is even more at odds with the world community. These freedoms were wholly or partly available in 144 countries, three quarters of the total, accounting for 64 percent of the global population by 2001. China, then, represents about 60 percent of the world's population that continues to live without any guarantee of basic freedoms.

For those concerned about democracy and freedom in our world, there is no more important place than China. To the extent that these things are the best guarantor of a just and fulfilling life for each individual and each community, as well as a stable world order, the country's continued rule by dictatorship is both a tragedy and a threat. A decisive step by China onto the road of democracy would by itself—in population terms—be no less significant than each of the previous "waves" of global democratization. Indeed, it might well bring many of the remaining dictatorships in the world through to democracy. A top aide to a former CCP leader notes that the impact of democratic breakthrough in China "cannot be overestimated. It will fundamentally change the balance between good and evil in our world."[4]

If the evidence of nearly two centuries of continuous global democratization is any indicator, China will indeed embrace democracy in the near future. This book attempts to show why and how that will happen.

The Struggle for Democracy

Democracy is a political system founded on an ideal. That ideal is the equality of individuals and their life goals. No democracy is perfect in realizing that ideal, but some are closer than others. Indeed, democracy is perhaps best understood as a process of striving to achieve it. Countries can be characterized by where they stand on the road. In Asia, highly democratic Japan and Taiwan compare to partly democratic India and Thailand and to barely democratic Singapore and Malaysia. Others, like North Korea and Burma, stand on the wrong side of an imaginary line that separates nomimal democracies from dictatorships. Along with them is China, the world's last great dictatorship.

While various experiments like benevolent kings or communitarian oligarchies have been tried throughout history to achieve equality, experience has shown that it is best achieved, and maintained, by democratic institutional arrangements. These fall broadly into two categories: elections and freedoms.

A democratic government is one in which both the legislature and the executive are fully elected by direct and universal suffrage on a regular basis. The elections must be free, such that voters are not coerced, campaigning is not subject to limits on speech, and parties can field candidates of their choice. They must also be fair, meaning they are administered by a neutral body, do not advantage incumbents unduly, and are not subject to wide corruption. Those elected must hold actual power, roughly reflect the interests of the community, and be subject to recall and scrutiny by the electorate.

The achievement of equality has also, in experience, been enhanced by the provision and protection of extensive freedoms for everyone. In theory, we could have equal but highly limited freedoms. But in practice this is impossible to achieve because it inevitably restricts the freedoms of some more than others. Certain freedoms have proven to be indispensable. They include freedom of expression, movement, association, and conscience. Equality also requires economic and social freedoms, both the freedoms associated with properly operating markets and the freedoms of equal opportunity and status.

Many countries have elections but not freedoms. In Asia, Singapore holds reasonably free and fair elections but imposes strict conditions on political and civil freedoms. Other places have freedoms but no elections. Hong Kong has a robust free press, a laudable judiciary, and extensive freedoms of association and protest. But its people cannot choose their leaders. A country can be undergoing a "quiet democratization" if freedoms are expanding, even if it does not hold elections, an argument that many have made for China. By the same token, a country can experience "democratic regression" if freedoms deteriorate, even as elections continue, something that commentators noted of Malaysia under strongman Mahathir Mohamad after 1981.

Since equality is the core concept of democracy, the institutions used to build it are constantly being revised and strengthened. The democracy of the nineteenth century was well short of today's democracy, which in turn will doubtless be seen in the coming century as hopelessly crude. Democracy may be described as the "current best practice" for achieving equality. It is a constantly evolving political technology which keeps changing in response to changing social needs, even when rulers and elites do not see the need for change. It is also a perpetual struggle to apply the technology fully and correctly, and to make sure that it is not replaced by an older one.

The American scholar Francis Fukuyama's famous endorsement of democracy as "the only coherent political aspiration that spans different regions and cultures around the globe"[5] is thus a statement of the obvious. While we cannot rule out the discovery of a better political technology in future—science fiction notwithstanding—Fukuyama remains, as it were, the final word. That is why more than 120 countries with mind-boggling differences of culture, history, and geography have embraced democracy.

Democracy produces more of the things that people want in order to pursue their life goals. The United Nations Development Program notes that democracy produces better government in terms of broad participation, rule of law, transparency, responsiveness, consensus orientation, equity, efficiency, accountability, and strategic vision.[6] Policies are better thought out, more accepted and thus enforceable. The political system is more stable. Empirically, democracies weather crisis better than dictatorships because the response takes place within the political system, not by overthrowing it.[7] Political power, because it is dispersed and equally monitored, is also less susceptible to misuse. Political pluralism teaches tolerance and understanding. The act of voting makes citizens more engaged with their communities and countries, strengthening their sense of self-worth and making them bulwarks of the institutions of democracy.

Dictatorships often point to their superior efficiency and vision over democracies. But rarely do those claims stand up to scrutiny. China's vast $25 billion Three Gorges Dam project, a tribute to the vision and effectiveness of dictatorship, may have been one of the greatest policy mistakes of the twentieth century.

Internationally, democracies produce peace more than war for the same reasons that they resolve domestic conflicts better than dictatorship, an insight first described by the German philosopher Immanuel Kant in a 1795 essay *Perpetual Peace*. While Kant focused on popular aversion to the financial costs of war, the modern version of his "democratic peace" theory includes popular aversion to the human, moral, and political costs of war. Empirically, a democracy has never gone to war against another democracy.

Democracy does more than just allow freedoms. It also makes an economy more innovative, sustainable, and robust. It excels at allowing capital, ideas, and labor to be freely organized and reorganized as technology and entrepreneurship develop and interests change. Contracts are enforced, property is protected, and policymaking is fair and transparent. Democracy enhances optimal investments in education, alleviation of poverty, equality of opportunity, policy legitimacy, effective regulation, and rule of law. It controls corruption. Taxes are easier to collect and external shocks can be managed better. To quote the United Nations Development Program (UNDP): "Countries can promote human development for all only when they have governance systems that are fully accountable to all people—and when all people can participate in the debates and decisions that shape their lives."[8] Socially, democracy is popular because it ensures the freedoms—to vote, to rabble-rouse, to attend church, to achieve self-respect—that allow people to attain satisfaction. By creating an environment which recognizes the equal worth of each individual, democracy provides the system under which people can realize and express their individual worth. Through democracy "society liberates itself from traditional or feudal forms of domination to participate as an agency in its own self-definition."[9] In doing so, democracy generates its own support. A state that respects, even encourages, the diversity of its citizens gains their allegiance.

Democracy does not presuppose anything about a culture or society. Indeed, it is the most culturally sensitive system yet devised. To call it "Western," whatever that means, is to ignore its roots in universal principles of individual psychology and social organization. The West is neither uniquely nor necessarily democratic, nor are other parts of the world uniquely or necessarily authoritarian. Attempts to portray democracy as "ethnocentric" are undermined by the wide number of successful and devoted liberal democracies outside the West and by the frequent setbacks in the West itself. Aside from its universal—universal because it has no coherent refutation—core value of individual equality, democracy is not "value-laden" at all.

Today, to take Asia, countries as distinct as Confucian Japan and South Korea, Buddhist Thailand and Mongolia, Chinese Taiwan, Hindu-dominated India, Catholic Philippines, and Islamic Indonesia are all functioning democracies. Liberal and tolerant Asians like the Thais—with their mainstream transvestite competitions—would be surprised to find themselves described as more "authoritarian" than the conservative and cautious Swiss. The potential for democracy or dictatorship lies amongst us all.

Democracy implies no undermining or discarding of the unique aspects of a country's culture, merely a better way to organize them fairly and productively. Indeed, democracy brings out and celebrates cultural distinctions. The identical architecture of Moscow, Beijing, and Pyongyang shows how dictatorship does the opposite. Says one scholar: "The evidence for this pan-human possibility has been educed so many times such as to put the factual claim about cultures lacking democratic potential to rest as a deadly error worth burying once and for all times."[10]

Democracy does not automatically make a country well-governed, peaceful, rich, and free. If that were the case, the Philippines and India would both look like Germany. Nor can it promise to create a "democratic society" of selfless individuals all striving to bring justice to others. What it can promise is to make a country better governed, more peaceful, richer, freer and more liberal than it would be under dictatorship. It takes each country's particular inheritance of social, geographic, and cultural traits and makes the most of them. It takes every country closer to the ideal of equality than would any other system.

Given the moral and practical attractions of democracy, why do so many dictatorships continue to survive? Certainly, the reason does not lie in popular desires. No people has ever chosen to install a dictator who promised to curtail basic freedoms. Nor has any people ever voluntarily relinquished their right to vote. Rather, the survival of dictatorship, in China as elsewhere, can be attributed to the same factors that made dictatorship the norm in human history until very recently: a vast disparity in resources of rulers over ruled.

The achievement of democracy depends on an unprecedented leveling of the playing field between leaders and their subjects. It usually results from economic and social change which broadly empowers society. Without it, human society has always tended toward dictatorship. When the leveling happens, rulers find they cannot govern except with the consent of others.

Democracy is rarely bestowed by idealistic rulers upon their people. Nor does it come about because of a sudden eruption of democratic behavior within society. It results from a crisis of dictatorship. It is only after democracy begins that rulers and ruled alike begin to learn and accept the rules of democracy. An important adage which we will return to repeatedly puts it thus: democrats do not make democracy, democracy makes democrats.

That is why frequent hand-wringing about the undemocratic behavior of people in China is strictly speaking irrelevant. Democracy usually comes first as a result of a crisis of governance, idealism second as a result of a growing endorsement of the norms on which it is based. That will especially be the case in a society ruled by an ideal-destroying dictatorship for millennia.

Of course, the factors that create democracy can also tear it apart. Economic crisis, ethnic tensions, or external shocks can upset the leveling of society that makes democracy possible. A fragility of the institutions created to include and listen to diverse social groups can do the same. But short of complete social breakdown, democracy usually fails because elites step in to subvert the system, not because people waive their rights. More important, the problems of renewed dictatorship are almost always worse than those of imperfect democracy.

For those who dislike the messy and plebian nature of democracy, it is easy to slip into an intellectual searching for a more "ideal" conception. Nondemocratic systems appeal to those who, in the words of a former Canadian prime minister, "are disinclined to seek solution in temporal affairs through the mere counting of heads."[11] Indeed, it would surprise the millions of people living in countries which have fought, even risked their lives, for the right to choose their own rulers in recent decades that a "democracy malaise" has taken root in some long-established democracies. There, many have come to take their democratic rights for granted, or assumed they did not matter much. They in turn project those doubts upon others, questioning whether peoples in developing countries can, or should, be able to select their own leaders. They worry that democracy is rooted in "Western" culture, or would bring disorder to some nations, like China.[12] The supercilious disdain for televangelist politicians of the West leads to a comfort-seeking in the well-read dictators of the Third World, their "stability," "remarkable growth rates," and "modernizing vision."

For a start, all evidence points to the fact that democracy does quite the opposite, making countries more stable, more peaceful, and more able to grow. Had India been a dictatorship, it would have been a Middle East of conflict and poverty, a nuclear one at that. Instead, it is a unified and stable country that, having abandoned socialism only in the early 1990s, has grown quickly since then. Had China been a democracy since that ill-fated election of 1912–13, it might well be another Japan today.

In any case, those who advocate dictatorship, in China or elsewhere, have a burden to show that the people of these countries, if given a chance, would agree that it was a better system and endorse its continuation. Western business executives may laud the six-lane expressways slicing through rural China, but the peasants who stand fenced off from the fast lanes might, if given a chance, prefer other public spending, on hospitals and schools. Those who praise dictatorships find it hard to explain why people rise up time and again to overthrow them. To quote one Indian writer echoing Churchill: "It is not the finest product of the desiring human intellect. But it is certainly more practicable than other more promethean conceptions."[13]

At a deeper level, then, the struggle for democracy is a struggle against the authoritarian potential that resides darkly in every society and in every individual. It is the struggle against our desire to project our own moral conceptions upon society. It is the struggle against treating others worse than we would have them treat us. Democracy represents a break in every country with its prevailing political culture. It represents a universal drive toward one ideal against the universal prevalence of another. Every country, China included, needs to "break" from its past to achieve democracy, just as the United States needed to leave behind its slavery, colonial aristocracy, and anti-Indian genocides in order to achieve democracy. To say, then, that democracy is "incompatible" with any country's culture is then either a statement of the obvious (because it is incompatible with the prevailing culture of *every* undemocratic country) or patently false (because the world's 120 democracies have all overcome their authoritarian cultures and learned democratic ones). The same applies to China.

China's Democratic Potential

How is it that China, one of the world's most inventive and culturally rich human civilizations, remains in the grip of dictatorship? The question may seem trivial when we survey the long sweep of history a hundred years from now. It took democracy nearly a century to take root in France and the United States after their late-eighteenth-century popular revolutions. In the twentieth century, great nations like Russia and Japan fell under the temporary spell of dictatorship after early democratic breakthroughs before regaining their feet. In China too, democracy will probably be seen as delayed, but nothing more. People will talk of the aberration that was the People's Republic of China. Books will be written, indeed many are already appearing, about the deep cultural roots and decisive historical march of China's democracy.[14]

Keeping that notion in mind is important because it helps to focus attention on the events and actors that thwarted democracy in China in the twentieth century, rather than on maudlin laments about the country's "plight," as if it suffered from some unspeakable disease. China remains under dictatorship not because of deep-seated, unchangeable "factors" but because its leaders, its neighbors, and some bad luck conspired to suppress the democratic urge time and again. One need only recall the pessimistic tomes written in the 1970s about the Philippines—pointing to its resource-based economy, colonial history, conservative Catholic church, impossible geography, and entrenched business oligarchs—to be reminded of how things can change. Likewise for any number of Eastern European countries which today live in stable democracies after decades of communist rule.

Many excuses have been offered for dictatorship in China. Begin with China's 3,000-year-long imperial history, dating back to the Zhou dynasty. This was long a staple of the retarding legacies argument. A dominant and centralized dynasty run by a single emperor held power closely and treated society as mere subjects. Unlike ancient Rome, China's emperors did not appoint deputies or large senates to help them govern. Unlike feudal Europe, they did not decentralize power to provincial lords and burghers. The result was an inherited system that China found hard to shed.

This argument both overstates the strength of imperial China and understates the potential for change. The rule of emperors in China was under constant threat from rebellions, disobedience, and allegiance to rivals.[15] Emperors were denied patronage rights, the norm in feudal Europe, relying instead on a meritocratic examination system. There was no patrimonial lineage. Indeed, the very right to rule, the mandate of the gods, was revoked from those who governed poorly, prefiguring the contractarian tradition of modern Western liberalism. In addition, countries with far stronger imperial traditions, like Japan and Thailand, where the emperor was worshipped as a king, were able to escape that tradition and create thriving democracies quite easily when conditions changed. China is no more destined to suffer the rule of kings than any other country.

Social and cultural factors are more commonly advanced today, not least by frustrated Chinese democrats themselves. Many cite China's ancient Confucian social order. Within this order, the individual was imagined only as part of a larger group—the family, the clan, and the Chinese nation. Dissent was frowned upon. Elitism thrived. The problems with blaming Confucianism on China's democratic failure are both its interpretation and its modern-day relevance. Confucianism did not necessarily mitigate against democracy. The individual's duty in society was to seek a just or moral outcome, the bedrock of modern democracy. The moral rule of the emperor, meanwhile, echoed the procedural justice of democracy. In addition, the emperor was charged with improving the welfare of the nation; his mandate of heaven would be on the line if he did not. Court advisors were tasked with remonstrating when he went wrong. Religious toleration, derived from the strongly liberal doctrines like Buddhism and Taoism, existed in China long before it developed in the West as the precursor of liberalism.[16] As one scholar wrote: "Confucianism stressed that all could be educated; Daoism focussed on freedom; the Legalist school of philosophy was making all, including the rulers, equal before the law; and Mohism was premised on egalitarianism and the yin-yang school on compromise."[17] From the vantage of the Middle Ages, smart money would be wagered on China, not Europe, as the future birthplace of modern democracy.

In modern times, Confucian culture has been successfully used to nurture democracy in Japan, South Korea, and Taiwan. Just as Christianity has nurtured both terrible dictatorships and wonderful democracies throughout the world, so too Confucianism can be used, or abused, for opposing purposes. That Confucianism in China became a tool of dictatorship was more choice than inevitability. As one Chinese scholar wrote: "Liberalism is not an import. It's a basic value deeply embedded in China's traditional culture."[18]

In any case, other cultural and social influences play an equally important role in China today as inherited tradition. Delving into Song dynasty poetry for clues about modern-day China is like perusing Beowulf to comprehend modern-day Britain. The undemocratic attitudes that China's people display on many issues is entirely normal for those living under dictatorship. It is a result not a cause, as shown by cross-country survey data of how those attitudes change under democracy. Most surveys, as we shall see, reveal that by the end of the twentieth century. China's people already had a minimal degree of "democratic attitudes" needed to sustain democracy.

Another commonly cited explanation for China's democratic failure is underdevelopment. Mixed in here are several overlapping issues: poverty, illiteracy, peasants, and population. The common idea is that the incremental advances of economic and technological change kept the Chinese people poor, illiterate, scattered, and out-of-touch for most of the twentieth century. This "peasant mass" was not conducive to the growth of an empowered associational life in cities that could act as both the champion and bulwark of democracy. Even today, the argument goes, with a population of 1.3 billion, 70 percent of it in rural areas, 220 million people still living on less than a dollar a day, and 145 million illiterates, this great mass remains an insurmountable obstacle to democracy. In the words of one elitist Chinese scholar living in the West, talking about democracy in China today is like "playing the piano to an ox. It is too sophisticated a concept for such an unsophisticated audience."[19]

Without a doubt, underdevelopment is a useful descriptive device because, as mentioned, democracy is closely tied up, historically if not by necessity, with a leveling of the playing field between rulers and ruled. But while it may describe the conditions that have allowed elites to subvert democracy, it is far from being an iron-clad explanation. Many large countries with human development levels close to that of China—including India, Bangladesh, Turkey, the Philippines, and Indonesia—have functioning democracies today. Poverty might trouble democracy. It certainly does not validate dictatorship.

The argument is also weakened by the fact that since the early 1990s, it is those same listless, ignorant, and parochial peasants in China who have been electing their village leaders and running their village affairs with great aplomb. The indifference or ignorance of many peasants about national issues is, again, a result, not a cause, of dictatorship. Were they to have a voice, they would be as informed and involved as their counterparts in India, perhaps democracy's most enthusiastic electorate. Today, telephones and televisions have spread to every corner of China and local elections have been carried out under the most deprived conditions. Some scholars in China are now prepared to dismiss the underdevelopment argument entirely. "In fact there is no necessary connection between democratic levels and economic and cultural and other levels," wrote two Shanghai scholars.[20]

Finally, nationalism is a force which has been used to bury democratic urges time and again in China, as in many countries. China was both the Greece and the Rome of ancient Asia. Yet its relative decline, which began in the fifteenth century and culminated in its extravagantly-named "century of humiliation" at the hands of the dominant West in the nineteenth century left a deep psychological impact. Rulers have been able to assert that democracy was a threat to the rebuilding of national greatness, diverting attention from the damage wrought by their own despotism. "When there is a conflict between democracy and nationalism in China, nationalism always wins," write two Chinese scholars.[21]

Yet perhaps more than any other legacy, China's legacy of modern nationalism has the potential to support democracy, just as it did in India and Taiwan. Since the May Fourth enlightenment movement of 1919 to the time of Tiananmen in 1989, nationalism inspired pro-democracy movements against corrupt and tyrannical rulers. Before seizing power in China, Mao Zedong appealed to nationalism as the reason for giving self-determination to China's minority peoples, arguing that liberation from tyranny was the benchmark of national greatness. Indeed, this same logic allowed liberals in China to urge the introduction of democratic elections at the village level in the 1980s. Now, as we shall see, there is an emerging thread of nationalism in China that for the first time concedes the right of ethnic groups to self-determination and portrays nationalism in terms consonant with democratic ideals. Nationalism is increasingly linked to personal dignity, international responsibility, and internal freedom. This democratic national identity is growing strongly.

A country's legacies are for the most part contemporary social constructs that change with time. Some are more rooted in fact than others. None are permanent. China's rulers have successfully interpreted the country's inheritance in antidemocratic terms for more than a century. Their dictatorship has in turn produced the very behavior that further justifies this interpretation. Yet their ability to do so is weakening and the potential for reinterpretation is vast.

Thus, the direct and immediate explanation for China's failure to achieve democratic orbit since the last emperor was chased out of the Forbidden City in 1911 is the behavior of elites. Since then, six key figures—warlord Yuan Shikai, Nationalist leader Chiang Kai-shek, Communist China's founder Mao Zedong, and his three successors as paramount leader, Deng Xiaoping, Jiang Zemin, and Hu Jintao—have chosen to subvert democracy. It was in their hands that the power lay and it was on their watch that democracy was postponed despite popular pressures.

That they were able to resist democratic reforms is a result of specific historical circumstances that played into their hands each time. It is important to keep in mind the contingency of those circumstances, how they might have been different in the past and how they might be different in the future. Throughout the twentieth century, China's rulers made decisions based on self-interest that made it politic to repress democracy. Society was too weak, international pressure too sporadic, or the incentives for regime reformers too unappealing. Assertions that the normal drive toward democracy was either absent or that it was doomed to failure, notes one scholar, on closer analysis prove to be "ridiculous rationalizations of readily comprehensible political defeats."[22] In the next chapter, we survey how those political defeats came about.

2

Broken Promises

The Republican Failure

There can be no better antidote to pessimism about democratic prospects in China than to revisit the exhilarating political debates that resounded through the country in the first half of the twentieth century. From the late Qing dynasty until the communist takeover in 1949, China's intellectuals and politicians were abuzz with proposals to bring real democracy and freedom to their ancient land. The debate was usually open-minded, cosmopolitan, and fair, a reminder of the democratic potential that lies in China and has never left.

That China failed repeatedly in this period (and in the subsequent half century), to achieve a stable democracy is a testament to the historical chance and weakened society that allowed elites to make expedient decisions to stifle democracy. The twentieth century was a period of broken promises for Chinese democracy.

In the late nineteenth century, the first patently democratic reform proposals emerged. A proliferation of public protest and reformist writings espoused the public right to participate in state affairs. An indigenous political and civil rights discourse was born with pamphlets accusing the ruling Manchus of depriving the Chinese of their inalienable rights. A Hong Kong-educated medical doctor named Sun Yat-sen, later honored as the father of modern China, developed a broad political platform, the Three Principles of the People, that called for fully elected government and a separation of executive, judicial and legislative functions.

The late Qing rulers responded to the democratic urge with reforms that might have led to a constitutional monarchy, as in Japan. Confucian exams were abolished in favor of technocratic criteria for bureaucrats. A coherent economic development program—China's first election promise—was announced. Public submissions on policy were received. Yet a reluctance to embrace real democracy only stoked the forces of revolution, symbolized by

Sun's formation of the Revolutionary Alliance in 1905. A last-ditch effort by Qing officials to stave off overthrow by convening 26 provincial and one national representative assembly came too late. More than half of the provincial assemblies turned on their imperial patron after Sun's alliance began an insurrection in central China in October 1911. Four months later, 21 centuries of imperial rule ended with the birth of Republican China.

What followed was a noble attempt at democracy that fell to the schemes and devices of a series of authoritarian warlords. Sun Yat-sen's newly formed Nationalist Party, or Kuomintang (KMT), swept to victory in the 1912–13 elections. Yet tensions persisted between parliament and various regional warlords who had led the uprising against the Qing. From 1912 to 1928 there were 43 cabinets in Beijing, about one every four months.

Despite the ultimate failure of democracy to congeal, the brave experiments and remarkable creativity of the period remains notable. Several studies show how quickly a supposedly deadened, unorganized, and deferent society suddenly burst into active engagement and organization at every level.[1] The May Fourth Movement of 1919—sparked by China's weakness in the face of Japanese demands after World War I—consciously asserted the need for liberal democracy in an outpouring of pamphlets and soap-box speeches. Thenceforth, intellectuals took democracy as the measure of China's progress from the depredations of imperial decline.

By 1928, Sun's successor as KMT head, General Chiang Kai-shek, had unified the country with a series of military campaigns and launched China into a decade-long flirtation with one-party fascism now known as the Nanjing Decade. This of course was not happening in isolation from world events since democracies worldwide were falling to radical movements of the right (Germany and Italy) and left (Russia and Portugal) in the interwar period. The crisis of faith in democracy was not unique to China.

The KMT's promotion of "tutelary democracy" was backed by liberal intellectuals who, as elsewhere in the world, were suddenly attracted to the allure of strong government. Yet the experiment with an alternative, as elsewhere, proved disastrous. The KMT appointed the government and sapped powers from the parliament. Strong-arm police tactics silenced domestic critics, while endemic corruption and economic mismanagement undermined other sources of legitimacy.

Popular resistance to the KMT dictatorship forced Chiang Kai-shek to convene a national assembly in 1938 to act as a pseudo-parliament and to map out plans for a return to democracy. Foreign diplomats hastened to the opening meeting in Hankou in July, attended by 167 delegates chosen from prominent national, regional, and minority figures. Leaders across the political spectrum heralded the overture. But Chiang, while mouthing support for the assembly, had little intention of respecting its feeble writ. Circumstances gave him a perfect excuse: Japan—one of the many nations whose democratic transition had been reversed by military rule after World War I—launched an all-out invasion of China in 1937 and not for the first time China's leader would argue that genuine democracy was a threat to national strength and unity. The horrors inflicted on China by the Imperial Army would also stoke an enduring sense of victimhood that would prove yet another large stone for democratic forces to remove from the road to freedom.

The failures of the KMT led to a groundswell of support for a new political party that promised not only national strength and economic justice but also genuine democracy. The Chinese Communist Party (CCP), founded in 1921 and outlawed by Chiang Kai-shek in 1927, was an alternative agent for change. Its sporadic battles with the KMT, leading up to a final and conclusive civil war that lasted until 1949, reflected an underlying public debate about whether left-wing progressives or right-wing authoritarians were more likely to realize the ideals of the May Fourth movement.

From its birth, there was always a deep split between the letter and the spirit of the CCP. It was to the latter that China's people adhered, and have ever since. The letter of the CCP was Marx's view of a proletarian overthrow of capitalism, and Lenin's use of the Party as an instrument of state repression and terror. The CCP would duly appoint learned scholars of Marxism and sing the Internationale. But those things were always on the fringes of public perceptions of the CCP, which was viewed in more indigenous terms. The spirit of the CCP was a socially progressive, economically pragmatic, and politically democratic force. Many in China could, and did, ignore the fine print of the Party, attending instead to its grand spirit. Joining or supporting the CCP was intimately tied up with opposition to the KMT.

The CCP's first constitution, in the Jiangxi highlands where it carried out experiments in communal living, was nothing if not democratic. The dreamy Peking University librarian with the thick peasant inflection who soon led the Party, Mao Zedong, on several occasions in the late 1930s and early 1940s slammed the "fake democracy" under the KMT, calling for real multiparty democracy and guarantees of civil and political freedoms. What China needed, Mao averred, was neither the communist party dictatorship of the Soviet Union nor the business-dominated "bourgeois democracy" of the West but a "new democracy" where "there should be no monopoly of power by a single party, group, or class."[2] When, in 1945, the KMT argued that direct elections were impossible because China's people were inexperienced with democracy, Mao retorted: "If you want to learn to swim, you have to jump into the water." Democracy theorists could not have put it better.

Mao's China

Riding a wave of public support as China's great social and political democratizer, Mao and his Party finally ousted the KMT from power in 1949. With the push of an electric toggle at a ceremony on October 1, a new flag rose over China, that of the People's Republic of China.

The mere restitution of political and social order in China after a tumultuous four-decade interregnum was a boon for democratic prospects. Indeed, democracy appeared to be close at hand. Like every one of his predecessors, Mao at first made a show of fulfilling his pledges of democracy. CCP members accounted for less than half of the first central committee of the provisional government formed in 1949, and bare majorities of the cabinet and vice premierships. The eight political parties that had sided with the CCP in the civil war were given prominent cabinet posts.

The first constitution of the PRC, passed into law in 1954, was a reasonable first move toward full democracy. China was a "people's democratic state" made up of "a broad people's democratic united front." Citizens were equal, had the right to vote and stand for office, and enjoyed freedoms of speech, press, assembly, belief, association, demonstration and protest, privacy, and movement. Supreme state power lay with a National People's Congress, or parliament, which would pass laws and appoint the State Council, or cabinet, and its premier. There were also three local levels of people's congresses. At first, only the lowest level congresses would be directly elected. Those legislators would then appoint members to the next highest level and so on up to the NPC itself. In the first round of elections, 278 million people (86 percent of the electorate) voted into office 5.6 million local parliamentarians.

Though it was conferred with "leadership" of the whole system, the CCP's overarching role in the political process could be seen as a sort of benign tutelage to replace the oppressive tutelage of the Nanjing Decade. It was, after all, a party that promised to make people "the master of their own house." Little surprise that this "new China," inspired hope. Boatloads of prominent overseas Chinese returned to the mainland aboard steamers from the U.S. and Europe. Hundreds of Western intellectuals made their own mental journeys to the side of the CCP, seeing in it the seeds of a progressive postcolonial order in Asia.

Lying buried in the CCP, however, were several signs that Mao, as those before him, would ultimately renege on his promises. Of course, communism and communist parties, whatever their national variations, were founded on a basic rejection of power-sharing, no matter Mao's protestations about Soviet-style dictatorship. No lawyer, reading the fine print of the foundations of the PRC, would have advised their client to sign up for citizenship. No less important were the imperial and tyrannical pretensions of Mao. Against the advice of planners, he made the Forbidden City his home and hoisted his portrait onto the rostrum over Tiananmen Square. Whatever his avowals of support for democracy, they quickly proved expedient in the face of the autocratic temptation. Asked about the PRC constitution, which he helped to draft, Mao replied: "I don't remember a thing about it."[3]

Democrats made a last-gasp effort in 1956 to force the CCP to make good on its promises (as their counterparts were doing in Budapest). The so-called anti-Rightist movement launched by Mao in response signaled the beginning of a two-decade retreat from those promises. In the twenty years to 1976, China went through the most violent and deadly episode of dictatorship in human history as Mao paraded his cruelty, cheered on by sycophants inside the Party, especially Zhou Enlai and Deng Xiaoping. Chinese scholars estimate that one of every nine people in China—the equivalent of 70 million people in 1956—was killed or disabled as a result of the blood-letting against dissent and difference launched by Mao.[4] From the anti-rightist campaign to the Great Leap famine of 1959–61, and then the Cultural Revolution of 1966 to 1976, China was wrenched by the brutality of CCP rule. Alongside those national disasters were hundreds of regional ones associated with the fanaticism of Mao—like the suppression of a mass uprising in Tibet in 1959 or the collapse of two dams built for propaganda purposes in Henan province in 1975 that killed 300,000 people. Moderate Western estimates of the death toll up to 1976 range from 40 to 55 million, including the 30 to 40 million killed by the Great Leap famine.[5] Within a generation, a country full of hope became synonymous with unspeakable cruelty and fanaticism.

The vulnerability of the state, and society, to internal Party conflicts was most marked in the Cultural Revolution, where factions battling for supremacy created a vacuum of leadership at the top. Power was held by local military committees, while police took over the courts. The NPC failed to meet even once over the entire decade. The irony was that the CCP would later decry the era as a failure of democracy rather than dictatorship, using it as yet another excuse to postpone political liberalization.

Mao died in 1976 and was immediately entombed in Tiananmen Square, a symbol of China's failed democratic dream. He left a deep scar on China, one that arguably created a more insurmountable obstacle to democracy than any of the alleged antidemocratic conditions that preceded his murderous reign. By 1976, 60 percent of the population was living in poverty and the average income was about 15 cents a day.[6] Society was forced into disinterest and selfishness. Debate and participation were pushed to the sidelines along with other basic freedoms. The CCP's deadly embrace of the state meant that the state failed to develop as a separate entity and govern with reasonable insulation from ruling-party conflicts. It also meant that the normal give-and-take interactions between society and state were recast as a battle for supremacy between society and Party. "The result," as two official scholars would write candidly, "was that China lost the whole basis for citizen's political participation. . . . That's the reason why China remains unable to systematize its democratic system."[7]

Still, there are some mitigating legacies from this period. First, it is important to see these years as aberrant rather than as a confirmation of China's tyrannical destiny. In a global context, this was the period in which many postcolonial "second wave" democracies, especially in Africa, were descending into similar tyranny. Reversals also occurred at this time in countries that later reclaimed their democratic path, such as Spain. It was also a period in which most communist countries descended into a freeze. Czechoslovakia underwent intense Stalinization and ideologicalization from 1957 onwards, a period that ended with the Prague Spring of 1968 and finally redemocratization in 1990. In that sense, Mao's horrors, though worse, were consistent with what was happening elsewhere.

In addition, the much-reviled mass campaigns of the era were, in one light, a basic form of political participation and included some of the ideals of democracy. The so-called "four bigs" encased in the 1975 constitution—the right to speak out freely, to air views fully, to hold great debates, and to post one's views on political posters—were consistent with democratic ideals, even if the whole notion was badly abused and directed by leaders. The right to strike was briefly made constitutional in this era.

Finally, one can see some parallels with the impact of the bloody religious wars of post-Reformation Europe that gave rise to liberal and tolerant ideals, and ultimately to democracy, there. The rural areas that suffered most under Mao later became the first to embrace economic reforms and the most enthusiastic organizers of village elections. As two Chinese researchers found in one county that had been devastated under Mao: "These people suffered the most from the dictatorship of the past so they cherish their democratic rights even more. They take an active interest in politics and make sure to elect the right person to lead them."[8] As one Western scholar noted of the legacy of tyranny: "Only when you have learned what life is like in a political order where you are totally dependent on the whims of distant and unresponsive leaders will you acquire a visceral hunger for democracy."[9]

Post-Mao Reforms

The death of Mao marked the reversal of the dictatorship's high tide in China. After this period China resumes its post-1911 trajectory of seeking the foundations and forms of democracy. We can draw a direct connection between the story we left in the early 1950s and the post-Mao reform era. Control over society loosens, government is institutionalized, and power is decentralized.

By the mid-1970s, China, like other communist states, was suffering from stagnant growth and high repression. One or both had to be amended. Tens of thousands of Beijing citizens marched on Tiananmen Square in 1976 calling for an end to the Party's despotism. In Eastern Europe and the Soviet Union, where an urban elite would not relinquish the perquisites of economic control, the solution to the regime crisis was less repression. Dissident authors and embryonic trade unions were allowed to emerge in an uneasy peace.[10] But China was different. Since it remained largely rural, it could launch significant economic reform merely by empowering farmers and local governments—bypassing any potential resistance in state industry and the central bureaucracy. That meant it could also keep a tight lid on dissent. In urban areas, meanwhile, economic reforms were launched through a massive giveaway of public resources. Cadres and government officials at every level were sanctioned to make use of their administrative and political powers to enrich themselves. This resulted in pervasive corruption. But it also ensured a strong urban constituency behind the economic reforms to match the rural one.

Thus the new "social contract," initiated at this time under Deng Xiaoping provided for wide economic and social freedoms in return for political fealty. The state freed society and decentralized power, retreating to the citadel of uncontested rule. Henceforth, the CCP's legitimacy would depend on its performance alone. These were new waters for any communist regime: to maintain power without controlling the economy. Beijing was empowering its people not with ballots but with money. The breakup of communes, the sanctioning of local revenue-raising by rural enterprises, and the end of state-guaranteed employment all weakened the Party's hold on society. Citizens needed real news in the media, laws to protect them, and looser migration and dossier controls to pursue jobs. GDP growth between 1979 and 2000 was 8 percent, double the average of the previous quarter century. The state-owned sector's share of national industrial output fell from 78 percent in 1978 to just 25 percent two decades later, bringing China to an era in which the state sector was an archipelago of strategically controlled islands in a sea of private business.

Deng knew that economic reforms demanded changes in political techniques. The Party, he said, should "concern itself with major matters, not minor matters." The term "political system reform" (*zhengzhi tizhi gaige*) came into the Chinese lexicon in a speech given by Deng in 1980 warning about "bureaucracy, over-concentration of power, patriarchal methods, life tenure in leading posts, and privileges of various kinds" within the Party leadership. As part of these "political reforms," voting was reinstituted within the Party and there were new mandatory retirement ages for cadres at various levels. Courts were revived as semi-independent bodies, although Party committees continued to make the final decision on major cases. Citizens gained the right to sue government for misgovernance. Suits against the government jumped from 5,000 in 1987 to more than 100,000 a decade later. Military members of the governing Politburo fell from more than half in the Mao era to just 10 percent from the 1990s onward. The military ranks were trimmed from 4 million to 2.5 million.

Within the wider political system, the Party sought to revive the modest participatory schemes of the 1950s. The NPC resumed meetings in 1975, while a law passed in 1979 expanded the scope of direct elections up one level to include county legislatures (people's congresses). Village government also became dramatically more democratic with the passage of a law in 1987 allowing villages to elect their own leaders. Deng even promised that "general elections could be held in China half a century from now, sometime in the next century."[11]

What is abundantly clear, and became tragically so later, is that Deng had no intention of launching a process in which CCP would eventually have to compete for power with other parties, as the KMT did in Taiwan. The political reforms he envisaged were many things—institutionalization, liberalization, decompression, call it what you like. They were not democratization. The wily patriarch "pushed China into a political reform craze" noted one popular book published in China. "But unfortunately the results were not what people were hoping for."[12]

Under this new dispensation, the Party's "zone of indifference" widened. Only those representing a credible and imminent threat to CCP rule were now crushed. But crushed they were. First in 1978–79, then in 1985 and 1986, and finally on a huge scale in 1989, China's political scene was buffeted by mass demands for democratic political reforms. All of them were put down.

China was not unique in its renewed yearning for democracy. The "Third Wave" of world democratization began in southern Europe in the late 1970s.

Philippines president Ferdinand Marcos, fell to a "people power" revolution in 1986 after 21 years in office, while Thailand's military relented and allowed the country's first general election in 1988. In 1986, the KMT in Taiwan, now under Chiang Kai-shek's son, Chiang Ching-kuo, agreed to begin a slow democratization that would culminate in its loss of power 14 years later. The growing strains in the communist regimes of Europe were symbolized by the negotiations in 1988 between the Solidarity trade union and the Polish communist leadership.

The failure of China's movements to bring about a democratic breakthrough is testament to historical contingency, political expediency, and the power of the state in the face of social demands. This was especially true in 1989. Like virtually all democratic revolutions, the 1989 protests began over issues of livelihood and misgovernance. Students sought an end to official corruption, a free press, more funding for education, less inflation, and greater social freedoms. It was rare to hear calls for the CCP to step down. Still, the main student group did demand that that whoever took over in the CCP "must have democracy as their starting point and must introduce political reform to make China democratic."[13] Party leaders were in no doubt of the implications of the movement:[14]

> Democracy is a worldwide trend, and there is an international countercurrent against communism and socialism that flies under the banner of democracy and human rights. If the Party does not hold up the banner of democracy in our country, someone else will, and we will lose out. I think we should grab the lead on this and not be pushed along grudgingly. — *Party General Secretary Zhao Ziyang*

> We should grab the initiative by launching democratization now, while the leadership role of the Party is relatively strong. — *Party elder Bo Yibo*

While the movement was ultimately crushed by a well-armed military, many contingent factors could have swung fate in the other direction. Revolutions depend for their success on both an organized opposition movement and a disorganized leadership and both were plainly in evidence. The Beijing student movement was well organized and had strong sense of solidarity. The movement spread to 341 cities (three-quarters of China's total) and brought between 200,000 and 700,000 people onto the streets on peak days, encompassing an estimated 100 million people, a tenth of the population.[15] As "autonomous workers organizations" began to form in late May, the fiber of the protestors grew more stout. "Another major political mistake might cost us all of our remaining popular support," one top leader warned.[16]

Within the regime, the liberals had significant backing. A third of the standing committee of the NPC called for a convening of an emergency meeting, which might have led to a negotiated solution with the protestors. Indeed, Deng agreed in mid-May "to make clean government the centerpiece of our whole political reform and then to tie everything else—democracy, rule of law, openness, transparency, supervision by the masses—to that centerpiece."[17]

That the movement failed appears more and more a result of luck and happenstance. Among the protestors, student leaders failed to sideline radicals in their ranks, making a negotiated pact more difficult. As for the regime, the presence of a raft of long-lived Party elders made negotiations less likely, unlike Taiwan, Russia and Spain where the death of ageing strongmen had cleared the path toward democracy. Meanwhile, NPC chairman Wan Li had rashly left on a visit to the U.S. and Canada in mid-May and was detained in Shanghai on his return, unable to convene the body's standing committee.

All of which is to say that we need not take the Tiananmen failure as yet more evidence of the doomed democratic project in China. To quote Bao Tong, personal aide to the liberalizing Party chief Zhao Ziyang: "Tiananmen was a cry from the people long suppressed, a call to take hold of their own destiny. Without a broad and deep social basis, it would have been unthinkable."[18]

Tiananmen, then, was a prelude to a successful democratic breakthrough. It contained all the elements—nascent civil society, global linkages, livelihood issues that became politicized, spontaneous organization, negotiations between the regime and protestors—that elsewhere made for success. It was the latest instance of how historical chance, elite expediency, and a weakened society can undermine the democratic dream. But it came close and, in retrospect, probably signaled the end for the CCP. Like Budapest in 1956, Prague in 1968, and Warsaw in 1981, Tiananmen in 1989 was a failure that foretold later success.

The Last Days of Dictatorship

As in the Nanjing Decade, the failed transition to democracy in the 1980s was followed up a period of authoritarian reassertion in the 1990s and 2000s. In these decades, China's leaders, and not a few of its intellectuals, were tempted by the thought that the country's age-old crisis of governance could be solved by some exotic new form of authoritarianism.

This is an era in which the CCP is headed first by a cautious and uninspired engineer, Jiang Zemin, and then by a faceless puppet of Party factions,

Hu Jintao. Since it is the contention here that they were presiding over the last years of dictatorship in China, it is tempting in a brief narrative to skip over the period entirely. Yet there are developments in this period that will have important implications for the timing, nature, and results of China's move to democracy.

In its desperation to claw back unchallenged political power after 1989, the CCP accelerated the pace of social liberalization and state institutionalization. All but the largest state enterprises were put on the auction block, while the Party withdrew further from the media, education, and individual lives. The rule of law and the role of local people's congresses in policymaking gained ascendancy over Party fiat. Expanded tolerance for open protest—worker actions for back wages and pensions are a good example—became irrevocable. The military was professionalized, losing any political or economic clout. In short, the Party responded to the popular pressures of Tiananmen with an even less intrusive and less arbitrary state. In these respects, democracy was likely to be more durable once achieved.

In other respects, however, the foundations for democracy were weakened. Widened income inequalities, worsened ethnic tensions, and an enfeebled state treasury all spelled trouble for the future. Meanwhile, the spread of corruption to virtually every level of government—not just those in special positions as in the 1980s—meant a longer climb back to a trustworthy and efficient bureaucracy.

Achieving democracy was also going to be more painful. The CCP failed to grasp the nettle of political reform in an era of sustained economic growth and global stability. As a result, it would have less control over the future course of democracy compared to far-sighted authoritarian regimes like the KMT in Taiwan. China in the post-Tiananmen era has switched from being a country where democratization might have come through the planned and deliberate moves of those in power to one where it will likely result from a hasty and messy withdrawal in the face of crisis.

Thus in the post-Tiananmen era, China's quest for democracy was delayed, but not derailed. China entered into a sort of "tutelary democracy" like that proposed by Sun Yat-sen earlier in the century. Indeed, the parallels with the Nanjing Decade are strong. The CCP shifted from being a dictatorship of the left to a dictatorship of the right, a change symbolized most starkly by the decision in 2001 to invite leading capitalists into the Party. Through this and other shifts, the Party transformed from a revolutionary shock brigade of the working classes into a governing representative of the country's new elites. Democracy was now besmirched not as "bourgeoisie" (the left-wing Marxist jibe) but as "Western" (the right-wing ethnocentric one). Pro-democracy forces were now attacked not for opposing Mao's "leadership" (the left-wing slight) but for embracing his "chaos" (the right-wing one). The flawed universalism of Marxism was replaced not with the compelling universalism of liberal democracy but with a new right-wing exceptionalism of China's "national conditions" (*guoqing*). While the 1980s can be seen as containing the seeds of this shift, the post-Tiananmen era sees it entrenched as official policy. CCP rule is no longer justified as the engine of history but as a source of instrumental payoffs: economic growth, social stability, and national greatness.

As in Franco's Spain or Bismarck's Germany, this is a period of "blood and iron" rather than "speeches and majority decisions." Democratic inklings are crushed in order to "save China" with development and unity. That matters because it suggests where the challenge to dictatorship will gain adherents, less from the cosmopolitan urban elites who prospered from the post-Tiananmen social compact, and more from the normal constituency of the left—peasants, workers, social activists, religious groups, the poor, and the remote. Unlike in the 1980s, when the CCP was besieged by urban elites for holding high the banner of an undemocratic left-wing ideology, from the 1990s it comes under pressure mainly from the vast unwashed for adhering to an authoritarian right-wing ideology. Within the Party itself, leaders who aligned themselves with the downtrodden become the main voices for democracy.

Even if China after Tiananmen looked more like Franco's Spain than Gorbachev's Russia, the regime was no more entrenched than its erstwhile colleagues in dictatorship. The same forces that had brought others down would do the same in China. Indeed, there is an irresistible historical parallel with the democratization of Russia. In both places, the initial break with the totalitarian past (Khrushchev's 1956 speech denouncing Stalin, Deng in 1981 on Mao) was followed by a period of political liberalization that came to an abrupt halt with a hardliner backlash (Russia in 1968, China in 1989). There followed a period of political stasis which in the Russian case culminated after two decades in a regime crisis and a democratic breakthrough. Can China be far behind? The answer seems obvious. In the next two chapters, we survey the reasons why.

3

The Bane of CCP Rule

The PRC System

The People's Republic of China calls itself a democracy. The CCP regime asserts that people's rights are fully protected, government is accountable, participation is widespread, elections are held, and more. If we are to argue that China will embrace democracy, then it is worthwhile to establish first that it is not a democracy at present.

The CCP came to power in 1949 in order to remake China. Like all Marxist parties, its goal was to uproot society and remake it in a new image. The Marxist goal of communism was effectively abandoned with the reform era. But the revolutionary nature of the Party did not change. It continues to see its purpose as chasing utopia—"a strong and prosperous, culturally advanced, democratic socialist nation" according to the state constitution—not governing for the ever-changing aims of a diverse society. CCP elites decide the direction of the nation, not the loveable and monolithic "masses." Party rhetoric is filled with words like "struggle" (*douzheng*), "enemy forces" (*didui shili*), and "victory" (*shengli*). The PRC political system was designed to control and transform society, not to facilitate its development.

The Party is constitutionally endowed with the "leadership" of China's political system. This leadership includes the right to monopolize political power, to control all state and social organizations, and to define the nature and limits of public discourse. While the CCP has undertaken extensive liberalization in the reform era, none of these three powers has been relinquished. That is, while society has been largely freed from state control, the potential writ of the state, and thus its dominating influence, remains vast. Some scholars maintain that the PRC is still a "totalitarian" state because of this simple, if bothersome, fact.[1] In international comparisons of the nature of political systems, China consistently ranks as one of the most undemocratic nations on earth.[2]

In a democracy, those in power are deemed to "represent" the society they govern, that is to broadly reflect the considered views of their society on political issues. This is achieved through a combination of devices, from elections to public debate. Lacking such democratic means, the CCP would need to be an inherently representative party in order to justify its rule in democratic terms. Yet it is far from representative. Among its 65 million members, only 17 percent are women (compared to 49 percent nationally), 6 percent minorities (10 percent), 5 percent farmers (60 percent) and 43 percent college educated (4 percent). Most CCP members are college-educated urban Han males, "a network of bureaucratic elites with the training and connections to hang onto power."[3]

Some polls purport to show that the CCP enjoys significant popular support. Yet they are usually heavily biased in favor of educated urban elites.[4] More broad-based polling reveals deep mistrust and dislike of the CCP. In the late 1980s, the approval ratings for the CCP appear to have been at about 30 to 40 percent.[5] In the 1990s, although no reliable polls were done, that rating may have fallen further given the malaise in the countryside. One Chinese scholar describes a "widespread contempt for those wishing to join the Party, a view of officials as a self-seeking exploitative class, and pervasive political indifference."[6] Indeed, state leaders and Party planners have remarked openly that the Party faces a crisis of legitimacy.[7] In the words of Li Ruihuan, a member of the Politburo standing committee from 1989 until 2002: "People's criticism, denunciation, resistance and opposition to the Party and to leading cadres has come to the boiling point. The CCP membership has grown bigger but its strength is weaker than ever."[8]

One stop-gap solution to the legitimacy problem is to allow a certain amount of outside representation in the CCP-led system. Representative institutions can fill in some of the "democracy deficit," in authoritarian regimes by improving decisionmaking. But the problem is the same as those of trying to make the Party representative: the goals and power of the Party are non-negotiable and thus outside help can do no more than make the Party slightly less dysfunctional and appear slightly more democratic.[9] As we shall see, some forms of participation unintentionally provide resources for change. But claims that they somehow provide a substitute for democratic participation are wrong, recalling the credulous reports by Western scholars on Yugoslavia's worker councils and community boards of the 1960s and 1970s.

The National People's Congress in particular is a pageant of legitimization and ineffectiveness. As a whole, it has never rejected a single piece of legislation nor a candidate for a cabinet position. "Many of the deputies are so old they can't stay awake during the meetings. They snore so loud we have to alert staff to do something," one delegate complained at the 2002 session.[10]

The aim of legislatures in authoritarian states, notes one scholar, "is to de-politicize public life, and at its extreme, to make it one great celebration of the regime." Such rituals "are a means of giving a sense of involvement without power, thereby blunting popular resentment at their effective political exclusion."[11]

Like political participation, China's legal system is a tool of Party dictatorship more than a restraint on it. The Party often does follow the law but this is meant to make its rule better, not to make China a more just country. When the two clash, Party rule wins. To quote one handbook for cadres: "The judicial system of China is an important tool of the people's democratic dictatorship under the leadership of the CCP. . . . In the course of handling every case, the people's courts should assiduously implement the Party's line and policies."[12]

As a result, when citizens try to control the state using the legal system, they are taking a gamble. A peasant in Guangxi was put in a labor camp for three years by angry local cadres after he sued them in a provincial court over a government farming scheme that had cost him his livelihood. A crusading lawyer for workers rights in the central province of Henan was jailed for two years without charges by local cadres who did not like the way he was making their economic work look so tawdry.[13] During the "Strike Hard" anti-crime drive which began in 1995 and brought 15,000 people a year to the gallows in the late 1990s, trial procedures were regularly waived in order to produce results. As one scholar in China puts it: "Laws in China are used as a tool of the government to control the society rather than as a tool of the society to control the government."[14]

China is thus a country with a deep democracy deficit, one that cannot be remedied without challenging the CCP's dominating role in the political system. In the absence of sufficient outside pressures, it has refused to forego this domination. But those pressures are growing. In the words of a former top Communist Party official, "the democracy deficit created by the absolute power of the Party" is pushing China toward political opening. The only question, he noted after the change of Party rulers in 2002, "is how long the new Chinese leaders will resist."[15]

A Metaphor for Transition

If the story of democracy in China since 1912 has been one of repeated failure, why should we believe that the future will be any different? What evidence is there that conditions now favor a rapid and decisive democratic transition?

Imagine a road intersection where traffic is directed by a single policeman. For many years, the flow of vehicles is minimal. The policeman asserts his prerogatives with grand flourishes, when he is not dozing off. But there is little pressure for change. Then, as more people buy cars, congestion grows. The policeman proclaims his critical role, but he has little idea of which traffic lines are longest. In any case, he favors certain cars over others, asserting that he alone understands the "fundamental interests" of all drivers.

Frustrations among the excluded drivers grow as they are forced to wait long periods to get through the intersection. Others resent the mere fact that their passage depends on the whims of an unfair and corrupt policeman. Some drivers jump medians or try to maneuver in front of others, making everyone's journey slower. Horns are sounded everywhere against the policeman and other motorists. Nearby intersections are also affected.

Finally, the crisis reaches a climax. Two angry drivers seize the podium and oust the policeman, who shuffles away with little protest, worn down by his inability to manage the congestion. Soon they are joined by others. After a brief discussion, the drivers agree that the only fair way to manage the intersection is to install a set of traffic lights keyed to the amount of traffic coming from each direction. They have heard that such schemes work well elsewhere.

Tensions remain high while the lights are installed and drivers take turns directing traffic. Once the new system goes into operation, some drivers continue to run red lights. A mini-crisis erupts one day when the lights fail. But soon everyone accepts and abides by the lights and the system is given a back-up power supply and better wiring. Drivers also agree on a new traffic abatement scheme to reduce congestion, making everyone's trip faster. Tensions subside.

This metaphor describes how social and economic change (the growing congestion) which is not accommodated fairly in the political system (the incompetent and arbitrary policeman) can lead to a democratic breakthrough (the blockade and agreement on a new scheme) given the right conditions (the use of horns, the initiative of a few drivers, the existence of an alternative scheme, and the policeman's weakness and resignation). It highlights how democracy comes about because of a stalemate in the struggle not just between rulers and ruled, but among the ruled as well (otherwise the drivers of Mercedes would take over as traffic cops, presumably favoring their kind). It reminds us that democracy is often a solution to crisis and a "conservative" move by parties who want to preserve the freedoms they had in the past. It also highlights how drivers might, and usually do, prefer a slightly off-kilter system of lights to the arbitrary waves of a very good traffic policeman. It also points to the challenges of making democracy work later on (the operation of the lights, the abatement scheme).

It is far from certain that this stylized sequence of events will actually occur at every intersection. There are many other alternatives. The traffic policeman could sheath himself in a walled podium with electric fences and fire bazookas at offending or threatening drivers. Or he could hire some assistants to help him manage the intersection more effectively, acting as de facto traffic light sensors. In most countries, the "logic of authoritarianism" was eventually overwhelmed by the "logic of democracy." But this is a possibility, not a certainty.

Today, Beijing asserts, in effect, that it already has a perfectly good traffic lights system, indeed one that is better than "mere" traffic lights because it magically convinces drivers to stay off the roads and helps certain important cars to get through faster, making society better off than it would be with the plebian, selfish, and uninspiring lights. Yet China's people are less convinced of that claim than ever before. Their perceptions about the need for democracy are growing. So too are their abilities to bring this change about. In this chapter and the next, we survey respectively those demands and resources—the critical background conditions for democratic transition and consolidation.

Given the riot of information available on present-day China, it is of little surprise that reasonable people differ on where those conditions are leading. Some predict imminent CCP demise, others perpetual CCP rule. The contention here is that these factors are shifting decisively in favor of democratic change. On the demand side, the costs of dictatorship are increasingly attributed by society to the lack of democratic government. The "hidden costs" of China's transition to markets without the corresponding transition to limited political power are increasingly apparent.[16] The irrational and repressive state looms larger in people's minds. The state is less able to attune itself to society's demands and when it can it is often unable to meet them. No less important, democratic government is increasingly seen as a viable alternative to the present system.

On the supply side, liberalization and institutionalization are empowering the very changes that they were introduced to keep at bay. The growth of a broad and stable middle class and an autonomous civil society armed with more information than ever, coupled with emergent legal, electoral, and parliamentary ideals of constrained state power, are nudging China in the desired direction. The emergence of a strong reform faction inside the CCP is doing the same. As one scholar notes: "Even if the Chinese people were content with their authoritarian culture, socioeconomic forces have a transforming power."[17]

Time does not favor the CCP. The world's longest-standing ruling parties—Mexico's Institutional Revolutionary Party and Russia's Communist Party—both succumbed to the parable of the traffic policeman after 70-odd years in office. The CCP will have ruled China for 70 years by 2019, surely approaching its upper limit. As one Western scholar noted: "The costs of maintaining the existing system are high and the pressures for change are enormous."[18]

State and Society

Does China want democracy? Three quarters said yes in a survey in 1988, even if definitions of democracy varied. In more recent polls, that proportion has remained virtually unchanged. Political reform regularly tops the list of "pressing matters," in the minds of citizens and cadres alike.[19] In the words of a group of scholars in Shanghai: "Economic and social development has greatly touched off the desire for the expression of mass interests and political participation. But channels and opportunities for political participation are far from adequate to accommodate these demands."[20]

Of course, as with every society, China contains a diversity of views on the need for fundamental political change. Beijing University graduates leaving to pursue a higher degree in the United States before returning to a lucrative position in China (if they return at all), will typically sing the praises of one-party rule. A landless Anhui peasant gathering scraps of cardboard along the railway tracks in Bengbu will, by contrast, have nothing good to say about the Party.

While the university graduates' opinions convince many outsiders that China is going to be the great exception to the global democratization wave, the peasant's outlook is probably a better reflection of where popular opinion stands. And unlike the past, popular opinion is increasingly in a position to make itself heard in China. As one scholar in China notes: "The growing friction between the democratic consciousness of the people and their demands to take part in politics and the delayed arrival of legal and reasonable channels of democratic participation could easily cause turmoil."[21]

Before plunging into an examination of how demands for the replacement of the CCP with a democratic system have arisen from the economic, social, international, and political spheres of present-day China, it is worthwhile making a few general points about why China's people believe the present system needs fixing.

Authoritarian regimes are inherently weak. Feedback from society is deficient, society's role in supervising power weak, and norms of elite conduct unstable.

Communist regimes have an added defect: they are ideologically as well as politically separate from society. In states like the PRC, where the regime ideology has also become a living lie, that drawback is severe. Worse than advocating ideals that society does not share, the regime advocates nothing at all. Legitimacy is then based wholly on performance, economic and otherwise.

In a democracy, society both defines the limits of the state and regulates its power. In a dictatorship like China, the state does these things and does them in the interests not of fostering individual development but of protecting its monopoly of power and privilege. As a result, society is constrained and misgoverned while the state is lawless and corrupt. What should be a creative friction between the two becomes one of destructive friction or corrosive favor-seeking. The state favors certain companies, individuals, and political groups over others and represses those who claim equality. That gives rise to a gamut of problems, as explained in our metaphor of the badly run intersection. China is essentially a badly-run intersection at present. "In China today, we need to restrict the powers of the state, and enlarge its responsibilities. Only democracy will allow us to achieve this two-fold change," writes one Chinese scholar. Or to quote a prominent reformist Party scholar:[22]

> Our present system . . . is suited to class struggle not economic development. It is suited to mass movements not the coordinating and orderly management of society's activities. It is suited to personal fiat and rule by man not to democracy and rule of law. The result is that to a large degree our economic and cultural life has been politicized, statized, administrationized. Its natural autonomy and independence has been severely limited.

The resulting tumors of dictatorship—corruption, misgovernance, injustice, instability, and repression—have sparked cries from a wide range of people for a better political system. Corruption is widespread in modern-day China, far more than in neighboring Taiwan or ex-colonial Hong Kong, with which it might be usefully compared.[23] Power without restraint corrupts, and China is full of it—businessmen, students, policemen, judges, cadres—everyone is giving or taking bribes—what one book in China called "China's pain."[24] As the exiled economist He Qinglian wrote: "Corruption has become the biggest polluter of our political and economic systems and a poisoner of our society and people. Solving this is a big issue for the CCP because in history there is not a single corrupt government that has not fallen from power."[25]

The misgovernance that hampers the country's development is no less pervasive. Policy-related errors are the norm. Half of the arable land lost to desertification since 1949 resulted from policy mistakes. The country's banking crisis stems directly from failed state enterprise policies. Mass protests over urban housing reforms result from a lack of consultation. Attempts by China to assert a leadership role in Asia founder on the lack of transparency in its foreign and military affairs.

In major cross-country surveys of governance, such as those by the UNDP and the World Bank Institute, China fares reasonably well when compared to its peers among lower middle income countries. Government is more stable, lawful, and effective than in similar countries, but regulation, transparency, equity, participation, and corruption remain problematic. What separates China from democratic countries at similar levels of development is that governance shortcomings are attributed to the political system rather than to parties and politicians. As a result, every policy zig-zag, elite feud, massive corruption case, and unexplained decision is met with contempt for the system rather than contempt for just the players. Just to retain the same levels of allegiance from its people, the CCP would have to deliver much better governance. In the event, it cannot. As a result, localized protests and anarchy are the norm. Cadres live on a fragile day-to-day dispensation from the people. The Party admitted widespread local instability in a 2001 book on social frictions across the country.[26] One mainland author has written an entire book on what he calls "the phenomenon of irregularity" (*shifan*) in China, also known as "going off the tracks" (*yuegui*). Economic reforms without political reforms, he says, have created a game with no rules. Until the political system changes, he says, China will remain in a state of "social disorder, chaos and upheaval."[27]

The rise of "illegal" activities is a response to this failure. "As a result of the lack of channels, some people are seeking to express and participate outside the system, creating political instability. This includes the resort to protests and violence," notes one scholar.[28] Such "participation" is not a healthy part of a system that is working but a dangerous manifestation of a system that is patently not working. Unlike protests in a democracy, people in China are demanding that the system be changed, not upheld.

Restraints on freedom, meanwhile, mean that one of the world's most creative cultures is a global backwater of technological, intellectual, and cultural innovation. China's best scientists, writers, film-makers, and would-be politicians can only flourish abroad. Pervasive injustice and the systematic and widespread unfair treatment of individuals means that resentment against the system is high.

Of course, as our metaphor reminds us, not all frustrations are directly aimed at the state. Drivers feel frustrated with each other too. The retarded state-society relationship means that society engages in internecine warfare. Writers in China write apocalyptically about the pervasive breakdown of social trust and social fabric under CCP rule. One writes of a country living "in a black hole" of social norms and expectations in the absence of a public space to debate these things. Another writes of a country "covered in lies."[29]

None of this is to diminish the modest achievements of the CCP since it began undoing the damage it wrought in the first 30 years of its rule. Since 1978, and as part of its bid to remain in power, the Party has affected a successful transition to a market economy and a more free society. It has opened China to the world and integrated it with the rest of the Asian region. The CCP-led government picks up the trash, catches robbers, issues passports, and manages a stable currency. The trains even run on time. It is better than the state of anarchy into which some nations have fallen. But is this the standard against which we should hold China?

Given its cultural endowment, there is no reason why China is not the Germany or Japan of Asia. Instead, it is a relative backwater by every measure except that of brute size, hardly a mark of success. Democracy would not make China perfect, but it would make it far less imperfect than dictatorship does. There is virtually no issue—be it the enforcement of business contracts, the response to health crises, the making of policy through public input, or the conduct of an effective diplomacy—that would not be improved by a successful democratic transition in China. Many if not most of the problems of China—like casino stock markets, financial crisis, environmental degradation, AIDS crisis, high suicide rates, misgovernance, and international credibility problems—are to a large extent a direct result of CCP rule. CCP rule is the biggest generator of political instability in China.

As mentioned, global experience shows that whatever a country's problems and whatever its inherited legacies, democracy almost always makes things better than they were under dictatorship. To take Asia, democracy does not turn Thailand into Singapore but it prevents it from becoming Burma. Democracy does not turn Taiwan into Japan but it prevents it from becoming North Korea. The Philippines and India, two cases of large poor countries that are whipping-boys for antidemocratic advocates, would probably have broken up long ago into failed states were it not for democracy.

Arguments by CCP propagandists and some Western observers that China is somehow "unique," in its governance needs, making dictatorship indispensable in order to bring about the same improvements in individual welfare that democracy provides elsewhere, have little grounding in comparative political experience. Comparisons between the alleged "success story" of China and the alleged failures of India and Russia are common. If the comparisons included not only hard indicators of socioeconomics but also more human issues of fairness, dignity, equality, and social dynamism the failings of dictatorship in China would loom larger. In any case, the possibilities of those countries are different. Cultural endowments, historical legacy, and economic choice probably mean that India is living with a lower wealth potential than China under any system. The proper comparison is not India under democracy versus China under dictatorship but each country under either democracy or dictatorship. In both cases, evidence suggests democracy wins hands down. Concludes one Party reformer: "Taking the first step toward democracy is the key to China becoming a modern nation."[30]

Of course, this assumes the feasibility of democracy and successful transition to it, the subject of parts 2 and 3. For those who believe the Chinese are incapable of running a democracy, those potential gains do not exist. To quote one pessimistic Western scholar, under democracy "the political process would be dominated by a relatively small number of powerful elites, urban groups, emerging new influentials (notably private businesspeople) and foreigners; and the bulk of the population, including urban marginals, and the vast rural population, would in all probability be disenfranchised, in reality if not in form."[31] Yet that is a perfect description of China today. It is a result of dictatorship, not democracy. The rural population could not be more disenfranchised, "the world's biggest population without political representation" according to one leading scholar in China,[32] while foreign businesspeople could not be more frighteningly influential.

In any case, China's people themselves increasingly reject the view that they are incapable of sustaining a democracy. As one scholar commented after an in-depth study of a city in Henan province: "Civic, legal and equality consciousness is being quickly raised by the development of the market economy. . . . In the face of such deep changes, the system based on repression is out of step with people's expectations."[33] Or as another scholar noted: "For a China long ruled by feudal dictatorship, without democratization the modernisation drive will ultimately fail."[34]

Thus have China's people reached a point where they believe democracy is necessary for creating a healthy economy, society, and polity. The demands for civil and political liberties, writes one scholar, have generated a whole new liberal mainstream in China "strongly committed to a free society of responsible individuals." Since democracy is the only system known to ensure such liberties, he says, "the opportunity for China to finally get on the liberal democratic track is not inconsiderable."[35]

Sustaining Economic Growth

Economic growth has become the central justification for continued CCP rule since Mao's death. While the economy may decide the fate of individual governments in a democracy, in China it determines the future of the entire political system. As one Party scholar wrote: "If we are unable to unlock the productive forces of society . . . a socialist system will lose the support of the people and be in real danger of overthrow."[36]

Have there been gains in material welfare in the reform era? The answer is undoubtedly yes, using the broadest indicator of welfare, the Human Development Index calculated by the UNDP. In the two decades to 2000, China's HDI index rose by 31 percent. That gain was comparable to the 33 percent gain registered by India over the same period. While this does not sustain claims of a "China miracle," it does reflect a modest overall improvement in living standards. By 2000, the average Chinese was living to 71, compared to 63 in 1975.

The Party claims credit for China's material advance since 1978, arguing that without the firm hand of dictatorship, important infrastructure projects would have been delayed, foreign investment deterred, and market-oriented reforms impossible. Yet that argument has several flaws, all noted in China. For a start, of course, the CCP has been essentially cleaning up the mess that it created in the first three decades of its rule. Second, actual gains have been fuelled largely by one-off redistributions of capital and labor away from agriculture into industry and services, and by the marketization of the economy. This decentralization and liberalization, the withdrawal of the state from economic life, is little related to the alleged benefits of strong authoritarian rule. Third, the gains captured by income figures are certainly overstated. GDP growth has probably been overstated by a fifth in the reform era as a result of statistical exaggeration. Meanwhile, China's given level of GDP overstates the resulting welfare because of unproductive investments—ill-considered and ill-built projects as well as social and environmental degradation.

Like Bismarck and Stalin, CCP rulers pride themselves on opening new superhighways and power plants. Yet these are often badly underused. The 3,300-megawatt Ertan dam (roughly half the generating capacity of the Grand Coulee dam), loses hundreds of millions of dollars a year because most of the power it generates cannot be sold. About 90 percent of the 143 airports built by 2001 were operating at a loss. The same logic—high investment but little gains in welfare—applies to foreign investment. A total of $400 billion poured into China between 1979 and 2001. Yet this flow was largely attracted by the country's distorted economic system—everything from a lack of finance for private enterprises to regional market barriers.[37]

The lack of open political institutions also has bred widespread economic corruption. That matters because it undermines claims that the CCP has gained legitimacy from the reform era. While the sanctioning of corruption might have made it easier for Beijing to launch reforms, it has also undercut the value of those reforms. Corruption is variously believed to be the equivalent of between 10 percent and 20 percent of GDP. Foreign investors like American foods company Pepsi and British automaker Rover both found their local partners engaged in corruption in 2002.

One result is that China's income inequality now rivals some of the most skewed countries in Latin America or Africa. Throughout the 1990s, only the richest one-fifth of people in China saw their incomes grow at rates equal to or higher than overall economic growth.[38] Poverty has fallen from around 32 percent to 11 percent of the population since reforms began. But those people did not vault into the middle class. Rather, they scraped across the imaginary line from starvation to survival. This is reflected in the measure of overall inequality, the Gini coefficient, where a figure of 0 represents perfect equality (everyone earns the same) and 1 represents perfect inequality (one person earns all the income). China's Gini expanded from 0.15 in 1978 to 0.45 by the turn of the century. Some commentators, pointing to the vast underreporting of income by the rich and the in-kind privileges and benefits they receive, put the true figure at 0.5 or even 0.6. The Party is well aware of the consequences: "If this income gap is not controlled within a certain range, it will shake people's faith in the Party and could even kill the reform effort," says a top-level report on threats to Party rule.[39] The attempts to explain-away income gaps as a result of markets rather than political unfairness increasingly fall on deaf ears. Notes one journalist in China: inequality "is the natural result of a feudal political system married to bureaucratic capitalism."[40]

The impact on workers and farmers, 70 percent of the population and the very social groups that the CCP is supposed to favor, has been dire. Wages have fallen, conditions have worsened, and job security has virtually disappeared. The official urban unemployment rate of 3 percent is reckoned to be closer to 10 percent if unregistered and temporarily laid off workers are taken into account and will reach 20 percent by 2010. In a democracy, workers can protect their interests by forming unions, lobbying politicians to maintain minimum wages and safety standards, and using the notion of social contract to garner support in an open society. All of that is prevented under CCP rule. Moreover, with no input into the political system, workers cannot influence Beijing's fondness for capital rather than labor-intensive growth, nor can they moderate Beijing's export drive with demands for a living wage and safe work conditions. Beijing pours tens of billions of dollars into senseless "techno-nationalism" projects like a Mars mission, a high-speed magnetic levitation train, gargantuan water engineering projects, and cutting edge semiconductor factories while the majority of its urban and rural workforce endures income stagnation. Some layoffs in the state sector were inevitable with reforms. But the "democracy deficit" has made the adjustment much worse. Efficiency gains might have been more evenly distributed, the timing and method of adjustment more favorable to workers, and the national growth strategy one that provided more new job opportunities. The ineffectiveness of the state-sponsored All-China Federation of Trade Unions, now seen as a tool of ty-coons, has spawned a whole underground union movement as well as fre-quent protests by disgruntled workers. By 2002, Beijing had 41 workers in jail for advocating worker rights. "Employers can organize business associations but workers cannot organize their own unions," complains one scholar in China.[41]

Even less can be said for the country's 850 million rural-dwellers, and especially the 600 million who still rely on farming, who have been subjected to systematic and explicit discrimination throughout PRC history. In the re-form era, that has manifested itself in a yawning urban-rural income gap, which doubled to a level of five to one by the turn of the century, 60 percent of which one scholar attributed to policy rather than natural causes.[42] Yet income measures alone cannot capture the full extent of welfare losses suf-fered by the peasantry as a result of the PRC's Stalinesque policy of squeezing the countryside to build the cities. Controls on internal migration in place since 1955 have prevented the normal process of income equalization. The 100 million migrant workers who find their way into towns and cities cannot secure adequate education, health, or housing. Those who remain in the countryside suffer from low public investment in rural education and health and controls on their economic activities like the right to own land. According to the WHO, about 80 percent of China's health budget is spent in cities, while less than 10 percent of peasants have any health protection now versus 90 percent in the Maoist era.

Unlike workers, peasants do not have even a state-sponsored representative body, the formation of which has been long resisted by Beijing fearful of the political impact. They are counted only as one quarter of a person in the apportioning of seats to the national parliament. One peasant advocate in China calls the entire system "a contravention of international human rights agreements and an insult to people's dignity . . . an exploitation of people based on a lack of equality, rights and respect."[43] In the absence of organized representation, rural China is now alive with mass protests involving tens of thousands of people. They take the form, according to one official report, of "putting up posters, destroying crops, burning haystacks, exhuming the ancestral graves of cadres, and direct attacks on Party leaders and government offices."[44] One intellectual who made a four-month trek through the villages of the Yellow River sees one solution to the plight of China's peasants: "The critical aspect of political reform at present is to push forward democratization."[45]

Now switch gears. Assume that all the injustice, inequality, waste, costs, and pure heartbreak of the marketization of China's economy between 1978 and the end of the twentieth century was somehow worthwhile. A bigger question is whether the same program is sustainable in the first decades of the twenty-first century. If the argument for democracy was not compelling at first, it is certainly compelling now. For the same democracy deficit that hampered and misdirected the gains of the first two decades of reform is now preventing China from creating sustainable growth for the coming decades. Note two scholars in China: "The biggest advocates of political reforms today are not academics and intellectuals but economists and businessmen who appreciate most keenly the need for political reforms to keep up with reforms in their areas."[46]

Here we consider five aspects of sustainability: innovation, effective regulation, safety, environmental protection, and financial health.

Gains from reallocations of labor and capital out of industry are likely to dry up as a source of growth by 2015, according to the World Bank. The gains from marketization will also end sometime in the first decade of the century. Already, growth is more and more dependent on fiscal stimulus, without which, the premier Zhu Rongji said in early 2002, the economy "might have collapsed."[47] That means China's economy will have to rely more and more on technical improvements to grow. As is well known, innovation thrives under democracy. It requires open information sources, free debate, guaranteed rights, and secure contracts—of the sort that only democracy has proven consistently able to deliver. The necessity of democracy to spur technological change was noted in a famous speech by liberal Party elder Wan Li in 1986. A prominent scholar of the Central Party School repeated the call a decade later: "The serious lagging of political reform is now a major obstacle to sustainable economic growth."[48]

Yet at present, China's technical innovation capacity is woefully low. Its best scientists and entrepreneurs go abroad—82 percent of engineering, computer science, and physics graduates from Qinghua University left the country in 2001[49]—or register their companies abroad, because of the uncertainties of pursuing their vocations in China. Its home-grown companies, nurtured on clientelist ties to the state, find they cannot compete in world markets. All that creates a pressing demand in society for the openness and security of democracy. As one economist wrote in a state report: "There is not a single successful market economy in the world that is not also a democracy."[50]

Closely tied to innovation is the need for effective regulation. Here, reform China may have created one of the world's most badly regulated economies. Smuggling, counterfeiting, fraud, extortion, tax evasion, gangsters, and cronyism thrive on a scale never before seen. Half of the four billion contracts signed every year are fraudulent in some respect, according to official estimates. An estimated 40 percent of all products made in the country are either fake or substandard. The central government estimates that 80 percent of private entrepreneurs avoid taxes in some way. Meanwhile, two-thirds of the biggest 1,300 state enterprises keep false accounts.

The costs of this are real. Credit cards, checks, and e-commerce cannot develop. People die from fake booze. A black market in human organs thrives. Long-term private investment is stifled. Critical public investments in research, social welfare, education, and health are impossible. Public assets are privatized, plundered, and left to rot. Growth becomes almost impossible. Without free newspapers or opposition parties, the control of wrongdoing becomes stalled by closed political networks. The argument for CCP-style reforms, wrote three U.S. economists, "may be overlooking the social tensions being created by the asset-stripping, corruption and macroeconomic instability" which "may cause a popular rebellion against the regime."[51]

A strong central state could, in theory, impose order and regulations to create the "economic society" necessary for a properly functioning market economy, as Chile did in the 1970s. But in China, the decentralization of power that accompanied reforms and the rise of crony business networks both mean central edicts are a weak tool. Indeed, it is the state itself that is involved in most of the malfeasance. The only way to create the "economic society" of markets and rule of law is to limit political power. One Beijing scholar notes that the argument that dictatorship would spur growth by reducing the "transaction costs" of democracy has been turned on its head by the reality of widespread scams and inefficiencies bred by the closed political system. "The price we have paid is considerable, even massive. This is why it is urgent to begin democratic political reforms."[52]

Safety problems also stem from the lack of political oversight. Road safety is a good barometer of a state's ability to regulate a growing society. China's annual road carnage was 106,000 people in 2001, making it the world's most dangerous place to be in a vehicle, measured by deaths per vehicle on the road, and twice as deadly as in 1985. A person is 30 times more likely to die when getting into a vehicle in China than in the United States. Other types of accident are no less frequent: workplace accidents—everything from factory fires to flooded mine shafts to firecracker explosions—took another 25,000 lives in 2001. One mainland writer compares the response to accidents with that in newly democratic South Korea. "When a bridge collapsed in Seoul in 1995, the mayor resigned and seven city officials were arrested. But in China we have a daily parade of major accidents and the only thing that happens is that the relevant officials are praised for their work in the relief effort."[53]

Ineffective regulation is perhaps seen most starkly in environmental degradation. Official and unofficial estimates put the annual losses due to pollution (both direct costs to agriculture and industry and indirect costs to health and buildings) at the equivalent of 4 to 8 percent of GDP. In addition, ecological damage (deforestation etc) is estimated variously at another 5 to 15 percent of GDP per year. This means that the economic value of China's natural assets is being reduced in a way that will constrain long-term growth.

There is also a cultural capital degradation that is harder to estimate. UNESCO officials constantly decry the degradation of the country's great cultural sites. Soaring new hotels have marred the riverside scenes of once-idyllic Guilin, while waves from tourist boats have eaten away at the river's Buddhist carvings. Cable cars have covered the country's once-sacred mountaintops.

This environmental disaster was not a necessary accompaniment to economic growth but an avoidable result of a lack of political pressure and open society. One farmer in Inner Mongolia who tried to prevent the illegal logging of hillsides near his home was arrested after he found evidence implicating local officials in the problem.[54] Scholars call the Three Gorges dam decision in 1992 a massive policy failure that relates directly to the closed political system. Saving China's environment, according to the World Bank, requires "a significant change in development strategy" that includes "public participation in environmental decision-making."[55]

Finally, the financial crisis bred by Beijing's flawed state enterprise reform strategy increasingly constrains growth prospects. By allowing corruption to steal away the best parts of the state sector, Beijing is left controlling the dregs. The state's big four banks are politically mandated to lend to these losers irrespective of performance. The result is a banking system where perhaps half of all loans are never going to be repaid. To keep savings flowing into state banks, the government mandates low interest rates and limits the activities of private and foreign banks (something unlikely to change despite WTO promises).

Public confidence in state banks is weak. One result is capital flight. Estimates vary but a safe middle ground is that around $25 billion was leaving China every year at the turn of the century, most of it never to return. Another result is that finance is pushed underground. As much as half of all the money in the country's stock markets, a total of $100 billion, comes from illegal investment schemes.[56] The state's use of the 1,300 listed companies as vehicles for the enrichment of local cadres causes wild swings in official policy. It also creates dangerously unstable fiscal conditions. The amount of outstanding public debt as a percentage of GDP exceeds 100 percent if pension and implicit guarantees to the banking sector are included.

Internationally, the pressures for a better financial system are immense. Analysts expect the Renminbi to become the world's fourth most heavily traded currency once it is convertible, expected around 2010. As the steward of one of the world's major currencies, Beijing will need a predictable and open monetary policy-setting apparatus. Yet the current system fails to deliver that because financial policy is driven by the changing imperatives of sustaining Party rule.

Overall, the picture is of an economy that could profit from a heavy dose of democracy. China's economy has grown quickly but unevenly, unsustainably, and even dangerously. Crisis looms on many fronts, from peasants to pensioners, from bad loans to bad products. What might have been a South Korean or Taiwanese style emergence into a relatively equal and robust market economy has instead become a Latin American-style land of corruption and inequality. "In delaying the introduction of democratic reforms," notes one Chinese scholar, "the Chinese have missed the best chance to provide an equal start for everyone in the marketplace."[57]

It's never too late to curtail the losses of course. Many scholars in China now hearken back to Deng Xiaoping's words that political reforms are the real marker of economic success. "If the top priority of China's rulers really were stability through the difficult times of remaining economic reforms," concludes one Western scholar, "then they would already be working assiduously to democratize China."[58]

The Social Malaise

On a chill winter's day in Beijing, a father and his daughter strolled into Tiananmen Square to watch fluffy snowflakes floating to the ground. As the snow accumulated, the girl rolled a small clump into a chair-sized ball. Her father placed a smaller one on top with a few pebbles on the front and two sticks at the sides. The first snowman of winter was born.

Within minutes, a soldier appeared. No one had approved the building of the snowman, he barked. It was therefore an "unauthorized structure"; in a single kick, his knee-high black boot toppled the frosty-looking threat. A poem later appeared on the Internet describing the event.[59]

Snow is falling on Tiananmen
Pure the snow falls, just like one of your dreams

Suddenly a soldier's voice thunders
"Making a snowman? Don't you know what place this is?"
Smashed beneath the soldier's gun
Left behind are only his cruel boot marks
Black marks imprinted everywhere
Abruptly the child's song is stilled
The world falls silent
The entire world is benumbed

Please forgive me, my child
I have failed in my duty
I am at your side
But I cannot help you
The cowardice of your father
Of tens of millions of fathers
Gave rise to that rifle's insolence

Father can give you a comic book
Father can take you to McDonald's
Father can give you a robot toy
But father cannot give you Tiananmen
He cannot give you a little fun today

How absurd will China's future be
When a snowman cannot be build in the country's heart?
China's flowers cannot let loose their child's spirit
The snowman has no right to exist
The child's spirit has no right to exist
Dreams have no right to exist
To whom does Tiananmen belong?

As philosophers from Confucius to Kant have noted, man is essentially a moral being whose life goals are defined in terms of his ability to pursue a moral conception of what is important and worthwhile. Economic benefits and market freedoms certainly help with this quest. But they are a means to an end. Just as critical, perhaps more so, are guaranteed rights and freedoms so that people can pursue their chosen dreams. Some people dream of building a snowman in Tiananmen Square.

Whatever the material gains of the reform era, they are far from proof that China's people should be happy with their rulers. While some prosperity has come to some parts of China, freedoms, rights, and justice remain highly undeveloped. If so, the philosophers tell us, people's deepest aspirations will remain at best only partly met. It is no coincidence that revolutions against tyranny often happen in economically growing countries—Poland, South Korea, Brazil. Partly that reflects the empowering of societies. But the motive for change (as opposed to the means) is also grounded in the fact that material gains alone do not satisfy human needs. To quote the UNDP: "The most benign dictatorship imaginable would not be compatible with human development because human development has to be fully owned. It cannot be granted from above."[60]

In China, the moral being is increasingly making its presence felt. While the introduction of markets did enhance freedoms, the failure to reform the political system meant that a whole new dimension of injustice arose. Material gains were unfairly distributed to corrupt cadres, privileged urban-dwellers, men, the healthy, the smartest, and the well-connected. If we view society as a fair system of cooperation, then there is a good argument that China is worse off today from a moral, and thus a fundamental, point of view. As one mainland scholar wrote: "If there is no democracy then we should discount our livelihood greatly and in fact we are living just an idiot's existence. Without democracy the significance of the Chinese people is very limited."[61]

Some, especially among the disadvantaged, express their discontent by championing a return to Maoist ideals, if not practices. Scholars and intellectuals, meanwhile, have launched a whole new "anti-GDP" discourse which rejects the idea that material gains should be the marker of success. "We need to ditch the growth-centered strategy and choose a new strategy based on social development . . . grounded in humanism and justice, one that holds high the banner of fairness and morality," writes economist He Qinglian.[62] Another scholar, writing in a book published in Beijing in 2000, calls for a return to "ethical and human-centered" development instead of "GDP as the sole criterion of truth."[63]

While the space for individual behavior has widened in the reform era, this is not the same as freedom, which means being free from the very possibility of arbitrary state interference. China's people still live with the risks of attracting state attention. As a result, they develop strategies of behavior to avoid it and develop a sense of the self as subordinate to state power. The state may interfere less, but it dominates just as before. In the U.S.-based Freedom House rankings, China, receiving a civic freedoms score of 6 (with 7 the worst and 1 the best), keeps company with the likes of Vietnam, Rwanda and Bahrain. Fear of the state, relates one mainland scholar, is "deeply ingrained . . . in the minds of the Chinese people."[64]

At the personal level, this has a devastating impact. China is among Asia's most dispirited countries, alongside North Korea and Singapore, an unlikely achievement given its rich traditions of humor, sociability, and zest for work. When you step across the border into Guangdong from Hong Kong—Cantonese societies both—the joie de vivre of life in a free society is replaced by the torpor of life under dictatorship.

Dictatorship impoverishes individual life in China by limiting the space for self-realization. The lack of individual rights creates a society of passive subjects rather than engaged citizens. One mainland scholar paints an eerie portrait of a society characterized by "disorganized hedonism, a disregard for justice and, above all, a devastating poverty of moral and cultural resources for self-critique and self-betterment."[65] A former Chinese official describes the same malady: "Under this dictatorship, on the surface everyone is happily dancing, but in their bones they are slowly becoming paralyzed. One person of great potential after another is sent off to death. . . . In the end, every one of them has been given a burial by dictatorship."[66]

Many avoid that burial by fleeing the country. About 60,000 a year emigrate to North America while an equal number leave for Hong Kong, many bound for points beyond. Untold thousands drift illegally into Southeast Asia, Russia's Far East, and Japan. China's finest writers, like Nobel laureate Gao Xingjian, live abroad. The ones who gain fame at home attract audiences by penning stories about moral turpitude, hedonism, and cynicism. "Chinese literature in the twentieth century time and again was worn out and indeed almost suffocated because politics dictated literature," Gao said in his Nobel acceptance speech. "If the writer sought to win intellectual freedom the choice was either to fall silent or to flee."

Others respond with suicide. More than 300,000 people a year take their lives in China, a rate of 21 per 100,000 people, double the rate in the U.S. and India, and comparable to Japan's much-publicized and bemoaned rate.

The highest concentration is among rural women, who suffer from the PRC's lack of enforced individual rights on several levels.

Beijing's response to demands for individual rights is shot full of contradictions. Claims that individuals are perfectly happy without rights—busily engaged in stamp trading or mahjong games—reflect the high costs of trying to exercise such rights not the lack of demand for them. The few brave individuals who try to assert such rights quickly find themselves staring at prison walls. Meanwhile, Beijing's claims that rights to subsistence must supersede political rights—even if that were empirically proven, which it is not[67]—beg the question of why the 90 percent of China's population that lives well beyond subsistence is not given more rights. Claims that "group rights" must be considered, meanwhile, disguise the fact that not all groups are allowed to organize and claim attention. China's gaping income inequalities and systematic discrimination against its largest group, peasants, gives the lie to Beijing's claim to protect groups.

As elsewhere, attempts to discredit universal rights standards prove in China to be a shabby excuse for dictatorship. To quote one leading liberal in an article in a Guangzhou newspaper: "At root we are all people with the same basic desires. . . . Do the Chinese willingly live in a prison with no rights? . . . Do we wish someone else to keep our mouths shut?"[68]

Ineffective social policy and debased social capital are prominent macro-level results. Social policy covers many areas: here I consider just three: health, housing, and population. In all three, the essential problem is the same. The lack of public input into policymaking means they are either misguided or lack legitimacy or both. Implementation either fails to address problems or faces resistance.

China has achieved significant gains in overall health during the reform era. Life expectancy has risen by eight years and infant mortality has halved. Those gains largely reflect increased income, which has improved nutrition. The provision of health care for the least advantaged, however, has steadily deteriorated. China ranked 188 out of 191 in the World Health Organization's rankings of fairness in financial contributions to health care in 1997.

Beijing is unable and unwilling to respond effectively to health crises. Democracies are better at handling epidemics because of open information flows and pressure on politicians to act. The successful response to AIDS in Brazil, Thailand, and India proves the point. China, by contrast, faces the worst AIDS epidemic outside of Africa. It is expected to have 10 to 20 million AIDS victims by 2010, the most of any country. Yet the leadership's response, given a lack of public pressure, has been to ignore or downplay the problem, a shortcoming the UN has decried with increasing alarm. The same handicaps were evident in the handling of the SARS crisis that gripped the country in the first half of 2003.

Urban housing reforms, forcing people to buy and manage their own homes rather than depend on state flats, have not been accompanied by greater social participation in the making of urban housing policy. Decisions on zoning, property taxation, utilities, and much more lack popular legitimacy. In 2001, for example, the municipal government of Guangzhou forced all residents to remove metal gates from their apartment doors claiming that the gates gave the city a bad image. After police had torn down thousands of gates, the plan was abandoned due to open resistance. The *China Youth Daily* quoted one local scholar saying that the incident proved that dictatorship not democracy is the more costly system. "My teachers used to say socialism was superior to democracy because we could make decisions fast. But what are the costs when those decisions are wrong?" he wondered.[69] Across China, housing-related issues are now one of the fastest-growing sources of open protest. This issue is bound to rise in importance as urbanization, which went from 18 percent in 1976 to 36 percent by 2000, continues.

Finally, population controls have had an unnecessarily negative impact on society. Beijing claims to have averted 340 million births from 1979 to 1998 through its controls—essentially one child for urban dwellers and a second for rural residents if the first is a daughter. Partly, the statistics are overstated since many births of females go unreported. An estimated 80 million people have no legal existence in China. More important, the results should be compared to what might have been achieved through voluntary family planning, investment in female education and opportunities, and the free provision of contraceptives. The Nobel-winning economist Amartya Sen has shown how the same results can be achieved—and have been in countries like Thailand, Indonesia, and parts of India—even while protecting individual rights.

China's draconian approach—the approach of dictatorship—has had dire collateral consequences. By 2000, the ratio of newborn boys to girls was 117 compared to 107 in 1982 and a world average of 105, mainly a result of underreporting of girls and sex selective abortion forced by the one-child policy. Birth control policy is one of the main drivers of bad relations between cadres and farmers, the subject of literally thousands of physical attacks of rural cadres responsible for fining or aborting "excess births." It is also, not incidentally, a source of major official corruption for officials who take bribes to look the other way. Whole patterns of behavior are created—cohabitation, migrant life, etc—to get around the policy, robbing the country of productive lives. About 150,000 babies a year, mostly girls or disabled, are abandoned on the streets, a few of which are lucky enough to be adopted abroad.

Some argue that Beijing should just switch to a policy of voluntarism. But lacking the broader democratic pressures to create the necessary infrastructure—targeted poverty alleviation, a focus on women's rights and status, an end to population control as an indicator of cadre success—this seems unlikely. As with so much in modern-day China, the state cannot simply borrow "advanced techniques" from elsewhere and graft them onto its dictatorship. In the words of one expert: "Genuine voluntarism cannot live in the midst of China's regulatory and punitive administrative culture."[70]

The decline of social capital is another dimension of China' social malaise under the CCP. Crime has risen so high in the reform era that many travelers prepare special "robber purses" to hand to thieves who waylay their buses or trains. The crime rate reached 163 crimes per 100,000 people in 1998, triple the rate in 1978. Even so scholars say that this is probably a vast underreporting. There were 4,000 police killed in the 1990s versus 1,000 in the 1980s.[71] As with corruption, it is misleading to blame the rise in crime on marketization or social transition. The real problem is the lack of accompanying political reforms.[72]

Beijing's response to crime hearkens to the worst aspects of dictatorship: mass blood-letting and little due process through periodic "strike hard" campaigns. During the period 1997–2001, an average of 15,000 people a year were put to death or shot dead by police, accounting for 97 percent of the world's judicial executions in 2001.[73]

Social capital, the glue that allows members of society to undertake cooperation without formal arrangements, is a resource that underpins successful market economies as well as successful societies. It emerges through the norms and expectations of a society built by free individuals. In posttotalitarian states like China, social capital is at its lowest. The collapse of the top-down ideology and the failure to empower society to forge its own replacement creates a corrosive situation of expanding individual choice but no social norms. Notes one scholar in China: "When the state gives up direct control of people's lives, people have no idea of how to consolidate and secure their personal positions, and on what basis to have relations with other people."[74]

The results of China's degraded social capital are all-too apparent. People lie and steal as if it were the most natural thing. One Chinese scholar calls the country "a nation of hypocrites."[75] Books with titles like "China Covered in Lies" and "Can We Trust Anyone These Days?" pack newsstands. Rather than normal open channels, rent-seeking, backdoor methods, and plain screwing your buddy thrive. In the words of one scholar in China: "China is now in a state where every social class has a strong feeling of being exploited by the others, leading to a situation where each class condemns the other and does not trust the other. As a result, there is no mechanism to restrain people, which inhibits political stability."[76]

Of course social capital can be built outside the political sphere from cultural sources like religion, ethnicity, tradition, or rationalism. Indeed, as in the Cultural Revolution, Chinese society seems to hang together mainly because of these things. But alone, these things cannot sustain the system without regeneration from within. Political imperatives mean that regeneration is difficult. State constraints on religion, for example, driven by a well-founded fear of morally committed and organized believers, prevent the development of civic culture. The ongoing repression of the Falun Gong group, a qigong sect that rocketed into public attention when 10,000 of its members surrounded the Zhongnanhai complex in 1999, is the best example. The official *China Society* magazine called the crackdown "stupid": "In today's China . . . there is no effective ideology. Life in a faithless, isolated, insecure society in which people cannot tell black from white is just the same as a life in hell."[77]

In the end, society can only be rebuilt through freely associating individuals recognized and treated as moral equals by the state. That is a conclusion spreading far and wide as the social malaise deepens. Notes one scholar: "China's ethical slide can only stir up renewed political debate about the need for democracy."[78]

A Troubled Diplomacy

While China is a poor country with little impact on shaping the norms of international behavior at present, it has a linchpin role in Asia's security and economic development and will probably enjoy a rising profile in international diplomacy in coming decades. As a constructive partner, China could, like India, enhance Asian regional security, play a prominent role in seeking global equality, hugely assist international environmental efforts, and enhance world cultural diversity. As a menace, it could cause a lot of damage. Because of its border disputes with India and Russia, claims to Taiwan and an archipelago of reefs in the South China Sea, 400 nuclear warheads, and around 30 long-range nuclear missiles, China is a potential headache the world could do without.

That means the question of whether China has a government prepared and able to conduct a foreign policy that enhances stability and development in the world matters for everyone. At present it does not.

The mirror-image of the CCP's domestic goals of reordering and controlling society are its global goals of reordering the world system and dominating Asia. The CCP has defined its main aims in diplomacy as realizing by mid-century a *qiang guo meng*, or "strong country dream." It seeks to create "a new world order" and draws under its tattered standard outcast regimes like Zimbabwe, Cuba, and Burma. All this is at odds with the expectations of a responsible power in the twenty-first century. That notion is a state that helps to maintain global peace, uphold human rights and promote democracy. Beijing's outmoded view of competitive and inviolable state power clashes loudly with prevailing international norms. It seeks to join the world community while rejecting world norms and rules. As a result, it faces a constant "crisis of international respectability."[79]

Putting aside the interests of the world, this is a major concern for China itself because powers that run amok in the world system are usually brought to heel in a way that makes them suffer the most. By portraying itself as an aggrieved power demanding respect lest it cause trouble, Beijing encourages the rest of the world to treat it with "caution and circumspection."[80] As one Chinese writer notes: "China needs to make a fundamental choice: whether or not to stand on the side of world freedom and democracy, which represents the mainstream and direction of our time."[81]

Of course, Beijing is not alone in debating international norms. In Asia, for example, India, Malaysia, and Indonesia, to name a few, are constantly seeking to influence global norms, as they should. An open policy process allays fears of neighbors—a big reason why nobody fears India even though it frequently spouts anti-Western bombast. China's outlier foreign policy might be less of a concern if its political system were more democratic. Since it is not, it turns what might be constructive criticism into destructive dissonance. As one liberal reformer put it: "If we don't launch political reform, we'll bring upon ourselves the dread and disgust of the world."[82]

A democratic government, as Kant first began to outline, tends to make and implement foreign policy the same way it does domestic policy. Multiple voices contend and debate in an open setting until a consensus is reached and cooperation and peace sought with neighbors in the interests of making individual lives better. Kant's democratic peace—the proposition that democracies do not fight one another—is one of the few iron laws of social science.

China's undemocratic system produces the opposite: secrecy, extremism, and aggression. As in domestic politics, the CCP imperative of identifying and crushing enemies and admitting of no weakness makes it a bad diplomat. Without the legitimization provided by regular elections, the regime must seek popular support through external aggression. In the experience of the last British governor of Hong Kong, Chris Patten, China's diplomats acted like "guerilla fighters" rather than negotiators: "The Chinese system meant that their negotiators would have no room to question their instructions, would not always know the overall strategy behind the negotiations, and would have only one order and that would be to attack, to surrender no ground, and to come back with a clear-cut victory."[83]

Journalists and scholars are rewarded not for questioning state diplomacy but for fanning nationalist flames. Those who do the opposite find themselves imprisoned or the subject of virulent official attacks. The military, meanwhile, which dominates security policy and comes to the fore anytime there is a more general foreign policy crisis, "displays a distinctly insular and non-cosmopolitan worldview."[84] In short, the lack of a democratic system makes everyone a hard-liner.

Some argue that the PRC system allows for a consistency in foreign policy not subject to mere "domestic interests." Yet the consistency on things like noninterference and UN policies is a sign of a weak state. China has little choice if it wants to retain some voice. But that could easily change as its power grows, as the occasionally lamentable behavior of the United States shows. Second, consistency is of value only when the policy is consistently positive for the world system. China's is not: it consistently threatens Taiwan, consistently maintains ties to rogue regimes, and consistently scuppers UN attempts to uphold globally accepted human rights standards. It's a consistency the world could do without. Far better would be an open if erratic policy that was more constructive. As we shall see, even a more aggressive China in democratic transition might be preferable.

The failures of CCP diplomacy can be seen best in its border empire: the two inland regions conquered by the Qing dynasty—Muslim Xinjiang and Buddhist Tibet—and coastal entrepôts claimed by Beijing after their decol-onization—Hong Kong and Taiwan. Empires are difficult to maintain at the best of times given scarce resources and antipathy toward the colonizer. The difficulties are compounded by the fact that China is not a world leader, or representative of the world's advanced ideas. That means Beijing is forced to rely solely on old-fashioned, and expensive, coercion. Yet the cost—not just financially as in Tibet and Xinjiang but also politically as in Taiwan and Hong Kong—is a huge drain on the state and its people.

Today, Xinjiang is rocked by constant bombings and riots against Chinese rule, more than 1,000 "violent incidents," in 2001 alone.[85] Tibet is less in turmoil but is a bigger black mark on Beijing's global profile, "the single most negative factor as far as China's international image is concerned" according to one European parliamentarian.[86] Taiwan, meanwhile, is the biggest sore point in U.S.-China ties and a major threat to China's domestic well-being since an attack on the island would almost certainly cause sanctions on China. In Hong Kong, where voters regularly cast two-third of their ballots for pro-democracy candidates, rule from Beijing since 1997 has resulted in a clear deterioration of rights and a concomitant increase in domestic unrest.

A democratic nation limits these costs either by granting the colonies independence or by providing them with enough autonomy to accept imperial rule. Democracy has ensured national unity in diverse countries like India, the Philippines, South Africa, Spain, and Canada. By contrast, autocratic empires break up when the center's resolve weakens, as it did in Yugoslavia, Russia, and Indonesia. Beijing unwittingly portrays itself as the world's last great autocratic empire by citing those examples to justify CCP rule. Yet it cannot pursue a "democratic foreign policy," in its near empire because that would redound at home.

It was not always so, of course. In the early days of communist China, Mao and Zhou Enlai were indifferent to the future reclamation of Taiwan and Hong Kong and imagined a Tibet and Xinjiang living in high autonomy with a voluntary federation-like relationship with China. Yet as the communist state veered toward tyranny in the late 1950s, the external manifestation was a hardening of positions on empire. The KMT had gone through the same U-turn in the 1930s. Today, democracy is the only solution left to the crisis of CCP rule in these places. No amount of PRC leniency or concessions will resolve the illegitimate nature of PRC political power in the eyes of the colonized. Beijing leaders implicitly acknowledge the legitimacy problem in noting that, in the Tibet case, unrest rose in the 1950s and 1980s when accommodating policies were pursued.[87]

Within the rest of Asia, China's "strong country dream" generates significant unease. One example is the Shanghai Cooperation Organization, a regional security pact set up by Beijing in 1996 with its four Central Asian neighbors and Russia. Central Asian members fear that Beijing's agenda is to control their oil resources and isolate them from the West. Russia fears expanded PRC influence in Central Asia. As a result, two members have since negotiated bilateral security pacts with the United States, while the organization played virtually no role in the U.S.-led anti-terrorist war on its doorstep in 2001–2002. One scholar calls the group "stillborn."[88]

Suspicions of China's intentions also explain why Singapore, Thailand, and the Philippines maintain loose but clear alliances with the United States.

The region's countries have not been reassured by Beijing's behavior in the South China Sea, where it asserts ridiculous claims to sovereignty over reefs and islets as far as 2,000 kilometers (1,240 miles) south of Hong Kong, and backs them up with military expeditions and installations. Like its near empire, Beijing cannot admit of a democratic solution to these claims without undermining its rule at home.

It is in relations with Japan, however, that the costs of CCP rule are greatest. Japan brings out the worst of CCP: jealous and racist cultural resentment at a Confucian land populated by "pirates and midgets" that is richer and more successful than itself; rabid anti-foreign nationalism unable to seek reconciliation for the wounds of World War II; and fear-mongering portrayal of renewed Japanese militarism to justify its own stern rule at home.

Like other Asian nations, China suffered extensive loss of human life and property from Japan's war in the region in World War II. However, unlike other countries, notably South Korea, China cannot accept Japan's apologies and seek reconciliation, because its founding legitimacy was grounded partly in the war against Japan—its national anthem is an anti-Japanese folk song written in 1935. War history is used, and abused, to legitimate CCP rule. Schoolchildren are not told of Japan's frequent apologies, and adults are not reminded that the United States and the KMT helped force Japan out of China. In a country where most museums are shabby and uncared for, the Anti-Japanese War Museum in suburban Beijing spares no expense. Chinese do not know that Japan is the country's largest aid donor or that it built Beijing's new airport. Beijing's claims that Japanese militarism is reviving ignore the cause of cautious Japanese rearmament: concerns of a rising and aggressive China which are not allayed by its opaque political system.

The costs are enormous. Asia's potentially greatest economic relationship is dogged by suspicions. Japanese companies suffer waves of consumer activism over small issues because the CCP has created a society that believes the war ended yesterday and Japan is not contrite. Meanwhile, Japan and its people cannot even begin to imagine China as a responsible partner in Asian security. Like Taiwan, Japan can only hope, and argue, for a democratic government in China, while worrying that a CCP-led China may follow the warlike path of so many nationalistic authoritarian regimes before it.

With this background in mind, China's relations with the West, and the United States in particular, seem more amenable to understanding. Beijing's relations with every country are troubled primarily by its political system and the imperatives on which it is built. While other countries can act intelligently to manage that and contain its impact, it would be foolish to believe that any country, certainly not a West whose very existence is considered a challenge to the CCP's post-1989 ethnocentric chauvinism, could have good relations with Beijing. U.S. analysts trying to understand and improve ties to China would do better to look at the pathologies of authoritarian regimes than at wrongly essentialized cultural differences or the shortcomings of foreign policy-making in a democracy. As a leading U.S. State Department official put it: "It is no accident that our closest relationships—our true partnerships—are with fellow democracies. Societies that are like-minded are more likely to see the world similarly."[89]

The same goes for China's relations with Europe. Beijing imagines the European Union as a Western bloc without all the human rights hang-ups of the United States. At times, Europe—in particular France—fulfills that promise. But more often—whether its Swedish attempts to mediate Tibet, Catholic countries' concern about religious freedoms, or post-communist Eastern European leaders promoting democratic change—the hope is dashed by the same normative concerns that drive U.S. policy.

In the end, Beijing cannot escape the fact that its political system is incompatible with strong relations with the majority of the world's countries. As leading liberal Bao Tong notes: "China's need for democracy is all the more pressing because it has a growing world role and responsibility in an unstable region."[90]

Political Dysfunction

A state's capacity to govern is determined not only by its ability to manage and enforce its writ over society—the subject of the previous three sections. It also depends on the internal cohesion of the state: its ability to cooperate, divide up tasks, and maintain the allegiance of officials. Merely keeping the political system from tearing itself apart is a mighty task for communist regimes, which have proven to be particularly vulnerable to internal dysfunction. In their Alice in Wonderland world, what is "rational" for a given cadre is usually anything but good for the polity. Lacking popular accountability, decision-making processes are often held in thro to personal rivalries. This problem worsens as widely-respected elders of the revolutionary era die off, as China's did in the 1990s. With no one holding the right of final decision, power disperses. The political parallel to the looting of China's state economy is the parcelling out of political power to complex networks within the Party and state. Among the grossest manifestations of this in the PRC are factionalism, corruption, and regionalism.

The spread of factions based on family-like loyalties is a key weakness. Personal factions exist in democracies too but they are much less threatening.

Democratic leaders who promote cronies are accountable to electors and to the glare of media and opposition scrutiny for the results. The CCP, by contrast, must assert that all promotions are based on merit alone. Since that is patently untrue in so many cases, legitimacy suffers. So does governance: incompetents are promoted while policy becomes hostage to factional battles for power.[91]

While the Party has constructed a façade of rules-based elite politics since Mao, much evidence suggests little has changed. In the Jiang Zemin era alone (1989 to 2002), no less than six Politburo members were purged after losing out in factional battles. Of the nine new members of the Politburo standing committee chosen in 2002, only two reached their positions on the strength of merit.[92] What norms exist—like the idea that top leaders should retire at 70—are unwritten and subject to frequent violation or misuse.

Lower down in the political system, the same dynamics are at work. Since local officials are evaluated and promoted based on the views of their superiors "most cadres spend their time chasing promotions and not governing," noted one Chinese scholar after a study of a city in Henan province.[93] The term "self-operators in the Party" (*dangnei getihu*) refers to cadres who spend most of their time building up their personal networks. Each has an army of private secretaries, policy aides, and other hangers-on who shuttle back and forth to Beijing holding secret meetings with potential allies. Party journals frequently admonish cadres for worrying more about their *guanxi* (personal connections) than their governance. One scholar of China believes the failure to reign in factions "could yet prove to be a fatal flaw," in the PRC.[94]

Political corruption is another fatal flaw. In the ten years to 2002, more than 1.5 million cadres were punished for corruption, an average of about 430 per day. About one in seven of them was sent to jail. Corruption pervades inner political life—bribes are paid for promotions, housing assignments, official trips abroad, anything that requires another cadre's chop. "Money politics," that smear hurled at Taiwan and the United States by the CCP to besmirch democracy, is so pervasive as to be the norm in China.

Just about every government department has an "overseas student," an official who has absconded with state funds and fled abroad. Internal figures said there were 7,236 such officials by early 1999 who had taken a total of $16 billion of state funds out of the country.[95] Entire housing developments in the United States are populated by the spouses and children of corrupt cadres. As a female cadre in the novel *Heaven's Wrath*, an allegorical novel about a major corruption scandal in Beijing says when asked where she gets her money:[96]

My friends say there is no place like China when it comes to getting money from the state. In other places, even the president has to account for every guest he has over for dinner because there are opposition parties watching him. Not so in China. The Communist Party rules everything and arrests anyone who confronts them. Those of us who have officials as our sugar daddies know this best of all. I don't want to leave China. It has been very good to me.

Of course, the immediate cause of corruption is the economic powers put in the hands of cadres by reforms. But even in unreformed communist states, corruption was widespread, reminding us that the root cause is unconstrained political power. Blaming market reforms is a cop-out. Corruption was no less widespread in the pre-reform era, when cadres sold scarce grain on the black market and took money to exempt youths from mandatory rustication. Its monetary explosion after Mao should properly be pinned on the failure to introduce political reforms alongside market reforms, not the market reforms themselves.[97]

Political corruption introduces extreme dysfunction into governance. It means that incentives are oriented toward who pays and who receives. That explains any number of governance problems—from unenforced industrial safety standards to silenced people's congresses. Factional networks can easily sidetrack corruption investigations—as almost certainly happened when Jiang Zemin protected a former Party secretary of Fujian province from a smuggling scandal in 2001. As former top leader Li Ruihuan charged:[98]

> We in the CCP cannot seem to implement successful supervision of ourselves. . . . Over the course of twelve years we have eight or nine documents, but still no top leader is willing to reveal his income or property, or that of his spouse or children. Why did an advanced political party . . . come to this pass? . . . If we want to change the situation and to effectively prevent and check corruption, we must constrain and supervise power

Or as a former CCP official put it: "What are power holders and rich men in China afraid of? They are afraid of openness, transparency, revelations, journalist interviews, public condemnation, direct elections, legislatures, hearings, testimonies, public trials, the leaking of insider scandals. In a word, the corrupt fear democracy. Without democracy, corruption will never be curtailed. Just chanting anti-corruption without democracy is like going fishing in the middle of the forest."[99]

The scourge of regionalism, finally, does not refer to the assertion of regional interests. That is normal in any political system. Rather it refers to the informal and ad hoc response by local governments to the central government's unpredictable and opportunistic use of its powers, which in the unitary government structure of China remain absolute. Lacking any federal structure in which powers are shared, and any constitutional provisions to back that up, central-local politics in China are characterized by a constant battle over how far and how absolutely Beijing's powers should extend. The situation is exacerbated by the uniquely inefficient parallel "party-government" structure that provides means for both central and local cadres to further frustrate policies they dislike or impose policies they prefer. Officials from interior provinces cannot make formal submissions for a change in coastal development strategy based on policy aims of redistribution. Instead, they resort to fear-mongering to raise the specter of social and ethnic instability in order to attract economic development funds. Beijing responds with threats of its own, or by employing factional networks to quiet local officials. "The main sources of whatever unity exists," writes one scholar, "are political blustering and Party networking from the center, hardly a formula to inspire loyalty and confidence."[100]

Regionalism also means that Beijing has a remarkably vague idea of what exactly it governs. Estimates of things like arable land, industrial output, and local finances are pure guesswork. Beijing often sends "work teams" to the provinces to check on fire standards, uncover off-balance sheet "piggy banks," and crack open local smuggling rackets. As in ancient times, statistics and information are political tools, closely guarded and manipulated by officials at all levels in their own interests. Local cadres cover up instances of misgovernance with alacrity: When a state journalist reported on a sham irrigation scheme built by officials in one township to impress upper level officials, he was jailed for 13 years on trumped up charges.[101] One mayor in Hubei province was praised in the official press for creating extraordinary economic growth and eliminating poverty. Then it was discovered that his claims were all bogus. Two accurate figures were eventually tabulated however: the value of bribes that he pocketed ($100,000) and the number of young women that he bedded (107).[102]

Here as elsewhere, the democracy deficit stands in the way of solutions. Being unaccountable, the central government is not willing to create a federal structure in the interests of good governance. Even if it were, federalism could not be grafted easily onto China's political system. For one, the constitutional guarantees would be weak and the threat of Party-imposed fiat omnipresent. In addition, handing absolute powers from one level of government to another would not solve the fundamental problem, namely that power is unconstrained. Concludes one mainland scholar: "Federalism would require political reforms to expand popular participation and elections at the local level."[103]

In politics, then, as in the economy, in society and in its dealings with the world, China could use a big dose of democracy. It would not be an elixir. But it would be a useful tonic. That is a view gaining wide acceptance in the country as scholars, journalists, social and business elites, and not a few Party reformers gasp at the costs being exacted by the delayed political transition. In the next chapter, we survey the forces that will bring it about.

4

Resources for Change

Tocqueville's Paradox

I hope to balance the gloom of the previous chapter with a great deal of optimism in this one. For just as the depredations of the Maoist era provided fertile soil for the birth of modern-day liberalism in China, so too the flawed nature of reform has fostered the development of forces that will bring democracy to life.

Most regimes will choose to empower society in order to avoid immediate overthrow, as the CCP did in 1978 and reiterated after its near-death experience in 1989. It is, however, the essential paradox of all reforming authoritarian states that the very changes the regime undertakes to stave off its immediate overthrow ensure its eventual demise, as Tocqueville noted with respect to Louis XVI's belated attempts to create representative institutions in the year before the French Revolution.

The liberalization of society in China's reform era has given actors at every level the means to begin shaping the state. Private businessmen demand open and fair policymaking. Market-driven media introduce new ideas and uncovers political malfeasance. Global democratization brings unprecedented "border effects" crashing into the country. Inside the Party, an emphasis on the rule of law gives proto-democratic groups new life in backing drives for constitutionalism.

At the same time, the state has been forced to transform and weaken its totalitarian powers in order to foster reforms. Government ministries handling health, education, the economy, defense, and civic society are driven more and more by professional demands, less and less by the ideological demands of the Party. Doctors seek to cure patients rather than prove the superiority of socialism. Younger diplomats try to manage global issues rather than export revolution.

The relinquishing of authority has a snowball effect as society reshapes its newfound privileges in its own interests. Ideas and organizational resources in the economic, social, political and international realms are mixed together for achieving society's goals. The imperatives of competition emerging from the market economy, for example, have spilled into newspaper rivalries for readers. This in turn has provided a platform for political reformers to publish their articles in hot-selling publications like *Southern Weekend* newspaper or *Caijing* magazine.

Beijing's remit over society is thus already "inhibited" by society. Attempts to retake that control come at huge cost, as shown by the attempted extermination of the Falun Gong religious sect from 1999. Some regional governments have embraced this newfound weakness as a relief from the travails of governance: "small government, big society" was the strategy pursued in southern Hainan province in the 1990s and later taken up in varying degrees elsewhere. But that relief will be shortlived. For society will soon demand to be the master of the state, not merely its equal.

To take one well-known example, Poland was one of the economically fastest growing and socially freest countries in Eastern Europe in the 1970s. Yet it was also the first to experience major unrest and then democratic transition in the 1980s. Popular resources and expectations eventually outran the absolute gains provided by reforms. In China, as in Poland, absolute gains may simply empower society without reducing demands for democracy.

In some countries, like Taiwan, South Korea, Greece, and Spain, society was empowered as part of an explicit program of democratic change. Not so in China, where it has happened as part of a strategy to prevent such change. But the results will be the same. Notes one Chinese scholar: "Further economic progress will necessarily deepen changes in state-society relations, which will push China toward democracy."[1]

Of course, the CCP retains formidable resources. Its six million men in military and police uniforms can be deployed with brutal efficiency when needed. Its significant control of information allows it to set the tone of debate and attack alternative views. The pervasive role of the state in economic and social life has stunted the growth of civil society. Any linking up of social actors to demand democracy is resolutely repressed by the CCP. Evidence from around the world reminds us that delegitimated authoritarian regimes can survive simply by mustering more threats than can a demobilized and scattered society.

Yet the paucity of "diverse alliances," in present-day China need not lead us to conclude, as two leading Western scholars did, that it "bespeaks a fundamental weakness in their capacity to challenge state power beyond the realm of the single issues and local grievances."[2] Such alliances need not be formed prior to the critical moment of democratic transition—the subject of

Part 2. Bulgaria, Cambodia and Romania, to take a few examples, had similarly fragmented societies but experienced a burst of organization at the critical moment. We need not be able to identify a "government in waiting" to know that actors and networks are everywhere that could rise to the occasion—as they did in the early Republican era and again in 1989.

What may be more important is the development of multiple, often contending social forces all with an equal claim to fairness and attention and roughly equal resources to pursue it. For it is the "prolonged and inconclusive political struggle" among increasingly powerful social forces that can give birth to democracy.[3] Not only the struggle between society and state, but also the struggle *within* society provides the critical foundations for democratic breakthrough. To return to our metaphor of the intersection, it is the quest for fairness not only from the traffic policeman but also from fellow drivers that fuels the transition.

The resources for democratic transition described in this chapter are also critical resources for building and consolidating democracy later on. The creation of a market economy, a society with wide social freedoms, a political system using the rhetoric of legality, procedure, voting, and even democracy, and extensive interactions with the world—all these provide a solid foundation for China's future democracy. In stark contrast to Russia, where democratization occurred with an unreformed state economy, a near totalistic control of society, international isolation, and political ossification, China will have begun transitions in these areas already. That alone may not outweigh the downside of China's reform sequence—liberalization before participation. But it certainly provides a measure of consolation, as well as hope for the future.

The Privatization of Economic Life

Lu Guanqiu is a former rural cadre from Mao's days who took over his village's machinery company and turned it into one of the country's biggest auto parts makers, the Wanxiang Group. At the annual meeting of the National People's Congress in 2001, Lu submitted a motion demanding that the central government take new measures to enhance law enforcement and market regulation. Rule-breaking was so widespread in the economy, he charged, that it was threatening his company's future. There needed to be courts and government inspectors with the independence to crack down on malfeasance, no matter who was behind it, his motion said. Asked later about the motion, Lu said it required one thing above all: political reform.[4]

The example of Lu and thousands of other restless made-goods of the post-

Mao business boom are a reminder that economic change is the bedrock of the supply-side revolution in China. The resources created by economic reform have empowered society, creating powerful agitators for change. The impact is slowly making its presence felt in the political realm.

Even if China's economy had not grown one bit in the reform era, the reintroduction of markets would have had a profound effect on politics. Properly working markets share many of the underlying principles of democracy—the equality of actors, fair and open competition, law-abidance, and freedom of choice. By fostering autonomous interactions among individuals, markets also stimulate social mixing and build up norms of compromise and tolerance. Everyone's interests, not just the majority and certainly not just the minority, are taken into account by markets. They are a powerful bulwark of freedom.

China's move to markets was largely completed by the turn of the century. More than 90 percent of commodities, virtually all labor, and probably two-thirds of the capital stock were bought and sold in free markets. The state no longer told people where to work, what to buy, or who to deal with. Shanghai's elites came into close contact with Anhui peasants whom they hired as maids. Shenzhen became one of the first truly national cities as workers flocked to factories there from every province. In the cities, markets became a stage of "transgressive" activities against authoritarianism as consumers and marketers did their own thing.[5]

Whatever the flaws of the markets—and they are many—the impact on society was great. Researchers in China now talk openly about how the market economy "opens the door to political reform" and is "a training ground for democracy."[6] Under a communist regime reluctant to compromise its writ over society, writes one scholar, "a flourishing market economy is the most effective way to limit government power."[7] Or as another professor at the government's top training school wrote:[8]

> Through the experience of markets, there is a basis for civic consciousness and political participation. The power for democratization grows. People begin to think of paying their votes in return for the services of politicians, who are expected to engage in open competition among rivals to prove their worth and win office. In the end, people demand to be full citizens, not subjects, in politics just as they are in the economy. . . . In China, the principle of competition is leaking into the political system.

The creation of new wealth is another way that economic reforms have had a positive impact on democratic prospects. Economic development has long been considered the single most important factor in political liberalization worldwide. With it comes a middle class seeking protection for its assets and a voice for its interests. Wealth can also act as a sort of universal solvent in the political arena: as people use their wealth to gain education, they become more aware and tolerant of competing claims of their diverse society. In addition, greater absolute wealth reduces not only the relative costs of compromise (even if the absolute amounts at stake rise) but also fears of losing out from democracy.

Authoritarian governments can also gain legitimacy and power from economic growth, of course. But as the strong global correlation between wealth and democracy reminds us, the exceptions only prove the rule. The much-maligned modernization paradigm—where development leads to democracy—remains empirically if not necessarily true.[9] In Asia as well as in Latin America and Europe, democracy came earliest and fastest where there was strong and broad economic development. Africa's democratic woes are a reminder of the opposite.

Several attempts have been made, using empirical studies, to guess when democracy will sprout. Scholars have argued that above a certain GDP per capita a country enters a "transition zone" where democratic pressures resulting from economic and associated social development grow. Some say the entry point into the danger zone occurs around $3,200 (in 2002 dollars adjusting for price differences across countries). Another researcher found that political pluralism became highly likely once a country reached $4,500. Yet another research project found that the probability of democratization in a given year doubles as income per capita grows from $1,700 to $8,400.[10]

With a price-adjusted GDP per capita of $4,500 by 2003, China is clearly in the danger zone. Even discounting to take account of measurement problems, the amount of wealth in China is probably already sufficient to finance democratic transition. With every passing year, that is even more the case. In cross-country and cross-time comparisons, the CCP regime is living on borrowed time.[11]

Another widely studied indicator of democratic prospects is the size of the middle class. In China, as elsewhere, the middle class seeks a recognition and protection of its growing interests from the state, mainly through improved legal guarantees and openness. While the middle class rarely embraces the idea of democracy per se (fearing the votes of the poor), historically its agitation on its own behalf has led to just that. Using pure income and asset measures, China's middle class probably accounted for between 10 percent and 15 percent percent of the population at the turn of the century. Researchers in China have estimated that this compares to 17 percent in the United States in 1950 and 14 percent in Japan in 1975, suggesting that China is already in a position to sustain nascent democracy. If a broader definition is used to include all administrative and service staff, government clerks and teachers—essentially everyone who's not a worker, peasant, unemployed, or below the poverty line—then the middle-class figure rises to around 30 percent. On this basis, the share will rise to about 35 percent by 2010, according to one estimate.[12]

The political implications are already being seen. As one mainland scholar wrote in a Beijing-published book:[13]

> The middle class has already had a lot of impact on one-party rule, as shown by the [CCP policy since 2001 of expanding its constituency to include the middle and business classes]. . . . The middle class is increasingly in control of information and power resources in China, which is changing the CCP's past monopoly of these things. . . . In that sense it provides a safe pavilion and strong force for political, economic and social modernization. . . . Given their demands for political participation, the middle class will certainly promote political reforms within the CCP as well as domestic democratization.

Or as one long-time Western student of democracy wrote:[14]

> As it gathers more momentum and begins to generate a more urban, educated, wired, and middle-class society over the next two decades, economic development is going to generate enormous pressures for political change in China. People are going to want more say over their own affairs. They are going to expect less hierarchical control from the state and ruling party, and more accountability of political leaders to the citizenry. There will be decidedly less tolerance for corruption and abuse of power, and more readiness and ability to organize in protest of it. There will be significantly greater aspirations for personal and political freedom, and for greater pluralism in sources of information and choices of leaders. . . . If the more politically aware, autonomous, and resourceful social actors that economic development will generate do not find channels for participation and protest within China's political system, they will mobilize outside the system, possibly to bring it down.

Business leaders are one group that may mobilize for change. They played a key role in the democratizations of Spain, Brazil, South Korea, and the Philippines. Prior to transition, they organized into powerful business lobbies that brought new openness from the state. At the time of crisis, they defected to the side of reform.

Of course, democratization can also be delayed when business interests collude with the authoritarian state. This was long the problem in South America. It has also been an impediment to change in China, where the private sector got its start in the 1980s and 1990s by forging close alliances to the state.[15] Beijing's private computer company, Stone Group, which funded political reformers and supported the 1989 protestors, was anomalous.

Yet by the turn of the century, China's new business elite was showing signs of following in the well-worn footsteps of its counterparts worldwide. As bureaucratic (and military) control over the economy waned and the number of new entrants in each sector grew, the payoffs of pursuing patronage declined steeply. Not everyone could be a "privileged entrepreneur" when there were two million private companies and 100 million people in the private sector accounting for 50 percent of GDP. State favoritism was now a grounds for legal action. The new generation of private entrepreneurs is also more educated and more worldly than the first. They have more self-respect and less tolerance for engaging in demeaning *guanxi*. They also have reputations to protect from an increasingly aggressive business press. As a result, many entrepreneurs have begun to agitate for equality and openness from government. Private industry associations once thought a handmaiden of the local Party committee have begun to seek political change. Attempts by Beijing to control the rapidly proliferating local business groups are failing for the simple reason that at the local level, power resides more and more with the companies and not the bureaucrats.[16] "Private business owners have begun to express strong desires for political participation and a consciousness of their group interests," says one government researcher. "They're looking to take part in public affairs."[17]

The trends will continue. World Trade Organization entry and financial reform will increase bank lending to private companies (which are 90 percent self-financed at present), further dampening crony ties. A constitutional amendment on the table since 1998 would make private property "inviolable" and "protected" alongside state property. That change, if combined with tax and spending policies aimed at redistribution, would be a powerful agent in support of democracy by undergirding equality in both political and economic spheres.

The CCP has tried to expand its cooptive powers by inviting private entrepreneurs to join the Party. As a Party Organization Department book said: "We cannot afford to lose this camp."[18] But the change in 2001 was greeted with indifference. In one survey, just 8 percent of entrepreneurs expressed a desire to join the CCP.[19] In short, China's new breed of entrepreneurs have little interest in saving a dying regime. They prefer to stay on the outside. At a certain point, one hardline Party journal warned, "the capitalists will rise up and destroy the Party lock, stock, and barrel."[20]

Declining state economic power, both productive and fiscal, is the flipside of the move to markets and the emergence of an empowered middle class. In the past, state factories were the main channel through which the state exercised totalitarian control over society. State employees are vulnerable to ideological education and bureaucratic controls. With the state sector now accounting for only 30 percent of GDP—the private sector accounting for 50 percent and agriculture 20 percent—and just 10 percent of total employment, this tool is seriously degraded.

Fiscally, the rise of a private sector, ad hoc decentralization, and the increasing costs of governing a complex and growing population have eaten away at central finances. State revenues fell from 31 percent of GNP in 1978 to 11 percent in 2000. Income, sales, and social security taxes—typically half of total state revenues in market economies—account for just a few percent of tax revenues. Government debt is the equivalent of more than 100 percent of GDP when unfunded pension promises, local government debt, and bank restructuring costs are included. In mid-2002, premier Zhu Rongji publicly begged the country's richest private entrepreneurs to begin paying taxes, an echo of the shifting balance of power between lords and vassals in early modern Europe and a reminder that the management of public debt has been historically closely tied to the rise of democracy. Ultimately, short of engaging in a fire-sale of state land and infrastructure, Beijing will be forced to find a new accommodation with its "heroic" citizen-creditors that respects them as equals.[21]

With the loss of state resources goes the loss of the regime's ability to "buy" support from urban residents. Since one-off gains from marketization and sectoral shifts are nearly exhausted and state fiscal, banking, and corporate resources are depleted, the "social contract" of urban residents accepting CCP rule in return to material benefits will soon be broken. Notes one Chinese scholar: "The social contract has helped the communist regime insulate itself from pressure for democracy but will ultimately undermine its rule."[22]

Finally, foreign economic linkages are also acting on balance to undermine Party rule. To be sure, the CCP has managed to corral some of these resources for itself. PRC state firms now raise millions of dollars on overseas stock exchanges and foreign companies in China, which crowd out more politically active domestic entrepreneurs, account for about a fifth of corporate taxes. As one Party book stated baldly: "The foreign-related economy holds great potential for providing resources for the political system."[23]

But whatever early impact globalization had in bolstering one-party rule in China, that impact is changing. The influx of foreign investors is weakening the cronyistic ties that local governments once had with foreign companies.

Large portfolio investors in mainland securities like the California public employees pension fund (Calpers), overseas labor rights activists, and regulators in Western markets have begun using their leverage to pursue openness and accountability. As this happens, the "normal" pro-democratic impact of business—which promotes meritocracy, transparency, rules-based systems, information opening, codes of practice, and competition—is coming to the fore.[24] As one political reformer in China noted of the new generation of foreign executives in the country: "They don't know how to speak Chinese or take local cadres to lunch. They expect to work hard and enjoy the results. That is going to change everything."[25]

Just as Spain's quest for entry into the European Community from 1977 to 1986 encouraged the formation of government structures that reflected the imperatives of democratic rule, so too China's entry into the WTO will put unprecedented pressures on the political system. China's stock market regulator, the China Securities Regulatory Commission, intends to hire foreign nationals to improve its operations. The same impetus will be at work across the entire regulatory system. As China's semi-official annual political report of 2001 put it: "The secrecy and unresponsiveness of governments at all levels in China simply does not accord with the needs of WTO entry . . . We need to make all information public, make leaders compete for office, and increase public participation in political affairs in order to improve the efficiency of government to meet this challenge."[26]

New Ideas

In 1996, the newly established China Confucius Foundation filed a lawsuit against the Ministry of Culture alleging illegal interference in its activities. The ministry had tried to force the Confucian scholars to move their office from Beijing to Shandong province. When they refused, the ministry sent a gang of thugs to the office to haul away equipment and lock the door, "seriously encroaching upon the foundation's legitimate rights and interests," the suit alleged. In an out of court settlement, the ministry backed down.[27]

As with the economy, the dismal picture of social life under CCP rule is considerably enlightened by signs that society is finding ways to resolve the crisis. Tocqueville's prophecy is being fulfilled in modern-day China through a burst of new ideas and the creation of new organizational resources with which to put them into practice. Tracing these changes in values and ideas is difficult, notwithstanding the occasional appearance of litigious Confucians. Yet they are arguably the motive force of political development. Retrospective work on the failure of authoritarian regimes almost always dwells in the end on the ways that society quite literally outwitted the state.

New ideas of all sorts to replace the totalitarian values of the state are critical to the formation of an ideology for an opposition movement. By forging critiques and alternative views of central public issues, they disarm the regime's ability to lead by sheer will. These dissenting views need not be widely held. Only a small but critical mass of alternative opinion is necessary to provide the normative backing for the ad hoc solution of democracy when dictatorship reaches crisis.

Several surveys taken in the 1990s found mounting evidence that this critical mass already exists in China. According to one survey, "20 to 30 percent of the population of China have attitudes favourable for democratic behaviour," a level comparable to already functioning democracies in Italy and Mexico.[28] Another survey that compared democratic attitudes in Hong Kong, Taiwan, and China showed how China was already at a level comparable to Taiwan when it launched its successful democracy in 1988 and would continue to embrace democratic attitudes more widely as education expanded.[29] In cross-country comparisons of the strength of various values of toleration and self-expression, which are strongly correlated with democracy, China already enjoys levels that should sustain a democracy like those of Taiwan, Greece, or Poland.[30]

Even in the 1980s, as we saw, the Party was losing control of China's values as the pro-democracy movement grew. By the turn of the century, further liberalization and international integration, as well as rising education levels — 60 percent of the labor force now has secondary schooling or higher — had created even wider space for new views. In rural areas, as we shall see, the conduct of direct elections has had a profound impact on widening the scope of ideas.

In the cities, the transformation is even more profound. In contrast to the "anti-social individualism" that gripped the cities with the first bursts of freedom in the 1980s, by the turn of the century, a genuine "sense of community built on rational individualism" was emerging to take its place.[31] Citizens are putting a greater value on notions of justice and equality over notions like authority and responsibility.[32] Artists who engaged in cheap political pop art in the 1980s are now concerned more with human inquiry, drawing attention toward the individual and away from the state.[33] Of course, as we saw in the last chapter, the spread of this responsible civic ethos faces real limits under the CCP system, where autonomous associational life is wrecked at every turn. But its appearance helps gird the forces that would bring about change.

So too does the appearance of liberal intellectuals. Rare is the country that has overthrown an authoritarian regime without an intellectual leader. Intellectuals can provide the critical rhetoric and moral backing to disarm opposition to democratic change. In their writings on both historical and present-day issues, intellectuals can create dissonances that undermine Party's hegemony over discourse. In the USSR, the flood of reappraisals about Stalin's rule that appeared in 1987–88 opened a window of truth, a "return of history" that made it impossible for the communist regime to carry on. Through such acts, "the demand for truth" becomes as important as "the demand for bread" within segments of society. Again, they need not be the majority—usually they are not—to have a great impact.

In both 1986 and 1989, university professors and students were at the forefront of political agitation in China. As with entrepreneurs, there is some evidence that they retreated from that role in the 1990s by seeking clientelist ties to the state. But the recognition of the problem is now open and arguably has caused a reversal, a "reawakening" of the liberal intellectual mission now celebrated in many Chinese books.[34] Writer Yu Jie's collection of essays, published in 2003, was called "Refusing Lies" (*Jujue huangyan*), echoing Lech Walesa's remark on the growth of "a communion of people who do not wish to participate in a lie." A healthy scepticism toward the state—one fostered by its repression—has allowed intellectuals to reemerge at the forefront of political change. Among them, noted one scholar in China, "the core concepts of Western democracy—namely elections, participation, equality, and freedom of expression—are now widely accepted."[35] Indeed, China is arguably better endowed with liberal intellectual leaders than was the Soviet Union or any Eastern European country. As a Chinese scholar put it: "The liberalism expressed by some non-Party intellectuals is a vital part of the ferment leading toward political change."[36]

Finally, diverse and often democratic influences are also flowing into China from abroad. By 2002, there were 350 McDonald's restaurants in China. The national soccer team went to the World Cup in 2002 under a foreign coach. The number of outbound Chinese tourists reached 6 million. Meanwhile, about 400,000 graduate students and scholars had gone abroad since reforms began. The creation of a large PRC diaspora, in addition to starving the CCP of resources, has a profound cosmopolitanizing effect at home. Attempts by Beijing to portray life in a democracy as dangerous and alienating increasingly fail. New ideas spill off the flight from Los Angeles along with boxes full of Hollywood films.

Many of these global cultural influences are embodied in the awarding of the 2008 Olympics to Beijing. Merely organizing such an event would bring new people and ideas into China, not least the Olympic Charter's explicit "respect for universal fundamental ethical principles" and "preservation of human dignity." Citizens in Beijing quickly grasped the regular visits by IOC commissions as means to demand better treatment on issues like urban redevelopment. There are close parallels with South Korea, where the coming of the 1988 Olympics games was an important impetus for regime change. As in South Korea, China's people will be keen to show a "new face" to the world by 2008.

Of course, the cosmopolitanizing and liberalizing impact of globalization on Chinese society needs to be squared with the apparent emergence in the 1990s of a powerful nativist and illiberal nationalism. As mentioned, nationalism has a long and infamous history of being used by elites to discredit or subvert democracy in China. The CCP's launch of an official patriotism campaign in 1991 and its frequent resort in the 1990s to "nationalism on demand" from angry young males was nothing new in this respect.[37] Yet the mainstream, as opposed to official, nationalism in present-day China may be one of the most potent democratic forces.

Throughout the reform era, students protesting against foreign slights repeatedly turned their attentions to the failures of CCP rule. This transformation is latent in the nature of nationalism. The search for national dignity contains many of the same notions—equality, fairness, justice—that underlie the quest for personal dignity. The great political philosopher John Rawls contended that a people's demand for respect from other nations is rooted in the same moral philosophy that generates the individual's demand to be treated equally and fairly domestically.[38] In the process of seeking their due globally, people begin to seek their due at home as well. Notes one Western scholar: "The politics of individual dignity, far from being antithetical, appears to be parasitical on the idea of national dignity."[39]

We have seen evidence of this repeatedly. Wei Jingsheng wrote his famous democratic declaration to show that China's people were neither "spineless weaklings" nor "devoid of any desire to improve their lot"—a direct linking of democracy with national dignity. When Beijing won the Olympics in July 2001, the streets of the city were suddenly packed with celebrants, all of them acting with unaccustomed camaraderie, respect, and civility. "I haven't seen this sort of feeling since Tiananmen," one weeping young woman entrepreneur told me. National dignity and individual dignity are closely linked.

A second point is that the quest for national identity usually brings to light the diversity inherent in any culture, providing a new stimulus for democracy's equal treatment of all. Some of China's nationalists increasingly identify themselves with the long tradition of modern Chinese nationalism and Chinese cultural pride, not with the CCP regime. Loving China no longer means loving the CCP, if it ever did. Especially in the south, a new egalitarian and cosmopolitan culture has taken root that challenges the CCP's northern autocratic culture.[40] The result is that people begin to reinterpret the regime's propaganda about the need to avoid democracy as the need to avoid an inclusive national identity. The new national narrative sees regionalism and federalism as a good thing to prevent dictatorship. Democracy is portrayed as a unifying force. It was no coincidence that the biggest demonstration against the June Fourth massacre occurred in Guangzhou, where 50,000 people held a peaceful protest on June 5, 1989, or that the flame of that movement burns brightest in Hong Kong at the annual June Fourth vigil there.

As India and Taiwan have shown most strikingly, nationalism can be a powerful force for both achieving and sustaining democracy. It provides resistance to despotism and glue to hold together a country during the transition. A sense of belonging, of national identity, is critical to creating a democracy. So too is a pride in one's cultural traditions. In China, nationalism is helping to tip the balance toward, not away from, democracy.

In all these respects, the burst of new thinking in contemporary Chinese society undermines arguments that China is trapped in a fossilized culture that cannot support democracy. Earlier we rejected notions of a deep-rooted antidemocratic strain in China's culture, arguing that its democratic potential was as great, if not greater, than elsewhere. Of course, the converse of the adage that democracy produces democrats is that dictatorship produces dictators, norms in society at odds with democracy. But it is clear that China has already escaped from the prison of antidemocratic ideas, a remarkable feat living under CCP rule.

As one mainland scholar concludes: "China has discovered that dissent, diversity, and plural ideas and values are not incompatible with social order. . . . [Thus] the major cleavage in Chinese political culture today may not be between the advanced intellectuals and the backward masses, but between a people ready for more freedom and political leaders afraid to grant it."[41]

New Societies

New organizational resources—the media, civil society, rule of law, and open protest—are the other dimension of social change. Again, these remain deeply retarded by the communist state, with all the resulting negative consequences described in the last chapter. Yet we already see the emergence of a critical mass that has put the CCP on the defensive.

The explosion of the media in China is a tangible expression of the Party's loss of control of ideas. Consider the numbers in 2003: close to 7,000 news-papers and magazines, of which maybe a fifth have their own Internet sites; more than 500 publishing houses, of which only a third are directly controlled by the central Party or state; more than 3,000 broadcast and cable television stations; 70 million regular Internet users; and the world's largest mobile phone population: 250 million chatterboxes talking up a cacophony of competing ideas.

As a result, China is now awash with information that would have been considered seditious as recently as the early 1990s. Chat sites created to support the Party, such as the Strong Country Forum of the People's Daily, are used to launch criticisms of the Party. About three quarters of respondents to one survey said that the Internet gave them "more opportunity to express their political views," while 68 percent said it gave them more opportunities "to criticize government policy."[42]

Beijing tries to stem the flow through periodic crackdowns on newspapers and magazines and the blocking, according to one study, of 19,000 politically sensitive Internet sites.[43] But it is a losing game, especially given the impact of the Internet and mobile phones in creating the socioeconomic and geography-defying "communities of understanding" that are so inimical to dictatorships. The failing controls—the blocked Internet sites account for only 8 percent of the total potentially subversive sites—have increased calls for an end to censorship since it is insulting to a society already in-the-know. As one scholar noted: "The only effective way to stop [press] liberalization would be to resume full-scale subsidies to all the media. But that is beyond the capability of government."[44]

The media have another organizing impact through the work of investigative journalists in uncovering political problems. Malfeasance in the corporate sector, as covered by magazines like Caijing, is an open field now. As one study noted, this new breed of journalists is remarkable in being concerned with issues of justice as well as truth.[45] Official corruption and misgovernance remain more sensitive, but still provide wide room for honest reporting. In two incidents in 2001—a mining disaster that killed 300 in Guangxi and a fireworks explosion that killed 40 schoolchildren in Jiangxi—the media rejected state lies and reported the truth, forcing officials to recant. Dogged reporting into the affairs of the China Youth Foundation's charity for poor areas, Project Hope, finally uncovered evidence of long-rumored corruption in 2002.

Of course, since the line is unclear, many journalists end up in jail. The CCP regularly tops the odious list as the regime with the most journalists under lock and key worldwide, two dozen in 2001.[46] But the Party faces a losing battle. Journalists jailed for reporting corruption or misgovernance become causes célèbres at home and abroad.

Civil society, organizational life not controlled by the state, is critical to the lead-up, transition, and consolidation phases of democratic change. Authoritarian governments make little allowance for autonomous social groups because the state and its official social groups are supposed to represent all interests. Yet any degree of market and social freedoms will lead to a diversity of interests that seeks its own organizations. As they pursue those interests, social groups put dictatorships on the defensive, drawing attention to instances of poor governance and at the same time robbing them of their normal social support. Suddenly, two scholars note, the emperor "is seen not only naked but also unaccompanied by his usual retinue."[47] At the critical moment, as we shall see, civic society presses elites to embrace democratic change, later helping to sustain it through the turbulence of early consolidation.

Given this importance, it's no surprise that vast attention has been paid to the rise of social groups in China, both by the regime and by outside observers. At the end of 2002, there were 135,000 officially registered "social groups," in China. More than half were sub-national level groups, reflecting China's size and diversity. Of these, as one would expect, the most economically advanced provinces accounted for the bulk. Books about "civil society" (*shimin shehui* or *gongmin shehui*) and "civic organizations" (*shetuan* or *minjian zuzhi*) now crowd the shelves in China.[48]

The variety and the scope of the civic groups grow by the day. Academic, business, and professional groups account for most of the officially recognized bodies, little surprise given the Party's fears of losing their support. But the growth of associations representing women, environmental causes, homeowners, new religions, charities, recreational pursuits, and folk culture is astonishing. Taxi driver guilds, temple fair associations, soccer fan clubs, and female journalists' groups have sprouted with the grudging endorsement of a state no longer able to manage every aspect of society. The Falun Gong meditation group that surrounded the CCP's office complex in 1999 with 10,000 adherents to protest being de-registered was a stark reminder of a rapidly organizing society.

Some scholars argue that China's civic groups cannot play the same role they did in other democratizations. That is because the ones that are politically engaged are closely controlled by the state, meaning they do not restrain or reclaim state power. Others advocate ideals that are highly undemocratic. But the standards of civic groups under democracy are not those we should use for those under dictatorship. As with so many aspects of the resources for transition, we should be concerned with showing merely that a "critical mass," not a fully developed, pro-democracy civic society exists. From this developmental viewpoint, civic society in China is already reaching the critical mass that will make it an effective resource for transition.

While Beijing officially demands that civic groups be state-sponsored and that their behavior be consonant with state policies, formal compliance often masks actual divergence.[49] Despite fantasies of an orientalist bonding between state and society, all evidence suggests that civic society in China is developing exactly as it did elsewhere—in opposition to state power. The best evidence is Beijing's frequent repression of groups. In 1998, Beijing passed new laws to crack down on groups that were "politically problematic, seriously interfering in social and economic order, or illegal," along with others that were "redundant" or "badly managed." Two years later, the number of groups had fallen by 30,000, or 20 percent.[50] If China's civic groups were indeed pioneering some new Asian values approach to helping the state, then why would the state react against them in this way? One Party hard-liner provides the answer: "Some social groups have tried to cast off or weaken Party leadership over them. In some cases a small number of groups have only focussed on their own interests, seriously affecting political stability and unity."[51]

The second issue is whether these groups are putting in place the foundations of democracy. Many worry that China's "uncivil society" would bring chaos or new dictatorship if it overthrew the CCP. To be sure, China has its fair share of antidemocratic groups—as every society does. As in developed democracies, many of them are avowedly unpluralistic. But it also has a large number of proto-democratic groups focused on women's rights, liberal intellectual thought, or public charity. More important, civic societies which grow up within a dictatorship often take on nondemocratic colors as a result, just as people do. Evidence from elsewhere shows that this changes quickly with democratic opening. For that reason, the proper focus should be less on the antidemocratic potential of some groups—a potential that like all cultural potentials can be used for good or evil—and more on the extent to which these groups are managing to reclaim and restrain state power. Much evidence suggests it is great. Civic groups, writes one scholar in China "are helping to lay the foundations for a diverse, rich and democratic human society."[52] Or to quote another: "The gradual creation of a civil society is creating favourable conditions for China's future democracy."[53]

In a similar way, the accidental openness in China's nascent legal system is being used by society to forge a new relationship with and even change the state. One example of this new relationship is the Administrative Litigation Law, under which 100,000 suits were brought against mostly low-level government officials and departments in 1999. Others laws, like the State Compensation Law and the Administrative Penalties Law, have contributed to society's control of the state as well.

Like so much else, these seeds, planted to address a crisis of governance, have grown far larger than intended. Vigilante-like judges have appeared in localities where the crisis of governance is worst and made names for themselves by taking on powerful Party units.[54] The country's corps of 117,000 qualified lawyers and 10,000 law firms as of 2001 is also producing a whole new class of people who use the legal system to fight for justice, the entrepreneurs of legal limits on the state. People like Shenzhen worker's rights advocate Zhou Litai and Beijing-based lawyer's rights agitator Zhang Jianzhong appear by the day. While the CCP still imagines rule of law as a tool of legitimization and policy implementation, there are openings for law as a mechanism to bind the state and protect individuals. The norms it embeds are norms of fundamental, unalterable legal rights and of a state that is subject to limits.

Finally, the resort to organized and open protest has gone from a rare and daring act in the 1980s and early 1990s to a normal part of everyday life by the turn of the century. It is now a widely used and tolerated means of voicing protest. Party journals and books chronicle the rise of "sudden and mass incidents" which usually involved some degree of violence or disruption. In recent years, there have been frequent outbreaks of riots by peasants over taxes, minorities over religious repression, workers over unpaid pensions, parents over tuition fees, townsfolk over corrupt cadres, city-folk over urban redevelopment, taxi drivers over new license fees, and soccer fans over bribe-taking referees.

Protest is best known in rural areas, where anti-government riots have become so common that a Beijing University thesis called them the "mainstream" method of political participation.[55] One protest movement by relocated residents from the Three Gorges dam area began in 1979 and was still ongoing as of this writing.[56]

In cities, meanwhile, riots over urban housing and welfare and mass marches on government offices are commonplace. In one riot in 2000, residents of a township in Jiangsu burned 24 police cars and injured 50 policemen in a protest against the merger of their township with another. An informal movement of residents in Shanghai regularly foils heavy-handed urban redevelopment plans with protests, sit-ins, petitions, and even appeals voiced by the city's aggresive tabloids. Thousands of workers marched and picketed in Liaoning province the same year over unpaid pensions and state factory corruption.

For practical and normative reasons, police are increasingly allowing the protests to continue. Usually, the use of force makes things worse, as police and Party manuals since Tiananmen have been at pains to stress. More important, within the police there is a growing sense of professionalism that portrays officers as upholders of public order, not Party rule. This change, to which I return below, is monumental. It is a prelude to the defection of coercive forces that is critical in democratic transitions. Prior to that, it helps to empower the organization of social protest by reducing the costs of protest, thus providing an important resource for democratic change.

Of course, one might argue, as some scholars have, that the growing incidence of open protest is likely to strengthen the authoritarian clamor for law and order. As social tensions grow and as armies of unmarried young men — 30 to 40 million by 2020—emerge looking for release, the CCP will find new adherents to its calls for strong government.[57] Yet this conclusion goes against evidence of how China's people frame the problems and solutions to their crisis of governance today. More and more they frame it as a failure of strong government, not a call for more. In the words of prominent political reformer Li Fan:[58]

> Since 1989, there has been a constant outbreak of small-scale protests, sit-ins and marches. But the state has not conceded any major political freedoms. It instead relies on out-of-date police-style repression. . . . If the state does not undertake political reforms to meet these needs, the results will be even larger turmoil. . . . At a certain point, society will simply rise up and break down the constraints on freedom.

Democratic Diplomacy and U.S. Policy

International factors are playing an important role in shifting the balance in favor of democratic transition in China. Indeed it may be said that the global environment for a successful democratic transition in China has never been better. We have already seen how international economic and social factors are working to promote change. Here we consider explicit political linkages.

International political factors can occasionally be all-important in democratic transitions. In some cases—Japan, Grenada, Afghanistan, Iraq—democracy was imposed from outside even though domestic democratic forces were weak. In others—Greece, Portugal, Argentina, and even the USSR—democracy resulted partly from a failed foreign war. Usually, however, international political factors play only an indirect if powerful role, magnifying and empowering forces already at work inside a country. This is the case with China.

It is unlikely that the CCP would be ousted by a foreign power for, say, weapons proliferation, or by its own people, say after a failed attack on Taiwan. But global politics is being felt inside Zhongnanhai in other ways: through diplomatic policies, indirect border effects, and an increasingly active global civil society.

The diplomatic environment never imposed dictatorship on China of course. But as elsewhere, the uncertainty of the cold war bolstered the arguments of antidemocratic forces at home. With the cold war ended and new regional conflicts being solved through bipartisan global cooperation, this danger is removed. No longer can external threats be used to argue against democracy, as they have been throughout modern Chinese history. Just as the end of the cold war removed obstacles to democratic movements in the peripheries of the United States and the USSR, so too it has had a wider impact in Asia. A country can democratize today with excellent prospects of emerging with an independent foreign policy.

In China, this balmy international climate has encouraged policymakers to urge the government to cast off its discourse of threats and victimization in favor of a more mature and cooperative diplomacy.[59] It was just such a change in the external policies of the USSR, Gorbachev recalled, "that was the starting point for everything" that changed at home.[60]

Indeed, the end of the cold war marked the onset of a global diplomacy that explicitly favors democracy. "Democratic diplomacy" is of course rooted in normative ideals. But it is also hard-nosed realism: promoting democracy in other countries makes them more stable and open, thus protecting global security from militarist aggression; opening channels for international cooperation on transnational issues; and providing better prospects for global economic growth and redistribution. The EU has an explicit democratic condition for membership that has encouraged democratization in southern and eastern Europe. Several democratizations in Asia—Taiwan, South Korea, and Cambodia—have been greatly influenced by the quest for diplomatic acceptance from the West. In Africa, the old dictatorship-friendly Organization of African Unity was dissolved and replaced by a new democracy-friendly African Union in 2002 linked to an aid-for-democracy funding scheme from the West.

China thus finds itself confronting a diplomatic environment strongly tilted in favor of democracy. Democratic countries give significant support to village elections, people's congresses, human rights dialogue, and rule of law initiatives in China. Beijing hopes these things can bolster its legitimacy and governance without compromising its power. Democratic countries hope otherwise. As Japan's prime minister put it at China's annual Asia development forum in 2002: "The three values of freedom, diversity and openness are the driving forces behind peace and development in Asia. . . . It goes without saying that freedom refers to democracy and human rights politically," institutions whose coming to every country, he remarked, was "inevitable."[61]

China also finds that the United Nations system, long a friend of corrupt and brutal Third World dictators, is increasingly part of the same democratic diplomacy. Several UN programs and policies now have explicit democratic conditions attached to them. The agency's human rights commissioner, its covenants on human rights, and the "democratic governance" item which tops the UNDP agenda are all reminders of this. Nothing could be more upsetting to Beijing's argument that democracy and human rights are "Western" than to see UN democracy and human rights initiatives being pursued with vigor by an African secretary general and a Thai human rights commissioner, as in 2002. In the words of a U.S.-based scholar: "Beijing cannot escape the fact that the normative agenda of international society has expanded, as have the ambitions of China's domestic political reformers."[62]

The CCP thus engages the international system at its peril. China was a member of 55 international governmental organizations by turn of the century, up from 21 in 1977. While Beijing sought to maximize the publicity value and minimize the responsibilities of such engagement, the mere act of joining created new structures and powers for reformers in the state.[63] Domestic human rights advocates, for example, rushed into print a collection of international human rights standards the moment that Beijing signed the two UN covenants on human rights, calling it a "citizen's reader."[64]

As with domestic rule of law, the CCP's embrace of international rule of law has tied its hands. By involving itself more and more in the UN system, notes one scholar, Beijing has "crossed the Rubicon," in which it can no longer provide any coherent rejection of global democratic norms while simultaneously seeking to be a part of them.[65]

Like all democracies, the United States has a strong self-interest as well as moral compulsion to promote democracy in China. Merely by keeping the peace and encouraging openness throughout Asia, the U.S. makes a major contribution to China's democratization. Indeed, a U.S. policy that focuses assiduously on encouraging and supporting democracy in Asia as whole is perhaps the best friend of democracy in China.

From a prescriptive point of view, if one accepts the normative underpinnings of democracy as well as the practical evidence of the international costs of dictatorship, then the single overarching aim of U.S. policy toward China should be to bring about as rapid and smooth a transition to democracy as possible. While there is wide scope for reasonable differences on policy means, there is little scope for differences of aims. Every policy needs to be framed with reference to helping China's people to achieve their long dream of a free and democratic country. It is important to keep in mind that in China democracy accords with popular wishes. Too often, U.S. policy specialists imagine the PRC as a representative government whose policies reflect an essentialized "Chinese worldview" that is "deeply rooted and readily apparent."[66] Yet in light of recurrent pro-democracy protests and demands and in the absence of any popular legitimization of the CCP government through free elections, there is no basis for this assumption. The CCP's policies in all likelihood do not represent a "Chinese worldview," whatever that is, but a struggling regime's last-ditch attempts to stay in power. As two scholars note, referring to the essentializing views of Harvard University professor Samuel Huntington, authoritarian regimes the world over exist because they crush democratic urges, not because those urges are absent: "U.S. policy should not fall prey to Huntington's inability to distinguish between the regime line of the moment and the underlying dynamic that gives hope to so many Chinese people."[67]

To be sure, a democratic China would have its own distinct "worldview," as do democratic Japan, India, and France. But it would be one grounded in shared norms and ideals that have popular backing, in other words one both moral and legitimate. Moreover, as with U.S. policy in Latin America, a failure to pursue democracy as the primary goal risks undermining Washington's future credibility. A United States which is not a friend of democratization in China cannot expect to be a friend of a democratic China. One prominent Chinese democrat suggests the establishment of a "China Reform Promotion Fund," a sum of money promised to a newly democratic China with funds earmarked for poverty alleviation, farmers, unemployed, and the retired.[68] This idea follows closely the Bush administration's establishment of a Millennium Challenge Account in 2002 to reward democratic reforms in aid-giving.

Democratization theory suggests that this kind of "ethical engagement" with China is the best means to foster change. The Clinton administration pursued an admirable policy of low-level engagement with China but one that often fell prey to unethical behavior. High-level summitry with Beijing—culminating in a plan to build a "constructive strategic partnership"—as well as incautious business and military exchanges meant that the purposes of engagement were often forgotten. Much of this changed under the administration of George W. Bush. But the Bush policy erred in the other direction: useful engagement on health, rule of law, and military openness was put on hold along with the inadvisable summitry and military technology exports. Meanwhile, the 2001 terrorist attacks on the United States had a baleful influence in moving Washington's global policy away from the encouragement of political pluralism toward narrowly defined security aims.

In high-level dealings with the CCP, the United States should be open and unremitting in its calls for political liberalization. Washington should make it clear that while it respects China and its people, it cannot engage CCP leaders in any meaningful partnership. High-level contacts should be used to raise the costs of repression, proliferation, or aggression by Beijing. Washington should press for the release of dissidents and the relaxation of controls on religious freedom in return for modest concessions on high-level exchanges. Such exchanges would include careful but consistent engagement with reformist individuals in the military, government, Party, media, judiciary, and scholarly communities. As we posit in Part II, the CCP will likely be "extricated" from power by a breakthrough elite composed of reformist individuals inside the regime. Investing in them makes sense.

Of course, practical necessity means that Washington needs to have some degree of contact with the conservative leaders of the CCP regime. Matters of trade, the environment, crime, weapons proliferation, and the like need to be tackled at high levels. Yet there seems little justification for extensive summitry with Beijing. Investing in the current leadership risks underinvesting when preparing to deal with a post-CCP government. As one U.S. scholar commented: "We seem to be simultaneously betting on the current regime and recusing ourselves from any consideration of the crisis it will almost certainly face before long."[69]

This "post-CCP-oriented" policy would also include making it clear that the United States would be a friend of a democratic China and would welcome its role in sharing the burdens of Asian security and leadership. Even if a rump CCP emerges as the dominant party after democratic transition, something we predict in part 2, this would not prevent high-level engagement, for it would be a legitimate government.

At lower levels, engagement should be fuller *and* more ethical. Business should be encouraged, but under the rubric that it helps to make China a more free country. U.S. companies should be barred from outfitting or cooperating with China's coercive forces. Chinese companies that raise capital in the United States should be vetted closely. Overall business ties would not likely suffer: Beijing has proven to be thoroughly pragmatic in matters commercial. Beyond commercial policy, U.S. government agencies should be encouraged to engage with China. At present, many of them, such as the National Endowment for Democracy and USAID are hampered by their ban on involvement with a country whose government is not officially committed to democracy. This restraint makes little sense, as many observers have noted. In the philosophy of global justice of Rawls, China would be a "burdened society" where weak liberal political and cultural traditions—kept that way by dictatorship—struggle to gain preeminence. Low-level assistance to China in terms of education, health, welfare, rule of law, and much else is not only practical but also just. Withholding it on the grounds that China is burdened by dictatorship is both unjust and illogical.

Low-level engagement can and should include an explicit and open commitment to democracy, for two reasons. First, any democratic country has to be true to itself, to meet the same standards of openness and explicit policy aims in foreign policy as it must at home. Otherwise, those policies can go dreadfully wrong, as they did in Vietnam. Foreign policy experts soaked in Sinology who argue for a soft, face-giving approach often forget that they represent democracies that demand accountability to their own people, a fact they might find troublesome but that is there exactly to keep tabs on that desire to be freed from popular control. The "domestic interests," in the United States which many a Sino-U.S. relations specialist bewails is exactly the point of representative government.

Second, as with business, there is no evidence that such a commitment would adversely affect most programs in China. Building a "democratic" China is an explicit goal of the CCP leadership, even if it intends to remain the sole party. On the ground, meanwhile, as we have seen there is already a strong growing consensus on the need for real democracy. The head of the UNDP reports that while Beijing diplomats opposed the agency's "democratic governance," initiative in 1998, local officials in China embraced the notion as a real solution to their governance crisis.[70]

China's people, and many of its reformist elites, recognize that peaceful evolution from dictatorship to democracy offers the best hope for building the strong and prosperous China of their dreams. The United States, along with the rest of the world's democratic majority, should help them in that quest. To a great extent, they already are. With a more focused and enlightened policy, much more could be accomplished. To quote one congressional leader: "We should feel free to talk past the regime and directly to the people."[71]

Border Effects and Global Civil Society

We live in an age in which the norms of democracy have become the gold standard of our time. This atmosphere has a significant impact on China that goes beyond diplomatic policies. The "border effects" of global democratization and the rise of a powerful pro-democracy global civil society are widely felt. As one Party hard-liner wrote about the "Third Wave" of democratizations of the late twentieth century: "The so-called Third Wave theory has had an impact on China, causing some liberal scholars to become quite active and in society a wave of liberal democracy thinking has spread."[72]

Traditionally, the "border effects" of nearby democratic change have been the most powerful international factors in democratizations; indeed this is one of the explanations of the three "waves." The near-simultaneous democratizations of Eastern Europe and Russia in the Third Wave are the best examples. But similar effects have been seen in Latin America, southern Europe, and Southeast Asia.

China is feeling those same effects. Of course, democracy in Western countries exerts a constant influence, not least because of the economic and technological prowess of the West. Those affects have been deeply reinforced by the Third Wave. Beijing now finds itself looking in from the outside on conferences such as the Annual Conference of New and Restored Democracies and the annual conference of the Community of Democracies. In Asia, democracy has become the mainstream system, accounting for 24 of 39 governments by the turn of the century. Attempts to erect a cover for dictatorship under the rubric of "Asian values," as with the attempts in the past to subvert democracy in Africa through appeals to tribalism, now lie discarded. The Council of Asian Liberals and Democrats (CALD) brings together democratic parties of Asia into one forum and helps to share indigenous experiences with democracy, further evidence of the pan-human universality of democracy. As one Chinese liberal writes: "China has no reason to miss the opportunity to join the mainstream of human civilization."[73]

China's people look abroad and see those in allegedly inferior tributary nations like Cambodia, the Philippines, and Thailand lining up to choose their leaders and wonder why they cannot do likewise. When a newly democratic South Korea jailed two former presidents in 1996 for subverting democracy and taking bribes, it caused a sensation in China. "The trial was of great significance to all of Asia. It told us that modernization must have political standards," wrote He Qinglian.[74]

Within Asia, the examples of Taiwan and India stand out. Taiwan's successful democratization launched by Chiang Kai-shek's son on his deathbed in 1986 has proven to be a powerful example to people on the mainland. Not only has democracy sustained an economic powerhouse, but it has also endeared Taiwan to the global community. U.S. backing for Taiwan is singularly helped by its democratic and free system.

Beijing's attempts to discredit democracy in Taiwan by showing the occasional fist-fights in its legislature have boomeranged with the developing popular admiration for the Taiwanese ability to struggle over policies. Attacks on corruption in Taiwan serve to draw attention to far greater and less manageable corruption in China.

Scholars frequently point to differences between the democratizations of Taiwan and China. Yet on close inspection, those differences are narrowing rapidly. Taiwan's need to gain U.S. support in the wake of the diplomatic defections to the PRC in the 1970s is today paralleled by Beijing's need for international recognition in the post-Third Wave democratic environment. Taiwan's emerging opposition parties and civil society of the 1970s is today paralleled by China's nascent civil society, growing middle class, and reformist regime insiders. The KMT's legitimacy crisis on Taiwan was no worse than the CCP's legitimacy crisis on the mainland.

Indeed, some enlightened CCP leaders may see the Taiwan example as a model of how to retain power for as long as possible during democratic transition, as the KMT did until losing out in 2000. As one scholar sums up: "If one needs to find an example that points a way out of repressive authoritarianism for the CCP, there is not better choice than that of the KMT."[75]

The example of India is less politicized but arguably more profound. Asia's two great ancient civilizations are a study in contrasts today. Both are poor and populous. But India's flourishing democracy and extensive freedoms serves as a contrast to China's callous dictatorship and repressive environment. As mentioned, India almost single-handedly refutes arguments that large, poor countries cannot sustain democracy. It takes a Herculean effort for anyone to argue that India had better conditions for democracy than China because of, say, a British colonial heritage or a tradition of society being separate from the state, embodied in people like Gandhi. According to most estimates, India had far worse objective conditions given its extensive poverty (two-fifths of the population), unparalleled ethnic and religious diversity, and neighboring nuclear threat in Pakistan. "For opponents of democracy in Asia," writes one Indian intellectual, "the history of this experience is a warning of what can be done."[76]

A more pressing matter is whether India is an argument that China *should* embrace democracy. Certainly, many a Western investment banker, conservative academic, or stability-minded diplomat has replied in the negative. But that line was increasingly being challenged in China by those who see the benefits of democracy in India. Materially, India has improved as much as China in the Human Development Index since 1980, even though it began economic reforms a decade later. On the issue of sustainability, India's entrenched and stable constitutional order, its less extreme environmental degradation, and its lesser income inequalities suggest its gains are also more lasting. If India's impressive growth rates of the first years of the new century continue, this side of the argument will look stronger yet. Credit ratings agencies are making those points already.[77]

More important, there is a growing sense that India's protection of rights and freedoms and justice makes it a bigger miracle, given the obvious lack of expansion of these in China. One domestic critic of CCP rural policies returned from a trip to India in 2002 and praised the country for not unjustly forcing the burdens of reforms onto its farmers.[78] Likewise, the leader of Hong Kong's biggest pro-Beijing political party returned from a trip to India in February 2002 "struck by the upbeat outlook that almost everybody seemed to have" despite the country's poverty and communal tensions. "Indians," he wrote, "believe in their system of government. . . . If democracy means a slower pace of reform . . . Indians seem to recognize this as a price worth paying. . . . People do not easily find fault with a system built on common values."[79]

Beyond Asia, the democratic experiences of Russia and Eastern Europe have had a significant impact. Beijing's eager propaganda about the rough start for democracy there in the early 1990s had given way to grim silence by the turn of the century as the countries emerged with functioning democracies and strong economic growth. Of the 28 new democratic states created in 1989–91, 25 were considered either consolidated or moving in that direction a decade later.[80] Even those in China who express shock at Russia's loss of great-power status are being challenged by others who point to China's failure to achieve even middle-power status because of its political system.

Beijing's line that Russia shows the importance of delaying political reforms is today widely refuted in China by academics and some liberal leaders. A Chinese Academy of Social Sciences book on the collapse of the USSR issued in 2001 asserted that an over-concentration of power, not political reforms, caused the USSR's collapse. As one liberal writes: "Those who say the USSR and Eastern Europe show that we must not undertake political reform have got cause and effect mixed up; it was because of their lagging political reform that the system failed and resulted in collapse."[81]

Border effects also result from an increasingly well-organized and influential global civil society that takes democratic norms as its basic principles. This includes human rights groups like Amnesty International, labor rights groups like the International Confederation of Free Trade Unions, or democratic and legal-building institutions like the Carter Center or the Soros Foundation. The influence can be seen in an internal speech in 1992 by senior leader Luo Gan on reforming China's internal migration controls: "Some Western human rights organizations have raised this as a human rights issue, which has seriously harmed our country's reputation. In order to take away this excuse for attacking China as well as meet our own development needs, it makes sense to reform the system."[82]

As part of this global civil society, the overseas Chinese democracy movement has remained a factor in Chinese politics since 1989. U.S.-based groups like the China Alliance for Democracy, China Democracy Federation, and the Chinese Federation Development Committee push for a nonviolent overthrow of the CCP. Hong Kong, meanwhile, is home to the 1989-era Alliance in Support of Patriotic Democratic Movements of China which organizes an annual June Fourth vigil—the biggest annual political protest in the ex-colony—and to the Democratic Party, the most popular party in Hong Kong, which argues frequently and fervently for democratic change in the mainland.

Beijing would like to think, and its propaganda organs frequently write, that the overseas democracy movement is divided, weak, and discredited. Yet the positive coverage of its activities in virtually all mainstream Chinese-language newspapers and magazines published in Hong Kong and overseas gives the lie to that claim. Elitists may wash their hands of the boisterous groups. But on the ground they are invariably viewed with respect by the Chinese publics.

If the story of democracy in the nineteenth and twentieth centuries was one of closed polities in which lord and peasant battled for supremacy, political development today takes place in open polities where the peasants are backed by a militia of international forces. Border effects, no less than diplomatic policies and international economic and social exchanges, are helping China's people to cast off centuries of feudal domination. Notes one mainland scholar: "With China now joining the world political and economic systems, democracy has attracted a lot more attention from the people. Realizing a democratic reality in China is now an inevitable trend that no man can stop."[83]

Political Decompression

In the Spring of 2000, an article appeared in the popular *Southern Weekend* newspaper written by Ren Zhongyi, a former Guangdong province Party chief closely associated with the pioneering spirit of the reform era. In it, the wizened Ren declared that the Party had become dictatorial and conservative. The country needed laws that applied to everyone and a parliamentary system that wielded real power, he wrote. "The people are the boss. There should be no personality cults and no dictators."[84]

Two years later, a former top aide to Mao, Li Rui was making similar noises.

The Party should be subject to a new constitutional court and the national legislature should meet more often to consider laws. Freedoms of speech and assembly should be enforced, while censorship of the media should be lifted. "Only with democratization can there be modernization," wrote Li.[85]

While the CCP's harsh rhetoric and repression of open dissent makes it seem a formidable force, on the inside there are many signs of change. Since reforms began and with only a brief interruption after 1989, the CCP has been undergoing a quiet internal transformation that has fatally weakened the cohesiveness essential to its long-term survival. At the same time, quiet proto-democratic changes have been sprouting inside its own political institutions. This "creeping democratization" is a critical resource for change, one that disarms the Party's opposition to democratic transition and creates the institutional foundations that will help to consolidate a new democracy.

Of course, other changes have enhanced the internal vigor of dictatorship. The CCP's ideological collapse has given it more flexibility in pursuing any and all means to stay in power—including, for example, colluding with big capitalists and raising funds by privatizing state industry. Its new generation of technocratic leaders can talk the talk of modern leaders, gaining popular commendation. Professionalized army and police are more adept at crushing popular protest by deploying hi-tech tools.

But on balance, the very attempts by the CCP to appear and act more democratically while jealously preserving its monopoly of power appear to be sinking, not saving, its rule. Within the regime, the collapse of communist ideology has created a state more attuned to the needs of professional governance than revolutionary rule. One Western scholar has talked of the "quiet revolution from within" as cadres turn their attention away from political-ideological education toward attracting foreign investment, running local companies, and levying taxes.[86] A parallel process of professionalization driven by the demands of governance has sapped the revolutionary ethos out of the Party as bureaucrats seek to grapple with pressing needs to manage healthcare reforms, expand schools, and balance the books.

Cadres who join the Party today find that while its ideology is a "living lie," it has yet to be replaced by an alternative vision. There is no longer any moral claim on Party members, most of whom join the Party in order to boost their job prospects. In most surveys, fewer than 10 percent say they want to bring about communism. Popular perceptions of the Party as a closed oligarchy of rent-seekers hurt the esprit of members. This is like the loss of social capital in society: cooperation becomes impossible because there is no longer a shared understanding of "what it's all about."

As a result, inside the Party there is now a market of competing ideas.

Various factions seek to ground their views in their own interpretations of society's needs, leading to a diversity inside the Party that reflects the diversity in society itself. The result is a polity that increasingly resembles the "authoritarian pluralism" that existed in South Korea, Hungary, or Taiwan prior to their democratic breakthroughs. Internal advocates of democratic change compete on an even footing, and gain support. Such pluralism grew quickly in the 1980s, leading to a rupture and a defeat for reform advocates in 1989. Since then, the hard-line forces have weakened considerably, symbolized by the retirement in 2002 of Tiananmen mastermind Li Peng and the demotion of his top representative to last place on the nine-member Politburo standing committee. The death of most Party veterans of the civil war has removed another significant barrier from the road to change.

One of former Party chief Jiang Zemin's top advisors admitted openly in a 2001 interview that there existed a "freedom faction" within the Party that believed in launching democratizing reforms.[87] That faction has gained adherents as a consensus has grown on the need to restart political reforms, stalled since 1989 and has issued several clarion appeals for political liberalization.[88]

The resurgence of the liberal faction was heralded in 1995 when former vice premier Tian Jiyun called for direct elections for government officials, eventually all the way to the top. "Some people want multi-candidate elections. This would be a very good idea through which the people can express their will. . . . I think this kind of system will become a trend in China."[89] Former Politburo standing committee member Li Ruihuan, meanwhile, echoed that appeal in internal speeches and called for partial media privatization to gird the new political opening. "This is the natural trend of the times and history," he said.[90] Cues like these from the top have encouraged a host of reform-minded thinkers in Party institutes like the Central Party School, the Chinese Academy of Social Sciences, and the Central Office (or General Office) to tender a number of proposals for serious democratic change.

On the opposite side, there have also been calls for the creation of a neoauthoritarian state, a dictatorship completely stripped of its ideological baggage and focused on rule of law, efficient civil service, and rule by highly educated and competent technocrats. This model is highly attractive to many regime insiders since it holds the prospect of resolving the legitimacy crisis without a loss of power. Most Party cadres, while putting political reform at the top of their agenda, want administrative streamlining and inner Party liberalization rather than a freer media or stronger legislatures.[91] A senior researcher in the Central Office broached the idea of a "legal democracy," in China under which the CCP would gradually introduce a Singapore-style democratic system ruled by laws.[92] Another highly publicized proposal came from a vice minister of economic reform, whose blueprint for transforming the CCP into a broad ruling party under the supervision of media, laws, and limited public participation excited much debate in 2001.[93]

Democrats respond that such proposals fail to solve the key problem of over-concentrated power. Others call the system elitist or unworkable. In any case, the main importance of this debate inside the Party is that it creates the very balance of forces, the pluralism, that makes the later choice of democracy more likely. In that sense, the elitist neo-authoritarians—along with the orthodox ideologues, the corrupt economic reformers, and many other factions in the Party—play a positive role in bringing about democracy because they encourage debate and fragmentation. It is, as one Western scholar noted, "evidence both of the uncertainty that haunts China's political future and of the serious possibility that a democratic transition might be in store."[94]

The impact of this pluralism can be seen in the increasingly popular and inclusive nature of political discourse. The discourse of authoritarian regimes is typically one that draws a clear line between rulers and subjects, producing an identity among people as residual subjects (like the masses, or *qunzhong*, and the "old hundred names," *laobaixing*) outside the ruling elite. At the same time, authoritarian discourse telegraphs a strictly apolitical "unity" of the interests of the subjects (in China, the focus on the "big picture," or *daju*, and as well as on universal concerns of "eating one's fill," *chibaofan*, or "raising children," *sheng haizi*). Regime oligarchs use stylized language and a preponderance of third person nouns (the state, the people, the Party) in speeches to signal these relationships. A democratic discourse, by contrast, considers rulers as simply chosen representatives of the people (in Chinese the word representative, or *daibiao*, or even politician, *zhengke* which remained a dirty word in the CCP lexicon) and society is assumed to have its various partisan interests (another dirty word, *jubu liyi*) and personal viewpoints (ditto for *geren guannian*).[95]

While the complete transition to a democratic discourse awaits the transition to democracy itself, the signs of this move are already apparent. The breakdown of the authoritarian discourse in the PRC has been heralded by the likes of Zhu Rongji, premier from 1998 to 2003, who spoke in an off-the-cuff vernacular and often referred to himself and to his role as a politician. Official scholars, meanwhile, breaking from the tradition of court literati, increasingly write of the state and Party in the third, not first person, which breaks down the unified identity of the "rulers."

In this and dozens of other ways, the CCP has created a hall of mirrors in which it can no longer focus the attentions of its members. Whatever the news from the battlements erected against the plebians, inside the castle the knights are losing patience with the king. Talk of democracy inside the castle is seen by many knights as the way to democracy throughout the kingdom.[96]

The failing belief in the CCP's god-sent right to rule and the rise of internal pluralism are fateful changes. Attempts to replace one form of autocracy with another become impossible with so many competing interests. Two Western scholars note, in light of the internal differences which brought down communist rule in the Soviet Union, that "there is no transition whose beginning is not the consequence—direct or indirect—of important divisions within the authoritarian regime itself."[97] Notes one Chinese democrat: "The best hope for democracy in China is the evolution—or corrosion or split—inside the Party itself."[98]

Alongside this internal decompression is a pageant of new external political devices. Expanding local elections, stronger people's congresses, and various moves to entrench constitutional norms had gained wide currency by the early 2000s. Meanwhile, a gallery of outside remonstrators has restarted a lively and open debate in society on political reforms. The existence of this debate is a powerful resource for change, even if its predictive value may be limited. For just as we are looking for a "critical mass" of economic and social factors to support a democratic breakthrough, so too in politics a rumbling debate is the critical ingredient for wider systemic reform.

Village elections have been widely and rightly celebrated inside and outside China for showing the effectiveness of democracy in improving governance, not least because they are conducted among the great unwashed whom elitists frequently deride as unfit to choose their leaders. By the turn of the century, 13 years after the village election law was passed, about half of the country's 730,000 villager committees (representing about three-quarters of all villages) had been formed through popular multi-candidate elections. What began as a halting experiment has been embraced by peasants, who use elections to oust corrupt leaders, monitor the local Party chief, and improve governance. Party interference prompts petitions to higher level authorities or even mass resignations of village leaders. TV shows appear celebrating proactive elected village heads who confront Party officials. Border effects are evident as some candidates begin open campaigning from the back of blaring trucks, as in Taiwan. As one Chinese scholar wrote: "The country hicks who are always disparaged as being politically immature by urbanites are already electing their own leaders and enjoying the benefits of democracy. They have proven to be quick studies in the intricacies of elections and voting. Village democracy is the great starting point for the whole process of democratization in China."[99]

While they remain technically illegal, direct elections of governments in the country's 45,000 townships had "erupted," in a dozen places by the turn of the century. Much of the pressure is a direct result of village-level elections; peasants who have a say over village affairs demand the same say over township affairs. But there is also a welter of political reasons, from factional jostling in Beijing to local level careerism and bureaucratic rivalries. Many local cadres simply want to be on the right side of history—those in Walking on the Clouds (Buyun) in Sichuan province want to erect a sign commemorating their historic first township election of 1998.

The official endorsement of township elections, if forced on Beijing to resolve pressing governance needs, would be a major step. The sheer size of the areas—the average township has 13,000 registered voters—would require the creation of organizational structures, in other words nascent political parties. They would also require a freer press because not everyone could attend a campaign rally. In addition, the elected governments would likely leech significant responsibilities and resources from the township Party committees. No doubt this accounts for the reluctance to endorse township elections. Yet governance needs are pushing them forward anyways, heralding what would be a pivotal change in China's democratization.

The growing muscularity of local people's congresses is happening in parallel to elections. Like life in the universe, the appearance of vigilante congresses and delegates is made possible by sheer vastness, a reminder that a country's size can also be an asset to overthrowing dictatorship because of the variety of breakthrough points it can provide. Nationwide, 3.2 million people serve as delegates to people's congresses, an enormous resource for change. Of these, 3.0 million serve in the 51,000 directly elected township and county level congresses while the rest serve in the appointed congresses of major cities, provinces, and the national center. A law enhancing the powers of delegates is due to be passed by 2004. All this provides fertile soil for experimentation, just as it did in the Soviet Union where delegates to the local-level Congresses of People's Deputies began to find their voices in the mid-1980s, or in the late Qing dynasty where provincial legislatures ended up turning on the emperor.

Examples of local congresses exploding into action are now common. The congress of the northeastern city of Shenyang rejected the annual report of the local court in 2001, complaining of corruption. The Wuxi city congress stripped the local government of environmental protection powers the same year on the grounds that Party officials were involved in most of the polluting businesses. Congresses in many localities now use the term "order" (*zecheng*) rather than "suggest" (*jianyi*) when they comment on government policies, a signal that they are taking their promised legal status as "the highest organ of state power" seriously. The congresses are now awash with "political entrepreneurs" who are redefining the meaning of the bodies from tools of regime legitimization to tools of popular control.[100] Thus in a strange way, life is imitating art. The pageantry of democracy created by the Party to legitimate its rule is transforming into democracy itself. Since the congresses have both the constitutional and the moral high ground, the Party finds it cannot control its own creation. As the stature of the congresses grows, so does pressure to democratize them. Even conservative scholars agree that all the congresses should eventually be directly elected, even the national congress. As a frightened Party submits to the "supervision" of the congresses, it raises doubts about who the Party is supposed to represent, and why it alone holds power.

Surrounding all the institutional changes is a more general public debate about political reform. This is both a stimulus to institutional innovation as well as a result of it. Through it, scholars, journalists, and reform-minded officials have been able to set the agenda for political modernization in the country, portraying the Party as unwilling or unable to change. We can group commentators into two camps: constitutionalists and transformers.

The constitutionalists favor a gradual build-up of democratic foundations within the existing party-led system. They are the children of the great legacy of "change within tradition," in the Chinese state that goes back to the imperial era. Taking their role as remonstrating with the emperor on his own terms, they seek to guide him onto an enlightened pathway. In the PRC, that means reminding the leadership of the democratic laws and goals that remain in the political canon. This includes expanding direct elections for governments, empowering the people's congresses, enhancing the independence of courts, and liberalizing the internal administration of the Party.

The constitutional camp includes both "romantics" who believe such moves would consolidate CCP rule and "strategists" who believe it is the best way to undermine it. The romantics are concerned to stay ahead of the wave of change, preserving their perquisites while maintaining legitimacy. The strategists see internal reform as a more plausible path to CCP demise than external overthrow. Their idea is to recognize the CCP as a monarchy in a constitutional system while limiting its remit in government affairs in the interests of better rule. This would bring China closer to democracy even if the Party—like a Latin American military—is allowed to remain as "the power behind the throne." While awaiting the day when the CCP's ultimate prerogatives can be ended, this would also provide an important foundation for democracy by implanting the norms of constitutional behavior.

In the schizoid political atmosphere of the PRC, many activists dart unwittingly or not between the two poles of constitutional romanticism and strategy. But in the end, as we shall see in part 2, the difference may not amount to much. A drastically reformed CCP that managed to hold power in democratic elections would satisfy the wishes of moderates on both sides. Indeed, an argument could be made that the constitutional path is exactly the one that the CCP set out upon after Tiananmen, rejecting immediate change but embracing a host of fundamental changes in the relationship of the Party to state and society that took China closer, though still far, to the constitutional ideal. Citizens gained more legal rights and more control over social and economic life, the state was more constrained by the law and more professional in its behavior, the military was almost entirely removed from politics, and the Party showed signs of weariness in running the nation's life. Like the traffic cop of our earlier metaphor, it appeared worn down by the burdens of authoritarian rule. Hu Jintao urged a "comprehensive implementation" of the constitution shortly after taking over as Party general secretary in 2002, adding that "no organization or individual can have special powers overriding the constitution and the law." Little surprise that many already look to a post-CCP China.

Alongside the constitutionalists are the transformers, political reformers who urge more radical surgery on the body politic of China. Their main appeal is for a rapid transition to free and fair elections of all governments. "Ruling out direct elections might be accepted by people for a short time but as time goes by, this prohibition will increasingly not wash," note a group of Shanghai scholars.[101]

Of course, this group lives on the edges of official tolerance. In the late PRC era, Beijing held about 3,500 people prosecuted under the State Security Act plus at any given time about another 50,000 in three-year labor camp sentences for "disturbing public order." After initial tolerance, the Party crushed attempts by activists in the late 1990s to establish nascent opposition groups like the China Development Union and the China Democracy Party. But by the first decade of the new century there was a surprising amount of space for open debate on political transformation, such as existed in late-authoritarian Indonesia or Taiwan. As long as they did not use the phrase "overthrow the CCP" or seek to establish formal organizations, the transformers were free to make their point. Consider this quotation from a public magazine in China:

> The precondition for competitive elections within the Party must be that the ruling party allows competition among parties. If the Chinese Communist Party does not allow other competitive parties (jingzheng-

xingde dangpai) to exist, then it will lack internal competitiveness and the pressure to reform itself. Like every other organization, the Party can only become competitive in a competitive environment. At present, the [officially approved] democratic parties are not competitors and so cannot help the CCP to become more competitive. Can't we let them be more independent and compete with the CCP? Leadership is service [Mao said] and in any service you should have a choice. The CCP represents the interests of the greatest number of people so it should be confident that if it sticks to the truth and corrects its errors it can win victory in a multi-party competition.[102]

As more and more of a real "opposition" emerges in society among the constitutionalists and transformers, a real political system of "democrats" and "the regime" is emerging, the very polarity whose existence was so critical to democratic breakthroughs in countries like Russia and Poland. As with the wider community of intellectuals, artists, crusading journalists and jailed dissidents, it is not a question of whether they have the power to overthrow the state. In China as elsewhere, as we shall see, they almost certainly do not. Rather their influence is a more subtle one. They create a market of ideas and empower reformers inside the regime.

Thus the stage is set. Democracy as practiced throughout the world has proven to be the best known means of organizing political activity. It transcends cultures and conditions for the simple fact that it is sensitive to all. China's people have struggled to throw off the chains of dictatorship for more than a century. As the century turned, the possibilities for transition were immense. Society widely recognized the need for fundamental political change, and was for the first time in a position to bring it about. "The tragedies of China's history and of the lives of Chinese people have generated problems and issues which have forced Chinese liberals to try to bring democracy to China," writes one mainland scholar.[103]

There is an unprecedented opportunity for breakthrough. How will it happen?

PART 2
TRANSITION

5

Breakdown and Mobilization

Predicting Change

If the first part of this book was an elaborate exercise in stage-setting, then we have now come to the main performance. The task here is to narrate a plausible sequence of events that would bring about a lasting democratic breakthrough in China. In this "last mile" of democratization, the long development of liberal and institutional foundations reaches a terminus with the emergence of real participation and competition in politics.

As we saw, the recognition of needs and the balance of forces are now tilted decisively in favor of democratic transition. Many observers of China share this conclusion, but they differ on when the breakthrough will occur. Optimists put the event before 2010.[1] Others guess somewhere between 2010 and 2020.[2] Still more make predictions beyond 2020, perhaps well beyond.[3]

All of these predictions are plausible. Once the conditions for democratization are met, which I believe they are at present, the actual change can come as quickly or as slowly as circumstances permit. The collapse of an authoritarian regime numbers among one of the most contingent phenomena of politics. While the long-term forces that bring it about can be readily identified, the exact timing and path are highly volatile. Economic crisis can prompt popular protests that cause a regime to split and start a dash for democracy. During times of economic stability, however, such a split can lead to a democratic breakthrough that is phased and averts popular protest. Personalities emerge to take charge, leading figures die suddenly, uncertainty pervades choices, alliances shift like the sands.

To elucidate how a breakthrough might occur requires us to shift from the broad, long-term perspective of part 1 to a very narrow and immediate one. Here we will focus on three stages: the manifestation of crisis that provides the critical pressures and outlines for the democratic breakthrough; the "bargaining" issues of who and how the breakthrough occurs; and the immediate response to the change at home and abroad. The scenario I outline below is a rapid elite-led move to democracy prompted by modest popular protest linked to an economic or political crisis.

For the record, I would be surprised if this change were delayed beyond the year 2020. Nonetheless, caution is the byword in predicting both the timing and the sequence of CCP collapse. While it is possible to see the manifest failures of the PRC and its seemingly inevitable replacement by a democratic system, the regime "just might survive on inertia, complicity, fear of worse, chauvinism, the provision of guaranteed minimums, and the like" for several more years.[4] As with many a debased authoritarian regime before it—Czarist Russia, Ceausescu's Romania, Suharto's Indonesia—the CCP could muddle along for years or disappear in a flash. The actual timing of the event will reflect sudden opportunities and situations that are grasped by conscious individuals, something virtually impossible to predict.

So the following can best be described as a stylized scenario rather than a predestined sequence for democratic transition. The purpose is to raise and illuminate the relevant issues that any transition will face—economic crisis, popular mobilization, military response—rather than to provide an ironclad forecast of events. The battlements of CCP rule have survived one crashing wave of democratic agitation after another since 1949. Its foundations are now very weak and the waves grow stronger. Rip-tides and wind shifts may protect it from the next torrent for longer than we imagine. But history suggests it is only a matter of time before the sea rises again.

Gradual Democracy?

Imagine that you are CCP chief Hu Jintao sitting in an idle moment gazing through the winter-frosted window of a meeting hall in the Zhongnanhai leadership complex in Beijing. The country is now full of pressing demands for democracy and society is fully equipped, so to speak, to bring it about. You have read your history books. You do not have any ideological hang-ups about one system of government or another. But you want to retain your power, privileges, and interests. What to do?

There are two options. One is to do nothing on the political front and continue to direct attention to issues of administrative streamlining, economic reform, great-power status, social freedoms, international linkages, the Beijing Olympics, anything that seems to divert attention from questioning your right to rule. It has worked since 1989 and, with a little luck and stepped up repression, it might continue to work, at least until your term of office expires in 2012.

A growing number of "lively" scholars in society, people whose opinions

you trust, like old colleagues from the Communist Youth League, are artic-
ulating another view: waiting is not an attractive option. The longer democratic change is delayed, they say, the worse the problems become and the
more society is empowered. Regimes that waited too long saw their rulers
dragged from their offices and shot in the head. That's not quite the settled
retirement in the Western Hills of Beijing that you had in mind.

So the other option is to begin gradual democratic reforms. Many of those
scholars, and not a few foreign experts, have already proposed various schemes
that would take China through the last mile in a gradual, orderly fashion.[5]
The idea is that the CCP, sometime in the first decade of the century, would
expand direct elections to township levels, liberalize the media, and empower
the people's congresses with, say, all economic policy-making. That would be
followed in the next decade by expanded elections to, say, the provincial level,
the formation of opposition parties, and a formal separation of the CCP from
government. After that, the CCP would open the system completely and compete for power, expecting to win and enjoy a lengthy period as China's "natural" ruling party like Japan's Liberal Democrats or Malaysia's National Front
coalition. Just being a communist cadre is no longer an obstacle to change.
Since reforms began after Mao's death, the Party has sold off most state firms,
professionalized the civil service and military, embraced the concept of rule
of law, welcomed entrepreneurs into the Party, and allowed "bourgeois" thought
to suffuse society. A few ideologues still talk of the CCP's heavenly right to
rule. But you have no illusions: the Party must perform or be overthrown.

There is, however, one nagging worry: you may end up a loser. Authoritarian regimes that voluntarily initiated democratic changes in times of relative
domestic peace, like the Nationalists (KMT) of Taiwan, eventually lost power,
even if they enjoyed a considerable time to prepare for the day. Others found
they could not control the process and lost power overnight, as in South Korea.
Once rulers gave society an inch, it took a mile. Relax, say some scholars.
"Multi-party competition may be avoided for some time until the CCP has
completely transformed itself into an efficient and fully functioning social-
democratic party that is experienced and confident in running elections."[6]

Weighing up the two options, while you are attracted by the possibility of
voluntary withdrawal, you are too afraid of the consequences. You continue
to talk to those lively scholars and begin to drop some vague tidbits into
speeches about the need to "orderly expand democratic participation." Del-
egations are sent to Europe to study social democratic parties there. But when
push comes to shove, you flinch. "Why risk the 'achievements of the regime'
for the sake of the fuzzy long-term advantages advocated by the softliners?"
you say, echoing many a dictator throughout the ages.[7]

Would Hu be right? From the standpoint of the power and privileges of the CCP "interest group," evidence suggests that the answer is yes. Empirically speaking, gradual democratization only works when an authoritarian regime is in a position of still-overwhelming power vis-à-vis society. That allows it to exploit its supremacy to manage the process and to protect its interests along the way. Until it lost the presidency in 2000, the KMT had retained power for a remarkable 14 years after launching democratic reforms in Taiwan, twice as long if political liberalization is dated to the early 1970s.

But the CCP is not the KMT. The power of the CCP—in terms of its political legitimacy, its fiscal capabilities, and its ideological dominance—has weakened considerably in the post-Mao era. While it remains a dominant force when compared to society as a whole, it is probably not dominant enough to successfully carry out a phased political transition. If it did, the reforms would likely take on a life of their own. That is what happened in Gorbachev's Russia. Plans for regime-dependent reforms suddenly become society-dependent.

If the Party were to begin gradual reforms to crack down on political corruption, say, by giving the media a free rein or by establishing an independent anti-corruption body, the impact would be too great. The move would expose the hypocrisy and rot inside the Party for all to see. Township elections, with their open campaigning, would do the same. Such a move would also come at a time of unprecedented democratic expectations in China, partly fueled by developments abroad. If citizens in Shanghai were offered the chance to elect their own mayor, farmers in Anhui will wonder about electing their governor. A free press in Shenzhen would create pressures for the same in Guangzhou. The forces are unstoppable once unleashed under these conditions. That was the lesson of Gorbachev's failed attempt to control corruption and expand local democracy in the USSR.

As a result, Hu Jintao, or whoever sits atop the declining CCP, will not launch gradual democratic reforms. In order to protect the Party, he must avoid changes that will take on a life of their own.

It was not always so. The CCP could have successfully introduced gradual reforms in the late 1980s, when there were very open plans for a gradual democratization over a decade or more. Reformist Party chiefs Hu Yaobang and Zhao Ziyang outlined plans for reducing the role of the Party in a gradualist fashion that mirrored the phased erosion of state enterprises and planning in the economy. Deng Xiaoping even promised that China would be a democracy by the year 2035.[8]

Indeed, the phased introduction of direct elections at the village level beginning in 1987 was a classic case of authoritarian withdrawal. In this case,

an enlightened conservative, Peng Zhen, saw how decollectivization had created new pressures for good governance that Party-appointed village chiefs
could not accommodate. As a result of voluntarily ceding power, the CCP
enjoyed the privilege of guiding the development of village elections, often
to its advantage.

But it could not do the same at the national level today. Reformers inside
the regime cannot gain ascendancy in the absence of mass protests. Since 1989,
the Party has been on high alert against the emergence of "splittists" at the top
who might make a case for withdrawal. When liberal Politburo member Tian
Jiyun called for direct multi-candidate elections for state premier in 1995, his
speech was blacklisted and he was given a stern rebuke.[9] His standard-bearer,
Li Ruihuan, was purged from the Politburo standing committee in 2002.

The CCP will thus continue to reject political participation and sink into
deeper misgovernance. As a result, its fate will almost certainly be no different
from that of the communist regimes of Eastern Europe. Democracy will be
seized, not offered; and as a result it will come about in a short period. Communist China will end not with a whimper but with a bang.

CCP leaders are caught in a prison of their own making. They can refuse
reforms and face protests, or grant reforms and lose their jobs. As one Chinese
scholar wrote: "In recent regime transitions, autocrats compelled to liberalize
and democratize were, with few exceptions, driven from power because by
that time they had been thoroughly debilitated and delegitimized by their
own misrule. The cold and cruel logic of political reform—those who can,
will not; those who try when forced, cannot—has been tragically validated in
all too many countries."[10]

When China could, the top would not. Reformist Party chiefs in the 1980s
were purged by hoary Party elders. Now the Party cannot because society must.
At this late stage, it is no longer possible to navigate between the Scylla of
reforming and losing control and the Charybdis of not reforming and losing
support. "As yet no one has found a way to bring a Leninist state through this
narrow strait, and there is little reason to think that the current Chinese leaders
will have more luck or skill than their colleagues anywhere else," notes one
scholar.[11]

Or in the words of another: "The CCP may now be in a position where it
is so discredited and so unpopular that attempts at adaptation, such as meaningful elections, would hasten its demise rather than strengthen its support
. . . It is unlikely to sponsor the democratization of China's political system,
and unlikely to survive even if it tried."[12]

That compels us to consider the circumstances that might force change
upon the reluctant CCP leadership.

Metastatic Crisis

One important dimension of democratic revolutions is whether they occur in periods of broad-based prosperity and relative stability or times of economic and social crisis. While transitions are usually easier and more stable under the former conditions, most occur under the latter. Autocrats rarely relinquish power when they are in positions of strength and democratizers can rarely overcome the incentive problems of collective action when there is not a pressing crisis.

Asia is one region with several glorious exceptions to that rule. In the 1980s, leaders in Taiwan, Thailand, and South Korea read the runes of the long-term forces that would drive them from power and chose to initiate change when they were in positions of strength. As is typical, two of those transitions, in Taiwan and Thailand, took place over several years. That of South Korea occurred faster, an outcome more typical of crisis transitions.

What about China? Despite two decades of relative prosperity and stability, the leadership has balked at change. That suggests the transition will take place in crisis conditions. Since the Party will not launch democratic reforms because it rightly fears the worst for its position, the only thing that can initiate the process is a national trauma that prompts popular mobilization.

What will the crisis look like? More than 30 major dynasties, both national and regional, have wielded the scepter in China since the third century BC, and as a result "end of dynasty watching" is a fine art. The CCP has encouraged the view that its own lifespan is subject to the same cycle as past dynasties. By claiming to have come to power as a result of "objective historical conditions" rather than popular mandate, it has legitimated discussion about what those conditions are, and whether they have changed.[13] If they have, dynasty-watchers say, it's time to watch for portents of collapse.

In traditional Chinese geomancy, such portents have included a wide range of natural and man-made disasters. In a country as large as China, there are always such catastrophic events and those willing to ascribe cosmic significance to them. The SARS health crisis of 2003 was a classic example, fuelling metaphorical comments on the "contagion" of CCP rule. Given the scale of ecological crisis in China, it is also easy to point to any number of plagues that have swept the country in recent years as evidence of coming change: floods, locusts, or the ominous but unstoppable approach of huge Mongolian deserts to the borders of Beijing. The Chinese expression "the heavens fall and the earth splits" (*tian beng tu lie*) conjures up imagery of typhoons and earthquakes shaking the polity.

Also watched closely is the collapse of dams, surely a key reason why the twin dam bursts in Henan province in 1975 that killed an estimated 300,000 people were covered up and remain essentially a badly kept national secret. Certainly any problems with the Three Gorges dam would be read as signs of imminent change. But smaller collapses could be read with equal disquiet. Officials frequently wring their hands in public about the 33,000 dams in the country. A third of the total are deemed "defective," including 100 which are considered "large."

The collapse of sacred buildings elicits similar imagery. When "the clay crumbles and tiles sever" (*tu beng wa jie*) on a traditional Chinese house, it means the owner is ill-fated. The idiom was used to describe the fall of the first dynasty, the Qin. When the Dragon Pavilion in the central China city of Kaifeng collapsed in a rainstorm after being struck by lightning in 1994, officials put a news ban on the event until it had been repaired.

Geomancers also point to the growth of spiritual movements (such as today's Falun Gong sect and secret societies), moral rot (tattered social capital, pervasive official corruption), and national disunity (the election of a separatist party in Taiwan, the fleeing of Tibet's highest lamas abroad) as portents of dynastic failure.

While fanciful in their attractions, such portents are widely watched because they have a real connection to misgovernance. They may reflect a failing state that cannot afford to disinfect its hospitals, maintain its dikes, keep its officials clean, or protect its borders. In modern terms, they might signal the coming of the kind of crisis that has driven many an authoritarian regime from power.

How would a widespread national crisis begin in China? In one useful formulation, a Western scholar suggested that the key element is the emergence of "multiple metastatic dysfunction," in society.[14] Metastasis is when a disease like cancer transfers from one part of the body to another. Thus the phrase describes the spread of dysfunction beyond its initial boundaries—when a run on a local bank becomes a national financial crisis, or a failed bail-out of a national pension scheme becomes a fiscal crisis.

This formulation may overstate the conditions necessary for some authoritarian collapses but it is apt for Leninist dictatorships. They can usually contain single crises, preventing sparks from leaping across roofs. Thus it is a simultaneous exacerbation of low-level crises in several spheres that creates the environment for transition. Tragically, it also means that the transition is likely to be a bumpy one.

As we saw in the previous section, China's nodes of instability remained distinctly separate and "non-transferable," in the early 2000s. A conclave of scholars, government officials, and military strategists who met in 1998 to consider the question of China's stability concluded that the country was in a position of "stable unrest" where "numerous nodes of instability exist throughout the society, but with little apparent connecting tissue to create a critical mass." The attendees predicted that the situation would remain this way for "some time" but warned against complacency: "No reasonable analyst would be wise to assume . . . continuance of Communist Party rule in China."[15]

If indeed China was facing varying levels of economic, social, political and diplomatic crisis by the early 2000s, how might these nodes metastasize?

Economic distress—as opposed to purely social, international, or political factors—remains the best predictive variable of authoritarian regime collapse. It seems to be both necessary and almost-sufficient to bring down dictatorship.[16] So it seems reasonable to predict the same for the CCP's end. Typically, this means slowing growth and rising inflation. But steady growth and stable prices may mask other types of economic crisis that are just as powerful. In particular, growing unemployment, financial distress, and sectoral recession can all provide the economic crisis needed to prompt regime change.

The direct impact of economic crisis is obvious. Workers and farmers experience falling incomes while the middle class watches its savings and prospects do likewise. The indirect impact is no less important. It can lead to a defection of business leaders to the cause of reform by raising questions about the competence of the regime. The handling of economic crisis also puts huge pressures on the unity of the regime itself. It tears apart the coalition of interests that benefited from the status quo.

With a CCP regime committed to high growth, there is little chance that economic growth would be allowed to slow significantly. Given the cautious approach to international capital flows, it is also unlikely to be a Latin American-style balance of payments crisis. Still, this may merely shift the economic crisis to other spheres. Helter-skelter growth with poor governance creates "bad growth," as outlined earlier, characterized by low productivity, rampant lawlessness and corruption, huge inequalities, and financial turmoil. This low-key economic crisis has been underway since the mid-1990s. In such a situation, it takes just one major stock market scandal or bankruptcy to shift the balance of economic benefits against the idea of upholding the regime. Capital flight worsens the crisis. If foreign investor confidence collapsed, it could do the same: one analyst calculates that a 50 percent fall in FDI flows would cut GDP growth in half.[17]

Liberal activist Peng Ming imagines that in the first decade of the century, China's economy will face multiple metastatic dysfunction caused by slowing growth, high transaction costs, financial crisis, falling stock markets, wild swings in macroeconomic policy, and fiscal crisis.[18] A prominent Western student of China's economy, meanwhile, has predicted a fiscal crisis by 2006 or 2008.[19] Another scenario is a banking crisis.[20] A lack of capital account convertibility and limited foreign bank access to the domestic market were the only things standing between China's banks and collapse by the early 2000s. Yet those things were due to change with China's accession to the WTO.

We are not yet at the point of mass national protests for political reform. However, there may be large-scale strikes by workers over labor grievances, or a remote rural region may fall into anarchy as peasants rise up en masse over falling incomes, as has happened several times in China in the 1990s. Unlike in the past, however, this small-scale and dispersed protest cannot be doused with economic concessions for the simple reason that the indigent central state has nothing more to offer. The result: China begins heading towards "a swifter and more profound transition."[21]

A word of warning: metastatic crisis that brings an authoritarian regime to its knees is often seen only in retrospect. Only by examining the entrails of the former Soviet Union do we now realize how sclerotic and crisis-ridden the economy had become by the 1980s, once its last-minute resuscitation by oil revenues ended. For China, the crisis may already have begun. In a regime that lacks an adequate warning system, writes one mainland scholar, "problems get covered up and as a result economic issues become new breaking points of a political crisis."[22]

There are however signs to look for. Most important are signs that critical players are starting to defect from the cause of the regime. Business leaders may form independent groups calling for political reforms. Scholars may begin to openly say that the writing is on the wall for CCP rule. In the USSR, the appearance of articles in rival newspapers with diametrically opposite views of a new drama in 1988 signaled how divided the CPSU had become in the face of the secret economic crisis. Indeed, there were already tantalizing signs of this in China by the early 2000s, as we saw.

It is at this point, perhaps surprisingly, that many authoritarian governments have lost power. The mere crisis of governance causes a severe loss of morale in the regime and opens the way to the democratic solution. In countries with an organized opposition, the crisis has empowered the opposition to either win power in an election or seize power by overthrowing the regime, as in the Philippines in 1986.

Alternatively, where the ruling regime is an inclusive and mature coalition of interests, the crisis empowers insiders to seize the reins and launch fundamental changes—as happened in Spain. Even some narrow totalitarian regimes have lost power at this stage. The end of communist party rule in Bulgaria and Hungary, for example, was initiated by hitherto unknown reformist elites inside the leadership in the absence of any mass protest for political reform. In Bulgaria, younger elites within the Party launched a "palace coup" that displaced the discredited top leadership. In other words, the strategy of the reformers was to open up quickly to head off a slowly organizing opposition.[23]

But in China, the regime is unlikely to fall in the face of a mere crisis of governance, just as it did not in the USSR. The force of its repressive apparatus and its calculations of the dangers of withdrawal will remain unchanged. The CCP leadership will remain combative and inflexible. It is an authoritarian regime that while having disposed of its totalitarian past has yet to embrace a pluralistic future, either inside or outside. Its closet reformers, although widely known to exist, will remain too weak to seize the initiative because of a crisis alone. The regime may describe the problems as "transitional" and appeal to ethnic and national unity behind the banner of the Party's core leader. In some temporary crises, such as SARS, this may save the day. But in less tractable situations, history suggests that the crisis must move to the next stage: mass protest.

Popular Mobilization

When an authoritarian regime fails to respond to a prolonged crisis with political reforms, popular mobilization becomes more likely. The simple reason is that distress is suddenly transformed in the eyes of people from a broadly national issue into a narrowly regime issue. In the famous words of Tocqueville: "Patiently endured so long as it seemed beyond redress, a grievance comes to appear intolerable once the possibility of removing it crosses men's minds."[24]

The spark for mass protest may relate directly to the regime's failure to handle an economic crisis. Or it may be an unpopular economic policy, such as attempts to raise taxes, or changes to social welfare policies. Attempts to bridge the income gap with new taxes on the middle class, or new policies to ban migrant workers from cities, could do the same. Alternately, misgovernance on a huge scale could come to light. The National Auditor General— increasingly aggressive in recent years—might report a huge waste of infrastructure spending or an underestimation of state shares to be sold on stock markets. A revelation of massive mismanagement of public finances, over a showcase project like the Three Gorges dam, is another possibility.

China's history suggests that a nation-wide movement with the sense of mission to challenge the mandate of heaven of rulers might also be brought about by a purely political issue. Whether it was the May Fourth defenders of national dignity in 1919, the Zhou Enlai mourners of 1976, or the "patriotic" students of 1989, issues of high politics or national dignity have often played a critical role in mobilizing people against a background of economic and social crisis. A failure to defend the nation against an imagined foreign slight is one possibility. Another would be the persecution of a well-liked senior leader in the process of a factional struggle. The perennial issue of official corruption, a major grievance in 1989 and a problem whose magnitude and sensitivity has only grown since then, could also be at stake. In the Russian case, for example, the nationwide movement that eventually embraced 15 million people began with a small protest of just a few hundred people in the capital of remote Sakhalin province in May 1988 over corruption by the local Party chief.

Such sparks can start a fire when protestors know that they have some degree of support from reformers at the top. While those reformers were too weak to seize the initiative on their own, their presence exerts a powerful incentive to protestors on the street. Both in China and elsewhere, the existence of such elites has been an important incentive to popular action, where "fissures at the top provided the opening for mass action from below."[25]

As in 1989, the ability of protestors to come together quickly is well established in China. So-called "collective and mass protests" had become commonplace by the early 2000s. Civil society does not need to be strong for proto-civil society forces to emerge and mobilize to put pressure on the regime for political change. All the things we traced in part 1—growing social resources and ideas, state breakdown, etc.—come into play as collective action takes off. Suffice it to say that the means for such action in terms of material, organizational, ideological, social, and strategic resources in China's society are well established. The People's Power mobilizations in the Philippines in 1986 and 2001 came about suddenly and effectively, aided by pagers and then by mobile phones. China's wired population—250 million mobile phones alone—provides the same technical capacity for rapid gathering.

The scope and nature of the protests could vary widely. Popular mobilization need not be as widespread as in 1989, when somewhere between one-third and two-thirds of China's then-434 cities were swept up in mass protest. Given the needs and resources for change spelled out in previous chapters, the regime could be forced to embrace change as a result of a far less massive movement. We can imagine how loose coalitions of student reformers, laid off workers in independent trade unions, welfare groups, and disgruntled peasants could emerge to lead protests for political change.

The role of women might also loom large. In Latin America in particular, women played a leading role in the popular mobilization preceding democratic transitions. That role was less in evidence in the frozen communist states of Central and Eastern Europe, where feminism and gender equality were notions associated with the discredited state ideology. But more than a quarter century into post-Mao reforms, the plight of women in China looks more like the Latin American case. In that model, "women first become conscious of the effects of their political marginalization . . . in the context of a larger political crisis" and then "take their issues into the political arena . . . with the broader goals of changing both the substance and the style of politics."[26]

The coming together of these groups into a general mobilization against the regime would, as in the past, be spearheaded by hitherto unknown individuals who enjoy the support of protestors. In 1976 it was an obscure worker dubbed "Little Crewcut" and in 1979 a Beijing Zoo electrician named Wei Jingsheng. The cast of characters in 1989 was even more diverse. Recent studies of peasant protests show how it is the young farmers who are less risk averse and more engaged in political issues who take the lead and foment "revolution," not better known elders who have been part of the system.[27] This is of course a prelude to the functioning of democracy itself, where charismatic outsiders with mass appeal rather than traditional elites who remonstrated with the regime become the new powerholders.

The mobilization of society reflects demands for political change. We need not guess here about specific demands—1989 showed how an array of suggestions appears, many of them mutually contradictory. More important is that the protests reflect a questioning of the political order—the mandate of heaven—and demands for its change. While protests may begin over a specific issue or issues, they almost always transform into basic questioning of the system, and a quest for solutions. We need not specify yet what solutions may be proposed and embraced by elites. It is necessary only to note that the political system will become the focus of protests.

As one hard-line Party book aptly warns: "If our work fails, we cannot rule out that in the near future some regions will experience limited disturbances or even turmoil. . . . The forces which oppose CCP rule will use slogans of democracy and freedom to cheat people and make a great fuss about shortcomings in our work. They will want the CCP either to be overthrown or to voluntarily hand over political power to them. We must be prepared to deal with this situation."[28]

Violence

Popular mobilization is directly linked to violence. Typically, democratic transitions have been less violent than other revolutions because of the embedded ideas of tolerance and compromise as well as historical timing: they often take place against a background of authoritarian violence that has created a groundswell for nonviolent change. This in turn helps democracy to survive because its nonviolent habits and reputation engender popular support. More violent movements, by contrast, make political and social elites fearful of change and thus unwilling to offer concessions. They also create unstable democracies. Keeping violence in check helps democratic transition and consolidation alike.

At the same time, violence may prove necessary in some instances. It may be the only way for society to dislodge authoritarian rulers. Violence may convince social and business elites that the costs of upheaval are too great to bear where there is a reasonable assumption that non-radical opposition will emerge to seize power. Both the Philippines and South Korea along with Portugal had mass and often violent protests from radical groups leading to democratization and first elections.[29] As in so many instances in politics, limited violence may be necessary and morally acceptable in order to achieve a greater justice.

Fears of violence in China's case are widespread. One Chinese democrat worries that in China "a highly mobilized civil society may produce popular, radical and romantic politics rather than democratic politics . . . [that] may intensify the political struggle and make political concessions and negotiations more difficult."[30] But there is good reason to believe that violence will be both limited and unnecessary to bring about democratic transition. A deeply antiviolent strain in society at large and intellectuals in particular would likely constrain violence, as it did for most of the 1989 protests, when the independent trade unions favored a more violent approach but were overruled by the students until very late. Protest leaders such as Wang Dan in 1989 or Fang Lizhi in 1986 advocated peaceful protest, an appeal which resounded deeply with a society tired of the violence unleashed by the Party and eager to demonstrate its civility.

Nonetheless, democratic transition in China is sure to unleash communalist passions in which society organizes itself into identity-based groups — as protestors in 1989 marched under the flags of their universities or offices — and portrays the regime as a hostile tribe. In China, peasants identifying with their villages and workers with their factories are already the most violent, with ransacking of government offices and burning of police cars and public buses commonplace. Long-standing and immediate repression make the mobilization more radical than otherwise, just as the peaceful Falun Gong protestors became more aggressive as their post-1999 persecution dragged on.

Keeping in mind the causes of even this low-level violence, namely a long-repressed people forced to extreme measures by an unresponsive regime, will be important for a world watching events unfold in China. It was Mao who said that revolutions are not a tea-party. Those rising up to question his regime will prove this to be all too true. As the long-time democratic Wei Jingsheng wrote: "More and more people are ready to wage a war in exchange for a living, since they have lower and lower expectations for a peaceful evolution towards democracy."[31]

Violence could come from the state as well. In the face of growing protests, the possibility looms that inside reformers are too weak to gain the upper hand and protestors too weak to overthrow the regime. In that case, the regime would violently repress protestors and purge internal reformers. That is what happened in 1989, with tragic immediate and long-term results.

Will it happen again? Not likely. In other words, there will be no repeat of 1989, just as there was no repeat of Budapest in 1956 or Prague in 1968. Society in all its aspects is stronger this time and popular protests are better organized and more persistent. And reformist ideals have a firmer purchase at all levels, both within society and within the regime.

Generally speaking, pro-democracy movements in the late twentieth century—in the Third Wave that began in the early 1970s—did not face violent suppression. Either hard-liners waffled in ordering suppression or coercive forces waffled in obeying such commands. They saw both the need for change and the resources mustered by the reformers. It was not in their interest to act. Policemen and soldiers world-wide lay down their rifles and welcomed change. Tiananmen was the exception that proved the rule. "The carnations of Lisbon" not the "carnage of Beijing," to use Huntington's phrase, was the order of the day.

Next time around, China is more likely to fit the pattern. We can find little evidence that the PLA or the police forces or state security forces would step in to prevent a political transition. The "last argument of kings" is no longer available to the frightened monarchs of Zhongnanhai.

For a start, hard-liners would not likely order a suppression. Certainly there will be some in the top ranks arguing for a muster of soldiers to crush the movement with armed might—to give them "death and no burial" as one hard-liner argued in 1989.[32] But it is unlikely that the CCP leadership as a whole would order suppression. The death or retirement of virtually all influential old-time Party elders by the turn of the century is one important reason. Another, as we have seen, is that the resort to violence was frowned upon within the broader Party membership by the late 1990s because of evidence that it made matters worse. Attempts to crush even isolated groups, like the Falun Gong, were costly.

From several perspectives—moral, political, professional, and practical—the Party has now schooled its cadres in the idea that the use of force to crush unrest is no longer advisable. It would be difficult to suddenly reverse that exhortation. If the political elites are divided, any command to the military would be ineffective. As one analyst noted: "The PLA can only form a final guarantor of stability if the elements of the CCP which have influence within it act in concert. As Tiananmen has shown, this will not necessarily occur."[33]

Even if the regime did order a suppression, there are grave doubts that the PLA would follow. Certainly, China's coercive apparatus—a total of 6 million officers including 3 million police, 2.5 million soldiers, and half a million paramilitaries—has the manpower to crush a mass protest movement. But the PLA felt its dignity impinged by the riot control duties of 1989. The 150 PLA officers who decried the impending use of force in Tiananmen through an open letter to the Party leadership is a reminder of this. "To many in the PLA, implementing martial law compromised the basic ethic of the PLA which is to serve the people," notes one Western military analyst.[34]

Since Tiananmen, the coercive forces have undergone a quiet internal revolution of their own that has made them even less of a conservative force. Internal professionalism, a weakening of political-ideological education, a withdrawal from business, growing contacts with other militaries, and more interactions with society have all diminished the PLA's view of itself as the Party's bodyguard. It lost its last remaining seat on the Politburo standing committee in 1997 and retained just two seats on the wider Politburo for coordination purposes. Today, it thinks independently of the Party, a big reason to believe it would not obey an official command or tacit attempt by some to suppress popular mobilization.[35] The PLA's General Political Department, once at the CCP's beck and call, now reinterprets Party policies in its own interests and broadcasts its views back to the Party itself. That is why Party hard-liners have begun to worry more and more about the military's declining loyalty, openly warning of the military's trend toward "republicanization, statization, de-partyization and de-politicization."[36]

There is also a little-noticed pro-reform faction inside the coercive apparatus. One paramilitary forces scholar, Jiao Jian, in his 2001 book *The Abuse of Power: Misconceptions About the Use of Public Power* calls for wide-ranging new controls on Party power through public, legislative, and legal means.[37] The popular military-backed journal *Strategy and Management*, meanwhile, runs many articles on political reforms, often panning anti-democratic visions as unworkable.[38] Some Western scholars have argued that the coercive forces may see democracy as a way to preserve their interests, an issue we take up in the next section.[39] Indeed, coercive forces may be more "rational" than the regime itself. They may see that an attempt at violent repression that leads to the radicalization of mobilized groups will make matters worse. This was the lesson the police drew in internal reviews of the regime's crackdown on the Falun Gong.[40]

Having its own corporate interests to consider, the military would not want to take the risk of being on the wrong side of history. If it sees that the protests will be resolved peacefully and that whatever changes come, its interests (in terms of budgets and amnesties) will be protected, it may consider the costs of action as too high. The quiet internal changes in the military, writes one expert, "strengthens its sense of professional mission and corporate autonomy and its potential for making independent judgements about what the national interest requires."[41]

Might the military be a little too keen on political reforms? Some have imagined that under crisis conditions, the PLA might step in to assert a hitherto unknown ultimate authority over China. They imagine that well before any popular movement had a chance to bring democratic political reform, the military would seize power with promises to reestablish clean government with technocrats and rebuild national power, as did those in Pakistan and Iraq. "A formal imposition of military rule might come if the Party itself begins to split over the question of how to handle growing civil unrest," writes one Western scholar. "One can imagine a day when, instead of doing as instructed, a Chinese general will take over and then go on television saying in his first breath that 'Communism is nonsense, the Party is made up of criminals, and we have arrested them' and in his second breath that 'We are all Chinese, strong and proud of our homeland. We need order and discipline'."[42]

But the idea of independent action by the coercive forces seems highly implausible from what we know of the Chinese military (and police). Although it has long been involved in politics, China's military has never been an independent political force. There is no tradition of direct military rule in China even if there have been many militarized regimes. The Chinese model of communism emphasized the need to integrate the military into the political structure for the purpose of making the military obedient to the Party, not its substitute or partner. Like all coercive forces, its main concern was domestic stability and national sovereignty. The PLA has never enjoyed a messianic role as guardian of the state, as in Latin America.

Of course, the military may well be mobilized to maintain public order. As in 1989, soldiers might sit cross-legged face-to-face with idealistic students, grannies demanding their pensions, and peasants wanting to be paid for their grain. But there is every reason to believe that they would not obey an order to open fire, nor would their commanders seek to oust the CCP and seize the reins of power.

The elimination of the threat of military action is a critical factor ensuring that the slide to democratic transition continues. It allows the popular mobilization that will empower reformist elites to carry on. Without it, the reformers end up being purged. In addition, the very absence of military voices in the political sphere is also an important resource for reformist elites. Unlike civilian leaders, military elites are typically less able to "initiate, negotiate or adjust to" calls for democratic reforms because of their greater distance from society.[43] By staying on the sidelines, the military serves the cause of democracy in both ways.

Last Ditchism

In an attempt to prevent mass protests planned for 30 cities in February 1990, the Soviet leadership aired a Polish movie on television with full nudity called "The Sex Mission." It didn't work. But it went down in the annals of democratization as one of the most comical attempts at last-ditch efforts to save a dying regime, perhaps beating out only Gorbachev's attempt to clamp down on vodka consumption the same year.

As in Russia, and in the crumbling Qing dynasty, we can expect the CCP to pull out all the stops to save its reign. This might involve redirecting attention and making vague promises of change. Might the regime find a new enemy on its borders or lost territory that required recovery for national unity and dignity? Might a mass movement uncertain of its goals be easily sidetracked by appeals to nationalism or promises of cosmetic change?

Any significant concessions are unlikely, for all the reasons that made Hu Jintao balk at gradual democratization when things were still calm. The natural reaction of the leadership will be to reject the movement as a threat and to crush any reformers within the Party inclined to negotiate.

Still, the Party's weakened ideology raises the possibility of a formal offer of modest concessions. An existing regime leader could come to the fore with no intention of launching real democracy but with at least the wits to try to head off the regime's fall with promises of change. Such a scenario has been suggested by one neo-authoritarian scholar in China who believes that a Party faction could seize power and declare that "rule of law" will be the focus of work to control corruption and create a fair society. This faction would also outline a 20-year plan in which the CCP would become a natural ruling party by liberalizing its internal leadership selection process while continuing to ban opposition parties.[44]

But it seems unlikely that such a last-ditch rescue would work. "Partial reform" is possible only if the Party is in a position of strength, as it was in 1989. Indeed, this is arguably what happened in 1989, when the Party's promises of a stepped up anti-corruption drive and greater political openness had appeased much of the movement by the end of May. This time, however, it will be too late. Last-ditch efforts to offer rigged elections or more accessible government when the regime is already weak would only stoke popular mobilization. If Tocqueville's paradox was at work empowering society in the era of gradual economic reforms, it will be doubly strong at the moment of rapid political reforms. As Tocqueville famously noted: "The most perilous moment for a bad government is when it seeks to mend its ways."[45]

More ominous as a piece of "last ditchism" would be an attack on Taiwan. U.S. officials and many overseas democrats believe that there is a significant chance of an attack on Taiwan if the CCP is embattled at home. Indeed, China's strategic journals make frequent reference to this contingency: "The need for military preparations against Taiwan is all the more pressing in light of China's growing social tensions and unstable factors which some people, including the U.S. might take advantage of under the flag of 'humanism' to paralyze the Chinese government," one wrote.[46] Such a move would allow the government to impose martial law on the country as part of war preparations, making the crushing of protest easier. It would also offer the possibility, if successful, of CCP survival through enhanced nationalist legitimacy.

Yet the risks, even to a dying regime, may be too high. An unprovoked attack on Taiwan would almost certainly bring the U.S. and its allies to the island's rescue. Those forces would not stop at Taiwan but might march on Beijing and oust the CCP, or attempt to do so through stiff sanctions, calling it a threat to regional and world peace. Such an attack might also face the opposition of the peoples of Fujian, who would be expected to provide logistical support and possibly bear the worst burdens of war. They, like much of coastal China, look to Taiwan for investment and culture and have a close affinity with the island.

As a result, there are doubts about whether such a plan could be put into action. A failed war would prompt a Taiwan declaration of independence and a further backlash against the CCP at home, just as the May Fourth students of 1919 berated the Republican government for weakness in the face of foreign powers. Failed wars brought down authoritarian regimes in Greece and Portugal in 1974 and in Argentina in 1983.

Even if CCP leaders wanted war, it is unlikely that the PLA would oblige. Top officers would see the disastrous implications of attacking Taiwan. Military caution would also guard against the even wilder scenario of the use of nuclear weapons against Japan or the U.S.[47] At the height of the Tiananmen protests it appears there was consideration given to the use of nuclear weapons in case the battle to suppress the protestors drew in outside countries.[48] But even then, the threats did not appear to gain even minimal support. In an atmosphere in which the military is thinking about its future, the resort to nuclear confrontation would not make sense.

Beijing's last-ditch options will remain limited, then. It might try to calm the masses with promises of new spending or a crackdown on seafood banquets. It might even air some foreign beauty contests on television. But at this stage, it will be only so much bluster. The end of dynasty is near.

Collapse?

Would the entire PRC edifice simply collapse from the accumulated pressures of crisis and mass protest? In cross-country comparisons, "post-totalitarian" states like China are the most vulnerable to collapse because they are unable to respond creatively to protest and yet there is no organized opposition to assume control.[49] The East German regime was a perfect example. It simply collapsed when huge defections from the state occurred at every level and there was no organized opposition ready to take over.

In the German case, there was a neighboring fraternal state whose arms provided some cushion for the collapse. China would not have the same support. For this reason, the CCP and many of its supporters have warned of the dangers of collapse in words designed to scare the regime's opponents into quiescence.

Fear-mongering about the consequences of regime collapse in China has been a staple of PRC propaganda since reforms began. Deng said: "If the political situation in China became unstable the trouble would spread to the rest of the world, with consequences that would be hard to imagine."[50] Foreign scholars have taken up the histrionics with relish. One has worried about "societal disintegration" and even "the fragmentation of China into several competing polities."[51] Another warns: "At worst the resulting chaos from a collapsing China would have a profound effect on the stability of Asia and on the U.S. policy to guarantee the security of its Asian allies. At the least, China could turn to the West for economic relief and reconstruction, the price tag of which would be overwhelming."[52]

Yet these fears appear overblown or misplaced. First, as we saw in the last part, many of these dire descriptions are an accurate portrayal of China today. The problems of Party rule have created the very crisis that the fear-mongers allude to. China already has an AIDs crisis, an illegal emigration crisis, a pollution crisis, and an economic crisis. Given its well-established state and social cohesion, China has far more to gain than to lose from political liberalization.

Second, there is a good argument that governance in China will not collapse further even with a top leadership in crisis. The country actually functioned quite normally during the Cultural Revolution, when there was often no rule at the top, as a result of strong local governments and a social fabric that held together. At this stage, with popular protests in full swing, a military on good behavior and a regime trying to confront the possibility of change, there is no reason to believe that the country will abruptly disintegrate. As in 1989, in fact, there is every reason to believe that people will act better toward each other and that local governments will look kindly upon the movement, an outpouring of civic behavior linked to the ideals of democracy.

Finally, as above, if we are concerned with the creation of a more just system, then some degree of "chaos" relating to unstable government may be a worthwhile price to pay, including for the world. Claims by some U.S. foreign policy analysts that "there is as great a 'threat' to US interests from a weak and unstable China as there is from a strong and antagonistic China"[53] are based on a highly instrumental and even then flawed view of U.S., and world, interests. A world community committed to the principles of justice through democracy has an overriding interest in its realization in China. To the extent that instability in China worsens conditions for greater justice there or abroad, it would indeed "threaten" world interests. But if the instability, despite its costs, leads to greater gains through a more just order in China and, through it, abroad, then this is very much in the world's interest. Few Americans, French, Croats, Romanians, South Africans, Filipinos, South Koreans, or Indonesians would say the "chaos" of their democratic revolutions was not a price worth paying. China's people should be allowed to make the same choice.

Moreover, an alarmist view of growing popular mobilization against an authoritarian regime has too often landed the U.S. in particular on the wrong side of a democratic movement. During a visit to South Korea in 1986, then U.S. Secretary of State George Shultz voiced support for the military regime's rejection of opposition demands for a direct presidential election, calling such an arrangement "unusual." A year later, the regime conceded to the demands. The U.S., now portrayed as an enemy of democracy in South Korea, found its consulates and embassy the subject of popular protest.

A better policy from both normative and instrumental points of view, then, would be to call for a peaceful resolution of the protests and to lean on the Party to heed the voice of the people. This might require some quiet coalition building in the region to backstop the instability and fall-out. But again, from both normative and instrumental points of view, this is in the long-term interests of the world community.

China will not collapse, even in the face of metastatic crisis and popular mobilization. But it will certainly face grave instability. The best policy for the world community in responding to this instability will be to ensure that the democratic breakthrough occurs as quickly as possible.

The Eve of Transition

China, in our scenario, is now a country in tumult. Tiananmen Square, the vast 44 hectare square at the foot of the Forbidden City, is filled with thousands of the citizens that it was built to accommodate. But they are seeking the Party's demise, not its long life. Unlike in 1989, when the people made their point and headed home, this time they intend to stay until the job is done. Placards reading "Give back our China" and "Step down Hu Jintao" flutter in the air.

Foreign nationals are being withdrawn from the country and investors are closing their factories. A country that seemed to hold such promise has suddenly been revealed as dangerously unstable. The stock analysts and cheerleaders who ignored China's unresolved constitutional crisis are suddenly silent.

Party leaders are holding emergency meetings inside Zhongnanhai on the handling of the crisis. The Chinese expression for dilemma—*zuoyou weinan* or "danger on both left and right"—perfectly captures their plight: every choice leads to perdition. They rejected withdrawal in times of peace and now they certainly will reject it in times of crisis. They can neither repress nor appease the movement. What to do?

6

The Democratic Breakthrough

Extrication or Overthrow?

Broadly speaking, there are two exit routes for a CCP faced with popular protests that it can neither repress nor embrace: it can be overthrown by protest leaders riding on the wave of unrest; or it can be "extricated" from office by reformers within its own ranks.

In Asia, there have been examples of both. Thailand's military was extricated from politics through the efforts of the king and prominent politicians as pro-democracy protests mounted in 1983. A mass overthrow was evident in the People Power revolution against the Marcos regime in the Philippines in 1986. While overthrow is most memorable, it is the least common. One Western scholar calculated that only six of 33 democratic transitions in the 1970s and 1980s were popular overthrows, the others being withdrawals (gradual democracy) or extrications. Of the 10 communist regimes that fell in Eastern Europe and the former Soviet Union in 1989–91, perhaps only one, Romania, can be rightly described as a popular overthrow. Among the best examples of extrication were Russia and Hungary, where party elites engineered a democratic resolution in the face of a weak or disorganized opposition. Of the notable transitions since then, Indonesia and South Africa were both examples of extrications, although supported by mass action. In all, 29 of 41 democratic transitions in the Third Wave were extrications by elites.[1]

Regime-led extrication can be seen as a hasty retreat from the battlefield in the face of sporadic or mass protest or opposition. The regime turns and runs rather than being defeated. It is, I believe, the most likely path from power for the CCP. In this scenario, CCP reformers gain the upper hand and extricate the Party from office by establishing an interim leadership with promises of national elections and a new constitution.

The existence of extrication, indeed its common occurrence, is overlooked by many political reformers in China, who therefore pin their hopes for change on popular overthrow. Since voluntary withdrawal (gradual democ-

118

ratization) is unlikely, they embrace the other extreme of popular overthrow rather than the middle way of extrication. Peng Ming's China Federation Development Committee, for example, has formulated quite explicit plans to "attack" the CCP. Other democrats hope to see the regime collapse under the burdens of crisis. Few see the very real possibility of an elite-led transformation of the state spurred by modest pressures from below.

The belief in popular overthrow as the only means of political transition draws on the Chinese tradition of "revolution" or *geming*, a word whose Chinese rendering literally means "broken mandate." The implication, as one 1989 participant, Liu Xiaobo, notes, is that regime change is seen as necessarily violent and discontinuous.[2] "Each and every one of us has been a victim and a carrier" of the revolutionary ideal implied by *geming*, he writes.

Fortunately, there is some evidence that this historical curse is lifting as reformers learn from the past. A few democrats who once advocated violent change, like Liu Xiaobo and former Zhao Ziyang political reform advisor Yan Jiaqi, now advocate regime-led extrication.[3] They have absorbed the lessons that overthrows usually produce less stable democratic governments than extrications. They have also come to realize that overthrow is less likely.

The resolution of crisis through extrication reflects the relative strength of the state over society. Revolutions, democratic and otherwise, in which rebels truly "make" the revolution, occur only in countries with a significantly liberalized authoritarian regime and a strong civil society. This has been the leitmotif of democratic revolutions in Latin America, as it was in the Philippines. In cases where the authoritarian regime remains all-powerful and civil society is weak, the revolution is more likely to be "made," inside the state itself—through a crisis of state governance, a defection of elites to the cause of change, and much else. This was typical of Eastern Europe and the USSR.

Historically state-centered revolutions have been the norm in China too. Claims that Mao and his rag-tag armies "made" the revolution of 1949 do not stand up to scrutiny. Rather, he and his Red Army seized opportunities created by the breakdown of KMT governance and the invasion of China by Japan. In 1989, a revolutionary uprising failed for the same reasons: the state managed to right itself and deny rebels the opportunity for change. Rebel leaders— Zhao Ziyang and the students—duly shuffled off the stage when it was apparent that the "opportunity" no longer existed.

What about next time? To be sure, society in China has grown greatly in strength under post-Mao reforms. From our discussion in part 1, it should be clear that a mass protest movement in the early twenty-first-century would be better organized, better funded, and more clear of its purpose than in 1989. The growing sense of a need for political reforms, coupled with a more wealthy, connected, and organized society, mean that compared to the rag-tag tents-and-bedsheets crowd who demonstrated in 1989, a national move-ment would be formidably strong.

It would also be able to count on more robust international support, not least from the democratic rulers of the former communist countries of Europe and from the democracies of Asia. International civil society could also play a larger role, magnifying by many times the significant impact that material and moral support from Hong Kong and Taiwan had in 1989.

Some activists inside China see in these changes the seeds of CCP over-throw by a robust civil society: "There will be an organization of social unrest as the frequency of protests increases and the protests gain a certain amount of organizational and financial resources. . . . The demands for political free-doms will become more strident . . . But the state will not easily grant these freedoms. As a result, civil society may rise up and break down the obstacles to its development and create a new political structure by itself."[4] Another imagines a three- to five-year period in which "small protests are constant, the economy is stalled, fiscal crisis worsens, goods shortages appear, standards of living fall, social frictions increase, and faith in the political system is shaken." That crisis would prompt a last-ditch attempt by the Party backed by the military to assert control, which having failed, would spark mass protests lead-ing to the overthrow of the regime. "The use of force against protestors will be clearly insufficient to control the situation," he writes.[5]

Yet all evidence suggests that the state remains powerful enough to force the revolutionary change to take place on the inside rather than the outside. While the strength of society has grown manifold, it is not enough to over-throw the state. The lingering effects of the clientelist ties to the state that dogged the early development of private business and civil society in the 1990s will still be felt. The CCP had managed in the late PRC era to successfully neuter or co-opt most potential democratic opposition. This will make it more difficult for protestors to present themselves as a viable alternative to the regime.

To overthrow the regime, they would need a broad agenda with wide ap-peal, government-like structures including leaders, funding, and an amenable environment in which the regime cannot repress and indeed welcomes its presence. Many pro-democracy groups abroad have worked toward this goal, but with little progress beyond blueprints. In present-day China civil society remains too weak to produce and sustain this kind of alternate regime. The legacy of totalitarian rule is stronger than a few decades of reforms. Without societal leaders who represent well-institutionalized interests, the social movement will tend toward radicalization and a lack of coherence, factors which will mitigate against talks with the regime.

By contrast, the CCP-led state, though in serious decline by the turn of the century, remained strong enough to withstand overthrow. The coercive forces, though unlikely to suppress mass protests, were loyal enough to the state, and to the ideal of public order, to act to protect the state against violent overthrow. The CCP had also kept for itself a monopoly over other areas of the infrastructure such as telecoms, transport, and utilities. Says one scholar: "At least in its early stages, China's transition will be less negotiated than bestowed."[6]

This is not to say that protests will remain locked out of the process. Even in an extrication, mass mobilization is important because it is what prompts elites to begin responding to their problems. In Poland and Czechoslovakia, mass protests strengthened the hands of reformist elites but did not take their place, highlighted most dramatically by the Polish round-table talks of March 1989. That scene was echoed by the Tiananmen students meeting with state leaders in the Great Hall of the People two months later. We can expect that protest leaders would have audiences with the besieged regime again. They will shape and cajole the decisions of state actors. Popular unrest creates the conditions for initiative at the elite level. It will encourage the search for solutions within the Party. But it is there, inside the crimson walls of Zhong-nanhai, where the democratic breakthrough will occur. "Radical systemic change will not start at the top," notes one Western scholar, "but it will likely end there."[7]

The Heroes of Retreat

In the face of massive and growing protests but no imminent threat of over-throw, what will happen inside Zhongnanhai? As in 1989, when leaders hud-dled in long meetings debating the trends of the times and how the Party should respond, CCP elites will be forced to think beyond the immediate issues of crowd control and disruption.

Much will have changed since they were last in this position. There will be no hoary elders declaiming that they fought tooth and nail for the com-munist revolution and will not see it undermined by a bunch of idealistic students. Many of the younger members of the Politburo will be pragmatists to a fault. China will now be a significantly liberalized and globalized country.

Though the atmosphere will be tense and confused, the outcome of the meetings may still be predictable. Since the mid-1990s, and drawing on the period of the 1980s, a strong reformist faction has emerged inside the CCP which believes in the inevitability of democratic change. This group is complemented by a significant number of elites in the national parliament, business community, and scholarly community who share their views. Now will be the moment when they can lead China to democracy. Crisis and protest will have emboldened them to action, and impressed its need upon others.

Those who come forward to embrace democratic change were described by one writer as "the heroes of retreat."[8] That is because they have the courage and the wisdom to be the agents of systemic improvements that would otherwise come at greater cost. Chinese democrats have pointed out that their past reformist leaders have been, by world standards, conspicuously unwilling to engage in the heroics of change.[9] Hu Yaobang and Zhao Ziyang both humbly accepted the Party's censure and shuffled off stage, even though their power was surely as great as that of Yeltsin, who took to the streets and stared down a battalion of tanks.

This time around, however, it is the less demanding heroism of retreat that will be called for, and there is every reason to believe that it will be in plentiful supply. The acknowledged extent of the problems of CCP rule and the popular movement for change will make the risks of action less. China's heroes of retreat will be made inside Zhongnanhai.

In formal terms, the combined pressures of metastatic crisis and popular mobilization will lead to an elite split, or more accurately, a redefinition and widening of existing elite splits. As discussed, China's politics has been riven by factionalism, some of it policy-based, under the CCP. Now the policy content of factionalism will grow and come into the open. One scholar in China wrote: "The political crisis will lead to the creation of two competing groups in the leadership, one arguing for an immediate opening of the media and democratic participation in order to solve the crisis, the other arguing that it is exactly because of the crisis that these things cannot be allowed because they would expose more bad things and further damage faith in the government."[10]

Experience shows that a democratic breakthrough can be launched by any actor at any time. Nothing is for certain. As two experts on China note: "Individual personalities and historical contingencies—factors which remain stubbornly immune to the best predictive efforts of social scientists—play a decisive role in translating popular unrest into . . . political transformation."[11] Here we will describe the creation of a "breakthrough elite" drawn from reformers inside the regime and bolstered by semi-official elites in society.

We can divide elites in the central regime in Beijing into three groups: democrats, moderates, and conservatives. The latter certainly includes those who have long opposed democratic reforms and who were most closely associated with the 1989 crackdown. That means ex-hard-line premier Li Peng and his allies like security chief Luo Gan. Stalwart hard-liners among Party elders would include people like Song Ping and Deng Liqun.

On the democratic side will stand open and avowed liberals like elders Li Ruihuan, Wan Li, Tian Jiyun, and Qiao Shi. The democratic group will also include the jailed Zhao Ziyang. The critical role of purged liberals in democratic transitions has been seen time and again, from Taiwan's Chen Shui-bian and South Korea's Kim Dae Jung to South Africa's Nelson Mandela and East Timor's Xanana Gusmau. Zhao's personal aide, Bao Tong, and the personal aide of Hu Yaobang, Lin Mu, have remained active and high-profile voices for democratic change since their mentors were purged. So too has Li Rui, a former deputy head of Party organization and private secretary to another one-time democratic hopeful, Mao.[12]

The democratic group might also include those outside the regime acting in some remonstrative role, among them National People's Congress (NPC) insiders with strong liberal credentials like Wang Jiafu, or outspoken NPC women delegates like Li Baoqun and Wu Qing. Or they may include members of China's "democratic parties" who make their voices heard in the Chinese People's Political Consultative Congress (CPPCC). Party intellectuals are critical too. The Central Party School's Wang Guixiu is among the boldest advocates of democratic reforms. Others making the same arguments on economic grounds include prominent economists like government advisor Liu Guoguang, CASS member and Tiananmen participant Yu Guangyuan, and rural policy critic Du Runsheng.

Standing between these groups will be the moderates—the great swing factor. This group includes noncommittal pragmatists as well as more committed neoconservatives, both of whom share the conservatives' aversion to democracy and the democrats' desire for political reforms. Those gathered around retired elder Jiang Zemin include possible fifth-generation leaders Wang Gang, Xi Jinping, Bo Xilai, and Li Tielin. Most important could be the role of Jiang's protegé Zeng Qinghong, appointed to the Politburo standing committee in 2002, the author of the CCP's late moves to embrace pluralism in the 2000s and a man who in internal speeches made it clear he favors direct elections at all local levels and the introduction of new political parties.[13] Along with him, former premier Zhu Rongji and his successor Wen Jiabao are also moderates who would side with pragmatic reformers.

Party general secretary Hu Jintao may not be the person to lead political change, yet is also not likely to oppose it. The son of a family of tea merchants from central Anhui province, Hu spent his formative years in the unremitting climate of China's west as a water engineer and then cadre. In his ten years as designated Party heir from 1992 to 2002, he developed a reputation as a capable administrator and moderate reformer, overseeing important changes like the military's divestment of its business empire and new rules to encourage merit in the civil service. After coming into office, Hu took steps to make the Politburo more transparent, raise the profile of the constitution, end pompous send-off ceremonies for officials going abroad, and rebuild Party legitimacy through closer attention to the poor. Like Gorbachev, he appears to be a "Leninist romantic" who believes the CCP could work with better internal management. But his generation has less emotional investment in CCP rule and is less averse to democracy as a result. He too should be classified as a moderate.

This division of personalities is based on their known pre-crisis profiles. Yet these profiles can change once crisis begins. The new conditions mean that the fault lines may appear in new and surprising places. Gorbachev was an unlikely reformer when he came into office, but proved to be a hero of Russian democratization because of his pragmatic decision to embrace change. For other moderates or conservatives, their previous views may simply have changed, unbeknownst to others. Ren Zhongyi is a good example of the "sudden reformer," a longtime Party elder whose earlier-mentioned reformist article in the *Southern Weekend* newspaper in 2000 came as a surprise to many. Peng Zhen, the conservative who pushed for village democracy, is another example.

The key for a successful extrication is for democrats to be stronger than conservatives and for them to gain the complicity, if not outright support, of moderates. While conservatives may remain dead-set against change, moderates may swing to the side of reform because they believe that the costs of continued crisis, short-term and long-term, are higher than the risks of change. For both rational and normative reasons, they may be convinced by the democrats to isolate the conservatives and opt for democracy.

In the days and weeks that the breakthrough elite takes form, it will be critical for the would-be heroes of retreat to engage in secret consultations with several groups: regime moderates; the leaders of the protest movements; and the coercive forces. Communications play a big role in allowing the democrats to allay fears and build support for democratic change. If they are severed—as in 1989 when the Party General Office under Wen Jiabao was cut off from all information flows with the imposition of martial law on Beijing on May 19—it can hamper the movement. Again, technological advances like mobile phones and the Internet provide China as a late-comer with a great advantage.

Talks with regime moderates and protest leaders create the middle ground necessary for a successful transition. Both groups agree to support an elite-led transition as a compromise rather than back extremists in their midst.

Also both need to be able to exclude radicals on their sides, radical hard-liners in the regime and radical democratizers outside the regime. This "middle ground" to be staked out means that dissident pro-democracy groups in China and abroad would also likely not be part of the reformers. Their exclusion would ensure the reformers gain the support of moderates.

Keeping hard-liners isolated will be easier than it was in the USSR. By the early 2000s there had already been a significant clearing out—by death or retirement—of the old-time CCP elders who might oppose change. Veterans of the Long March were all but retired while most leaders had little recollection of the civil war or Japanese invasion. That means there is no overarching "power behind the throne" to step in and prevent democratic transition, a role than Deng Xiaoping and other Party elders played in 1989. Under Hu Jintao, no elder has the prestige to unilaterally intervene in a major political crisis. Chinese liberals are right to see in this great hope for a successful breakthrough.

This shift of calculations and allegiances is almost always imperceptible. Yet in state-centered democratizations it is the critical breach. Suddenly, there is a viable alternative to the regime created from within the regime itself. As the old adage puts it, China already has a formidable democratic opposition ready and waiting to assume office: it is called the CCP.

The heroes of retreat emerge with a goal to compromise, even accept, the demands of society for political change. They recognize the need for such changes and believe they can control and win early elections. They believe that the potential benefits of a decisive shift towards democracy outweigh the risks of trying to uphold a faltering authoritarian regime. They may also be induced to seek reforms to save the economic order or gain international commendation. Their well-timed and wise exercise of a rapidly diminishing ability to control events serves their interests better than inaction.

The strong likelihood that the PLA will remain on the sidelines (and thus not be a key elite in the transition) is a good thing, as mentioned. This is less because civilians are more democratic than the military—something questionable in China—but because they are typically better able to work out pacts and compromises because they operate under a less hierarchical system and have more regular contacts with the public. However, to the extent that the police, PAP, and PLA are allied with the reformist elites, it could well be as a liberal force promoting transition. All the literature on comparative transitions suggests that the military can be a positive force for change because it seeks to protect its corporate interests and is quick to disassociate itself from a regime that has lost support. The types of pro-reform writings contained in military-backed journals like *Strategy and Management*, or written into books by people like PAP Colonel Jiao Jian, hint at this potential in China.

One intriguing question is the role that local elites might play. As outsiders not sullied by involvement in the central leadership and often with strong track records in local government, such leaders can emerge at the height of crisis. One scholar speculates that a reform-minded regional leader who is associated with China's southern-style liberal and inclusive national identity could emerge to lead the nation toward democracy.[14] Another foresees "an attempt at change from above starting the process, but then stalling and being superseded by action at the local and regional level that goes farther than what was intended."[15]

These political elites at all levels will be joined by social elites. China has a large number of quasi-official elites who, while not likely to join mass protest will also stand outside the political elite. Scholars Pan Wei and Liu Junning and economists Wu Jinglian and Hu Angang hold a semi-official status as elites of a society always closely enmeshed with the state. The movement of such elites to join and support the insiders can add to the momentum for change.

Along with wider elites in business and the military, these groups may share the antidemocratic beliefs of the regime. But they do not share the regime's interest in maintaining power "at all costs." The regime may seek to forestall their defection by last-minute threats and inducements — recalling how the CCP sought to bring entrepreneurs into the Party in the late PRC era. But those attempts may backfire, as they have in other transitions, accelerating the defections.[16]

The importance of these social elites cannot be overstated. Typically, communist regimes have fallen to narrow and often radical reformers without a broad coalition because pluralism in society has been so underdeveloped. China may be an exception to that because its market reforms had, by the turn of the century, created modest pluralism that mirrored that in the advanced Eastern European countries like Hungary and the former Czechoslovakia. Having a broad and moderate coalition is critical to an unruffled passage from crisis through to functioning democracy. "Reformers should thus pursue support-building with special vigor and timeliness," notes one student of communist regime collapse.[17]

The defection of business elites in particular has been a key moment in many authoritarian regime collapses. The corruption, arbitrariness, unfairness, and impositions of the regime are weighed against the likely results of democracy and the business elite decides to throw its weight behind the cause of change. Business leaders focus on specific policy failures of the regime and recalculate the costs of democracy. In the Philippines, it was the formation in 1984 of the Makati Business Club of business leaders, and to a lesser extent the church-backed Bishops-Businessmen's Conference, supporting the presidential bid of Corazon Aquino in the breakthrough February 1986 election that is seen in retrospect as a critical leg of support for the overthrow of Marcos.[18] Aquino promised to dismantle monopolies and lessen red tape: this reflects the quest for a level playing field when a crony-based system breaks down in the face of new entrants. In China, as we have seen, in the early 2000s, business leaders had become more outspoken about the costs of CCP policy failure.

The creation of this "democratic breakthrough" group obviously depends on many factors. Insiders need to have the resources of incumbency while outsiders the resources of society. Both need to calculate that change is the best option.

There is a strategic game underlying this choice. If you are a member of the regime and believe democratic change is inevitable, the best solution is to be the first to launch it, or certainly not the last to endorse it. As one student of the Russian transition has shown, when the forces urging democratic change are weak, regime reformers who try to launch democracy will be purged (as happened to Yeltsin in 1987 and Zhao Ziyang in 1989). But once those forces are strong, even undemocratic elites will suddenly embrace the democratic course (Gorbachev in 1990) as the payoffs of doing so increase.[19]

To quote a former U.S. national security advisor on China's future: "The process that I envisage will involve political unrest or other circumstances that impose upon the Party the necessity of change; the Party will have to come to an accommodation with these pressures, or else eventually face a revolutionary situation. To some extent, I am betting on the prospect that the Chinese political elite will be intelligent and realistic enough to see that it must make the necessary accommodations."[20]

As mentioned, the elites are empowered by protestors. In that sense, there is a sort of implicit symbiotic relationship between the two. Early elite splits encourage mass action which in turn further empowers reformist elites. At the critical juncture, the leverage of the reformers is critically shaped and determined by the nature and extent of popular mobilization. These stirrings on the ground provide the breakthrough group with the resources needed to pursue its agenda.[21]

We have seen evidence of this pattern in China before. In April 1976, protests erupted in Beijing against the removal of wreaths in Tiananmen

Square commemorating Zhou Enlai, including sporadic violence and fights with police. Society was in no position then, and is in no position today, to march into Zhongnanhai and drag the Politburo Standing Committee into the Avenue of Eternal Peace in shackles. However, the outbreak empowered elite reformers led by Party veteran Ye Jianying to overthrow the Gang of Four shortly after Mao's death. As one insider account put it, describing how popular mobilization spurred elite action:[22]

> [The Tiananmen protests] produced highly favorable circumstances for the arrest of the Gang of Four, acting as a general mobilization and dress rehearsal. Without it, the Gang of Four would not have been arrested. Because of the protests, Ye Jianying and other Party veterans were able to hear the voice of the people and survey the size and strength of China's robust society. The fall of the Gang of Four would not have been as decisive or quick otherwise. The people took things into their own hands and made history.

How the heroes of retreat gain power need not trouble us here. It could be a formal vote of the Politburo, or of the full Central Committee if progress towards "inner Party democracy" had gone forward in the years leading up to the change. It could equally well be a palace coup, a night of the long knives such as ended the reign of terror of the Gang of Four in 1976. Since we are positing an extrication rather than a withdrawal of the CCP, a coup is certainly possible. Typically, it is only in withdrawals where no one gets purged. On the other hand, a coup might prove unnecessary if those purged were promised a graceful exit and a secure retirement. This has been the norm of purges in the post-Mao era. No less than ten Politburo members were purged in the reform era and all allowed to live out their lives in peace. If it could convince incumbents of the inevitability of change—pointing to the "size and strength of China's robust society"—the breakthrough elite might be able to seize power without force.

The Politburo is now under new leadership. The alliances are forged and the consensus readily apparent. A fateful choice awaits. It's time to make history.

The Pact

The core issue that is resolved by any democratic pact is the disposition of political power. Reforming authoritarian regimes like China's may have covered some distance in redressing this problem through liberalization and institutionalization. But the path leading down the "last mile" to democracy, where competition for and participation in political power are made universal, lies yet ahead. The CCP's pervasive and damaging "leadership" of the political system must be broken for democracy to begin. The breakthrough will not appear magically from the creation of a coalition of well-meaning elites. There is, in the words of one scholar, "no asymptotic approach to freedom."[23] Rather, democracy needs to be explicitly and formally embraced.

We have assumed all along that this is indeed the intention of the reformers who seize power. Here we look more closely at the content of the pact and how it comes into being.

The content of the pact is closely related to the motivations the parties have for embracing it. There are really two separate forces pushing the elites to embrace democracy. One, the weaker of the two, is a normative belief that democracy is the best thing for the country. While a critical mass exists in society that holds this view, it is probably not felt deeply at the top. Even political liberals may have reservations about full-scale democratization. The second force however is the critical one: democracy is the only solution to the political crisis. Any attempt to recentralize power or repress protest would lead to fissures and breakaways because it would be illegitimate. The only legitimate solution is to offer everyone an equal voice. This is why democracy so often results unintentionally from crisis in authoritarian regimes. It is the only way for elites to lead their nations out of a political impasse.

It is important to stress this instrumental rather than normative reasoning since it will likely be paramount in China's case. In the face of popular pressures and a breakdown of an internal consensus, the "selectorate," which has the power to install or remove the head of the regime, confronts alternatives to autocracy.[24] It may consider broadening the franchise to more groups within the regime to make it into an oligarchy. It may consider allowing some elites in society to become members of a new ruling coalition—a new United Front—as a sort of aristocracy. Or it may decide to throw the doors open completely to create a democracy. The more is the diversity and autonomy of constituent parts of the regime, the more likely it is that democracy will result. History shows it does not take much. In Eastern Europe and the USSR, as in so many Third Wave democratizations, "multiple centers of power contended with one another from within the state and no one coalition was able to establish its hegemony." As a result, "projects to maintain authoritarianism or establish new authoritarian constitutions failed."[25]

China will likely follow this path. It takes just a few disgruntled members of the selectorate to spoil attempts to create a new autocracy, or some form of oligarchy or aristocracy. They may all be self-interested. But like a feud inside the mafia, it usually leads to demise. The only system they can all agree on that will ensure they are not trodden by others is democracy. They all hope to reach into society and use their imagined support there to defeat their rivals.

This was the case of Gorbachev in USSR. It also was Poland against the Solidarity strike wave. It was even Greece in the wake of the Cyprus invasion debacle. Democracy offers the only workable way out of a national crisis. In Taiwan, the KMT wanted to maintain national stability while the opposition wanted to cash in on its growing popularity.[26] As even China's 1989 experience showed, at the time of crisis, while not everyone was agitating *for* democracy, none except a few hard-liners at the top were arguing *against* democracy. It is in that sense a "fortuitous byproduct," in which "circumstances may force, trick, lure, or cajole nondemocrats into democratic behavior."[27]

Next time around in China, democracy will be the only solution to both long-term and short-term crises. The breakthrough elite will argue, backed by a political will and power that it could never have mustered in the pre-crisis period, that democracy will allow the Party to compete and to do well, as remnant communist parties did in Eastern Europe. They will argue that "democratization is the best path for the CCP to take in terms of its own narrow interest."[28]

Those advocating democracy for idealistic reasons will be in the minority. Most people will want a clean and accountable government, rule of law, and more freedoms. The breakthrough elite will likely promise all these things—along with national unity, social stability, economic development, even cultural revival. Undemocratic elites who have proposed various non-democratic or pseudo-democratic solutions will find themselves embracing democracy too as the only means to their own pet projects. As one scholar noted: "What matters at the decision stage is not what values the leaders hold dear in the abstract, but what concrete steps they are willing to take."[29]

The democratic decision can be thought of as an almost perfectly controlled experiment in social decisionmaking such as was used in the theories of the political philosopher John Rawls. Since everyone is living behind a "veil of ignorance" about the future, the only system they can agree on is one based on equal rights. The terms of the transition typically change later as the veil is lifted and various forces realize, and use, their relative strengths. For now, the focus is on face-saving and risk-sharing for everyone.

That said, there is still a deep underlying reason why elites embrace a normatively desirable system. The instrumental script should not obscure the normative stage on which the elites are acting. The reason, after all, that mobilized society does not accept anything short of democracy is that years of debate and reflection have brought enough of them to the conclusion that this is the only fair way of making decisions. In that sense, what appears to be a pragmatic solution is, at a deeper level, a forced embracing of an ideal solution. Elites may prefer a Magna Carta-like limit on authoritarianism but that kind of "limited democracy" quickly loses support from society, which in China by the early twenty-first century had seen the rest of the world embracing full democracy. While we focus here on the elites, it is these "background" conditions that push them to embrace democracy. On their own, they might choose a rigged system with strong authoritarian features. But the looming presence of mobilized society—whether it's workers on the streets or intellectuals in advisory positions—makes it harder to embrace anything short of full democracy.[30]

How will the breakthrough be announced? Some scholars imagine a "political southern tour" (*zhengzhi nanxun*) in which a reformist leader "breaks out" of the system and makes a speech on the need for democratic reforms, replicating Deng Xiaoping's 1992 southern tour which focused on economic reforms.[31] Others imagine a grand Party meeting where the reform leaders announce the change in policy as the latest "ideological liberation" of the reform era.[32] The leader of the reform faction might address the nation on television. The protests had shown the great patriotism of the people and their concern about the future, he would say. The Party is now ready to embrace changes. Both scenarios would likely involve a sudden eruption of the "democratic discourse" described earlier. A leader would suddenly begin talking in the first person and in the informal language of democracy.

Still others believe that the democratic move might be signaled by a reversal of the official verdict on the Tiananmen Massacre. The movement would be declared as just and patriotic, while many political dissidents jailed under post-Tiananmen laws would be freed. Zhao Ziyang might reappear in public. This issue is bound to come up early, if not immediately, in any democratic transition because it remains so inextricably linked with the whole issue of political reform. No democratic breakthrough could remain coherent without embracing the pro-democracy ideals of Tiananmen, just as economic reforms under Deng required a reversal of the original verdict on the 1976 Tiananmen incident. It would also make strategic sense for a breakthrough elite uncertain of its powers to wrap itself in the good feelings of Tiananmen to bolster its power. As former Party aide Bao Tong wrote: "Those who reverse the June Fourth verdict will inherit the benefits of this great legacy, they will win the hearts and minds of the Chinese people, as well as sincere respect and applause from around the world." Or as he later put it: "Whichever leader reverses the Tiananmen verdict will gain the upper hand in politics."[33]

At some point, this will lead to an explicit commitment to plans for democracy within a reasonably rapid period. That is, the participation that has long been denied to Chinese people will be expanded to embrace virtually every adult and with the power to choose executive authorities at the top. Immediate freedoms of the press would be unveiled along with a crackdown on judicial and government corruption. Existing governments at all levels would remain in place pending arrangements to expand elections to the top. The NPC would become the "highest organ of state" as promised in the constitution. The Party would relinquish its special powers over the political system.

It is possible for the pact to be more limited, of course. The promised introduction of some form of "minimal democracy" as the first move in which elections are held but still guided in some way may be seen as striking the right balance between new "positive" freedoms to take part in public life and the existing "negative" freedoms from interference and fear already through market reforms. Consideration of introducing full-blown democracy would be deferred to a national conference. Reluctant elites hoping to maintain power may successfully sell such a program as a guarantor of smooth transition. Reformist writer Wang Lixiong's proposal for the direct election of legislators at local levels who would in turn choose legislators to higher levels is conceived precisely as the sort of bounded pact that might be more politically feasible to start.[34]

There may also be some "secret" aspects of the bargain not known to the public. They would concern power-sharing and guaranteeing everyone's interests. The ex-CCP head might want his son's business interests protected, while the Guangdong governor might want promises that rich provinces will not be given a shakedown in post-transition revenue-sharing arrangements. The protest leaders may have promised to endorse the regime democrats with promises of funding for their first electoral party. The regime democrats may have promised an inquiry into the role of Li Peng in Tiananmen. The democratizing elite might even strike a bargain with the outgoing regime, promising some form of "cohabitation," at least for the initial period until elections are held.[35]

Some of those secret bargains may be not so secret, as for example, limits on new political parties or democracy to be introduced only on an "installment plan" over a decade or more, as in Taiwan. There may be a compromise with the antidemocratic forces. Poland's Solidarity is now accused of betraying its followers by striking a power-sharing agreement with the ruling communists in 1989. Yet given contingencies—the realities of the future interim regime's power—that might have been the only way to avoid a more tumultuous transition. The breakthrough elites may have to promise, for example, an upper house with extensive representation for the defenders of the ancien regime, even if this does not make it into existence later on.

The chance of this, again, depends on the influence of civil society on the elites: the stronger it is the harder it will be for them to limit the pact. The more serious is the economic crisis and the more mobilized is society, the harder it is to limit reforms or participants and to grant special amnesties or protections for the interests of the old elites.

In order to keep the military onside, the reformers may issue some form of immediate amnesty for past human rights abuses to ensure that the coercive forces—military, paramilitary, state security, and police—are less inclined to fight the changes fearing for their own futures. Such amnesties were seen in many countries during the democratic transition—Chile, Argentina, and Spain. In China, those responsible for the Tiananmen Massacre and the Falun Gong crackdown will want to know they will not be brought to book for following CCP orders. Of course, the balance to be struck in this amnesty cannot alienate those who hope for justice. So the amnesty has to be suitably vague. In the same vein, military leaders will want some indication of future budgets for them, promises of their role in the appointment of future military leaders, and a definition of the military role in politics under democracy.

The need to strike some face-saving and interests-saving bargain with the anti-reform elites is a reminder of their important role in this delicate time as potential spoilers.[36] Again, this is one of the "undemocratic" aspects of transitions that can help the transition itself but can pose problems for the new democracy, a battle scar that takes time to heal.

Continuity may be the byword of the democratic breakthrough. It is entirely plausible to imagine that it would be announced in the name of the CCP. The reformist elites could hearken back to the 1911 revolution, the May Fourth Movement, Mao's pre-1949 promises of democracy, the democratic humanism of Hu Yaobang, Deng's promise of democracy by 2035, or Jiang Zemin's theory of a more representative and inclusive polity. One Western scholar, noting the rediscovery of Mao's populist and democratic persona, notes how the reformers could win converts from those who feared a discrediting of Mao—as Lenin's supporters clung to his memory as the Russian communists fell—by pointing to their being his true successors—even if an objective evaluation of Mao would make him anything but democratic. "If Mao is popular, then democrats may win popularity by embracing Mao, reimagined as a democrat," he writes.[37]

Likewise, the radically pragmatic teachings of Deng Xiaoping could be a touchstone for democratic change. "It doesn't matter whether we are a communist dictatorship or a multiparty democracy, as long as the system brings economic growth, social peace, and national strength," the reform elites might say, echoing Deng's use of an old Sichuanese adage that it doesn't matter whether a cat is black or white as long as it catches mice.

A key point here is that it will be possible for a CCP-led reformer to promise competitive elections even in the name of the CCP. Gorbachev and Chiang Ching-kuo both recognized the need for opposition parties as part of democratization plans, along with greater media freedoms, hoping to maintain power as the natural ruling party. Sharing political positions might be seen as consistent with maintaining political power if the latter is defined by the ability of the CCP to set the broad agenda and guide the country.

Thus, a high degree of continuity may be expected with the old state even as the reformers overthrow its fundamental tenet—the CCP's monopoly on political power. This is typical of most democratic transitions where "the overthrow or transformation of the state is not necessarily the primary object or result."[38] The changes will be announced in the name of continuity, or preserving the gains of late PRC era, rather than radical change. Stability, development, and national greatness, the rallying cries of the late CCP, will be the new ones too. The PRC may remain in name. But the democratic moment will have come. As the saying goes: "If things are going to remain the same, some things are going to have to change."

Alongside the political pact, there will need to be a socioeconomic pact, explicit or not, that embodies a new approach to the general welfare. Some aspects of this—like the promise of fair taxation exacted by Guangdong leaders mentioned above—may be tied up in promises of political support, a preview of the new political economy of a democratic China.

But much of it will be a salve to the protest movements that forced the transition on reluctant elites. As we have seen, China differs significantly from the USSR, where welfarism and planning had a lock on state power at the time of transition. In China, those things have long ago fallen away, giving rise to jarring inequalities and a tattered social safety net. "A successful democratic movement will require a social program that addresses the poverty and social divisions in Chinese society," notes one scholar.[39]

The socioeconomic pact will likely include promises of proper welfare and benefits for workers and peasants, a crackdown on tax evasion, possibly even a renegotiation of some high-profile showcase foreign investment projects. Workers might be rewarded with the promulgation of the right to strike and organize independent unions. Peasants might get their long-sought-after farmers association (*nonghui*) and the right to free internal migration. What is important here is not "who gets what" but "how we decide." A country long thought to be frozen will now be awash with competing interests and competing ideas of the just polity. All will want their just desserts.

In this way, the heroes of retreat will forge and announce a democratic pact that, with all its messiness and complexity, extricates a troubled regime from the burdens of rule. As during the 1989 protests, reports of the change will be confused and often mistaken. The actual outcomes will depend on many contingent factors yet to come. But a historic shift has occurred: China is on the road to democracy.

Ending the PRC

In every transition from authoritarian rule, there is always a "democratic moment" when the people inherit the burden of rule from the regime. The crowds of Lisbon who adorned the rifles of rebellious young officers with carnations in 1974 followed this with feverish spontaneous "assemblies" to make grand plans for the future. It is this sense of victory, the sense of having taken history into their own hands, that is really the democratic moment.

In China, while the CCP may remain in charge of the state, responsibility for the future will now lie with the common man. Despite the elite-led nature of the pact and the strong elements of continuity, this will be a revolution indeed. The sudden end of CCP's unchallenged monopoly on political power, coupled with the broader breakdown of state identity and ideology that will result, will fit any "commonsense" definition of revolution, even if there is no guillotine or Declaration of the Rights of Man and Citizen. That was the retrospective lesson of the "silk revolutions," in some Eastern European nations, and it will likely be the case in China as well.[40]

This may be symbolized by a formal political act that ushers in the demise of the PRC. Constitutional changes require the approval of two-thirds of the NPC, so any new regime that wanted to remove the CCP's monopoly on power and embrace new rights would have to make this an early priority. Again, assuming the state crisis is serious and the democratic response enjoys general support, the NPC, although stuffed with CCP loyalists, could be expected to support the change.

The actual sequence of events—from coup to carnations to assemblies—will be a mixture of necessity and choice. Clearly, the ideal sequence would involve a relatively short period from crisis and mobilization through to breakthrough and pact. Reality may not be as simple. Hard-liners may hold up agreement as they bargain for concessions. Reformers may hesitate if protests escalate. Eventually though, the deed is done. The PRC comes to an end, in fact if not in name.

The removal of Mao's portrait from the rostrum of Tiananmen may not take place immediately, just as Lenin's tomb remained in Moscow. The elements of continuity will be strong and there will be a need to reassure citizens with the reassuring grin of the chairman. But the democratic moment may be symbolized in other ways, by the vacating of the Party's Zhongnanhai (Central and Southern Lakes) leadership complex so that it can be rejoined to Beihai (Northern Lake) public park, for example.

The CCP will have ruled China for 60 years in 2009. The previous records for a party's unbroken tenure in office were just over 70 years by both the Russian Communist Party and Mexico's Institutional Revolutionary Party. Whatever the exact date of democratic transition, the CCP will go down in history as one of the world's longest lived ruling parties. It will be a reign that ends for the same reason that other dynasties in China ended: the court lost touch with the people, was starved of resources, and finally rotted from the inside. It will also mark the end, for all intents, of the disastrous utopian experiment called communism that once engulfed the world.

Now we have brought China through the tense and historic move toward democracy. It is not the first such move in the country's history. But, compared to 1912 and 1949, the prospects for the creation of a genuine and enduring "people's republic" are now bright.

7

The Immediate Aftermath

The Interim Regime

Given the constellation of forces that will be pressing in on China's heroes of retreat from every angle, the immediate aftermath of transition will be delicate at best. Democratic transitions the world over show how the interim period—which typically extends from one to two years—is no less crucial to maintaining the momentum toward democracy and setting it on a proper course than the breakthrough itself. Like the smooth but swirling wake thrown up after the passing of a great ship, this period can be deceptively unsettled. The economy may remain in crisis, while society will leap into a frenzy of political activity under new freedoms with few norms or rules to follow. All this bears heavily on a fragile new leadership struggling to erect a new constitutional order.

Not for the last time, China's achievement of a democratic breakthrough through an elite-led extrication will pay dividends here. In general, extrication produces less unsettled results than mass overthrows or collapses where protestors seize state power, as shown by the tumultuous examples of the Philippines, as well as many Latin American examples, especially Chile under the Allende government from 1970 to 1973. An elite-led extrication allows for the orderly creation of a "caretaker government"—in contrast to the revolutionary councils or power-sharing governments that result from more mass-led transitions.

Caretaker governments are typically the most stable and effective types of interim regimes because they are both inheritors of state power and legality from the old regime as well as legitimated builders of the future democracy—a situation described as "backward legality, forward legitimacy."[1] Backward legality provides the interim government with the resources of the state—its bureaucracy, its meeting places, its law-making powers—to prepare the way for democracy. This can be useful as long as the interim leaders are committed to that project and those resources are still of some value.

Typically—as in Spain and many Eastern European cases—the first law they pass eliminates the political monopoly of the old ruling party (if not the party itself). They also tackle some issues of the transition pact that cannot await an elected government, things like laws covering amnesties for human rights abuses, rules to stem capital flight, and macroeconomic stabilization. The interim government also has to raise revenue and maintain public order. Not least, and the source of its forward legitimacy, it must make plans for a new political system.

China should be in a good position on all counts. A caretaker government could quickly deploy the old CCP system for new purposes. The rule of law and the legislative and judicial organs were respected and workable in the late PRC era, while the bureaucracy was increasingly professionalized. The CCP's "leadership" could be ended with the mere stroke of a pen. One of the great ironies of that change, as was noted in the case of the USSR, would be that just as the entire PRC political system is about to be revamped if not ended, the PRC constitution will suddenly come into full play for the first time. The interim NPC will briefly shine as "the highest organ of state power."

An immediate issue to be confronted will be the takeover of the assets formerly controlled by the CCP. A fracas for control of these assets—factories, bank deposits, houses, cars, and public records—has ensued in other authoritarian collapses where remnants of the old regime and elements of the emerging democratic polity have contended for control. The newly "stateless" CCP will have to be unburdened of these chattels, which in turn will need to be put under the impartial custody of the interim regime.

Keeping the civil service in operation is a crucial task. The dismissal of large numbers of bureaucrats is usually a mistake. In fact, old bureaucrats typically swing quickly into line—for rational reasons if no other—and that in turn ensures better governance. Moreover, the interim government's "backward legality" would be undermined if it engaged in a wanton and lawless purging of former government officials, whose positions after all were legal and whose loyalties to the old regime were necessary.

Given the mere size of China, the imperatives of governance make it necessary to compromise with the old. The caretakers will have to vet and reappoint a swathe of top leaders in roughly 65 ministry-level and cabinet-level bodies as well as in 31 provinces or provincial-level cities. Within the provinces, the same processes will be repeated covering something like 60,000 sub-provincial governments. How that process proceeds in each province and locality will vary widely. One can imagine that the situation will be more parlous for the ancien regime in inland regions where resentment runs highest. Police may find themselves in impossible situations as angry peasants ransack the offices of predatory county cadres.

Most crucial will be the need for the interim regime to set out a plan for the new democracy, which we consider in part 3. Given the inevitable challenges of democratic consolidation even in best-case scenarios, an interim government would be advised to avoid creating exaggerated expectations. Ideally, its rhetoric stresses the importance of immediate and mundane tasks, and on learning the messy business of democracy, not grand dreams and impossible amity. Again, having a caretaker government rather than a revolutionary council in charge of the newly democratic China will make this valued sobriety more likely.

There is always a danger of interim governments becoming permanent, claiming some degree of present legitimacy for ousting the previous "scoundrels" and asserting that the necessary preconditions for a successful move (or return) to democracy have not been met. Caretaker governments may try to introduce some form of "tutelary democracy" or to inhibit the holding of free and fair elections. Yet the fact that the interim leadership is not elected, and probably not representative either, means that this brings dangers of a backlash. Gentle pressure from the world community to set and abide by a transitional timetable could help ensure that it does not happen in China.

Sudden Politicization

CCP leaders and their propaganda organs frequently warned in the late PRC era that China would descend into widespread anarchy if a half century of authoritarian rule were suddenly lifted. Deng Xiaoping was master of such scare-mongering. "As soon as they seized power, the so-called fighters for democracy would start fighting each other," he said shortly after Tiananmen. "And if a civil war broke out, with blood flowing like a river, what 'human rights' would there be? With each faction dominating a region, production declining, transportation disrupted and not millions or tens of millions but hundreds of millions of refugees fleeing the country, it is the Asia-Pacific region, which is at present the most promising in the world, that would be the first affected. And that would lead to disaster on a world scale."[2]

Party scholars have echoed Deng's words, writing cataclysmic tracts about the results of any democratic breakthrough in the country. One, imagining an elite move similar to what we have sketched above, conjures up the set-piece dark scene of national disunity, economic collapse, and social disorder.[3] Another cautions: "The countries of Southeast Asia along with Japan, Hong

Kong and Taiwan should be prepared to handle tens of millions of refugees from China if a civil war breaks out as a result of political chaos and the fall of the CCP. . . . Half of the world would be pulled into a situation of instability caused by China."[4]

Even pro-democracy advocates have issued sober warnings: "The moment dictatorship collapsed, violent populist politics would appear. Every kind of social demand from every sort of group will appear like a volcano. Terrible recriminations, cruel struggles, all sorts of lawless activities will appear taking aim not only at those who supported dictatorship but also at rivals within the anti-dictatorship camp. All sorts of people will use the name of freedom and democracy to trample on human rights and rule of law."[5]

To some extent these predictions may come true. It is almost certain that the democratic breakthrough will result in some degree of street violence between those celebrating the change, those opposing it, and those simply seeking to take advantage of the unrest to loot, rape, and rampage. China was already a heavily armed country by the late reform era—evidenced by the fact that police confiscated thousands of firearms every year. From January 2001 to July 2002, there were more than 15,000 separate incidents of violent attacks on Party and government individuals and their property.[6] As one democrat writes: "The CCP cadres know all the blood debts that have built up over the years, which is why they fear democracy. The moment they fell from power a countless number of people and their families would come out to seek revenge."[7]

One could imagine scenes of violence in Tiananmen Square as pro-democracy groups trying to tear Mao's image from the rostrum battle with remnant Maoists intent on honoring his memory. With little tradition of compromise, street violence could be ugly. Some bloodshed is a virtual certainty. Writ large, the threat of such social conflicts remains the biggest fear of those inside and outside China about the immediate consequences of a democratic breakthrough.

But there are several reasons to believe that society's reaction will be less calamitous than imagined. Most important, a new regime which promises openness, elections and freedoms will not be a cause for rioting. Like the takeover of the CCP itself with its promises of a new era, "liberated areas" would be easy to manage. The "chaos" of China's past was always a result of illiberal policies—like Maoist movements or the deployment of military might against peaceful protestors in 1989—not of liberal ones. Even then, as has been noted, Chinese society remained remarkably cohesive and unaffected by high-level tension during the Cultural Revolution, in part due to the strength of family units.[8]

Indeed, the social atmosphere would likely be quite the opposite, recalling the heady feelings of mutual respect and love—a veritable Woodstock—that broke out during Tiananmen, or on the streets of Beijing after the city was awarded the 2008 Summer Olympics. This would be especially likely if the breakthrough elites have draped themselves in the flag and promised to "revitalize China" and encourage broad-based economic development in addition to introducing democracy.

Excluding the mostly contained minority areas, there are not major ethnic or cultural cleavages within China waiting to split open the moment the old regime falls. Unlike Indonesia after Suharto, India at partition, and the USSR, China is more similar to Asia's other democratizers like South Korea, Japan, Taiwan, Thailand, and the Philippines, which made smooth transitions to democracy after long periods of authoritarian rule partly thanks to their social cohesiveness.

Another reason to believe that the tensions would not lead to anarchy is the strength of provincial and local governments, one of the clear legacies of state-building under the PRC. While CCP leaders and many scholars continue to view China through the imperial prism of a vast unwashed held together by a grand central state, in fact, as we saw in the last section, regional power was already quite strong. Mao's one undisputed contribution to China was to erect a strong state, and his successors can claim some credit for having dispersed its powers.

High-level political instability is likely. Social anarchy is not. The self-serving "Yellow Peril" propaganda used by the CCP to try to scare Western governments into supporting its rule by invoking fears of thousands of migrants arriving in shipping containers off Orange County simply does not add up. As one democratic leader wrote: "Democracy will not cause social disorder. In China's cities today, people are very dependent on the stability of the system and would work to uphold it. Even if there were some riots and some clashes, there would rapidly be a compromise and settlement reached and peace would be restored. The new government would quickly take over from the old one and restore order. Democracy has been a long hope of the people. A democratic government would enjoy immediate support and people would draw together to maintain peace even if some people tried to destroy it. Those causing disturbances would have no market."[9]

Even when disturbances *do* find a market, the relevant normative question will be what degree of violence would negate the whole transition? That is, to what extent would the injustices of transition be acceptable as part of the process of eliminating the injustice of CCP rule? That question can be answered only by the people of China. Many democratic revolutions, as mentioned, have involved violence and unrest. Yet few citizens of today's democracies believe the price was not one worth paying. China's transitional violence will probably be limited. What violence there is may be deemed by its people as the acceptable price of freedom.

A less dramatic but probably more politically relevant question is how the interim regime will handle the sudden eruption of political participation in society. With new freedoms to speak out and organize, the interim regime will confront a boisterous polity the moment it takes office.

Among those who may feel aggrieved by the transition, ironically, are the very democrats who had long lobbied for change. Since the breakthrough will likely be elite-led, democrats may believe that it has been achieved in a nondemocratic way and call for a "completion of the revolution." Many democratizers, especially those excluded from the democratic pact, might accuse the new regime of having compromised too much with the ancien regime and not promised fast and full enough democracy. The mass protests might have empowered reformers to seize the day, but in achieving the breakthrough pact, the reformers may have locked the protest leaders out of the bargain. Overseas dissidents excluded from the transition would be immediate critics, as would those at home who were shouldered out of the way in the jostling of the transition. Tens of thousands of released political prisoners may join them.

It was this same tension that led to splits in the 1989 movement after one group had achieved talks with the regime. Post-1989 the often strident public disputes within the Chinese intellectual community about whether, for example, the U.S. government should endorse normal trade tariffs for the PRC or whether funding should be provided for village elections and judicial development, reflect the same latent tensions. In general, the narrower was the coalition that led the breakthrough, the greater the likelihood of renewed agitation by excluded groups. The broader the coalition, the less likely.

On the opposite side will be excluded hard-liners, the dislodged elites and their friends who sided with the nondemocratic camp. In the immediate wake of the democratic breakthrough, there will be a significant portion of the leadership at both central and local levels that fears the new disposition. Some will be deeply opposed to the democratic breakthrough. But most will be simply afraid of the uncertainties of the new era. With a newly freed press and civil society, they may fear the end of the corrupt gains from reform that constituted their reward for complicity. In addition, those who openly opposed the changes would rightly fear for their lives and safety. Some will fear mobs marching on their villas and throwing their mock-Renaissance furnishings into the street along with their half-dressed mistresses. They will, in the words of one scholar, rue the day when they "become high-profile targets of newly-activated political groups and their self-enrichment activities are subject to press scrutiny and populist attacks."[10]

In the turmoil of the initial coup, one can imagine many of them fleeing from their offices in cars toward airports where special planes sweep them to freedom. Their children and wives may by this time already be stashed safely abroad, along with their money, a backdoor exit that was already widely in existence for many senior cadres around the country by the turn of the century.[11] Will foreign countries like Burma, North Korea, or Vietnam offer them safe haven from the changes? Will they "rediscover" their familial links to Southeast Asia, as Peruvian president Fujimori did his Japanese roots? Certainly, many have children and relatives who are U.S. citizens. Might they end up living in obscurity in Hawaii, as Marcos did after his ouster? Or will they flood Canada and Australia as "business migrants" as did corrupt Russian officials?

Some who have not been detained or fled might seek to oppose the fragile new leadership. They might collude with disgruntled elements of the military who are angered by their service's inaction. This is what happened in August 1991 when hard-liners in the Russian Communist Party tried to oust Gorbachev along with Yeltsin.

The natural response of the unstable new leadership may be to crush the antidemocratic forces with repression and witch-hunts. This would be a mistake, not only for the reputation of the regime itself but also for the impact that it would have on bestirring this group. It might also have the effect of making the democratic leadership itself more extremist. In successful transitions, the new leadership has sought to conciliate hard-liners as far as possible. The ideal response is to admit, even welcome, this group's existence and its right to compete in fair elections in future. If other post-communist countries and China's communal traditions are any guide, retro-communists will enjoy significant support at the polls. The key for the interim regime is to steer this threat onto the open and democratic path.

Fortunately, China will have the odds in its favor. The ability of hard-liners to retire peacefully has been a hallmark of extrications, in contrast to overthrows. The exclusion of radicals in the opposition makes this more palatable at the political level. Moreover, there is a kind of mutual dependence between the interim regime and the ancien regime. The interim regime must respect the right to a quiet retirement of the hard-liners because it has one foot in the old order with its backward legality. It also wants to offer them a graceful exit so that they will not pose a threat to the new order. The hard-liners, meanwhile, must recognize the interim regime because it offers them the best hope to avoid jail, exile, or death. China had already established a norm of quiet retirement for purged elites in the late PRC era. There is every reason to believe it will be respected again.

Alongside the potential backlash from ousted leaders is a potential backlash from sidelined military leaders who had sought an early crushing of the democracy movement. Such figures may have failed to convince others at the time of mass protests. But they may find a larger constituency as military officers begin to consider the implications of the democratic pact for their own interests. Certainly, many, especially in the police force, will consider how the old days of easy money from corruption will end. The military will be less worried about this, given its withdrawal from business. But the pact itself will need to be one which makes most in the coercive forces confident that their corporate interests will be safe in the new era. If, as we posit, the new elite has emerged to promise more military money, an amnesty, and the protection of national stability and sovereignty alongside democratic reforms, there will be no pretext for action.

It was just such calculations that caused huge military defections from the antidemocratic backlash in Moscow in August 1991 when hard-liners in the Russian Communist Party tried to oust Gorbachev and Yeltsin. Most of the units simply did not respond to the hard-liners' appeal. Of those that did, a large group soon changed its mind and—composed of 10 tanks, 30 APVs, and 500 troops—surrounded the parliament in its defense, pointing their guns outward instead of inward. The leader of the defecting soldiers was Colonel Alexander Rutskoi, an Afghan war veteran and vice president of the Russian republic. He told the soldiers that they were as much a part of the new order as anyone else. "Today," he said from atop a tank, "the fate of the country, its freedom and democratic development are in your hands."[12]

International Reaction

No less than fears of domestic unrest, the threat of national disunity has been repeatedly invoked in China as an argument against democratic reforms. It is an issue that will appear frequently in the consolidation phase. Early on, it can stall democratic reforms if interim leaders revert to arguments for a firm hand to preserve unity. In the USSR and Yugoslavia, the threat of breakaway republics held up reforms at critical moments.

Tibet and Xinjiang would be the most likely sources of secessionist sentiment in the immediate aftermath of a breakthrough, although China's hidden diversity counsels us to keep in mind the possibility of division elsewhere. As the USSR example showed, the very triumph of "legality" and "constitutionalism" on which the interim government's authority partly rests creates new openings for separatism. In Tibet and Xinjiang, the "high degree of autonomy" promised to these regions under the country's laws will suddenly seem not just viable but also necessary.

Although Tibet's spiritual leader, the Dalai Lama, has publicly ruled out independence and sought only greater autonomy for his homeland, younger and more fiery Tibetans, especially those in exile, might seek to lead a new uprising against Chinese colonial rule like that of 1959. In Xinjiang, where avowed independence movements operate across the border, oases along the border with limited Chinese influence like Hotan, Kashgar, and Gulja could be the source of similar movements. Such activity could provide ammunition for advocates of less than complete democratization in China.

The threat of immediate breakaway is less pronounced for democratic Taiwan since the island is already totally self-governing and would be well aware of the consternation it would cause in Asia and the West if it were seen as having exploited a fragile move toward democracy in China — something it has long advocated — for its own ends. As above, it might also strengthen the hand of remnant conservatives in China. There would be little incentive for Taiwan to make a preemptive declaration of independence at this stage, especially given that the longer-term prospects of democracy in China would provide brighter hopes for its eventual peaceful achievement of this.

Indeed, there may be a role for Taiwan's leaders in supporting the changes. In the USSR in 1991, Boris Yeltsin promised to support the secession of Baltic States to gain their support and thus win the upper hand over Gorbachev by portraying him as "antidemocratic." A similar pact might be negotiated with Taiwan. A Taiwan leader could promise to support the reformers and not declare independence in return for a promise that the future Chinese state would recognize Taiwan's autonomy and drop threats of war.

Certainly there are normative reasons to wish that breakaway movements do not erupt anywhere in China at this stage. But the "window of opportunity" presented by the transition may be too tempting. Some leaders may see the possibility of a more nationalistic China in the early years of democracy and argue for an immediate dash for freedom. It would be critical for world leaders to make it clear that they would not, at this stage, support such division. Although later derided as his "chicken Kiev" speech, U.S. President George Bush was probably right in 1991 when he asked Ukrainians to defer a vote for independence, fearing that it would sabotage Russia's fragile democratic transition. We return to the long-term resolution of national self-determination movements in part 3.

The broader international reaction to the democratic breakthrough will be important as well. The international community will need to provide robust political and economic support for the move to democracy. Immediate recognition of the new regime and backing for its goals would be exigent. This would be especially true if the reformers are still facing the threat or even reality of an armed opposition to the change by some admixture of conservative and regional elites. Promises of financial aid and assurances that China's new government would retain its UN Security Council seat would be useful. Rhetoric, to paraphrase U.S. president George Bush after the collapse of the Berlin Wall, should not gloat about the end of CCP rule but rather express support for the bright new era.

Western nations will have to strike a careful balance between fortifying the new republic while not interfering in its transition. The U.S. military deployed naval vessels off the Dominican Republic to support its first elections there in 1978 and made overflights of the Philippines to support the new Aquino government in 1986. It would be advised to avoid such well-intentioned actions around China, because they would likely provoke nationalist reactions. The United States should not pretend that the new China is an immediate ally of the West, something that, in addition to being unlikely, might be seen as a revelation of a plot to "retake" China, "lost," in 1949. Nor would it be advised to offer its services in resolving outstanding issues of the transition, a job best left to the countries of Asia. Tiny Singapore, which is widely admired in China and takes a leading role in Asian political affairs, might be the better venue for this, as it was for the first meeting of top-level negotiators from China and Taiwan in 1993.

Washington and the West in general, then, might need to take a quiet back seat to the changes in China. It could tell Taiwan, Tibet, and Xinjiang to stay within the fold and warn other Asian nations not to take advantage of the delicate transition in China. It could offer financial and political support through international agencies. But its voice might best be muted.

At the same time, the world community will want to ensure that the costs of democratic transition in China are contained. There will need to be preparations for contingencies such as an increase in illegal emigration, the possible loss of management over China's nuclear weapons, and perhaps the eruption of health emergencies. All this suggests that the United States and its allies in Europe and Asia must have a ready-made plan for fundamental political change in China. At present, it is believed that such a plan exists only at the military-to-military level and focuses on strategic issues only. The need for a broader diplomatic and issue-oriented plan is pressing.[13]

China's neighbors would likely adopt an equally careful posture toward the changes for similar reasons. Although nationalists in India, for example, would see an opportunity to invade the disputed mountain pass between the two countries, such a move seems highly unlikely given the wider stakes for India. An untroubled and short transition in China to a more stable regime would benefit India in practical ways economic, military, and political. Moreover, as the world's biggest democracy it has a moral commitment to shepherding its giant brother along the same path. India's role could also be critical in moderating any Tibetan unrest since it plays home to the exiled leadership.

Many more contingencies too numerous to consider could turn for the worse through the actions of Asian neighbors. Southeast Asian countries could retake reefs in the Spratly Islands, a still unreconstructed North Korea could turn inward again without the pressure of a modernizing communist neighbor, Russian nationalists in the Far East could make incursions on borderlands given to China in a series of disputed demarcation exercises in the 1990s. The list goes on.

No less than in the breakthrough period, then, the transition period will bring to the surface a host of new issues that will confront a democratic China. The sudden eruption of these issues on the watch of a delicate interim regime makes them all sources of potential setback. We may find solace in the fact that most democratic transitions in the Third Wave with an equal onslaught of domestic and international issues — think of South Africa, Russia, and Brazil — succeeded in the end. Again, while it is useful to focus on the immediate and instrumental issues of transition, there is a deep and powerful normative undercurrent that has carried many countries through the same difficulties. The challenge for China and the world will be to minimize these costs of freedom.

PART 3

CONSOLIDATION

8

The Political Challenge

Will Democracy Fail?

The year 2012 will mark the 100th anniversary of the first and only election of a national government in China. It may be around that time when the country makes a second attempt to build an enduring democracy. Having successfully navigated the dangerous shoals of democratic transition, it now will face the vast and turbulent sea of democratic consolidation. Will it finally achieve a stable position among the world's democratic majority? Or will it fail again, falling back into a cycle of revolution and dictatorship that reflects a centuries-old crisis of state legitimacy?

There are two separate but related possibilities. One is an outright democratic failure that brings a return to dictatorship. This might come under some guise like "managed democracy" or "tutelary democracy." By failure, we mean a reversal that is *significant*, such as the suspension of elections or the banning of opposition parties, and *sustained*, meaning that such conditions last for more than one or two years. The other possibility is a democracy which, while not failing, experiences a prolonged and painful period of consolidation, characterized by frequent political crises, extraconstitutional behavior, and institutional weakness.

To return to our initial metaphor of the intersection, once the drivers have ousted the lone policeman and decided to implement a traffic light system, there are two threats. A single driver may seize the abandoned traffic podium and direct traffic with promises of restoring order. Even if this does not happen, adaptation to the new system may be slow. Some drivers may run red lights. Others may drive on days they should not. The newly installed lights may short circuit one day, bringing temporary disruption until they can be repaired.

History suggests that rapid and trouble-free democratic consolidations are the exceptions. In China itself, democracy failed in the Republican era, providing the conditions for a return to dictatorship. History is also littered with famous democratic failures. It took nearly a century for the French Revolution to lead to the foundation of a genuine democracy despite the democratic ideals of the revolution. Failures also grew out of Weimar Germany, Russia's democratic revolution of February 1917, Japan in the 1920s, South Korea in 1961, Budapest and Prague in the early communist era, and many postcolonial transitions in Africa and Latin America.

If we narrow our focus to the post-1970s democratizations, however, there are grounds for optimism. Most of the Third Wave transitions gave way to successful democracies, a reflection both of the stronger supporting conditions as well as the greater normative appeal of democracy by then. Of the 28 new democratic states created out of the collapse of Eastern European and Central Asian communist regimes in 1989–91, for example, 25 were considered either consolidated or moving in that direction a decade later.[1] Most of the modern-day democratic failures have been in Africa, where a nonexistent civil society, economic distress, and ethnic conflict have savaged the foundations of political order.

On that basis, there is reason to believe that China too will break the cycle of failure and achieve a stable democracy. It will begin its democratic age with a strong dose of normative support for democracy alongside the usual pragmatic supports related to the crisis of dictatorship. The belief within society that democracy will eventually bring about a "superior" point in terms of stable governance, a fair and just society, prosperous economy, and a settled international role will ensure that the difficulties of consolidation will not overwhelm the system.

Nonetheless, the process will be difficult. As Russia and Indonesia have shown, troubled democratic consolidations are common in large countries, characterized by regional secessionism, political turmoil, social upheaval, and economic volatility. Elsewhere, overly strong elites hampered consolidation in Latin America, while socioeconomic crisis was a factor for the rocky beginning in Eastern Europe.

Democracy may be a pacifying force in the long term, but democracies usually take years—if not several decades—to reach this stage. In the interim, the new system can unleash disruptive forces that test the very fabric of a nation. As China struggles with this aftermath, the main bulwark of democracy is a pragmatic one: there is no turning back. No one will acquiesce to the forfeiting of their democratic rights and no group is strong enough to bring this about by force. In any case, the spoils system that sustained the old regime cannot be reestablished. History's march of events makes a return to "the good old days," infeasible.

It may take several decades before the struggle to entrench democracy ends in China. While democracy will not likely fail, it will likely be ugly, very ugly at first. To quote one former top Chinese political advisor, discussing the post-transition scenario: "China will likely have to go through several more nationwide protest, strike, and student movements before it achieves mature democracy. It will have to get through several short-lived military coups, many local-level armed conflicts, many cases of major political scandal, the entry of bribery and violence into elections, and maybe a couple of cases where the national election results in a great dispute that brings constitutional government to the brink of collapse. Even so, China can surely march through the various stages of democratic development."[2]

A word of caution is in order. Here we are most of all in the realm of speculation. To say that we tread on uncertain ground in this section is merely to state the obvious. Democratic consolidation is a contingent process that depends on the already contingent transition that has preceded it. Before we were dealing in possibilities derived from facts, here we are dealing with possibilities derived from other possibilities. It is perfectly reasonable to posit that democracy will fail in China. I simply believe that it is more reasonable to predict that it will succeed.

Either way, this chapter may help to frame the possibilities so as to provide a basis for positive action by domestic and international actors alike. We should try to predict what the road will look like, where the potholes, unexpected exits, or U-turns may occur. To be forewarned of the difficulties of democratic consolidation in China is to be able to recognize those difficulties when they occur. As one Western scholar notes: "The imperative of making democracy succeed is almost inevitably going to appear on the political agenda. Consequently it is worthwhile even for a democratic opposition in a still-Leninist state to begin to contemplate how they would consolidate a democratic breakthrough, how they would quell the forces of those who could be attracted to alternatives to democracy."[3]

Legacies and Choices

There is a good argument, remember, that proto or pro-democracy legacies exist in China's long history, things like bureaucratic meritocracy, Confucian accountability, and Buddhist tolerance. China will be drawing upon this rich legacy as it grapples with the new demands of political liberalism. As occurred in South Korea and Japan, this heritage will await rediscovery as the country reimagines itself in democratic terms. China's people will suddenly be "ransacking the cultural attic, looking for the furnishings the revolution drove out of sight" to use one salutary phrase.[4]

The Republican-era legacy will be no less useful. The relatively rapid advance of Eastern European countries to functioning democracies in the space of a decade has been attributed to their pre-communist democratic legacies and to the relatively short period they lived under communist dictatorship. China too will be able to hearken back to its pre-1949 democratic episodes, the liberality and civil society of Shanghai and other Republican-era metropoles, and to its democratic thinkers, from Republican founder Sun Yat-sen to democratic scholar Hu Shi, a Cornell University graduate.

The PRC era, of course, will leave a mixed legacy. Certainly there are many antidemocratic legacies—the absolutism in political life, the atavistic security forces, the unreconciled historical issues—that will constrain democratic emergence. Still, it is worthwhile to recall that the worst phase of totalitarianism lasted for only two decades—from 1957 to 1976. Before and after that, Communist China was more like a soft authoritarian regime. There were also, as mentioned, some democratic legacies of high Maoism, not least the revulsion to dictatorship that it spawned.

The reform era, meanwhile, created much stronger foundations for democracy. The growing consensus on the need for democracy to solve the crisis of CCP rule provided normative momentum. Meanwhile, many, if not most, of the resources we traced in part 1 will help to consolidate democracy just as they helped to overthrow dictatorship. Economic growth, nascent civil society, the emergence of a liberal nationalism, international pressures, and moves to institutionalize and depoliticize state power will all help China's new democracy.

The political legacies cannot be overemphasized. Countries like Russia and Ukraine have shown that democracy can survive in countries without a strong middle class or civil society as long as the political system was sufficiently decompressed by the time of transition to make a reestablishment of autocracy impossible. Just as this pluralism and autonomy within the regime helped in the choice of democracy, so too it will act as a bulwark against a return to dictatorship. A professional bureaucracy, hardening legislatures, and a more adept judiciary will add to the supports. As one Western scholar notes: "By the time political transition occurs, a panoply of late-Leninist institutions may have enabled the [new democratic] state to manage society with increasing sophistication."[5]

China's real trump, however, is economic. In cross-country evidence, above a certain GDP per capita a democracy will survive "come hell or high water." Several scholars contend that the level is around $10,000 (in 2002 price-adjusted dollars). If so, then any democratic breakthrough in China—with a level of $4,500 in 2003—will be impregnable by around 2020 (or 2024 if we discount GDP by a quarter for quack statistics), assuming a modest annual per capita growth rate of 5 percent.[6] With every passing year, the probability of success rises. Another research project found that the probability of a return to authoritarian rule fell steeply from 2 to below 1 percent in any given year as income rose from around $6,700 to above $8,400.[7] Again, that means that democracy will be virtually unassailable in China by the end of the second decade of the century and more or less stable much before then. On other measures, China is already near a level at which its income is sufficient to make democracy indestructible.[8]

Of course, some factors will hamper democracy. The fiscal problems of the state, income inequalities, the authoritarian and illiberal norms implanted by CCP rule, and the regional strains of Tibet and Taiwan will be legacies that undermine democratic success. But in general, and unlike other former communist regimes, China's "democratic infrastructure" will be reasonably well developed by the time of transition. As a result, the eruption of political participation that defines a democratic breakthrough is less likely to breach the walls of systemic order.

The legacy of the transition itself is also important. Empirically, mass overthrows—as in Chile and the Philippines—have led to unstable new governments while elite-led transformations have the best track-record of success. On that basis, the elite-led transition posited here will help to ensure greater stability. At the same time, the economic crisis preceding transition along with the turbulent interplay of mass protest and pact-making leave any number of potentially explosive issues lingering in the public space. As with the interim regime, the main bulwark against this transitional aftermath is the new legitimacy of rulers in the democratic era. No longer dependent solely on performance, they enjoy a honeymoon with the populace, giving them time to act without immediate threat. That is why even messy transitions in the Third Wave gave way to stable democracies.

Finally, just as global border effects helped China through the transition, so too they should help its consolidation. There is every reason to believe that democracy will continue to dominate the international system. China will also enjoy the "latecomer advantages" of crafting its democracy according to the lessons of a century of democratizations elsewhere. The only danger would be an outbreak of democratic deterioration in the world's established democracies. That is why ongoing efforts in the U.S., Europe, and Japan to deepen their own democracies, including the pursuit of more ethical and law-abiding foreign policies, will be important for China's successful consolidation.

For argument's sake, it may be worthwhile to draw up a legacies scorecard for China, taking into account the many factors (critical ones highlighted)

Table 1 Democratic Legacies Scorecard

- Democratic pre-communist legacy: 2
- Severity of communist period: 2
- Small geography and population: 1
- **Developed market economy: 3**
- Limited crony culture and rentseeking: 1
- Significant middle class: 3
- **Strong civil society: 1**
- Aggressive media: 2
- Basic social freedoms: 2
- **Ethnic and religious unity: 2**
- Traditions of public compromise and public good: 1
- Democracy-compatible nationalism: 2
- Entrenched rights norms: 1
- Rule of law and independent judiciary: 2
- Institutionalized legislative process: 2
- Politically-engaged population: 1
- Experience with elections and political life: 2
- Organized democratic opposition parties: 1
- **Pluralism and autonomy within the former regime: 2**
- **Regulatory strength of state: 3**
- Fiscal strength of state: 1
- Weak military role: 3
- Favorable international environment/global support: 3
- **Elite-led, non-violent transition to democracy: 3**

that are generally assumed to be critical to democratic consolidation. We range the scores between one and three, where one represents an unfavorable condition, two a neutral condition, and three a favorable one. Then, based on the analysis of parts one and two, we might have the results shown in table 1.

The average score of all 24 factors is 1.9, and of the six highlighted factors 2.3. This is a suitable reflection of China's "mixed prospects." It suggests that China faces neither democratic hell nor democratic heaven but a sort of unsettled purgatory where democracy survives but is rife with problems.

Of course, even if these rough scores are accurate, deriving predictions from them is difficult. Some countries with high scores have experienced democratic failure, as in Argentina. Meanwhile, the three most frozen and undeveloped Eastern European countries under communism—Albania, Bulgaria, and Romania—had by 2002 defied all predictions and attained remarkably democratic and free societies.[9]

This is a salient reminder that beyond the "embedded" factors lies a vast unknown territory of contingent "path dependent" events. Whatever has preceded the breakthrough, the consolidation period itself is one of choices that can sabotage or support democracy. As with all democratic failures or successes, the behavior of elites is a big part of this uncertainty. Legacies are possibilities, nothing more and nothing less. Countries with strong pro-democratic legacies may nurture dictatorship, while those with weak legacies may foster democracy. As with the transition, the only thing that can "explain" where China heads will be the dynamics of the consolidation period itself, in particular the choices made by those in power. As with China's entire quest for democracy since the Qing, no one's decisions are scripted.

A few points can be made about the choices of elites based on experiences elsewhere. The simplest, if disarmingly bland, principle is that democracy succeeds when politicians act democratically. In particular, that means they act in two ways. One is to act inclusively, making a sincere and steadfast effort to embrace as many distinct voices as possible in decisionmaking. Inclusiveness ensures that every significant interest group is more likely to abide by the new democratic order. Whether it be ethnic minorities, laid off workers, victims of communist-era repression, stability-seeking business tycoons, or nationalistic military officers, attention must be paid to these interests in crafting the new democracy, perhaps more so than in future. For China, the challenges of meeting disparate demands will be huge. Not only will the new state need to recognize known groups, it will also have to embrace new groups previously excluded from public life. A people long schooled on notions of being singular and pure, of having an officially delimited structure of different groups, may wake up surprised by the army of unrecognized minorities, victims of unknown CCP horrors, transvestites, Hakka farmers, and hitherto little-known religious sects clamoring for recognition.

Second, elites should stick closely to the procedural norms of democracy. Proceduralism occurs when principled standards are met in the process of achieving something, when the means must abide by certain rules and cannot be violated for some higher ends. The opposite is consequentialism, where almost any means can be justified by the ends. We will see proceduralism (often called procedural justice or legal proceduralism) crop up again and again below. The idea is that society is engaged in a struggle to think and act in terms of procedures as much as outcomes, whatever the issue at stake. This may be an even greater challenge in a post-Leninist state that leaves behind a legacy of extreme consequentialism in policymaking. Weak evidence can no longer be used to convict a rapist in order to satisfy demands for vengeance. Peasants cannot be arbitrarily thrown from their land for a new business park bypass.

Put simply, in making choices about everything from new national symbols to reconciling economic conflicts, China's society will be engaged in learning democracy as it lives under democracy. In this respect, it will face monumental but by no means insurmountable challenges.

New Institutions

The first order of business will be to write a new constitution and establish new institutions of state. Along with the first national election, this stage can be considered the epilogue of democratic transition and the overture to democratic consolidation.

No less than other aspects of democratic consolidation, this is a path-contingent process. Scholars of China who make a close reading of elite discourse on the future shape of democracy in the country may be disappointed by what actually takes shape. In South Korea, for example, opposition demands for a directly elected president emerged in 1985 only in response to a gambit by the military-backed government to democratize the parliament while keeping control of the executive. In Thailand, an appointed Senate set up under the first democratic constitution was replaced by a directly elected one in 1997 in response to popular demands.

There is no fixed model for constitution writing. It can be done by the interim regime or by a constitutional assembly, elected or unelected. The resulting document may be put to a popular referendum or simply passed into law. In Asia, there are examples of constitutions drafted by the ruling regime with a referendum (Philippines and South Korea), by the ruling regime without a referendum (Thailand), and by an elected constitutional assembly (Taiwan).

Many theorists have argued the case for a strongly democratic constitution-writing process—one involving an elected assembly and a referendum—on normative grounds. This normative case is even stronger in the case of constitutions written in new democracies where the legitimacy of the former system was low and the socioeconomic consequences of the new system potentially huge.[10] But evidence from many transitions suggests that the most successful constitution-writing processes are the least democratic, involving unelected if broadly representative assemblies and no referendum.[11] That is because the relatively simple matter of writing a constitution can become hostage to insistent interests that emerge as part of the new political drama. It is important that those battles be fought on the electoral field rather than on the constitution-writing one. The window of opportunity for getting the democracy into operation may be small and cannot be further constricted by debates that in the end will have little relevance to the success of the democracy.

Fortunately, China may be well-served by its history. In both the Republican and Communist eras, constitution-writing was considered to be the prerogative of the state. Unelected but broadly representative bodies were created to write new constitutions in Republican China in 1938 and in Communist China in 1953. Hong Kong's mini-constitution, the Basic Law, was drafted by a similar committee set up in 1985. It is probable that China would choose the same path for its post-CCP system, an arrangement already endorsed by several Chinese democrats, although they differ on whether the resulting document should be put to a referendum.[12]

As in 1938 and 1953, one can expect that delegates would be chosen by the interim leadership from three broad groups: national figures representing a broad array of political, economic and professional sectors; local representatives from each province and major city; and representatives of ethnic minorities and possibly religious groups, women, and Overseas Chinese. The more representative the body, the more immediate legitimacy the constitution will have. There would be wide scope for significant input from Hong Kong, whose well-developed legal system and highly-skilled constitutional law community could be of great support. Unlike Hong Kong's Basic Law drafting committee, however, which took a leisurely five years to complete its task, China's assembly will be under pressure to act quickly. The first national elections will be expected within a year or so of the end of the PRC, meaning that a constitution will need to be passed well before that. The urgency of the task will be all the greater given that the "hollow" nature of the PRC constitutional order has left a residue of popular mistrust of constitutions.

While broad social and political forces will make or break democracy in China, the new constitution will be a useful support or a damaging impediment to that project. Constitutions can act as a touchstone for social pride in a new democracy, or a progenitor of new social tensions. Experience elsewhere shows that the process is more likely to succeed when it is conducted in full public glare, seeks consensus and outside inputs on issues, and borrows liberally from established laws and customs.[13] The resulting document will be more valuable when it does not attempt to encompass every aspect of society but rather confines itself to the basics of the political system. Values like development, morality, and nationalism are best left to be settled in the political arena.

At the most fundamental level, the new constitution will need to embrace the core value of democracy, namely the equality of individuals and their endowment with inalienable rights. This will be entrenched in the constitutional design, just as it has been for every major constitution promulgated in China since 1908. It will be followed by an extensive system of guaranteed rights and liberties for all, including the right to vote and run in regular, free, and fair elections.

Critically, no party or other force can be given any paramountcy over the constitution or exclusion from it. This, of course, assumes that there have not been any secret antidemocratic details in the transition pact, such as a promise to insert a clause asserting that all political parties must serve "state interests," or that the media must not cause "social instability." In Hong Kong, hardliners who were stunned by the colony's role in the 1989 Tiananmen movement inserted a clause in the otherwise highly democratic Basic Law requiring new laws against "treason, secession, sedition, and subversion," the passage of which in 2003 provoked half a million people to take to the streets in protest.

A formula for constitutional amendments would also be needed. Given China's regional diversity, which we come to below, the formula would need to ensure that the populous rural heartland, which will hold a near plurality in the national parliament, cannot push through constitutional changes against the opposition of coastal or minority regions. Some higher plurality level, like two-thirds or three-quarters, plus a regional distribution requirement (say at least one province from minority and coastal areas) might suffice to meet such concerns.

A more tricky issue will be emergency powers to suspend constitutional rights in the case of a state crisis. Most democratic transitions show that such a situation can emerge early in the consolidation phase. Framers need to make allowances for such crises in a way that will save the democratic project. If emergency powers are imposed too readily, the democracy can be undermined and discredited. If too laboriously, it can be vulnerable to sabotage. Russian president Boris Yeltsin's imposition of "special presidential rule" on two occasions in 1993 is now seen as a necessary stroke to break through resistance to democratic reforms from the Soviet-era parliament. Civil liberties were not affected and Yeltsin enjoyed wide popular and international support for the moves.

The conditions for emergency powers would have to be given in some detail, involving some phrasing like "imminent threats to security of the state or the constitution." Thus, while an armed rebellion would pass the test, the existence of an anti-constitutional party (say a secessionist party in Xinjiang) would not, unless the party were elected to office and moved to fulfill its promise. In Russia in 1993, the parliament had attempted to block a referendum and appoint a new president; both actions were clearly at odds with constitutional government.

The invocation of emergency powers would also need extra checks. In the 1989 Tiananmen crisis, martial law was imposed without the approval of the

NPC. A revised Martial Law Act of 1996 made NPC approval mandatory. That points the way to the necessary checks on the executive's imposition of emergency powers. The new constitution might also impose mandatory judicial review as an added level of safety. As one Chinese scholar has written: "A well-designed article regulating emergency power cannot resolve the complex problems of the transition, but it can provide a due procedure to resolve a crisis."[14]

In designing a new political system, delegates to the constitutional convention will have to strike a balance between preserving and breaking with the PRC political system. There is bound to be a significant group, tracing its intellectual origins to the constitutionalism project of the late communist era, that argues for continuity. With Party rule struck from the constitution, they will argue, the people's congresses at all levels, if directly elected, could assume their role as the supreme organs of state power. The premier would be chosen from the national parliament, along with his cabinet. A largely titular presidency appointed by the parliament would be retained. Political consultative conferences would remain and possibly gain new powers of review and supervision. Villages would retain autonomy along with minority areas.

This argument will be a convincing one, as it has been in most transitions where framers opted to retain large chunks of the previous system. It not only makes the transition easier, it also makes political sense. As Santayana wrote, the success of revolutions "is generally proportionate to their power of adaptation and reabsorption within them of what they rebelled against."[15] The greater institutionalization and empowerment of the people's congresses in the late PRC era will provide an existing structure for democracy. Building on those foundations will strengthen the sense that China has finally escaped from the tyrant's cycle of "broken mandates" (geming) that wipes away all that came before.

Some might argue for a stronger, directly elected president, claiming that the pressing needs of socioeconomic reconstruction demand a single leader above the fray of party politics who can push through necessary policy changes. Former Party reformer Yan Jiaqi, for example, has advocated a strong president with control over the military, foreign affairs, federalism, and overall state administration as well as the power to dismiss cabinets.[16] The experience of former communist countries in Eastern Europe and of former authoritarian regimes in South America shows that this can be dangerous. Not only are strong presidents—or "superpresidents"—prone to engage in patronage and cronyism. They also are vulnerable to what has been called the "authoritarian temptation," overriding democracy when things don't go their way and claiming "the national interest" is at stake. When combined with a fragmented legislature, a common result of the first few elections, the results can be disastrous. A parliamentary-oriented system is usually a better way for the flux of new competing interests to work out their differences without the additional complication of an external actor claiming to have discerned "the national interest" or to be "the hero of democracy."[17] In addition to this normative reason there is a practical one: conducting national elections for parliament will be a major job as it is. An additional election for president, with perhaps the need for runoff elections, might be unmanageable.

In China's case, the arguments of continuity and of the dangers of a return to Republican-era and later Maoist strongmen subverting the political process will bolster the case against a strong presidency. Indeed, most existing plans for China's new democracy already describe a state president who has only symbolic power, or who is in charge of only foreign affairs and defense while domestic affairs are entirely in the hands of the cabinet under the premier.[18] Nonetheless, a president appointed with cross-party support and great moral authority could be a unifying figure for the new democracy, an embodiment of the nation above the compromises of electoral politics.

The creation of the national parliament will be a prime issue to consider. It would be unlikely that a parliament could function with the 3,000 deputies to the present NPC. Yet in such a large country as China, reducing the number of parliamentarians to the several hundreds common globally would make each constituency impossibly large. India's 545 parliamentarians represent 1.6 million people each, surely the upper limit. The 437 U.S. congressional representatives have around 600,000 constituents each. One Chinese democrat suggests that each member of a new parliament represent two million people, which would create a house of 650 members.[19] For expository purposes, we make the arbitrary assumption of members representing 1.3 million people each for a neat total of 1,000 delegates. This would make China's the world's largest parliament, ahead of Britain's 650-strong chamber.

By going to a strictly representative system, the new democracy would be overturning the late-PRC era system that counted city-dwellers as four times a rural dweller and coastal areas more heavily than inland areas. The result would be a drastic shakeup in the seats held by each province, and within each province by each area. Inland and largely rural provinces like Henan and Sichuan would see their weight increase while coastal and urban provinces like Liaoning and Shanghai would see their share fall, as shown in table 2.

Some new features of the political system may be added to the old one. In the late PRC era, there was a growing espousal of an independent anti-corruption body to tackle official graft. Hong Kong's Independent Commis-

Table 2 Seats in a 1000-seat parliament

Area	Seats[a]	Change[b]	Cumulative Total
Henan	75	+15	75
Shandong	71	+3	146
Sichuan	68	+12	214
Guangdong	58	−1	272
Jiangsu	57	+1	329
Hebei	53	+9	382
Hunan	52	+8	434
Anhui	50	+9	484
Hubei	47	+1	531
Guangxi	38	+5	569
Zhejiang	36	+3	605
Jiangxi	34	+4	639
Liaoning	33	−10	672
Yunnan	33	0	705
Heilongjiang	30	−9	735
Guizhou	30	+6	765
Shaanxi	29	+4	794
Fujian	27	+3	821
Shanxi	26	0	847
Chongqing	25	+3	872
Jilin	21	−5	893
Gansu	21	+4	914
Inner Mongolia	19	−2	933
Xinjiang	14	−8	947
Shanghai	12	−14	959
Beijing	10	−12	969
Tianjin	8	−9	977
Hainan	6	−1	983
Ningxia	5	−1	988
Hong Kong	5	−8	993
Qinghai	4	−3	997
Tibet	2	−5	999
Macau	1	−3	1,000
33 Total			

a. Based on proportional representation. Each seat represents 1.3 million people
b. Compared to figures for the ninth NPC of 2,703 members, excluding Taiwan and PLA delegates and normalized to 1,000 seats

sion Against Corruption and Taiwan's Control Yuan, created from the designs of Sun Yat-sen, show how such institutions can help stanch corruption in a cronyistic political culture. Indeed, given that corruption will likely be a prominent issue in the overthrow of the CCP, the promise of such an institution in China may well be an explicit part of the transition pact.

Another possible new institutional feature would be a civil service examination system such as exists in Britain and Singapore and as existed in imperial China. Support for a merit-based bureaucracy spans the political spectrum in China. Rightists see it as a guarantee of rule by the educated, while leftists conceive it as an impediment to patronage.[20] In the raucous new era of electoral politics, a respected civil service might, like the state presidency, be a source of stability and hope.

There are bound to be calls for purges of old bureaucrats associated with the CCP. Fears that old personal networks would secretly control the country would run high. Yet the experience of Eastern Europe showed that bureaucrats rapidly swung into step with their new masters—seeing their self-interest in doing so—and that their retention helped maintain the effectiveness of the state.[21] In any case, the pressing demands of governance in the new era mean there is often not much choice. As in the interim period, retaining most of the existing civil servants will ensure that the new state has the capacity to carry out necessary reforms.

Although the late PRC era had seen a significant revamping of the ministries in lines with the imperatives of market and functionality, some further changes would be needed. The Ministry of State Security, the all-powerful CIA of China, would need to be disbanded and turned into an agency under the control of a home affairs ministry. There may also be demands for a separate regional development ministry.

Pulling the fangs from the military has been an urgent task in many democratic transitions. In China, it will be less pressing, for all the reasons that we saw in part 2. Nonetheless, it will be important to institutionalize the military's professional and nonpolitical ethos with new policies and structures. The Ministry of Defense will need to be transformed from a hollow shell established for the sake of foreign exchanges into the real command structure of the military once the Party's Central Military Commission is abolished. The military's mission will need to be stated exclusively in terms of external threats, and possibly disaster and emergency relief—paralleling the mission statement of PLA forces in Hong Kong—no longer in terms of supporting the ruling Party. The end of any political role will be symbolized by the military's loss of seats in the national and provincial parliaments along with the disbanding of the PLA's General Political Department.

More general policies to keep the military satisfied with its defense mission should include generous budget increases to pay for both arms acquisitions and better living standards, laws entrenching the aspects of amnesties agreed in the democratic pact, and a slate of new promotions. It would also be wise, and likely, for the number of troops to be slashed. One democrat suggests slashing the combined PLA and PAP complement from 3.5 million to 1.5 million soldiers while keeping the budget at two-thirds of its previous level to ensure fealty from the officers.[22] Those kinds of cuts were already being considered by top brass in the late PRC era as the military transformed itself. All this should make it easy for democratic China to dispense with the threat of military involvement in politics.

The court system will need some revamping as well. Most important will be the introduction of judicial review of laws passed by the national parliament, especially those bearing on constitutional essentials, something the PRC never allowed since the courts were servants of the Party, not guardians of the constitution. The new higher profile of courts, in particular the Supreme Court, will raise questions of judicial appointments. Who will be the first chief justice of democratic China? In this respect, as in so many others, the prior institutionalization of the state in the late PRC era will offer an important resource. The growth of the legal profession, the countless foreign-financed courses for training China's judges, and the norms of examining government behavior built under the Administrative Litigation Law will all come into play. Unlike other totalitarian states, China will have a head start in building the rule of law.

Though I will not return to the issues of building the bureaucracy, judiciary, and police again, it is worth remarking that the strengthening of these institutions is critical so that the state can carry out the tasks of economic and social refurbishment and political justice that democracy promises. This "state capacity-building" will be no less important in democratic China than it was elsewhere. In many of the areas outlined here—rule of law, federalism, emergency powers—the natural urge of democrats for constraints on state power will need to be balanced by the need for a measure of concentrated state power if the entire democratic "package" is to succeed.

Finally, the constitutional convention will have to consider the whole gamut of new symbols for the reborn state. What will it be called? The title "People's Republic of China" will likely retain strong emotive attachments. So too will the existing five-starred red flag, even though it is Marxist-inspired. The national anthem, a 1935 anti-Japanese war song, the March of the Volunteers, may also be retained despite its negative concepts of victimization and enemies. The central bank will issue new currency to celebrate the new state. But the world should not be surprised to find that Mao manages to hold his pride of place on the national specie. Adapting the legacy of communism to the challenges of democracy may entail holding onto past symbols no less than past institutions.

Federalism

The contentious nature of central-local relations in the late PRC era has led some to warn of a breakup of China under democracy. "Many people who thirst for political reform and faster democratization are concerned that it would threaten central power and thus oppose democratic political reform," says one mainland scholar.[23] Certainly any introduction of democracy without a devolution of power to the provinces would be risky. The Russian example showed how the launch of national elections without simultaneous devolution can be disastrous for attempts to create a workable federal state. Newly elected local officials come under pressure from voters to act in their interests and demand the power to do so. What's more, the imbalance of seats in the national parliament resulting from a strictly population-based scheme stokes demands for greater autonomy from smaller and more remote provinces — in China's case places like Gansu and Jilin (21 seats each). As a result, many scholars believe that a substantial and sweeping federalism will be one of the most likely institutional changes in a democratic China.[24]

The political arguments for a significant devolution of power in China will be powerful. Empirical evidence strongly supports the claim that smaller jurisdictions make democracy more successful, as seen in China's villages. It makes it easier to develop democratic values among citizens, increases the accountability and responsiveness of government, brings marginal groups into the public arena, enhances checks and balances on central power, and gives small national parties a chance to hold power at local levels. It also makes state finances more stable because taxpayers can more easily monitor the spending of their tax dollars.[25] This is not unimportant in a country where two-thirds of county governments run budget deficits. Overall, federalism will allow China to "mimic" the conditions of small states, devolving powers to 33 provincial-level governments with an average population of 39 million. They might in turn devolve power to the 3,200 counties, regions, and large cities that on average contain 400,000 people.

In many ways, federalism will be simply an entrenchment or formalization of the growing provincial power that arose in the reform era and made the PRC so prone to regional power struggles. But the new arrangements will go well beyond the ad hoc economic federalism and de facto political federalism that developed in the PRC. One prominent university professor in China predicts that federalism "will have a clear direction in future: legalization, systematization and coordination" to replace the current system's use of fiat, ad hoc policies, and bluster. This, he says, will be "a necessary component of democratic politics."[26]

According to one proposal made by a scholar and government advisor, the powers for provinces would include commercial regulation, economic and social development, education, healthcare, culture and sports, and basic infrastructure. The central government would be left with foreign affairs, macroeconomic management (including monetary policy), income redistribution, interprovincial commerce, foreign trade policy, and universal aspects of healthcare and education.[27] New fiscal arrangements concerning the sharing of tax revenues, especially new income, sales, and social security taxes, would be needed as well. So would arrangements governing redistributive transfer payments to poor provinces. In the PRC era, transfers were dictated by arbitrary political considerations, which forced needy provinces to embellish reports of their plight.

The break with the unitary state in which virtually all power resides in Beijing and is doled out to the regions as and when the center sees fit is bound to incite some opposition. Some will argue that it threatens national breakup and will make China a weak state. Yet throughout its history, China has been a loose confederation as often as a unitary state, despite the assertions of monistic historians.[28] Reasoned arguments will suggest that a real federalism will reduce secessionist tendencies and make the country better governed at all levels, as it has done in countries like India. There, an explicit and transparent federalism—rather than a de facto one that developed in the PRC—has created two-way virtues, making central authorities more sensitive to regional concerns while "widen[ing] the horizon of regional parties on matters of national importance" thus enhancing the loyalty to the national state of otherwise parochial local politicians.[29]

The introduction of federalism will be a historic move, the first attempt to end China as a unitary state and admit the regional diversity it contains. With single-party rule removed at the top, the gates will be open to a real federalism based on explicit and open sharing of power rather than the might-is-right, covert, and unstable power sharing of the late PRC period. The argument that democracy would bring national breakup would finally stand tattered as yet another poor excuse for dictatorship. Federalism will be portrayed as a bulwark, not a threat to the nation.

A second institutional change might be an upper house of parliament—like a Senate and perhaps constituted from the CPPCC—that is based on regional rather than proportional representation. This might be the solution to the weakened position of places like Shanghai, Qinghai, and Liaoning in the lower house. As in the Republican era, its members could be appointed by the directly elected provincial parliaments. An alternative, suggested by one scholar, would be to impose a "one province, one vote" body inside the national parliament when it was considering certain types of legislation, such as financial bills.[30] This would be in addition to whatever regional considerations are built into the formula for constitutional amendments. A constitutional court might also be useful to arbitrate on central-provincial disputes, something likely to loom largest in the first years of the new system.

Finally, there would be good arguments for a redrawing of some provincial boundaries. In the reform era of the PRC, the megalopolis of Chongqing was carved out of Sichuan province while the island of Hainan was separated from Guangdong province, both becoming provincial-level jurisdictions in order to meet developmental needs. One could imagine that in the interests of development, authorities may opt to create more provincial-level cities, such as the Yangtze River cities of Wuhan and Nanjing, or break up some large and easily divided provinces like Shandong, which was historically two separate states.[31]

One of the most detailed redrawing of boundaries as part of an imagined federal democracy in China comes from Peng Ming.[32] His plan includes six "self-governing provinces" (*zijue sheng*) where the central government handles only foreign affairs, defense, and some economic coordination, similar to the "one country, two systems" arrangements in Hong Kong. These would be Hong Kong, Macau, an enlarged Tibet, Southwest Xinjiang (with the capital as Kashgar), Eastern Inner Mongolia, and Hainan. Next would be 26 "autonomous provinces" (*zizhi sheng*) with a high degree of autonomy similar to that enjoyed by the special economic zones and would-be ethnic areas in the PRC. These would largely cover the minority and mixed areas of Western China and Manchuria. Beyond them would be another 52 regular provinces and provincial-level cities (*zhixia putong sheng* and *zhixia dushi sheng*), mainly in central and coastal areas. This 84-province federation would represent a more than doubling of the 33 provincial-level areas of the PRC, cutting the average population size of each unit to 15 million.

Federalism would also open the way to a minor but strongly symbolic change: the introduction of separate time zones. In a hangover from the imperial era, Beijing has long imposed a single time zone (Greenwich plus eight) on the whole country as a symbol of unity.[33] As a result, the farther west you go, the more time spent in the prolonged darkness of the morning. When you cross into Pakistan from western China, the clock moves back three hours. Many places keep an unofficial local time, forcing people to specify which is being applied, adding to confusion. Under the new federalism, there could now be four separate time zones, ranging from Greenwich plus six in Xinjiang to Greenwich plus nine in Manchuria. Many a foe of early morning starts in western China or of the confusing unofficial "local times" around the country would bless the new federalism of democratic China. As elsewhere, time zones would also save energy, reduce crime and traffic accidents, increase worker productivity, and cut health costs. More importantly, the introduction of time zones would be part of the process of reimagining the country, appreciating its diversity and its linkages to surrounding periphery countries rather than as an inward-looking monistic whole.

Secession

While a new federalism would significantly enhance provincial autonomy, it would not likely by itself avert the specter of secession in Tibet and Xinjiang. Indeed, experience elsewhere shows that, improperly managed, devolution can lead to a rise of secessionist pressures in minority regions. More than half of the 47 new states born between 1974 and 1997 were a result of the breakup of multinational countries following the introduction of federalism under a new democracy.[34] The USSR, Yugoslavia, and Indonesia are striking examples of how democracy resulted in secessionism and countervailing irredentism, creating conflicts that threatened the democratic project in the center itself.

Secessionist pressures are not an automatic result of democratization of course. In many countries—the Philippines, India, South Africa, Turkey, and Canada—democracy actually contained such pressures by creating federal arrangements with real regional autonomy for distinct regions and by making the national political system legitimate in the minds of minority groups.

There are no hard and fast rules, but in general, the stronger is the new democratic state and the greater the degree of cross-party unity among national leaders, the less are the chances of national breakup. A strong new state gives minorities confidence that their interests will be protected. Elite consensus, meanwhile, reduces the likelihood that a political party will use ultranationalist or irredentist claims to gain the upper hand over rivals.

The experience of Tamil areas in South Asia demonstrates the importance of a properly handled deal. In India, the central government helped create a largely Tamil state—eventually named Tamil Nadu—in a series of reforms in the 1950s. Tamil became the state's official language and locals gained greater autonomy over their affairs. The result was a prosperous and productive member of the new nation where secessionists found (and continue to find) that they had little electoral appeal. In Sri Lanka, chauvinist Sinhalese limited the rights of Tamils from the 1950s onward, leading to the outbreak of a violent insurgency for an independent Tamil state in 1983. As one Western scholar says: "An early, generous offer of autonomy, made before extreme separatist leaders outflank moderate leaders, may avert secession."[35]

What would happen in China? Secessionist tendencies, as we saw, remained strong in Tibet and Xinjiang in the late-PRC era because of the lack of autonomy and freedoms. Those pressures would certainly not disappear with the end of the PRC. This is a concern not only for its own sake but also because it could undermine the democracy itself.

Democratic principles suggest that the two regions should be allowed to conduct referendums on their status and relationship to the rest of China. Yet that prospect might cause irreparable harm to democracy in China. For one thing, the idea of "losing" Tibet or Xinjiang would be anathema to many. It would thus discredit the new system because of its inability to maintain national unity. The rise of ultra-nationalist leaders in Russia and Serbia in the late 1990s in response to ethnic insurgencies is ample warning of this. Han Chinese who supported democracy might quaver if it appeared likely to result in a division of the country. Democracy in China would then be under threat, just as the war against secession in Chechnya almost scuppered Russian democracy in the second half of the 1990s.

In addition, any consideration of secession would raise divisive questions about the boundaries and electorates of these regions. Would Han Chinese who had migrated on their own and lived in peace with the minority peoples be disbarred from voting in Tibet and Xinjiang? Which Tibetan areas outside the Tibet Autonomous Region would be included (they exist in four other provinces)? Would the Kazaks of Xinjiang be allowed to secede from a proposed Uighur state? There are also very real concerns about the rise of violent ethnic reactions against Hans, not to mention the strategic vulnerability of the places so close to unstable regions in Central and South Asia.

One can imagine an immediate referendum in multiethnic Lhasa or Urumqi being a disaster, recalling those in the capitals of Kazakhstan and Kyrgyzstan where ethnic Russians were in the majority. Extreme nationalist Han politicians would appear in these cities and gain electoral support. In the charged atmosphere, Tibetans and Uighurs would vote along ethnic lines out of fear, even if they were not ethnic chauvinists.

For all these reasons, several Chinese scholars have suggested a solution that is both principled and practical.[36] The new state should, they argue, impose a temporary constitutional ban—say of 10 to 20 years—on secession in the interests of creating a solid foundation for democracy. Such a limit on the "secondary right" of secession would be justified in the interests of the "primary rights" of civil and political freedoms, an acceptable trade-off in most normative political theories. Secession would be deemed unconstitutional in the interests of the protection and enhancement of basic freedoms in potentially secessionist regions.

In the meantime, real autonomy would be granted similar to that in Hong Kong. Beijing would approve whatever leader was elected to head the regions, provided they disavowed secession, and the central government would handle only defense and foreign affairs. Tibet's Dalai Lama (the current one will be 75 in 2010) might be appointed as that region's titular or religious leader and a civilian leadership constituted from among the Tibetan population, while a popular local leader in Xinjiang might be allowed to gain power there. Local police forces would be constituted in the regions. Several plans call for the withdrawal of the 150,000 to 300,000 Chinese troops in Tibet and the creation of an autonomous border protection force there. This would depend not a little on India's goodwill in allaying Chinese security concerns. The demilitarization of Xinjiang would also require similar moves by Central Asian neighbors.

In the meantime, émigrés would be allowed to return to both Tibet and Xinjiang and political prisoners would be released. Some sort of international monitoring of rights in the regions could be invited—a UN special envoy for Tibet and Xinjiang for example—to ensure that the ban on secession did not become an excuse to deny rights. If this rapporteur asserted that all was well, the regions would find little international support for secession. Over time, the theory goes, the real enhancement of rights in these regions would reduce secessionist pressures, allowing them to remain part of China while enjoying the religious rights and sense of self-respect that they were denied in the communist era. If it did not, then at the very least, the complex issues of secession could be decided within a more mature democratic polity.

Obviously, it will be easier to convince Tibetans and Uighurs to remain a part of China the more evidence there is of an improvement of rights and enhanced political status. The autonomy over local affairs promised under the PRC system would have to be implemented quickly. It might be appropriate, as part of the revamped federalism, to give minority regions a veto or opt-out power over constitutional changes, such as granted to Quebec in Canada. Long-standing grievances over everything from the location of military bases in pastoral land to official inquiries into historical issues would need to be addressed. And although secondary in importance, evidence of economic payoffs from remaining inside China would further blunt secessionist urges. International support could play a critical role in this respect.

Since we are predicting an elite-led democratization in China—albeit with bottom-up pressures—in a well-established state, there is reason to believe that such a solution could work. Both Tibet and Xinjiang could see in the new polity a chance to live at peace in a new broad-minded and free China, while Beijing politicians would not "play the national unity card" against these regions.

That said, there will be a significant danger that this ethical solution to a complex problem will fail. The experience of countries like Yugoslavia, the Soviet Union, and Indonesia shows that ethnic minority regions tend to make their dash for freedom the moment the authoritarian weight is lifted even where there is some prospect of a democratic federal state. Years of resentment against the colonial power are simply too hard to bottle up with reasoned arguments along the lines of "this is for your own good." Even with a special UN rapporteur declaring that rights are being respected in Tibet and Xinjiang, raw ethnic hatred may be hard to assuage.[37]

In addition, the very plausibility of the scenario sketched above—that a democratic China might be able to integrate Tibet and Xinjiang successfully—would encourage separatists to urge an immediate break. Fervent believers in an independent homeland would fear becoming another Quebec, Basque region, Puerto Rico or Tamil Nadu, where ultra-nationalist yearnings are constantly frustrated by the very reasonableness and tolerance of the "colonial" power.

The key then will be for outsiders and insiders alike to convince ethnic minorities that secession is not in their interest, whatever the law says. Influential countries and NGOs would have to lean heavily on politicians in minority areas—not just Tibet and Xinjiang but also in Yunnan, Inner Mongolia, and Guangxi—to refrain from secessionist politicking. In short, keeping secessionism from ruining China's democratic project will require a real commitment to the principles of democracy in these regions. At that level, stemming secession will be as much an issue of democratic learning as of national unity. Whether such a case can and will be convincingly made must remain unanswered. But the creative solutions of liberal Chinese scholars offers real hope. We return below to the longer-term future of these places.

The First Election

The holding of a national election in China will be the single largest event in the world. At present, that title is held by India's national elections, where 600 million people go to the polls. There, the task of voting requires 800,000 poll stations, 5 million poll station managers, a corps of specialized elections police, and two entire months. In China, there will be 900 million voters. Although infrastructure and technology will be light years ahead of what was used in the 1912–13 elections, there will also be 20 times more eligible voters. In logistical terms alone, democracy in China will not be easy.

Elections for the national parliament will need to be scheduled within a short time of the constitutional convention to ensure that the democratic momentum is not lost. At most, an interim government could rule for around two years in the face of a rapidly politicizing society. The interim government will need to appoint an electoral commission headed by a person of unimpeachable integrity to choose the method of election of parliamentarians, define electoral boundaries, conduct voter registration, set the rules for candidates and campaigns, and organize the voting days.

In the method of election, the choice is broadly between proportional representation, where parties gain seats in proportion to their share of the popular vote, and first-past-the-post, where seats are allocated to the winners in each constituency. Proportional representation systems are more inclusive but may lead to more unstable and inefficient governments, constantly trying to forge coalitions from a multiplicity of parties. When combined with a titular presidency, the results can be doleful.

In the PRC era, local people's congress delegates were elected through multiple-seat constituencies, a mixed system. Hong Kong shifted from a first-past-the-post system to a similar multiple-seat constituency system after the 1997 handover. There is thus good reason to believe that, in the interests of inclusiveness, some type of mixed system like this will be embraced in the new China too.

Given the size of the electorate, it may be advisable to conduct a two-stage campaign, with the national polls first, followed by the provincial and local elections. The remnant strong state from communist China would help immensely in the organization of the polls. Also, by the time China holds an election, computers will have greatly simplified the task, one of the benefits of a latecomer to democracy. The role of the United Nations, assisted by funds from supportive Western and Asian nations and from NGOs that support elections in new democracies such as the UN-backed ACE Project, could also be critical, helping to provide both technical expertise and moral support.

Who will contest the first election? The campaign will begin even as the constitutional convention deliberates on the new democratic structure. Political parties will form the moment they are legalized, probably before, and the campaign for the first election will erupt in earnest. Even if the transition pact has imposed some limit on the formation of political parties, or sought to retain some favored role for a continuist party created by the breakthrough elites, it is unlikely that such provisions will survive, a reminder of how the terms of the transition change quickly.

The creation of competing political parties becomes a necessity once universal suffrage is affirmed because parties are the only way to create coalitions

of interests and opinions. In new democracies, it is normal for a vast proliferation of new parties given the uncertainty and unfamiliarity of democratic
politics. The Beer Lovers' Party won a frothy 16 seats in Poland's first elections
of 1991, one of 29 parties competing for seats in the 460-seat parliament.
Indeed, political parties proved a boon to young democracies in Eastern Europe, where a weakened civil society was ill-prepared for the burdens of self-
rule. They channeled new social demands, acted as mediators with the state,
and integrated competing demands into viable governments. Along the way,
they showed "a reasonably strong capacity for responsible political behavior
and surprisingly high levels of commitment to democratic norms."[38]

The formation of political parties will be one of many significant milestones in China's democratization. The officially-sanctioned "flower vase" parties that co-existed with the CCP in the PRC era are certain to be displaced
by genuine new contestory parties. Their creation should be welcomed as a
first step toward a mature polity. As one former Chinese official predicts, once
national elections become a certainty, "we will see a proliferation of political
parties. The airwaves will be filled with candidates making speeches and debating policies. . . . We will see how the light of freedom brings out the enthusiasm, creativity and proactive spirit of the people."[39]

What kinds of parties will appear? By the late PRC era, China had an
emergent and distinct political spectrum, which we can loosely arrange in
terms of left, right, and center. This spectrum, including a vast array of what
were called "illegal organizations," is a good guide to the kinds of parties that
will compete in a democratic polity.

On the left, locally based groups representing peasants and workers—like
Hunan's Society for Reducing Peasant Taxes or the northeastern Association
to Protect the Rights of Workers would be common. They would gain their
support from those excluded from the spoils of China's reforms, possibly a
majority, as we have seen. They would be akin to a neocommunist movement,
basing themselves around the leftists in the CCP who had been shunted aside
in the late PRC era. Unlike in Mongolia, Russia and some Eastern European
countries, the mainstream of the CCP had abandoned Marxism even in the
late Mao era, focusing on holding power rather than realizing utopia. Those
yearning for communism will not likely try to resurrect it through the CCP.
Instead one can imagine a "New Communist Party" (xin gongchandang)
emerging to bear Marx's torch.[40] As in Russia, it would retain strong loyalties
from those who believed that the end of the socialist dream had been a disaster
for China and those fearing the economic and social impact of further reforms. The left might also include a noncommunist alternative based around

left-leaning intellectuals and the poor, perhaps named the China Welfare Party (*zhongguo fuli dang*).

On the right, more liberal, white-collar groups like the Alliance for Development or the China Development Union, representing coalitions of business leaders, liberal economists, and well-off urbanites, would also appear. Right-wing nationalists would likely find their home here too. Pro-democracy groups, like illegal organizations of the late reform era such as the Northeast Peace and Democracy Assembly or the China Democracy Party, might find their supporters on this side as well.

In the center would sit some form of continuist party constituted from the reform elements of the CCP who led the transition. It would of course enjoy the largest organizational resources and might be called the China Social Party or the China People's Party. This party would be a roughly centrist grouping that favors the market but also advocates a return to better welfare. But within its ranks would be wide divergences based on regional, economic, and ideological lines. Many of the candidates for the positions may be the former local CCP party secretaries not tarnished by the old regime.

Just as new parties would be permitted, it would be important not to limit or repress symbols of the old regime. Democrats might oppose the continuist party built on the remains of the CCP, while the breakthrough elites in turn might oppose a neo-communist party. Acquiescing to these demands would however threaten the legitimacy of the new system. Fortunately, the number of people who might oppose any suggestion of a communist return—in new or old garb—would likely be small. Unlike Chile or Argentina, where vast human rights abuses by the regime created a mentality of opposing its very reappearance, China had to some extent already made peace with the CCP by the late PRC era.

One way to envisage the riot of new parties is to imagine the politicians who might appear:

- An economist who argues for China's integration with world trading and economic system as the primary task
- an ex-CPPCC delegate espousing the type of corporatism and democratic harmony that will appeal to many
- a city mayor from a coastal city which has drawn in lots of foreign investment arguing for a Malaysian-style developmentalism
- an ultranationalist scholar arguing for limited democracy and a strong military
- a judge from the lower ranks who represents a Confucian-style morality and sense of justice

- a Buddhist-sect mystic who embraces ancient healing remedies and appeals to a forgotten era of kung-fu knights-errant
- a charismatic peasant mobilizing the vast village populations, abjuring the business suit for the homespun vest and arguing for a better deal for rural China

It is likely that the new polity will include far greater numbers of women running for office, and winning. Women have normally played a big role in overthrowing authoritarian regimes—as Beijing's Chai Ling, Taiwan's Annette Lu, and Hong Kong's Emily Lau remind us for the Chinese world—and continue to play an equally large role afterwards.

By contrast, one group that will likely not contest the first elections, at least not with any success, consists of the very intellectuals and activists who argued for democratic reforms in the late communist era. Since democracy is a system of representing various interests, idealists who represent no interests except the ideal of democracy cannot "represent" anyone, unless they go back to find a constituency after the communist collapse. Practically speaking, democracy activists often prove less than effective campaigners, having fought their struggles in journals and bookish circles. As one Western scholar puts it: "Democratization will not hand over control of policy to the proponents of democracy."[41]

The conduct of the elections will be an important litmus test of the new democratic spirit. Campaign violence, administrative blunders, and vote-buying will all be a threat. Experience suggests that the less ingrained are the "rules of the game," the more fraught are the first elections. On the other hand, even limited experience with elections under authoritarian rule can ensure that the first democratic polls are a success, as shown in Indonesia and Taiwan. A strong sense of the rule of law can also make the transition easier since people feel bound to respect the decisions of an electoral commission when the inevitable disputes arise. In China, of the 900 million potential voters, perhaps 300 million, representing half of those in villages, will have voted in a meaningful and properly conducted election by the time of the transition. Meanwhile, rule of law norms were basically established in theory if not in fact. On that basis, China has good prospects for a successful first election.

Typically, voter turnout and enthusiasm is high in first elections. This is a blessing since it ensures that the results are respected, especially when turnout exceeds half the electorate. Yet predicting the results is well nigh impossible. Empirically and logically, there are good arguments that the continuist party could do well. Taking into account China's weak corporatism, desire for stability, and the skewed distribution of organizational resources, it all augurs well for the success of a continuist party. In the first semi-free elections in June 1990, Bulgaria's Socialist Party, the ex-communists, won 47 percent of the vote and 211 of 400 seats.

On the other hand, as was seen in other countries like Poland and Czechoslovakia, the first elections can be occasions for strong votes against anyone associated with the old regime. The elections become an occasion for a thorough ventilation of the political system. Parties with strongly anti-continuist platforms do well.

A best guess for China is that a continuist party would take most votes. In that sense it would have the chance to become "hegemonic" — meaning having a predominant influence — like the dominance in the early years of democracy by the KMT in Taiwan, the Liberal Democrats in Japan, or the Congress Party in India. Nonetheless, in the interests of both inclusiveness as well as securing a strong majority, the dominant party may seek to build a coalition out of the scattered, regional-based parties which collect marginal seats.

Assuming that the results are declared legitimate and are accepted by most parties, we can at this point consider the transition to democracy as completed — even if the consolidation phase has only just begun. Having removed the CCP from power, agreed on a new constitution, elected the first democratic government, and eliminated "powers behind the throne," China will have made a successful democratic transition. Now comes the challenge of a successful democracy.

Rights and Interests

Beyond the first elections, we are peering at the journey of democracy in China through a misty lens. At best we can point to the rough outlines of the landscape ahead, if not to its likely impact. From here, we are less concerned with the sequence of events than with the setting. What will democracy look like?

The issues at stake can be broadly divided into two categories. One is *the struggle for rights*, the contention over the meaning and application of the universal and normative demands of democracy as the country goes through the growing pains of freedom. This can also be called the struggle for political justice. Second is *the struggle for interests*, the contention over "secondary" issues of macro-economic and fiscal policy, social justice, job opportunities, regional disparities and much else. This is the struggle for socioeconomic justice.

Typically, the struggle for rights looms largest in a new democracy. Since equality is the highest core value of democracy, other aims such as economic growth, national power, or cultural revival must now be pursued only in ways consonant with it. Fundamental rights can only be overridden in order to protect even more fundamental and extensive rights—as when protestors threaten the personal safety of bystanders. Basic liberties "trump" other aims.

Throughout history, democracies have failed because this core tenet was violated. Communism was a goal-based value system, a means to an end, which is why democratic rights could be shelved in order to "launch a sputnik" of socialist development. Likewise, nationalism, with its aim of national greatness, can make rights all too dispensable. The goals of economic growth or social stability likewise can provide the pretext for an overthrow of democracy when it fails to deliver these goods. Zionist Israel and Islamic Iran have troubled democracies because of the constant clash of rights with the imperatives of religion. In Singapore, attempts to uphold an imagined Confucian moral order mean that rights are suspended every time that order is threatened.

As a democracy matures and rights become settled, the struggle for interests takes over as the dominant issue of politics. Political debates are less about the banning of opposition parties and more about the funding of the national healthcare system. Those struggles are no less intense. But they are not taken as signs that the system is about to collapse.

The separation between the struggles for rights and interests is not hermetic. If the struggle for rights results in a victory for patriarchal nationalism over individual rights, as it did in Malaysia or Singapore, this can provide the pretext for giving certain groups better access to public resources than others. On the other hand, if the struggle for interests results in the rise of a dominant party which favors soaking the rich, for example, that may provide the basis for violating the fundamental rights of some. In both cases, there is a threat to democracy.

Both struggles are bound to be intense in China, so intense, indeed, that many will often despair of the country's future. As participation rises and identities are created within the new polity, levels of violence and disagreement may actually increase before they decrease into a Valhalla of responsible citizens solving their differences through civilized debate. A new liberalism in politics will provide a means of reaching consensus. But it will also generate even greater pluralism in the political arena. Conservative scholars will begin to wax nostalgic about the wonderland of authoritarian stability that was the PRC, as they did in Yugoslavia, Indonesia, and the USSR.

One thing is sure: as in France, with its bloody postrevolutionary century, and in Russia, with its troubled post-1991 era, the challenges of democratic consolidation in China will loom far larger than the transition itself. Overthrowing dictatorship is the easy part. Making democracy work is the most difficult, and unending, task of any society. For a China that toiled longer than others to remove the rock of dictatorship, this will be no less true.

Rights: Threats and Safeguards

The struggle for rights will be played out in an evolutionary and accretionary drama of speeches, court decisions, legislative actions, and public opinion. Through it, China will attempt to consolidate its democracy.

Predictions of a debacle in the struggle for rights are legion, grounded as they are in the baleful memory of Republican China's failed democracy. One scholar predicts that China after the first election will suffer from deteriorating law and order, political factionalism, an obstinate bureaucracy, and an ongoing crisis of legitimacy.[42] A journalist warns that China will likely join Indonesia and Russia as "messy states" where authoritarian rule gives way to corruption, political instability, violence, and secession.[43] A mainland native predicts "utter chaos under heaven."[44] Another warns: "The legislature will be so torn with conflict that it cannot carry out its constitutional functions; governments will have little time to implement a policy program before falling from power and governance will enter a state of semi-paralysis; money and violence will plague elections making them unfair; corruption will be rampant; and people's basic rights and freedoms will not be protected."[45]

Of course, all this may be true and yet not prevent the eventual consolidation of democracy. Ten years after its transition, Russia, for example, was widely considered a stable, if minimal, democracy. So too with China. While it is important to be honest about the challenges the country will face, it is still a large leap from there to predictions of outright failure. Most Third Wave transitions were a ultimately a success, and China's own scorecard bodes the same.

The challenges to rights faced in consolidation can be broadly grouped into state-centered and society-centered concerns. The former include weak institutions, weak norms of conduct among elites, and remnant authoritarianism. The latter includes things like violent, extraconstitutional social movements and popular illiberalism.

Every country's "biggest challenge" (or threat) to consolidation is different. The countries that confronted state-centered problems were diverse. Chile had to get the military out of politics. Pakistan faced persistent elite-level violations of democratic norms. In Taiwan and Thailand, weak institutionalization hampered progress. Society-centered challenges are no less varied. Colombia faced major anti-system movements from both the left and the right. In India and Indonesia, violent communal politics plagued democracy.

In China, the most prominent state-centered problems may be weak elite norms of conduct and remnant authoritarianism. In Eastern European countries where state repression was worst "communism was so harsh it destroyed the trust in the public good necessary for political cooperation or a modicum of honesty in public life."[46] In Bulgaria, both the former communists and the opposition made frequent departures from democratic procedures in the early years "each side justifying deviations from democratic norms by referring to the anti-system behavior of the other." The actions included invalidating local elections, election fraud, and jailing journalists. As two scholars wrote of this elite-led transition, similar to the one that we predict for China: "The revolution from above [spawns] a pattern of elite interaction that constrains democracy by weakening the commitment of key actors to its basic rules."[47]

In China, weak traditions of public compromise, a lack of political engagedness, a weak legislative process, and minimal experience with elections and public life could bring about the kind of paralysis noted by two students of democracy worldwide: "an increase in political cynicism and apathy, decline in effective political participation, and inability of the political system to generate stable, representative ruling coalitions."[48] If the process of state capacity-building is slow, it will further weaken the ability of the bureaucracy to implement legitimacy-enhancing policies.

Nonetheless, weak elite norms may be compensated for by strong institutions. As we saw in part 2, the coercive and organizational strength of the state created by the CCP is an essential bulwark against outright collapse. While the state became increasingly unable to govern properly in the late PRC period, it remained a large and powerful organization that could easily be reoriented for new purposes. It had rules for policymaking, a large bureaucracy, and a legal system. Corruption was widespread, but professionalization was increasing as education levels and technocratic credentials rose. The idea of cadres as servants of the public—symbolized by the national police force's switch from military-green to citizen-friendly blue uniforms in 2001—had begun to take root.

Since the agenda for governance should be clear, any new government in China should be able to make rapid headway in reorienting the state. By controlling corruption, empowering local governments and communities, addressing economic and environmental crisis, and providing an atmosphere of social enthusiasm similar to that in the 1950s, a new regime could enjoy immediate new legitimacy and political stability.[49] The old state will help uphold new institutions, ensuring freedoms and enhanced welfare. A new federalism that empowers provincial and local governments would make the state even stronger.

There is a flipside to the persistence of a strong state, however: the threat of remnant authoritarianism. Worldwide, new democracies have often experienced "a gradual erosion of the substance of democratic rule through intermittent repression of opposition groups, emergency measures, and declining integrity of legal guarantees," write two students of democratization, until "though still short of a formal transition to authoritarian rule, electoral institutions are rendered a façade."[50] Closet authoritarians may seek military support, portray the opposition as disloyal, and break constitutional norms.

The authoritarian temptation will loom large in China. The country's long legacy of dynastic rule coupled with the elite-led nature of the transition will leave a rich vein for would-be dictators to tap. If instrumental goals like social stability, economic growth, and national unity appear threatened, a strongman leader could quickly emerge to impose new clamps on "irresponsible media," "traitorous regions," and "bickering politicians." Such a leader might attempt to institutionalize those changes through limits on opposition parties and a weakening of parliamentary power.

This temptation may be supported by the unreconstructed members of the old security apparatus. While we have generally ruled out any overt military interference in politics, that leaves wide scope for a corrosive covert role. A totalitarian state's internal security apparatus is often the hardest to change given its ingrained traditions. When a pardons commission of prominent intellectuals in Russia released a convicted American spy in 2000, it noted that "the investigative organs of our country still bear the marks of the Soviet system, more so than society in general." In China, the very existence of the Ministry of State Security was often denied.

Even among new democratic leaders, a strong elitist tradition would help to feed the authoritarian temptation. Those who construe democracy as a means toward "scientific decisionmaking" and "efficient rule" rather than a just and fair working out of differences will contribute to this urge. They may argue that parliament should be reconstituted with a majority of seats elected by narrow franchises of business and social elites, much like the legislature in Hong Kong.

Some in society might abet the backsliding. Neo-authoritarians might be egged on by a people disillusioned by the poor performance of the new democracy on issues like the economy and effective governance. The foreign business community, which hailed warlord Yuan Shi-kai's "decisiveness" over Sun Yat-sen's "conspiracies" after the 1912–13 elections, might join the chorus, along with domestic business leaders pining for the old certainties of authoritarian rule. As a former Chinese official warns: "If our people lack patience with democracy and simply want a 'great leader' or 'outstanding politician' to step in and solve all the problems according to some vision, then the biggest loss of all will be the loss of democracy."[51]

If the reversion is significant and sustained, then China could slip from being a troubled consolidation to an outright democratic failure. Of course, the outside world and pro-democracy forces in China will have to be careful not to declare a "return to authoritarianism" too readily—as many did unfairly when former security service head Vladimir Putin was elected Russian president in 2000. If an election brings to power a continuist party with strong roots in the former CCP, this need not be prima facie evidence of reversion. Parties finding their roots in the old communist groups came to power in Hungary, Poland, Russia, and Mongolia; and a Francoist party did the same in Spain. None sought to implement a return to dictatorship. Like the rest of the old state, they adjusted quickly to the new democratic norms. Cambodia's People's Party, the inheritors of its authoritarian legacy, continued to sweep elections in the country after 1993, but at the same time presided over an enlargement of democracy—not just elections at local levels but also widened civic freedoms, a vigorous press, growing civil society, and norms of public debate.[52]

Fortunately, failed one-party dictatorships like the PRC are typically harder to reconstitute than military dictatorships because the former have been stripped of their resources while the latter remain a well-endowed and organized force (one reason why reversions to military rule occurred in places like Peru, Thailand, and Pakistan). Within the political elite, the same balance of forces that led to the initial democratic breakthrough remains to prevent a return to authoritarian rule. The multiplicity of actors, each with their own toehold in a new constituency, makes any "recompression" of the system more difficult. No influential actors can be sure that a newly-empowered autocrat will protect their interests.

In addition, moves by the state to limit the exercise of some political rights need not themselves be proof of democratic reversal. Campaign funding limits, limits on hate articles in the media, or bans on individuals facing criminal charges from holding office can all be consonant with upholding rights. The litmus test is whether rights are being restricted for the sake of other more extensive and fundamental rights or whether they are being restricted for nonadmissible goals such as purging political opponents or boosting economic growth.

Within society, the array of pro-democracy forces typically prevents backsliding despite growing disillusion with democracy. While new democracies have often faced the threat of a return to authoritarian rule, it has not come to pass. In Huntington's memorable phrase "nostalgia . . . is a sentiment, not a movement."[53] The middle class fears a return to cronyism and instability. The poor fear renewed economic crisis. China's civil society, especially that recently demobilized, would be an important bulwark. So too would the media and its ability to raise the specter of a return to dictatorship, as Russia's did throughout the 1990s. Whatever the attractions of strong rule, no one would vote in favor of a widespread curtailment of liberties. Newly independent courts, meanwhile, could play a role by striking down limits on rights or rejecting emergency powers. Openness and elections also tend to curtail the dreams of closet-dictators by bringing out their unsavory features.

No less important would be the international community, recalling the sanctions and suspensions of official contacts after Tiananmen. Assuming China has won wide plaudits for its democratic transition, it will not want to return to the dog-house of international relations by reversing its democratic gains. Eastern European countries and Russia were frequently steered away from the authoritarian temptation by pressure from the European Community.

In all, there are good reasons to be hopeful that China's millennia of authoritarianism will finally fade into irrelevance. As one Chinese democrat wrote: "The spirit of democracy will infuse the whole government. If the government tried to implement a new dictatorship, it would not be accepted by its own members. In addition, if it came to power with the support of the West, the new government would risk losing that support, even facing sanctions if it backpedaled."[54]

Society-centered challenges to democratic consolidation may loom less large. One well-known threat to new democracies, ironically, is populism. This does not mean popular participation in politics, the basis of democracy. Rather, it refers to popular desires to override the democratic process. The political system may generate stable governments, but they may be constantly challenged by street protests. This would arise if there was a widespread feeling in society that the "revolution" had failed and a "second revolution" was needed to complete the process. If the newly elected government appears as little different from the overthrown CCP, or if it is unwilling or unable to begin implementing the ideals of the democratic breakthrough, the threat of a second popular mobilization would grow.

One Western scholar of China believes that since the first government will be unable to deliver on instrumental goals of economic growth and political stability, "the prospect of a radical, possibly violent, political rupture would become more likely."[55] In the wake of the elections of 1912–13, for example, students, women, and the poor began agitating for the right to vote, arguing that the restrictions on the franchise deprived them of the fruits of revolution. This time, populism might arise from the marginal groups left out of the transition pact and possibly left out of the first elections. In distant Yunnan, an ethnic minority-led armed insurgency such as Peru's Shining Path (or indeed the "bandits" that continued to oppose CCP rule well into the 1950s throughout southern China) could emerge. The demagogues of this movement would gain their strength not from debates in the legislature but from "street politics." Some might resort to violence. Poor farmers seeking immediate salves for their plights might make use of new freedoms to storm the national parliament.

As mentioned, the very notion of dynastic change—the "broken mandate" or *geming*—is a cultural legacy that will fuel populism. Having overthrown the CCP, society may feel a heavenly righteousness that justifies any and all actions, democratic or not. Populist activity might also draw on the "mass movement" politics of the PRC era. While state-directed mass politics had been significantly weakened in the reform period, this era had seen the rise of spontaneous mass politics, as evidenced in the growing incidence of entire villages or religious sects that marched on government offices. More salient would be the degree of popular mobilization which preceded the democratic breakthrough. The more that popular mobilization was present in the transition, the greater would be the threat to normal representative democracy, with all the instability and impairment of democratic processes implied.[56]

The threat of populism is usually larger in countries that have experienced an elite-led transition, as we predict for China. Countries like Brazil, South Korea and Taiwan, where authoritarian leaders headed off growing popular movements by initiating change, typically faced an anti-establishment movement that felt "deprived" of a real revolution. In all three cases, the anti-establishment parties finally won the presidency around the turn of the century, topping successful efforts to keep populist pressures within the political system.

A key factor in mitigating this threat in China will be the degree to which the new government can gain legitimacy. It will also depend on the inclusiveness of the new government, something that bears on coalition-building in the first election. As with Brazil's rubber tappers or Mexico's urban poor, China will have to ensure that its dispossessed—the industrial workers of the northeast or the farmers of Sichuan—feel their interests are being heard inside the distant Beijing parliament.

Another society-centered challenge will be illiberalism. This may result from an undemocratic tyranny of majority rule or a tyranny of unelected top judges. Instances such as the passing of laws in newly democratic Ukraine, Estonia and Latvia to deny rights to ethnic Russians or the regular use of courts in Singapore and Malaysia to silence the media and purge political opponents are a reminder of how democratic institutions can be misused for illegitimate purposes.

Unlike the threat of authoritarianism, the threat of illiberalism reflects more deeply the strength of undemocratic norms in society at large—a fact that allows undemocratic leaders to "go through the motions" of democracy, as Hitler did in forcing parliament to grant him emergency powers. In some cases, leaders may even be forced by their electorate to act undemocratically. Indonesia's post-Suharto government refused to legalize the Indonesian Communist Party, banned in 1966, and allowed police to arrest people selling Karl Marx t-shirts, because of strong anti-communist sentiments in the country.

As we saw in the last section, illiberal beliefs and norms continued to be widespread in China's society in the late PRC era. The vast popular indifference, even support, for the government's brutal crackdown on the 100,000-member Falun Gong religious group beginning in 1999 was one example. Another was Beijing's racist exclusion of 5,000 non-Chinese, mainly South Asian, lifelong residents of Hong Kong from holding Hong Kong passports after 1997, a move that made them stateless yet attracted little concern even among Hong Kong's Chinese. To a certain extent this reflected the impact of living under dictatorship, where society is polarized and taught that politics is a process of identifying, labeling, and purging "enemies." Yet no doubt it also reflected some degree of latent illiberal feeling in society, such as has survived, even revived, in the mature democracies of the West.

There are four areas where illiberalism would likely appear: group discrimination, social morals, nationalism, and criminal justice.

The abolition of the PRC's legalized discrimination against peasants, religious groups, and minorities might face opposition in society. Urbanites unhappy with seeing their cities flooded by migrants might urge their politicians to reimpose a ban on internal migration. Uighurs who wanted to send their children to religious schools might incite the opposition of "scientific" educationalists in Beijing. Villagers speaking an unintelligible patois in some remote part of the heartland could declare a cleansing of outsiders, just as residents of Hong Kong's New Territories tried to exclude women from inheritance rights after 1997. The 10 percent of the country that is not Han Chinese and the 30 percent that does not speak Mandarin Chinese could face exclusion from public office under new laws passed by ultranationalists intent on "purifying" the culture.

Such group discrimination would strike at the heart of rights since it involves a systematic rather than just sporadic inequality. Averting it will require a national government and active civil society that exposes instances of discrimination and offers means of recourse—like ombudsmen, rights commissions, and legal mechanisms.

Closely related is the threat of attempts to impose a sort of Singaporean-style conservative moral order. Fukuyama describes a universal impulse in democracies for a return to an "older, purer set of values" as liberalism continues to generate and encourage a pluralism that many find jarring.[57] Iran's fledgling democracy was overthrown in 1979 by radical Muslims demanding a return to veils, prohibition, and religious rule. In China, conservatives could appear to demand continued bans on homosexuality and rock concerts. Others might hearken back to Mao's day of women in dowdy outfits and teenage partying limited to ballroom dance. One thinker, who is considered a liberal in China, asserts that China "cannot adopt the Western concept that 'anything not forbidden by law is the right of individuals' because this would destroy our concept of rule of law and social morals." He points to examples such as doctors who smoke and female university students who earn money as karaoke hostesses as instances of behavior that would be unacceptable even in a democratic China. His solution: impose "moral sanctions" and "social sanctions" as well as "administrative measures" and "disciplinary measures" on those whose behavior is considered "irregular" (bu guifan).[58]

As for nationalism, as we saw the contention between rival liberal and illiberal notions was growing in the late PRC era. Illiberal nationalism, such as that which encouraged racial slurs against Japanese or which applauded the terrorist attacks on the United States in 2001, was widespread, if not dominant. The emergent liberal nationalism would now be bolstered, as elsewhere, by pride in the values, institutions, and practice of public life in China seen as embodying shared notions of justice.[59] It will be a testing time for whether this new nationalism, whose emergence we traced, can grow strong enough to withstand its ugly counterpart. As one Western scholar noted: "Constitution-making alone will be a weak reed against hurricane-force antidemocratic gales" unless key players in government can draw upon "a deeply rooted popular democratic nationalism."[60]

Criminal justice is the other area where democratic norms will face illiberal pressures. Crime has risen to epic proportions in many newly democratizing states, notably South Africa and Russia. The end of the authoritarian state may open the way to a rise in violent and organized crime, even if democracy promises to address the fundamental causes of crime in a way that dictatorship could not. Certainly, it is likely that the social consensus in China will remain inclined toward a widespread use of the death penalty: China's

15,000 executions per year in the four years 1997 to 2001, accounting for 97 percent of the world total, were heralded in the country as a sign of success.[61] But for the first time there will be a real public debate on the value of capital punishment and more space for domestic opponents to air their views. Media exposés of unjustly convicted prisoners will introduce doubts into society. The illiberal desire for vengeance will be moderated by the growing democratic demands for due process and fair punishment. Even by the late PRC era, there was a growing awareness of the legal and social costs of draconian criminal justice, and a growing legal consensus that executions should be reduced.[62]

The battle against illiberalism in China will of course be the first step in an endless battle against illiberalism fought in every democracy, as the U.S. civil rights movement of the 1960s or the global debate on the use of the death penalty today reminds us. It will determine how quickly the country can move from the "starting blocks" of simple electoral democracy into the long, indeed endless, run to build a truly liberal democracy. Institutions ensuring that minority views are represented in elected bodies and independent courts that uphold fundamental rights will be critical bulwarks against illiberalism. So too will that part of civil society that supports democratic norms. Containing those impulses will require not only the commitment of government leaders but more widely of society as a whole.

As with the authoritarian threat to political rights, observers will need to be sensitive to the fact that China's interpretation of fundamental rights may differ in some respects from that of other democracies. The debate on where to draw the line is a normal and constant part of every democracy. Just as the limits on rights vary between Japan and Thailand, or between France and the United States, so too China will find its own way, probably leaning toward a more restrictive exercise of rights. If it chooses to pass laws against religious cults that manifestly threaten the safety of children, as France has done, that need not be a sign of a triumphant illiberalism.

In any case, we might be surprised to find that illiberalism was less powerful in China than many imagined. Taiwanese intellectual Bo Yang coined the phrase "The Ugly Chinaman," in the 1960s with his piercing critique of Chinese society as deeply illiberal. Yet that very society he critiqued, Taiwan, has changed immeasurably in that short time, becoming one of the first liberal Chinese societies, something once thought to be an oxymoron. Likewise, many believed that Serbs were deeply illiberal until they suddenly overthrew their elected tyrant Slobodan Milosevic in 2000 and sent him to the UN war crimes tribunal in the Hague. Other Eastern European countries that went through similar illiberal phases, like Bulgaria, Romania, and Slovakia, also veered toward the norms of political (though not necessarily social) liberalism eventually. Confucian fragments South Korea and Japan have proved how the liberal political project can work even alongside specific cultural values like consensus and nationalism, even emperor worship. King-worship in Thailand backed by draconian *lèse majesté* laws has given way to king-worship based on social voluntarism and genuine national pride.

In China too, illiberalism will be contained by the powerful influence of free and open public debate. The mullahs of "older, purer" values will face new challenges from the reason and humanity of democracy. China's political identity will be in full play, and with everything to play for.

Toward Consolidation

In the battle to consolidate democracy against all manner of undemocratic gales, society and state alike will be engaged in a torrid process of learning. There is a great scholarly debate about whether the classroom progress of society or the state is more critical to consolidation. The consensus seems to be that while the changing behavior of politicians is "preeminent," it cannot be isolated from the "stimulus and support" provided by society.[63]

This of course mirrors the relationship during the transition stage, where the actions of political elites, however decisive, are critically informed by the behavior of society. In China's case, the behavior of state actors will be even more important given the elite-led transition. The commitment of political elites, the bureaucracy, political parties, the coercive apparatus, and the judiciary to uphold democracy irrespective of any pressures from society will make or break the consolidation.[64] Democracy failed in China in the Republican era because of frequent departures from constitutional norms and resort to violence by elites. Many of those same tendencies will remain next time around. Yet China's elites will be further along the road to democratic beliefs than other countries — Bulgaria, Chile, and Indonesia come to mind — where democracy eventually triumphed. Moreover, if civic groups perceive backsliding or democratic deterioration, they can mobilize again, through newspaper columns, marches, petitions, and legal actions.

This learning of a constitutional culture is an important underlying element in the success of new democracies and has been widely studied as a result. It comes about as leaders, groups, and individuals — who in their personal lives might espouse antidemocratic doctrines — learn to espouse democratic ones in public life.[65]

Some learning will occur through explicit civic education. One can expect in China that supporters of democracy will stimulate wide-ranging discussions and debates on the normative values that underpin every successful democracy. Quasi-government organizations that promote public consciousness, like the PRC-era China Society for the Study of Human Rights, set up in 1993, or Hong Kong's quasi-government Committee on the Promotion of Civic Education, will become more prominent.

The expansion of civil society will also provide an important formal arena for democratic learning. Civil society is critical in democracy because it keeps the state within the agreed confines of action. A faltering or divided state can be bolstered by civic groups. An overreaching or illiberal one can be chastened. It is the invisible fiber that ensures liberty. One well-known political reformer in China with much experience in community-level democracy imagines a day when China will be characterized by the ideal situation of "a strong state and a strong society."[66]

Most of the learning, however, will be implicit. It will take place endogenously, through the very political struggles that threaten democracy. Through the fires of conflict, democracy will produce democrats who uphold the ideal of tolerance, a belief in pluralism, a suspicion of authority, and a deep-seated pragmatism. The long struggle to bring about political change will already have created some of these values—recalling that the Cultural Revolution bestirred modern Chinese liberalism. Now they will germinate at a faster pace.

The emergence of an elite commitment to democracy may seem irrational because elites in a fledgling democracy might have better chances for survival in the chaos of transition by acting outside the rules of the game, grabbing for power, and purging rivals. But the Third Wave democracies have shown that such a commitment can be rational for a variety of reasons.

Most basic, the new political elites may genuinely value democracy and the need to administer the new system impartially and consistently. In China the growth of beliefs in justice, political liberalism, and freedom among elites will powerfully help this cause. The mere belief in the possibility of a constitutional democracy among political elites can be one of the most powerful factors in making it a success.[67] One group of scholars found that worldwide such a genuine commitment was more likely in countries "where memories of past absolutisms convince key political actors that the dispersal of political power is a public good that should be institutionalized if possible."[68]

If so, then China, with its memories of emperors, Republican warlords, and Mao—not to mention his successors—will benefit, echoing one of the legacies mentioned earlier. The constant ferments of democratic discourse in China since the fall of the Qing—in the Republican era, the early PRC years, the "humanist" project days of CCP chief Hu Yaobang in the 1980s, and the reform faction of the CCP in the 1990s—reflects this emergence. By the turn of the century, many political elites had begun to widely regard the notion of democracy as an end of itself, and one that could possibly flourish in China.[69] As one official scholar wrote in a book published in 1998: "Even a strong state must not impede on personal freedoms."[70] The hope that China might create a democracy which surpasses those in the West—the so-called "surpass sentiment" (*chaoyue qingxu*)—would bolster this commitment.

Second, international pressures may help consolidation just as it helped transition. In Russia the vision of the "return to Europe" was a powerful influence shaping the behavior of politicians. In China, the vision of becoming the predominant power of Asia through cooperation with mostly democratic Southeast Asia, South Asia, and East Asia might do the same. So might a desire to attract Taiwan into closer union.

Third, it may become more and more electorally wise to be seen as a party or a politician who is a defender of democracy. Even if society is largely antidemocratic at first, typically one part of the electorate is critically concerned with protecting democracy and votes accordingly. Unlike other voters, who may vote for a variety of candidates, the pro-democracy voters choose the most democratic candidate.

One irony of this process is that the more deadlocked are political forces, the more quickly democratic norms may become entrenched. India, with its impossible diversity, is proof of this. China's huge potential struggles over interests, considered in the next chapter, may be a blessing in disguise. Successive elections will tend to bring into power politicians who are more and more committed to democratic norms because they find that this is electorally appealing under conditions of dire conflict. While China may have come up short on all the factors needed for an immediately functioning democracy in the late PRC era, every passing year would see that change. The numbers on its scorecard will shoot up quickly as learning progresses.

Of course, the lessons may be learned at some cost. Historically, the struggle for rights has led to a great deal of bloodshed in democracies, not to mention much political, social and economic disruption. Americans fought a civil war to end slavery, while in Asia the early years of democracy in South Korea, the Philippines, Cambodia, and Indonesia were accompanied by years of sporadic violence.

No less than democratic transition, velvet political change is rare when it comes to democratic consolidation. In the process of learning to be democratic, a society struggles, often violently, to overturn the legacy of authoritarianism. As with the violence and unrest of transition, every society will constantly evaluate whether it is a price worth paying. Time and again they have decided that it is. When Russian president Boris Yeltsin summoned a battalion of tanks to end an armed uprising by filibustering anti-reform parliamentarians in October 1993, some warned of the costs. In the ensuing battle, more than 300 civilians and soldiers were killed. Yet Yeltsin won widespread popular backing for his actions and there were no reports of military defections to the side of the parliament. Seen in the broader light of democratic consolidations, and in light of Russia's subsequent improving democracy, this may be one example of the "acceptable" costs of consolidation.

The same goes for China. Again and again commentators have warned that the struggle for rights in China will be a "protracted and difficult process."[71] We can probably go further and assert that there will be much violence and many deaths. This is not inevitable, but it is likely. If paralysis, populism, authoritarianism or illiberalism threaten the new democracy, pro-democracy forces will need to reemerge to repulse that threat, and violence may ensue. Foreign commentators might wring their hands about "the situation in China," but if the alternative is a steady collapse of democracy and a return to dictatorship then the people in China might find the struggle worthwhile.

With the rapid spread of democratic institutions at the end of the twentieth century, learned commentators in the West began to denigrate those institutions for creating formal elections but not real freedoms.[72] Often, they accurately described the pain of democratic transitions. But in blaming that pain on democracy, rather than the accumulated ills of dictatorship, and in prescribing a return to dictatorship, they were sorely out of touch with the very people whose interests they claimed to speak for. The problems of a return to dictatorship are almost always worse than those of muddling through with imperfect democracy. Moreover, this is a choice to be made by the peoples concerned. South Africans, despite their soaring crime, AIDS crisis, and economic slide, have no desire to return to apartheid, or any other form of dictatorship for that matter.

Survey evidence shows that people will rise up to fight for a new democracy if they believe that it is a truly democratic system. Empirically, people tend to believe this more when the new system has produced economic as well as political benefits, perhaps reflecting the coincidence of political and economic success. If regionalism, corruption, and factionalism plagued China's political system before, then perceptions that these things are being reduced will help. Since injustice, inequality, unfairness, and repression of basic rights was common before, if people experience improvements in these areas, they will support the new democracy more.[73] This is a reminder that it is the relative, not absolute, efficacy of the new government that will matter.

Even if the new democracy is plagued by infighting among parties, stalled legislation, ethnic insurgencies, street protests, and sex scandals, the mere recognition that this is a result of democracy may help to undergird an "irrational pride" that ensures legitimacy. As one scholar puts it: "Culturally, democracy remains a valued goal."[74]

This explains one of the great paradoxes of democratic consolidation—that disillusion with the results may be accompanied by support for the system. An explosion of open griping about political leaders may be one of the healthiest signs that people have accepted that democracy is a solution to tyranny but not much else. The beginning of realistic expectations and a sense of empowerment to criticize and even oust shoddy democratic leaders is the beginning of democracy's triumph.

Thus society may simply say that whatever the costs and whatever the instrumental failures, democracy is a good thing merely because it is democracy. As the years pass and China gains world praise for staying the course, its people, as elsewhere, will view their construction of democracy as a great achievement of their civilization, especially given that it was done in the face of a difficult legacy. This will help to make the system more stable as people develop pride in democracy, a pride that transcends instrumental outcomes. To quote one Chinese democrat: "People will have to understand that many problems cannot be solved simply with democracy. Rather it is to ensure that a bad government cannot stay in office, so that its destructive effects do not spread to every area, so that when people realize the government is bad they do not have to wage a war, coup, or violence to exercise their democratic rights and replace a government, but just have to cast their ballots."[75]

Typically, as in Eastern Europe, it takes a decade or more for a democracy to be consolidated. In Asia, democracies in the Philippines, Indonesia, and Cambodia took more than a decade to settle down. In Latin America, democracy remains unconsolidated in countries that made the transition to democracy in the immediate post-World War II era like Venezuela, Argentina, and Peru. When will the people of China be able to breathe a collective sigh of relief and say that their democracy is consolidated?

Some analysts define consolidation as an uninterrupted change of government after the first election. That would make the opposition victory in Taiwan's presidential election of 2000 the signpost of democracy's triumph there. Yet this may be an overly stringent criterion in new democracies with a dominant party. In India, Mexico, and Japan, for example, ruling parties continued to hold office long after democracy was visibly consolidated. By the same token, frequent changes of government in Latin America belied still-unconsolidated democracies. Since China's democratization is likely to be elite-led and therefore accompanied by the rise of a continuist, or hegemonic party, the change of government criterion would also be less useful. Democracy may be entrenched even if the opposition struggles to win seats.

Other measures of consolidation may be more instructive. One scholar looks for a polity in which constitutional norms are followed irrespective of results, all political interests are properly represented, all actors behave within the political system, and society itself takes an active role in upholding the system.[76] Another scholar says consolidation occurs when 70 percent of the public consistently says they prefer democracy to any other form of government and when no more than 15 percent say they prefer dictatorship.[77] On both these definitions, consolidation represents a fundamental shift in the political culture of authoritarianism. For the first time, the public is truly engaged and included within the political system, while the state and parliament are regulated by constitutional norms that do not brook violation.

Of course, consolidation need not involve a fully tolerant, inclusive, orderly, and public-minded polity. Such a utopia has never been achieved anywhere, even in "core democracies" like Britain and the United States, where these things reign only uneasily over opposing tendencies. In China, as was the case in Russia, democracy will likely achieve consolidation despite the continued presence of notable antidemocratic elements in state and society alike. The absence of the high-minded civic culture and law-abiding political traditions that some Western scholars see as critical to democracy's survival will no more condemn China to democratic failure than it did Russia — or the United States.

Consolidation does not require that everyone be democratic or liberal in their personal views, but only an agreed public way of doing things. The persistence of antidemocratic views and behavior in society need not be fatal. In the metric above, as much as 15 percent of the population may still be advocates of a return to dictatorship and another 15 percent advocates of other nondemocratic solutions. For better or for worse, many in society will see democracy as a solution to crisis and a means to instrumental ends — national unity, social stability, or economic growth. Yet as long as political elites and state administrators cling to the importance of the democratic vision, democracy will survive.

Beyond consolidation lies the vast realm of democratic deepening, where a country takes up fundamental issues like the equal value of political freedoms and the achievement of social and economic justice. The challenge moves from building a functioning democracy to building a perfect one. Having confronted the problems of entrenching democratic norms, a country now confronts the challenge of realizing democratic ideals. That road is a never-ending one of course. In the case of China, it is bound to be a centuries-long work in progress.

Political Life

What will democracy in China look like? While certain fundamental values and institutions are universal, democracy also allows for considerable variation in the details. Democracy is sure to be very "Chinese," just as it is strongly redolent of the local culture of every country where it operates. China can and must have its own values to fill in the blank spaces of democratic practice. "The sheer recognition that China's democracy may not be our democracy is a brave starting point," says one Taiwanese scholar.[78]

As with institutional design, the question can be seen broadly in terms of continuity and change. Many scholars argue that political culture in the PRC was more culturally than politically determined.[79] If so, then the aversion to open conflict among competing political parties, the spectacles of mass mobilization for political events, and the corporatist-looking interest groups might remain. But evidence elsewhere suggests that political culture in authoritarian regimes is heavily politically determined. As the Taiwan example has shown, Chinese cultures prove themselves every bit as keen to embrace open, pluralistic, contentious, and individual-focussed politics as other cultures when given the chance.

Take the issue of language. As mentioned, a universal trait of democratic transitions is that the language of politics shifts from the stylized and elitist language of dictators to the vernacular and populist language of the people. In Taiwan, the local Fukkienese dialect gradually took over from the imposed Mandarin of the Nationalist Party. In Mexico, the first non-PRI president began using local Mexican Spanish rather than the elitist European brand of his predecessors. In former French colonies, the local creole has replaced European French. India, going through a democratic deepening under the Hindu nationalist BJP party after years of Congress Party rule, has had ministers who speak neither English nor Hindi.

For China, this "universal" phenomenon will be manifest in a very "Chinese" new political discourse. Local dialects, which are spoken by 30 percent of the population, will flourish in public life for the first time. Cantonese will get its rightful due in the national polity, along with the distinct dialects associated with Fujian, Shanghai, Jiangxi, and Hunan. Provincial leaders will speak in their own local twangs. Foreign scholars of China will complain long and loud about having to hire translators because of the limits of their assiduously practiced court Mandarin, as they did in Taiwan. Meanwhile, a populist discourse will emerge as politicians personalize politics more and more. Speeches will be cued to prompt applause, not note-taking.

The "Chineseness" of China's democracy will also be seen in the nature and behavior of political parties, something we alluded to in the first election above. After a decade of volatility, the huge splintering of parties and interests in the initial period typically settles down as the struggle for rights is settled and the struggle for interests creates broadly united groups of several major points of view. The extent of this winnowing of parties depends on many factors. As a general statement, the more that the transition was driven by economic crisis and popular mobilization, the more fractured will be the polity and the longer it will take to settle down.[80] In Poland, for example, where crisis and mobilization were high, the number of parties in the legislature began at 29 in the 1991 elections, but fell to just six by 2001, when the largest party, the Democratic Left Alliance, held 47 percent of all seats, almost a plurality. In China, given an elite-led transformation, we can predict that a fairly bounded period of winnowing will take place. The broadly left, right, and center views that were already apparent in the late PRC era will coalesce around one or two national parties, perhaps holding alliances with provincial and local parties (of which there will be many).

Given the nature of the transition, China's party system is likely to be an elite-dominated rather than populist system at first. The elites in charge of parties will channel and control popular pressures, as in Thailand or Japan, rather than being controlled by them. This can be stable as long as elites in charge of parties satisfy popular pressures. When they fail to, a period of upheaval can lead to the rise of popular-dominated parties which eventually win power, as occurred in India and Taiwan in the 1990s.

Some aspects of China's collective and corporatist culture will surely color the practice of democracy. While claims of a uniquely collectivist nature of Chinese society are usually either overblown, ill-defined, or simply an excuse for dictatorship, this does not mean that a collective spirit will not remain, or even grow stronger and become a nurturing force. Japan's single ruling party and extensive social consensus-building, for example, accords with that society's collective streak. South Korea and France with their powerful trade unions are another example. Collectivist institutions, voluntarily formed, are perfectly at home in a democracy.

China's political culture since the late Qing has been suffused with a normative goal of creating a "great harmony" (datong) in the public sphere, wherein a civic-minded community is ruled benevolently by a virtuous leadership. Several Chinese scholars talk of wanting to avoid the confrontational and boisterous politics of countries like Taiwan or Britain and forge a pattern of "democratic harmony" (*minzhu hexie*) or "harmonious cooperation and consultative discussion" (*hexie hezuo, xieshang taolun*).[81] This distaste for open disagreement has its roots in the Chinese notions of not having public disagreements in which one or both parties would lose face and thus social standing. The idea of "glossing over problems to settle people's hearts" (*xishi ningren*) was historically rooted and later encouraged by the Leninist demands of democratic centralism of the PRC. It would certainly color political life in a democratic China, especially as the normal disruptions of democracy are played out.

There is nothing wrong with this. Indeed it is admirable, as long as it is not an excuse to infringe on rights or repress interests. Many democracies function without the slugfests of the Taiwan legislature or the puerile name-calling of the British-style parliaments. Still, the harmonious impulse may prove less than ironclad in China, with its ethnic and geographic diversity and the damage done to the collective spirit and deference to authority by communist upheavals like the Cultural Revolution. One would not like to see a Hui and a Hakka duking it out in the national parliament, but a more unvarnished politics is likely. While the frequent backstabbing and infighting of the overseas Chinese dissident community was to some extent conditioned by its exiled and excluded status, it may provide some preview of the realities of life in a democratic China.

One persistent feature of politics may be *guanxi*—the existence of a "hidden structure" of personal relationships that determines critical policy outcomes. This was not just a result of the Leninist polity but also a reflection of cultural facets of etiquette, morality, and emotion in China.[82] If so, then it will not die with the PRC. *Guanxi* politics and political corruption, so pervasive in Taiwan and in local elections in China, would remain a perennial problem in political life. This may reflect cultural as well as political legacies where democracy is seen as a simple exchange of favors ("your seafood banquet for my vote"). Yet the openness of democracy typically brings this problem under control.

Politics may also come to have strong overtones of traditional Chinese morality drama—as it has in Japan, South Korea, and Taiwan. A deep infusion of morality can be a positive influence in politics as long as it does not override rights. Appeals to behavior based on individual moral doctrines cannot be made mandatory, but they can and should play a role.[83]

Some will decry the revival of "feudal culture" evident in the reinfusion of traditional morality and the persistence of *guanxi* in politics. But on a normative basis, the people's freedom to choose and form their own identities is a good thing. We may not like the way democracy is practiced in China any more than we like the way it is practiced in Japan or India. But it will be incumbent on the world to respect China's democratic course provided it does not clash with universal democratic norms.

One key change for China's democratic politicians will be that they spend far less time than their predecessors in formalistic and pompous activities — meeting foreign businessmen, traveling abroad, presiding over ribbon-cutting ceremonies — and a lot more on the ground, especially in the villages, keeping their popularity high. This was always a key difference between leaders in India and China. The former spent far less time on publicity-making overseas travel and far more time touring the rural heartland and in off-camera policy-making. It was inconceivable that a CCP leader would make a *padyatra*, a foot journey through the villages to garner electoral support, as in India. When they darkened the doorstep of rural areas at all, it was in convoys of black Mercedes headed by a phalanx of sirening police cars. That would now change as China's leaders "discovered" their own heartland.

Another change in political culture may be the "depoliticization" of politics. After the consolidation period, economic and social issues will rise to the forefront of public life and issues of ideology, law, Party machinations, and constitutionalism will recede. Like all totalitarian societies, China was over-politicized, and by the late reform era there were signs of a strong anti-political undercurrent where people did not want to hear about politics because it gave them a "headache."[84] That means that political participation — the extent to which China's people become engaged in democracy — is hard to predict. Election turnouts may be high but out-of-election participation may be low. Typically, new democracies see a high turnout for the first election and then the population becomes "demobilized" as the thrill of transition gives way to the drudgery of consolidation.

One heartening new aspect of political participation will almost certainly be the rise of women. The PRC lagged badly on this issue, reflecting a general fact that authoritarian regimes — with their machismo, chauvinism, militarism, and intolerance — are usually no place for women. The highest ranking women in communist China, with the late exception of Wu Yi, elected to the Politburo in 2002, were always the wives or mistresses of senior CCP leaders. By contrast, democracy brings many more women to prominence not only because of the enfranchisement of women but also because women are more aligned to its political culture of tolerance, compromise, and empathy. Women usually play a prominent role in the overthrow of authoritarian regimes and in their subsequent consolidation.[85] In China, the roles of Tiananmen mother Ding Zilin, Tiananmen protest leader Chai Ling, environmental and political critic Dai Qing, Taiwan vice president Annette Lu, and Hong Kong democratic legislator Emily Lau remind us of this.

As in so many respects, democracy will bring out the latent diversity of a country long represented by Han males schooled in a particular northern plains culture. That political culture is bound to change dramatically. Many of the seemingly "deep-rooted" features of China's politics that orientalist foreign scholars harped upon will appear in retrospect to have been nothing more than the defile of dictatorship.

Local Politics and Hong Kong

Enhanced political freedoms and formal political devolution will give new prominence to provincial and local-level politics. For the first time, politics at the local level will assume the importance that it was long denied by a centralized and undemocratic state. The various identities and particular political cultures of each province and subprovincial region will emerge from a long sleep. Provincial political cultures developed over centuries will spring back to life.

The resulting China will bear some resemblance to the early Republican era, when local powerholders held sway. When people talk about "what's going on in China" they may well be referring to a constitutional crisis or an insurgent poor people's movement in a province rather than to the comparatively settled affairs of Beijing. "This loosely amalgamated China will be functional in many respects, but it will not be neat," notes one Western scholar.[86]

The struggle for rights within each province will loom no less large than at the national level. A consolidated national polity may mask regional enclaves of unconsolidated democracy. Some places will gain a reputation for being more liberal and democratic, while others will be rued as havens of intolerance. In India, West Bengal and Kerala are the liberal leaders, while in the United States, California and Vermont are ahead. In China, we might expect Guangdong and Fujian to emerge as pioneers of the new democratic politics. Meanwhile, more politically conservative places like Henan and Shaanxi may retain stronger vestiges of authoritarianism. Some places, like Shanghai, will be clean orderly cities while others, perhaps Guangxi, will be near-gangster kingdoms. Middle-of-the-road places like Shandong, Sichuan, Hunan, and Jiangxi will waver between traditional and reformist, collective and individual personalities.[87]

Overall, just as some provinces "blazed a trail" with the economic reforms and political liberalization of the post-Mao era, so too some places will lead the nation in creating a stable democratic polity. Beijing may recede in the political life of the nation, becoming merely the arbiter of the competing notions of the just polity that will emerge from powerful centers like Shanghai and Sichuan.

One part of political life that may change very little is village politics. Yet even here, despite being democratic to some degree, national-level democracy will exert influences. Candidates will ally themselves more closely with national issues and parties rather than maintain strictly parochial profiles. Real mavericks and plain crackpots, kept out of power in the past by matronly Party committees, will gain power in villages. China will be awash with stories of the village chief in some distant remote area who was elected with bizarre promises, recalling the mayoral candidate in post-Soviet Vladivostok who claimed he was the son of God.

The new prominence of local politics will be most marked in Hong Kong. Former Party patriarch Deng Xiaoping, in a typically self-serving warning, said that the fall of the CCP in China would see "the end of prosperity and stability for Hong Kong."[88] Yet from every possible angle, the opposite seems to be true. Hong Kong has much to gain and little to lose from democracy in China. (This also applies to the half a million people living in the nearby gambling enclave of Macau.)

Since Hong Kong is undisputed sovereign Chinese territory, there would be no question of secession; indeed support for an independent Hong Kong was weak even under British rule. At the same time, the Joint Declaration between Britain and China that formed the basis of Hong Kong's return to Chinese rule in 1997 was an international treaty lodged with the United Nations. Such treaties continue to have force when regimes change, and there is no reason to expect that a democratic government in China would want to renege.

But a democratization in China would create an immediate demand for full democratization in Hong Kong and election of the chief executive. Hong Kong is a virtually self-governing city-state which has been unable to achieve full democracy and whose freedoms and rule of law were constantly being challenged as a result of dictatorship in China, its sovereign after 1997. It is also a city overendowed with the ingredients for a successful democracy—a large well-educated middle class, a tolerant society, successful local elections, strong legal system, a robust free press, and more. Giving it full democracy—a promise Beijing made in the Basic Law—would make it better run and protected, would eliminate a source of criticism of China, and bolster a key entrepôt for Asia's economy. Autonomy would entail a fully elected legislature and chief executive to hold the "separate system" powers promised under the Basic Law.

Fortunately, one might expect that the new government in Beijing will look favorably on such demands. Still, it may well be that the development of democracy may proceed faster in places like Guangzhou and Shanghai, where a people long denied rights embrace them with greater vigor, than in Hong Kong, where the post-1997 period revealed a modest political apathy bred by the comforts of colonial rule.

Assuming that a new federalism comes into force in China as a result of democratization, Hong Kong will also fit more easily into the Chinese state. As a "special administrative region," in the unitary state, its relations with Beijing were troubled and confusing because of the lack of an institutional structure to handle central-local relations. With a new political and judicial apparatus able to manage and mediate central-local relations in a more regular and predictable way, Hong Kong will find that its relations with Beijing are less fraught. The forces of the PLA stationed in Hong Kong and Macau as an assertion of sovereignty might be withdrawn as a token of good will.

Hong Kong's economy would benefit far more from the spinoffs of a successful democratic transition in China than it would lose as a place with special status within a dictatorial state. It would be better off as an average city in a dynamic country than as a glittering exception on a dismal landscape. Certainly, as happened in the Great Leap Famine and the Cultural Revolution, there would be a danger of new immigrant influx if the transition in China goes wrong. But assuming it does not, there is little to fear. Indeed, the continued legal migration of people from China into Hong Kong—roughly 200 per day—could slow. As in the 1930s to 1950s, when Guangzhou and Hong Kong were seen as equally inviting—indeed Guangzhou was long thought superior—the creation of a normal polity in China would reduce the incentives to migrate to Hong Kong. This would help to ease intense population pressures in the territory, which had a population of seven million by 2002.

It may take decades before Shanghai or Guangzhou can match Hong Kong as a center of business services for Asia. But in other respects—quality of life, political dynamism, cultural vibrancy—the coming of democracy will narrow the gap quickly. Most important, everyone will be better off.

9

Refurbishing Economic and Social Life

The Struggle for Interests

What are the political implications of the PRC's mind-numbing legacy of social and economic injustice? And how will the political system mediate the claims of a free society in order to establish a new framework for economic and social life?

These are the basic questions of political economy, the interplay between the political system and socioeconomic conditions. If the "struggle for rights" of the last chapter revolved chiefly around the political system, the "struggle for interests" takes us deeply into a newly invigorated social and economic world.

As mentioned, these twin struggles are closely intertwined. Battles over social and economic justice both affect and are affected by battles over democratic norms. In China, a return to authoritarian-style rule could mean that peasants fail to win their share of welfare benefits. Conversely, the success of a party representing the populous rural heartland could create a majority government that is prone to override democratic norms.

In the early years of the new democracy, it is almost certain that issues of economic and social justice will loom large. No less that the struggle to embed democratic norms, the struggle to agree on a fair economic and social structure will be immense. For not only did the PRC leave China with severe problems of economic and social injustice—everything from underinvestment in remote and rural areas to the state's reneging on pension promises—but its intellectual and policy communities also heavily underinvested in these issues.

One can imagine sporadic outbursts over such issues in the aftermath of the first election: angry workers surrounding the luxury villas of former cadres who enriched themselves by skimming off state assets; foreign investors who built their factories on land stolen from villages fleeing in panic; the governor of Shandong province at the mouth of the Yellow River demanding an end to excessive upstream irrigation. Some business leaders, as one Party exile wrote, "will surely say that they felt safer in the old China than in the one promoting freedom and democracy."[1]

Even Chinese liberals express a profound disquiet at the socio-economic implications of democracy. As one writes: "To garner votes from the peasants, political candidates would promise things like an end to family planning and the privatization of land. They would promise fast economic growth no matter the environmental costs. This short-termism would have profound consequences. It would speed China's slide into oblivion."[2] Even with politicians behaving responsibly, the fragile new state may simply be unable to manage the country effectively. As we saw, state fiscal capacity was weak by the late PRC era, while regulatory powers were only slowly catching up with a newly-liberated society. Lacking the coercive powers of the communist regime, many worry, the new democracy may simply lose control. As one foreign scholar wrote: "Instability would reduce the government's ability to control proliferation, attack pollution, sustain economic growth, fight transnational crime, slow the spread of HIV/AIDS, and control the movement of people across the country's borders."[3]

As mentioned, evidence points to the opposite conclusion, that democracy makes population control, environmental protection, sustainable growth, and much else more not less amenable to effective governance. That said, there will no doubt be short-term costs of transition as the new polity finds its feet. As with the disorder in the political realm, this may be the necessary and normatively acceptable cost of moving toward a more just system.

If the costs are high, much of the blame will lie with the CCP's failure to choose a course that combined political and economic liberalization, such as ensured a smooth transition in Taiwan and South Korea. A democratic transition in China in the 1980s might have reduced the overall costs of transition. Instead, the country may face a path more like those faced in Latin America, the Philippines, and Indonesia, where new democracies had to overcome a legacy of extreme social and economic unfairness and inequality. Likewise, these long-term structural problems will be exacerbated by the economic crisis that precedes the democratic transition. The ghost of reform critics like economist He Qinglian will brood darkly over the newly democratic China. As one Chinese liberal predicts: "People will discover that democracy has not made their living standards better. Inflation will not be controlled, corruption will remain pervasive and the constant bickering in the legislature will give people a headache. . . . Government after government will fall from power in trying to deal with all the issues. People will realize that even though democracy has come to China, many problems have not been resolved." Or to quote another: "If democratization comes soon there will be no political reconciliation, but great popular anger and determination to reverse economic injustices. Then the outcome could be like [revolutionary] Russia all over again — the [rise of conservative politicians] producing a new Bolshevik revolution, leading to a new despotism once again."[4]

While a bumpy economic and social transition may be the inevitable and even acceptable cost of China's belated democratization, that does not make it less disquieting. The economic and social performance of any new democracy — even if it appears in empirical evidence to take a back seat to performance in the political realm[5] — can provide a critical boost, or a critical blow, to a new democracy. People expect higher incomes, better education, improved health, and modern housing. Poor economic and social results may not be enough to sink democracy. But they can gravely slow the process of consolidation.

In addition, the *way* in which social and economic issues are tackled affects the consolidation. Politicians help consolidation when they pay particular attention to the losers of the pre-transition and transitional economic and social crisis, since these people are most likely to sabotage the new order. Policies created through consensus gain legitimacy and are easier to implement. Conversely, a continuation of the PRC's exclusive and stipulative policymaking would alienate many citizens.

Still, there is reason for optimism about the struggle for interests, perhaps more than about the struggle for rights. In general terms, Marx's prediction that social and economic disputes would tear asunder capitalist democracies turned out to be wrong for the simple reason that such differences are not absolute and can always be reconciled. If half the population wants to soak the rich and the other half wants to maintain the status quo, they can always split the difference with a modest tax increase.

China's polity had already begun to learn this lesson in the late PRC era. After a spirited six-month battle in 1999 over a new national fuel tax to replace locally collected highway tolls, for example, the NPC struck a compromise with rural-based opponents of the tax that provided reimbursements for farmers and for non-highway fuel users. As one provincial governor put it, reflecting the assimilation of values of compromise and consensus in some instances of policymaking: "As a mayor or governor, you need to seek the people's support and understanding [to carry out] reforms that involve changing old ideas and reconciling diverse interests. [You must] win over the majority of people's support for each reform before moving ahead."[6]

Another mitigating factor in China's case is that it had become a much wealthier country by the late PRC era, a middle-income country. Demands for a fair-share from the have-nots can be indulged by the haves without jeopardizing their livelihoods. Unlike in low-income countries, the struggle for interests will not be a battle for survival in China.

Third, many countries facing crisis have often drawn on their national-ism—another example of how nationalism helps democracy—to draw to-gether in times of crisis. Hungary and Poland were able to do this, creating consensus on difficult economic and social policies in tough times. China and its belief in national cohesiveness—*ningjuli*—could do likewise. The honeymoon provided by the breakthrough to democracy could allow the first government to make difficult decisions on reform and growth policies. Such "rapid reforms" can increase the efficacy of the new state, bolstering its legit-imacy. Since we are predicting an elite-led transition with the rise of a con-tinuist party, the less fractured polity may make it easier to implement positive changes in the economic and social sphere.

In all these respects, then, China's struggle for interests may be easier to manage than many gloomy soothsayers predict. The eruption of wealth in the reform era provided the foundations for managing diverse interests in a plu-ralistic setting that is integral to forging socioeconomic pacts. Extending those lessons to the population as a whole will be a difficult but by no means insurmountable task.

Growth and Development

China's economic performance under democracy will be a great testing ground for competing claims about whether democracy supports or impedes devel-opment. The debate is ages-old and depends not a little on abstracting from the constraints of history. But even for mere descriptive purposes, China's economic performance under democracy will be closely watched.

Empirical evidence is ambiguous about whether democracy makes coun-tries grow faster.[7] Some scholars (not just the CCP) argue that democracy lowers investments needed for long-term growth and makes strategic planning impossible because it weakens the state. Others turn this argument on its head and contend that only a democratic state invests in the basic needs for long-term growth and only with democratic legitimacy can a state be strong and stable.

Studies purporting to show the benefits of dictatorship typically deal with short time spans that ignore sustainability. Dictatorships often achieve growth in environmentally, socially, or politically unsustainable ways. To take the latter, such studies usually fail to construct alternative growth scenarios that consider whether growth would have continued at its previous pace under dictatorship if a deposed regime had used violent repression to prevent the coming of democracy.

Democratization might result in a short-term economic slump. But it usually results in more sustained growth over the long term. It not only helps end the unsustainable dimensions of economic growth under dictatorship, but also lays more sustainable foundations for future growth through investments in education, alleviation of poverty, equality, policy legitimacy, effective regulation, and rule of law. A general consensus is that while GDP growth may be faster in poor countries with dictatorships not sustained through violent suppression, equity and welfare suffer, so that investments in people and political stability, the key to long-term growth, also suffer. For middle- and high-income countries, democracy wins hands down.[8]

If institutional framework is as important to economic performance as modern economists believe, then democracy as a superior institution should make growth faster than it might have been in China. It will reduce transaction costs for entrepreneurs by providing a stable and predictable framework where they spend less time engaging in clientelism, illegality, and rent-seeking. Democracy should lessen, but will not eliminate, the diverse forms of malfeasance in the PRC economy—corruption, smuggling, fraud, counterfeiting, extortion, tax evasion, cronyism, and gangsterism. The Russian experience saw them rise almost to Chinese levels with the sudden onset of both economic and political freedoms. China itself will have a head start in turning back the tide.

While the marketization and globalization of China's economy had been largely completed or set in motion by the late PRC era, the coming of democracy would also add new sources of growth. The private sector, which already accounted for something like 50 percent of GDP, would rapidly push out of business remaining state enterprises and would corporatize the smallholders of the agricultural sector. On the demand side, domestic consumption would leap upwards once deregulation of the financial sector reduced excessive savings.[9]

Growth could also be bolstered by a successful resolution of the country's financial crisis—in which the bad debts and pension obligations of state firms ate a hole in the balance sheets of both state banks and the central government. A big reason this problem could never be resolved in the PRC was that the CCP lacked the legitimacy to find solutions through a democratic processes in which every party agreed to give up something. In the late PRC era, about 10 percent of the 30 to 40 million retired state government or enterprise staff were not being paid their pensions due to the financial crisis.

Democracy will allow elected leaders to sit down with all parties and hammer out a real solution that cannot be reneged upon. A national commission might be set up—as was done in many Eastern European countries—to create accords that fairly resolve the complex issues. For the first time, everyone with a stake in the issue—taxpayers, workers, foreign lenders, shareholders, and pensioners—could be represented. This will release banks from the burdens of bad debt and solve the central government's looming fiscal crisis.

The state's fiscal health will also depend on an increase in official lending to China during the transition. This may be critical not only to help pay for the resolution to the bad debts but also because the new government may be politically committed to an expansionary fiscal policy to pay for new welfare commitments. Unlike in Russia, which was spending a quarter of its GDP on defense in the 1980s, China's state treasury will not gain a peace dividend from democracy. And unlike in the past when the central bank was a political tool of the regime, the new central bank in China would likely strike a more independent stand committed to stable prices and thus be unwilling to bank-roll an inflationary government splurge. What's more, if Russia is any example, tax collection may become more problematic in the initial years of democracy due to the weakening of the central state. An increase in lending from the IMF or World Bank may open up the contentious issue of conditionality, which provoked mass protests in new democracies like Indonesia and Brazil. As with the SOE dilemma, China will have to lean heavily on the legitimacy of its new democratic institutions to resolve the perplexing challenges of state finances.

With so many factors in play, it is impossible to predict how China's head-line GDP growth rate may change. Typically, the tumult of transition results in an immediate slowdown. But with its transition to markets largely completed, China could see growth rebound quickly, as happened in South Korea, where growth actually accelerated during the transition. As one Chinese democrat predicts: "With revamped controls on fiscal spending, a reduction in economic corruption, stepped up privatization of state firms, new borrowing from foreign markets, fair competition in markets, and new investments in the environment, the economy should be able to grow at 6% to 7% a year."[10]

The shift to democracy will also have a profound impact on the *way* that China's economy grows. All the previous modeling of China's economy will be out the window; a whole new set of assumptions and structures will need to be modeled. The appearance of new rights like the right to strike and organize independent unions, and the right to free migration will have deep reverberations. Wage rates will rise as a result of organization and lobbying (political and social) by workers.

As before, economic development will remain a pressing, even overarching goal of mainstream politicians. The notion of a "rich and strong" China was deeply embedded in popular consciousness in the late PRC period and would likely remain. Yet this goal will now be conditioned by questions of how far it should run ahead of other matters of economic and social justice, and how it should sit alongside the new importance of rights. Typically it becomes more difficult in a democracy to build dams, superhighways, and business parks because people and civil society mobilize to defend their rights and interests against the state. Fundamental rights to protest, seek legal review, and have contracts honored will mean projects need to be more carefully considered.

But while the rights-based state may provide for better compensation and due process, the imperative of development is likely to remain strong. Even in a democracy, the state has room to interpret the distinction between fundamental and secondary rights. Some of the 1.1 million people displaced by the Three Gorges dam, for example, might win better treatment and recognition of their interests. Yet the dam would go on. Protests that impede economic activity and erode foreign investor confidence will be managed by police and frowned upon by mainstream opinion, even though they will be legal and permitted. China will shift from being a "developmental dictatorship" to a "developmental democracy."

The crisis of China's environment will not be solved overnight by democracy. Population growth and a continued commitment to development—the two key factors causing environmental degradation in China—may not change. As one student of the problem wrote: "Even a democratic China could do little to change radically either the country's absolute population growth or its long-term environmental prospects, especially because the nation's quest for affluence transcends politics."[11]

Nonetheless, a democratic polity in which pressure groups and directly affected individuals can bring pressure and awareness to bear on environmental problems will hold out greater hopes for ameliorating the crisis. The increase in popular participation in environmental debates urged on China by the World Bank will now be possible. New voices will be able to challenge damaging development by making the costs better known. As such, the assumption that environmentally-damaging developmentalism "transcends politics" may prove less secure. Certain issues, water pollution perhaps, certain sectors, maybe paper-making, and certain regions, perhaps modernist Guangdong, will show vast improvements in the environment. The environmental impact of bridges, roads, electricity pylons, coastal reclamation and much else will now be considered more carefully. Thoughtless tourism development—like the defacing cable cars of Mount Taishan or the bird habitat ruining theme parks of Shenzhen—will be halted.

Several immediate and pressing environmental issues will be confronted. The Three Gorges Dam is intended for completion in 2010. A reopening of the book on the 185-meter wide $25 billion dam could mean that it is managed in a more environmentally-sound fashion. Other large projects, by contrast, could be stopped if people are made aware of the costs and dangers. A plan for a grand network of canals totaling 3,000 miles to carry huge amounts of water from the wet south to the dry north was criticized by Wen Jiabao, who became premier in 2003, as inferior to conservation and pollution taxes: "We must conserve water before moving it, control pollution before turning on the tap, protect the environment before consuming water. We must fully think through the economic, social, and ecological effectiveness of transporting water."[12]

The delay and reconsideration of Taiwan's planned fourth nuclear power plant after the election of the protest-based opposition party in 2000 is a perfect example of how environmental lobbies can work, even in Chinese societies. In China, new nuclear plants in Shandong and Zhejiang provinces could come under question, as could the country's long-term policy of boosting nuclear power from 1 percent of its energy supply from two plants in 2000 to 5 percent by 2020. An environmental lobby would raise the cost of nuclear fuel in China by compelling more stringent safety standards. Agitators might encourage better use of hydro power from the inland—like Sichuan's underused Ertan dam—rather than new nuclear plants in coastal provinces.

The nature of foreign investment in China will also change. To the extent that it was a function of a distorted domestic economic system previously, foreign investment may find the country is less attractive under democracy. Domestic companies will now have local sources of finance to turn to; tax loopholes for foreign investors will close; and artificially suppressed wage rates and other costs will rise. A one-fifth reduction in annual foreign investment—meaning about $10 billion—would probably knock several percentage points off annual economic growth.[13]

What will happen to foreign investors who invested so much in the goodwill and personal ties to the old regime? Sweet deals such as U.S. photo giant Eastman Kodak's 1998 agreement to invest $1 billion in China in return for a four-year ban on rival Fuji's entry into the market might be harder to strike. Foreign investors who had tied their fates too closely to privileged relationships with the state would suffer. Prudent foreign investors may already have distanced themselves from highly-personalistic projects by the time of the transition. Those that had not might suffer.

The nature of doing business in post-CCP China will change dramatically too. In particular, the opening of public debate will make business propositions much more politicized—recalling the highly political nature of major foreign business projects in the Philippines and India. Stronger regional forces will also put a premium on having a presence in more than just Beijing. Foreign executives, no less than anyone else, will suddenly be pressed to learn the complexities of a diverse country.

Typically, democratic transitions witness the convening of commissions to investigate the economic corruption of the outgoing regime, a process that can suddenly implicate all manner of respectable domestic and foreign companies. The long-standing attempts to recover the "Marcos millions," in the Philippines, for example, implicated several major international banks. Late PRC era flight capital—maybe $25 billion a year—may be the target of recovery attempts by the new government, uncovering the tangle of offshore companies and multiple citizenships held by top CCP cadres that had gone unnoticed. It may also turn up the mesh of ties between the corrupt CCP regime and foreign business. The paper trail in the U.S. of former Bank of China president Wang Xuebing, arrested in 2002 on corruption charges, is an advance look at the ignominy that awaits.

Social Welfare

Alongside developmentalism, a renewal of interest in social welfare is a likely result of democratic transition. Mainstream opinion is likely to favor a reconstruction of the social welfare system that fell apart in the PRC's reform era. The reform-era model of "growth without equity" would no longer be acceptable to the newly visible majority who suffered from the yawning inequalities of the PRC. Although China is unlikely to witness mass executions of its modern-day landlords, the "big portions" (*dakuan*) of the cities, a rebalancing of priorities is to be expected.

While its average income per capita may put China in the safe zone for consolidating its democracy, the sharing of that income will be contentious. At the very least, unaddressed income inequalities might threaten to keep China's democracy forever on a minimalist and weak footing—like India in the 40 years after independence under the Congress Party or Latin America in the 1980s and 1990s. A successful equity program will sustain growth by preventing political unrest and will buttress democracy by ensuring that the rich do not exert excessive influence. Greater economic equality will ensure that the political freedoms won through democracy will have a roughly equal value to each person.

Bringing equity issues back to center-stage would help create the sense of economic entitlement that makes the vast unwashed supportive of the political system. President Gloria Arroyo of the Philippines made poverty-reduction her number one task after ousting a corrupt president, Joseph Estrada, following mass protests in 2001. The lessons of Latin America should be warning enough that if economic inequality is not tackled, the new democracy will be under constant threat from antidemocratic insurgencies and rich political bosses.[14]

"On the day that we achieve public power with the support of the people, we need to be ready to treat the wounds of the past," writes Liu Guokai, a machinist and long-time democracy activist in China who fled to the U.S. in 1989 and became a truck driver. "We cannot just be an alliance of justice, we have to have a clear program of political and social change."[15]

Like many Chinese activists and scholars, Liu believes that some form of "social democracy" will return in a democratic China. Political reformer Cao Siyuan's suggestion that the CCP change its name to the China Social Party is prescient of this new thrust in politics. Socialism, at least as a rhetorical goal, will not die with the CCP. As one group of forward-looking Chinese scholars writes: "In our country's modern political development, a key question is how to manage the relationship between socialism and a democratic system."[16]

What would social democracy entail in China? The reintroduction of universal healthcare properly funded and the imposition of more progressive income taxes would be obvious changes. A recommitment to universal education and perhaps even affirmative action for disadvantaged rural-dwellers in university entrance and other areas might also be embraced. One democrat proposes a social welfare net covering medical care, education, and social security payments that would be funded by both central and provincial governments based on a formula under which richer provinces would bear more of the burden.[17]

Under the new social contract, China's commitment to controlling population growth will likely remain. Indeed, with a greater awareness of the environmental impacts and a greater sense of public responsibility in a newly autonomous society, there may emerge an even stronger commitment to family planning. One Chinese democrat suggests replacing the one-child policy with a simple taxation policy where you pay additional "population accumulation" taxes for every child born beyond the first.[18] The system would continue to exempt ethnic minorities and rural-dwellers who give birth to a female first. Those failing to hand over their taxes would be taken before newly established population courts or sent to the frontier to do manual labor. Coming from an avowed democrat who calls the plan "consistent with human rights," the seemingly draconian idea reflects the wide consensus on the need for strict population controls.

Yet democracy should make effective and just population control policies easier to achieve. As mentioned, the main flaw with the policies of the PRC was their reliance on coercion and administrative fiat. The normal tools of a democratic society—education, especially for women, alleviation of poverty, economic incentives (not penalties), and the like—were unused or misused. Genuine voluntarism within a proper regulatory system could finally work. Not least, China could once again enjoy funding again from the United States, which had previously been withheld because of concerns over forced abortions.

Finally, the new welfarism may see the emergence of some sort of corporatist structures, like cross-sectoral wage bargaining and new national unions for farmers and workers. Most studies of reform China suggest that a modest communitarian spirit continues to inform Chinese society even as it becomes more diverse.[19] That might translate into the type of loose corporatism as exists in Japan, Taiwan, South Korea, and Thailand—where companies agree to finance welfare programs and keep employment high in return for limits on wage demands and industrial action. Importantly, the state-directed corporatism of the PRC would shift to a society-directed style, one perhaps varying across regions.[20]

The debates on welfarism will create new splits in the left wing of China's political spectrum—a reflection of how economic issues will shape the party system. One Chinese scholar has described the fragmentation of the "new Left," in China among social justice advocates, political liberals, and fair market economists.[21] The demands of development and democracy may clash with the demands of welfare and each will have a different solution, he writes.

A sign of this emerging spectrum was a pro-worker book published by a group of "new left" scholars in 2001 (published appropriately enough by the Petroleum Industry Press) which warned against the wave of "liberalism" among economists that harmed the interests of the lower classes in favor of economic elites.[22] Scholars and activists will tap into a large constituency that feels nostalgia for the defenestrated CCP, or at least for the ideals it represented.

As with the new limits on helter-skelter development, the rise of social welfare as a key component of China's political economy will change the way the economy grows. Many foreign economists and business leaders will bewail democracy's bothersome and costly processes, as they do those of India and the Philippines. Yet the long-term prospects for growth will almost certainly improve. To quote the UNDP from its report on democracy and development in 2002: "Democratic governance can trigger a virtuous cycle of development as political freedom empowers people to press for policies that expand social and economic opportunities. From Indonesia to Mexico to Poland, moves toward democratization and political opening have helped produce this kind of virtuous cycle."[23] China stands a good chance of enjoying the same rewards.

Regional Interests

The political economy of regional interests will be central to the way that democracy changes China. India, Russia, and Indonesia are the best examples of large countries where regional interests have been at the center of the redefinition of the state under democracy. The regional political differentiation discussed in the last chapter will be accentuated by a clash of regional economic and social interests. Again, it is not just the solutions to these conflicts but also the way in which those solutions are reached that will critically define the new China.

With a democratically constituted parliament, the representatives of just ten provinces in the rural heartland will command close to a majority of seats (see table 3). That is sure to have an impact on how governments address the urban and coastal bias left over from the communist state. Former policies that discriminated against rural residents—everything from residence requirements to central investment decisions—will have to be renegotiated. Rural enterprises will demand a fair shake with urban industry in terms of public investment, production subsidies, and training. State requirements that forced heartland areas to grow grain to feed coastal areas will have to be dropped or reformed. No less than in the struggle for rights, the struggle for interests will witness the emergence from the shadows of China's long-hidden heartland.

The response of coastal regions to this new challenge will no doubt be a mixture of political bluster ("The fast development of Shanghai is good for all of China") and practical compromise. Shanghai and Guangzhou, for example, might agree to a significant loosening of residence limitations in return for a continued central commitment to building infrastructure in major cities. They might then be transformed into even vaster agglomerations of high-rise buildings and shanty towns like the teeming cites of Rio and Mumbai.

One reformer suggests keeping controls on residency only for major cities. Governments would then pour funds into building secondary cities and allow

Table 3   Regional blocks in parliament (1,000 seats total)

Rural heartland (459 seats)
  Henan, Sichuan, Hebei, Hunan, Anhui, Hubei, Jiangxi, Shaanxi, Shanxi, Chongqing
Coastal band (375 seats)
  Shandong, Guangdong, Jiangsu, Zhejiang, Liaoning, Heilongjiang, Fujian, Jilin, Shanghai,
  Beijing, Tianjin, Hainan, Hong Kong, Macau
Far West Minority Areas (166 seats)
  Guangxi, Yunnan, Guizhou, Gansu, Inner Mongolia, Xinjiang, Ningxia, Qinghai, Tibet

free migration to them.[24] Such a system was already emerging in the late PRC era. Urbanites and business leaders may not like it. But for the first time, China's poor will be heard and seen. Notes one scholar: "The impact of democratizing the system so that peasants can affect policy will be adverse to some urban interests. Chinese democrats, who are overwhelmingly urbanites, may fear this."[25]

The introduction of constitutional federalism will require a parallel "fiscal federalism" to share the costs of governance. A devolution of powers to provinces might worsen regional inequalities if rich provinces gain more control over their taxes. This can create injustice by variations in quality of public services especially health and education, especially between urban and rural areas. Under some negotiated fiscal agreement, the center might make transfers to needy regions using the (redistributive) taxes it gains from a new tax deal. It might also set minimum standards while better off places can exceed those standards if they wish. Such arrangements work best when the central government can exercise some supervision over how the money, ensuring that it is not frittered away on corruption and waste, as happens in countries like Brazil.

Even with attempts to create some rough uniformity in social services, some provinces will have a more egalitarian ethos than others. Some southern coastal provinces like Guangdong and Fujian will likely retain strongly individualistic socioeconomic policies, while more egalitarian solutions may appear in places like Shanxi, home to the CCP's wartime Yanan redoubt. Other provinces are hard to predict. Many are split between twin identities — Shandong with an identity split represented by cosmopolitan Qingdao on the coast and conservative Jinan inland. Sichuan has both a minority and a central plains identity.

Ironically, another result of the redistribution of political economic power under democracy toward central areas may be a decline in the privileges for far western minority regions — which will hold only 17 percent of seats in parliament. Because of their strategic and ethnic dimensions, these regions have long enjoyed significant state investment. As that investment declines, they might press for more control over their natural resources—Xinjiang's oil and gas reserves for example are a third of the national total.

In the new political economy of democratic China, provinces will also expand their ties with neighboring foreign states. Like the flawed "federalism" of the late PRC, such contacts had long taken place in an illicit and ad hoc manner. Officials in Shandong conducted an illegal and barely-secret trade and investment with South Korea prior to the establishment of official links in 1992. Officials in Fujian are frequently found out to have offered incentives to Taiwanese investors that breech state laws. Once devolution and democracy empowers provincial officials with the ability to engage in open deal-making with neighboring states, the relationships will change. Commercial envoys visiting China will go straight to provincial capitals to talk business. The main corridors of economic traffic will be reoriented away from domestic business toward border business—as they had already begun to do in the late PRC era along the borders of Indo-China, Central Asia, and Russia. The reopening of commercial routes between Tibet and India (the routes that Tibetan leaders like the Dalai Lama himself used to flee PRC rule) would invigorate the Tibetan economy by reconnecting it to its natural South Asian setting.

Just as seismic shifts in power-holding will occur at the national level, so too within each province we will see changes as traditional cities lose out to rural areas and to newer urban areas. Assuming that devolution went far beyond provinces to include devolution to counties and townships, it will also create a need in each province for a renegotiated fiscal agreement. In the late PRC era, two-thirds of county governments and probably a higher proportion of township governments ran budget deficits. These governments will have to be given control over new taxes and forced to be accountable to local citizens.

Unlike the NPC, the provincial and local people's congresses were constituted more closely along strict proportional representation by the late PRC era. Even so, the modest realignments caused by equal representation and the equal empowerment of all legislators will bring out the "hidden identities" of a given province. In Guangdong, for example, a province of 70 million people, the high-profile "golden horseshoe" of the Pearl River Delta will account for only a quarter of the seats in the provincial parliament under a population-based apportionment (see tables 4 and 5). The influence of fishing communities in the southwest and eastern coast will grow, accounting for nearly a plurality, while the poor western rivers and north regions will hold more votes than the Pearl River Delta.

This augurs for a significant change in the political economy of Guang-

Table 4 Seats in a 300-seat provincial parliament in Guangdong Province

Area	New Seats[a]	Change[b]
Guangzhou	29	−12
Zhanjiang	27	+3
Maoming	25	+6
Jieyang	22	+4
Shantou	18	−1
Jiangmen	17	−1
Meizhou	16	+1
Zhaoqing	16	+2
Qingyuan	16	+3
Foshan	14	−3
Heyuan	14	+3
Shaoguan	13	0
Huizhou	12	+4
Shanwei	11	+1
Yangjiang	11	−1
Chaozhou	10	0
Yunfu	10	0
Dongguan	6	0
Zhongshan	6	0
Shenzhen	4	−6
Zhuhai	3	−3

a. Population-based seats using 1999 census; each member represents 235,000 people
b. Based on distribution of 737 seats in ninth Guangdong People's Congress at 2002, excluding military seats and normalized to 300

Table 5 Guangdong Regional Blocks (300 seats total)

Pearl River Delta (74 seats)
  Guangzhou, Foshan, Huizhou, Dongguan, Zhongshan, Shenzhen, Zhuhai

Southwest Coastal (63 seats)
  Zhanjiang, Maoming, Yangjiang

Eastern Coastal (61 seats)
  Jieyang, Shantou, Chaozhou, Shanwei

Poor North (59 seats)
  Qingyuan, Meizhou, Heyuan, Shaoguan

Western Rivers (43 seats)
  Jiangmen, Zhaoqing, Yunfu

dong. Since 1995, the province has pursued a policy of "modernizing" the Pearl River Delta area. As a result, the delta has absorbed two-thirds to three-quarters of the province's annual outlays on capital investments in areas like transport, energy, urban development, and technology.[26] Under democracy, there would be intense pressure to reduce that share to something closer to the delta's 25 percent of the province's population. Even if a higher proportion, say 50 percent, can be justified on general welfare grounds, it is unlikely to be as skewed as the present levels.

A Free Society

Will China's society erupt into an orgy of confusion and anarchy once the restraints of authoritarian rule are lifted? Are warnings of an "uncivil society" emerging from the shackles of communist rule justified? In Albania, villagers burned libraries and ransacked community clinics and daycare centers when the communist regime fell. In Russia, crime and looting soared while artists went on a binge of cheap political pop art.

Even without these visible manifestations, the simple disappearance of a guiding ideology, a "truth," a powerful state that told people how to think and act, was a jarring change for many, especially outside major cities. Russian villagers and elders felt stunned and disoriented. The moral and ideological vacuum left by the end of communism can be crushing.

Rather than being pessimistic about post-CCP society in China, however, there is every reason to be highly optimistic. In contrast to the huge challenges of political and economic life, there is every reason to be sanguine about the future of social life. If China's society was in a state of "hampered development," in the late communist era, then under democracy it should enter a new phase of "unhampered development." All signs are that Chinese society should flourish under democracy. This is important because the embedding of liberal norms of tolerance and respect and the rebuilding of trust and cooperation within society, quite aside from their intrinsic worth, are important for democratic consolidation.

There are two main grounds for hope. Most obvious is that China had already traveled far down the road of social freedoms in the late reform era. Many basic freedoms like travel, job-seeking, living, social mixing, and even to some degree artistic expression and media diversity were entrenched. This suggests a society that has already come to terms with both personal autonomy and the end of ideology. The immediate reactions to social freedoms — reflected in behavior such as rising divorce, conspicuous consumption, public drunkenness, or political pop art — were well-established, even passé, in China by the early 2000s.

Second, if indeed China's transition is elite-led, not mass-led, then according to most other experiences of democratization, not just the polity but also society will continue to be "state-led." This means that there will continue to be a largely elite-defined and state-sponsored "national culture," much as one finds in France or Japan, with their elaborate state cultural organizations. In the short-term this means that there will continue to be a state role in defining morality and thought, much as in the Czech Republic or Hungary with their high-profile writers-cum-statesmen. The weakness of China's civil society should not hamper the development of a new national culture.

A successful transition to a free society does not of course mean stasis. As in other areas, democracy will bring wide-ranging changes to Chinese society, even if those changes build on trends well underway in the late PRC era. As stated at the outset, democracy does not undermine or threaten any country's culture. Indeed, properly implemented it strengthens a country's indigenous culture by bringing out the true pageantry of its people and positively encouraging pluralism. That is why in Taiwan, a free society, a remarkable preservation of traditional Chinese culture exists alongside a flourishing new rediscovery of native aboriginal and Fujianese cultures.

What will be the key aspects of China's new society and culture? Again, the answers can be found by applying the general experiences elsewhere to the Chinese case. Generally speaking, democracy makes a culture more populist and more varied, replacing the former elitist and monistic culture of authoritarianism. For centuries, China's mainstream culture has been an elitist one, forged by imperial writ and reinforced by CCP rule. Top-down culture in China was not just state-interpreted traditional Chinese culture. It was also the elite and packaged Western culture that elitist modernizers in China—from republican to communist eras—sought to implant in the country. The appeal for China's society to "converge" on some imagined monistic, Western-based "modernity" was no less elitist than that advocating a return to the study of Confucian classics. This elitism will recede as the country liberalizes under democracy. The old elite culture so divorced from everyday life—like "oil on water, or powder on the face"—will be superseded by a popular culture of visual images, urban life, and non-hierarchical social relationships. "Top down" culture will be replaced by a "bottom up" culture, in the words of one scholar in China.[27] It may include both traditional Chinese and imported elements. But those elements will be chosen and created by a state that is constituted and answerable to those below. China may remain a state-led culture and society, as in France. But there will be a significant rebalancing of elite and populist concerns within the state itself.

Even elements of traditional culture will be reclaimed by populist forces. In Hong Kong and Taiwan, this "neo-traditionalism," included elements like a popular prime-time TV drama about the worthy Judge Bao of the Northern

Song dynasty and a flourishing martial arts movie industry that produced such gems as the 2000 film *Crouching Tiger, Hidden Dragon* and the knights errant epic novels of Louis Cha.

On their own, Hong Kong and Taiwan have created something of a mini-boom in Chinese popular culture in Asia, and beyond, that at times can compete with the more powerful craze for Japanese popular culture. Chinese martial arts films, feng shui masters, and traditional-medicine doctors have penetrated Western homes as much as Japanese manga comics, teenage fashions, and electronic gadgets. A continent-sized Chinese culture now engaged in the same project could create an even bigger Chinese impact on global culture. What people knew abroad as "Chinese culture" would no longer be the dead culture of Tang horses, architecture, and noodles but the live culture of hit movies, rock musicians, and green tea-based sports drinks.

One aspect of neotraditionalism likely to make a strong showing are the traditional Chinese written characters so beloved of the overseas Chinese communities. Despite an official ban, they crept back into China in the 1990s, prompting periodic crackdowns from Beijing. While China is likely to retain its simplified characters officially, the use of traditional ones is likely to expand once the state no longer interferes in such realms of private life.

Even nationalism, that bogey-man of critics of the late PRC era, is likely to be popularized, as it has been in, say, Hong Kong. Nationalism will now mean a healthy pride in the country, in other words a "liberal nationalism" of the sort whose rise we traced earlier. The negative nationalism based on imagined foreign incursions would have little market, a fact symbolized by the spectacular box-office flop of *The Opium War*, an anti-Western propaganda film made by Beijing to "celebrate" Hong Kong's return in 1997.

Growing diversity will be a second dimension of the new culture and society of China. As noted by the writers of the fabled 1988 television series *Yellow River Elegy (Heshang)*, China's dominant authoritarian culture has long been primarily northern, inward-looking, and chauvinist. Many observers believe that democracy in China will unlock the cosmopolitan, outward-looking culture of southern China, which has had such a great influence in Southeast Asia as well as Hong Kong and Taiwan. As in Russia, which rediscovered its liberal and European heritage, China too will reimagine itself as a flourishing Asian nation with an enviable record of interchange with the rest of the world. One Western scholar noted that by the mid-1990s there was a trend toward reimagining China's patriots, its heroes, and its values in terms of the south and its villains and problems in terms of the north.[28] That change can only accelerate under democracy. With the unlocking of a more cosmopolitan Chinese culture, China may come to resemble Hong Kong and

Taiwan more and more, confident in its Chinese heritage and yet easily mixing with the rest of the world.

Even within the Mandarin-speaking Han population—accounting for roughly 70 percent of the population—a new diversity will be discovered. The peoples of areas like Henan and Hubei have long considered themselves separate from other northern Hans. The Hubei people's reputation for being tricky and querulous is symbolized in their nickname as "five-headed birds" (*wu tou niao*), a slight taken up with gusto by one Hunan-owned restaurant chain in Beijing trading under the same name. The Henan people, meanwhile, have a reputation as ugly and stupid, something that by the late reform era they were fighting to change with active efforts at self-promotion.[29]

China's elitist and monistic culture will thus be shattered with the coming of democracy, even if the country remains more uniform than astonishingly diverse India or Indonesia. It is a change to be welcomed, indeed celebrated. For it will reflect society's liberation from customs and identities imposed by centuries of dictatorship.

Dealing With History

Among the imperatives of China's new democracy will be the remembrance of the past. Authoritarian governments leave behind a field of unexploded historical landmines, not just victims of repression but more widely a whole area of forgotten, distorted, or misused history. Communist regimes in particular leave behind a legacy of history that was "produced," in order to justify their rule and whose legal monopoly on the past pushed alternative histories into oral or *samizdat* form.[30]

Dealing with the historical record is at once the most painful and the most necessary process for society in a new democracy. It is painful because it often involves assigning blame over episodes of repression as well as grieving for historical wrongs. It is necessary because without it, neither the polity nor society as a whole can escape the past and function properly.

Within the public sphere, confronting history is most critical. Obviously, it helps to delegitimate the old regime, excavating evidence of its abuses and undermining those pining for "the good old days." By the same token, it bolsters the new regime, making it the healer of past wounds and lending new legitimacy to institutions like the judiciary and police whose reputations may have been sullied by the past.

Merely by drawing attention to the functioning of dictatorship, historical reconciliation can help deracinate the habits of authoritarianism in politics—the authoritarian temptation and social illiberalism we discussed in the last chapter. No politician wants to be called "a dictator" when the awful dimensions of that term have become evident through historical aeration. Indeed, dealing with history is part of the struggle for rights itself. By putting honesty, truth, and an ethical reexamination of the past above other considerations, including the pain and even antagonisms of the process, a political system asserts the triumph of justice over expediency.

Within society, historical inquiry can build reconciliation and trust while providing cathartic relief, critical ingredients to democratic life. No society, and no person, can move into the future without confronting its past. Without it, note two scholars, a country is "burying not just its past but the very ethical values it needs to make its future livable."[31] Or as another scholarly project notes: without confronting history, "the transgressions of [authoritarian] regimes remain embedded in the society's collective memory and institutional fabric."[32] The wider recovery of history and memory begins a process of seeing one's past as one must see one's future: as one of conflicting interests, unclear moral choices, and halting progress. By overturning a self-serving version of the past created by dictatorship, a society opens the window to new interpretations, including the "discovery" of its liberal legacy.

Evidence is everywhere of how historical inquiry helps build democracy. A thorough introspection about Nazism and the Holocaust helped Germany to reemerge within 50 years as the center of European integration.[33] In Eastern Europe, the best performing new democracies were those where "a profound examination of the past occurred."[34] In South Africa and Latin America, official truth commissions that dealt mainly with human rights abuses calmed a great deal of social antagonism that might have destroyed young democracies.[35] Honest inquiry into historical tragedies like the plight of native Indians, slavery, and the Vietnam War have kept otherwise divisive issues from shredding the fabric of American democracy.

By contrast, those countries that remain at odds with their past find that the issue haunts their democracy. Japan's slow and half-hearted acceptance of its war record have prevented it from taking on a larger leadership role in Asia and remains a volatile issue in domestic politics, as evidenced by frequent political crises over school textbooks and visits by government officials to shrines honoring soldiers. In Cambodia, the government's foot-dragging over trials of Khmer Rouge leaders in the late 1990s delayed healing in society and remained a potentially system-threatening issue in politics.

China's huge undigested past will be a major challenge to the emergence of a healthy democracy. Few countries, democratic or otherwise, have experienced an era so bloody and cruel as did China in the twentieth century. Countries that experienced equal trauma, like Cambodia, will bear the scars for decades. The coming of democracy in China will discharge an explosion of historical memory, not just about major national events but also about hundreds of regional and local ones little known to the outside world. There will be a need to create a "livable past" as much as a livable present.[36]

A torrent of reinspections and revisions of history will flood out in the immediate years after dictatorship. People who have secluded their personal stories, photographs, and documents, and been deterred from seeking historical justice, will emerge like a silent army. The whole gamut of suffering under the wayward state will appear: mothers with forced abortions, families whose sons were jailed as dissidents, people executed for petty crimes, farmers whose land was lost to corrupt cadres. It is a potentially volatile stew of historical grievance. Lost voices like minorities, peasants, women, beggars, disabled, those from inland provinces and second-rate colleges will all come out and provide a rich tapestry.[37]

It is not just facts that will change; so will interpretations. The 10 million people killed in the consolidation of CCP power between 1949 and 1956 may be remembered not as enemies of socialism but as martyrs to the cause of individual freedom. The anti-Rightist movement of 1957, which killed another half a million, mainly intellectuals, will be compared to the Prague Spring; indeed this process had already begun in the late PRC era.[38] One book published in 2002 detailed how 2,000 of 3,000 inmates at a labor camp in remote Gansu were allowed to starve to death during the campaign.[39] The role of "reformer" Deng Xiaoping as the chief inquisitor for this campaign will be brought out, part of a broader reevaluation of Deng that will include his order to send soldiers into Tiananmen Square in 1989.

In terms of lives lost, the Great Leap Famine remains the worst atrocity of the PRC and a full examination of it cannot be avoided. Even in the late PRC era, books were appearing in China that laid the blame for the famine squarely on CCP policies rather than the bogus claims of bad weather or an adverse impact from the withdrawal of Soviet assistance.[40] The true place of this tragedy will be resisted by those who assert that it killed "mere" peasants or political criminals. Even among Chinese intellectuals living in free societies, less attention is paid to the deaths from this famine than to urban elites killed in other Maoist campaigns.[41] Yet by any standards, the 30 to 40 million killed in the famine demand the most recognition. Indeed, the famine could easily be classified as a crime against humanity under international law. Some well-loved CCP politicians, in particular Zhou Enlai and Hu Yaobang, could be censured for their roles in backing Mao in the policies that caused the famine. The inquiry is also bound to provoke a wider reexamination of the utilitarianism that remains stuck in China's political culture.

By contrast, less remained to be said about the Cultural Revolution since it had already been widely reviled and remembered in the late PRC era. Still, one important departure will be the remembering of the average people as well as the ethnic minorities, not just the Han elites and intellectuals, who suffered, accounting for the majority of the one to three million killed. Some signs of this new historical approach are already visible, for example in the photographic montages by one Beijing artist of family members killed in the campaign and in the work by Chinese scholars on the murder of 16,000 Mongolians and maiming of another 87,000 by zealous Maoists.[42] Writer Ba Jin's long-standing proposal for a Cultural Revolution Museum could be taken up at last. "We need to remember the common people, not just the famous intellectuals. . . . If their deaths and persecutions are not recorded, there is no guarantee that it will not happen again," the editor of one on-line memorial writes.[43]

The 1976 Tangshan earthquake, humanity's worst-ever urban earthquake with 250,000 dead, will also be subjected to new inquiries. At the time, Mao's cronies covered up most news of the tragedy, refused foreign aid, and turned it into an opportunity for regime propaganda and political repression in the Tianjin area. PLA General Chi Haotian, who served as China's defense minister from 1993 to 2003, is one leader who has already expressed deep regrets: "After it was all over, the more I thought about [the regime's behavior] the worse I felt. Guilty conscience, I suppose."[44]

All this will lead naturally to the question of Mao himself. There can be little escaping the fact that Mao is one of history's most evil people, along with other madmen of the left like Stalin and Pol Pot and a few of the right like Hitler.[45] In Russia, the vilification of Stalin had gone some distance before the democratic transition began, as symbolized by the "Memorial" movement founded in 1987 to commemorate Stalin's victims. Yet in China, Mao remained widely admired, even revered, in society. His entombed body and dominating portrait in Tiananmen Square and his preeminent position on banknotes and lucky charms reflected a celebration of his legacy that went beyond state propaganda.

Can a democratic society revere a mass killer? Certainly not. But the veneration of Mao seems to reflect two factors, both of which will be significantly eroded in an open society. One is simple ignorance. China's people know little of Mao's twisted personality, his use of violence to consolidate his position in the Party, or his constant flip-flops on issues like Taiwan and democracy. They have never been exposed to an open debate about his role. Merely being able to learn about "the real Mao" and to discuss his legacy in light of the new democratic norms being espoused by society will do much to discount the reverence he enjoys, as it has in overseas Chinese communities and Hong Kong. Indeed, the debate on Mao will reflect larger debates about the norms being contested in society at large. Each city with a soaring Mao statue—from Kashgar to Zhengzhou—will have to debate his legacy in this broader new context. Lenin's reputation in Russia, where supporters insisted his tomb remain on display in Moscow, was steadily chipped away by archival research that revealed such grisly details as his looting of orthodox churches during the famines of the 1920s. How many equally chilling directives from Mao must be lingering in the archives in China waiting for the light of day?

At a deeper level, the veneration of Mao appears to reflect a degree of self-loathing in some parts of Chinese society, one that was assiduously fostered by the CCP. By portraying the old China as weak and loathsome, the CCP was able to argue that the body count of Chairman Mao was a penance for the sin of being Chinese, a necessary self-flagellation for the inability to "stand up" to the West or "coagulate" as a nation. Lacking a strong sense of self and of the individual, China's people could imagine Mao's exaction in "mere," individual lives as unimportant compared to the stirring gains of the "Chinese nation." Once a democratic polity asserts the value of each individual, this will begin to change. Mao's blood debts will lose all mystical legitimacy. In this fundamental sense, the end of Mao worship will reflect the growth of a more healthy national psyche.

Even so, the Mao cult may never disappear completely. Some will argue that revering Mao as a nation-builder and patriot with a few faults is no different from revering George Washington, a soldier with his own kingly pretensions, who upheld slavery and waged war on Native Americans. Others will argue—as some have for Hitler—that he was a victim of insubordination and did not know the extent of trauma in the country. It took the French more than a century to disassociate themselves from Robespierre's reign of terror, while more than a decade after democratization more than half of all Russians still expressed a favorable opinion of Stalin. It should be no surprise if it takes the Chinese many decades to bury Mao.[46]

Finally, how will China deal with the Tiananmen Massacre? Reversing the verdict, as mentioned, may be part of the collapse of the PRC itself. But that will not solve the healing and search for truth. The official recognition and introspection in the 1990s over Taiwan's February 28 Massacre of 1947, South Korea's Kwangju Massacre of 1980, and Thailand's massacre of 1992—all killings of civilians by military dictatorships—marked important milestones in the democratizations of those countries because they showed that the forces of the old state and its values were now fully expurgated.

One thing is certain. Tiananmen has not been forgotten and will not be laid to rest without a significant and thorough-going reevaluation and memorializing of the tragedy. Hong Kong's annual commemoration vigil consistently attracts 25,000 people or more. A group called the Tiananmen Mothers has continued, like their counterparts in South America, to defy official intimidation to remember and inquire into the loss of their children. The publication in 2001 of a trove of official documents on the crackdown, *The Tiananmen Papers*, reflected the vitality of the issue inside the regime. June Fourth could well be declared a holiday to remember the martyrs who fought for democracy and civil rights.

For all these historical wounds, China's official approach to reconciliation will be an important facet of democratic consolidation. There are any number of official methods for recovering history, all of them potentially worthwhile. Every society must strike a balance between remembering and forgetting, revenge and reconciliation. Methods range from trials of former leaders and official truth commissions to monuments, national holidays, and memorials. Most evidence suggests that official activities succeed when they are consonant with feelings in society; reconciliation does not work when justice is sought, as it was in Chile and Argentina; justice does not work when reconciliation is desired, as perhaps the trials of Japanese officers by Allied forces after World War II have shown.[47] Again, it is a reminder of how government in a democracy becomes better attuned to society.

Of course, the government does not have complete control over the process. The mere arrival of freedoms usually stimulates a burst of remembrance, from activists lobbying for justice or filing civil suits against remnants of the old regime to new history, drama, and literature. Simply by opening up archives and guaranteeing freedoms for historians, journalists, activists and victims to re-create the past, a new government facilitates healing.[48]

Yet the official processes tend to concentrate most minds. The best guess is that China will lean toward reconciliation rather than revenge. This is both because elite-led democratic transitions typically give the ancien regime more control over the process and because, in any case, Chinese society had seemingly come to terms with much of the bloody history of the PRC by the turn of the century. It seems unlikely then that China will convene any sort of official commission to look into the past. No ex-communist country had such a commission, a reflection of weak civil society as well as the remnant impact of the strong socialist state in controlling information and protecting the past. Nor did they put on trial any of those associated with the past regime, as occurred in the wake of right-wing dictatorships worldwide.

Typically, the control of former archives becomes a highly politicized issue.

Communist regimes in Eastern Europe jealously guarded their past even after they fell from power, allowing state security organs to keep control of information with only limited public access. Likewise, the central Party and state archives in Beijing will doubtless be the scene of hurried paper-shredding or removal as the PRC ends. Luckily, China's glorious tradition of local archive-keeping will ensure that much survives.

Still, monuments are likely to be an important official act of memory, as China's vast museum and memorial to the Japanese invasion near the Marco Polo Bridge near Beijing or its Tangshan earthquake monument attest. This soft approach may be consonant with China's society's desire for reconciliation. The apparent ease with which China got on with normal life after the CCP declared the Cultural Revolution a "disaster," rehabilitated a million cadres, and overturned the 1976 Tiananmen Incident verdict suggests a willingness to reconcile and move on. Another reason for hope is that much of the historical healing over incidents like the Cultural Revolution and the Great Leap Famine is already far advanced through official and unofficial histories. China was far more open than the USSR in its late communist era and there are likely to be fewer shocks from the discovery of its past.

Beyond the tragedies of the PRC will lie a broader reappraisal and reinvention of history itself. This will make China a very unfamiliar place for outsiders and Chinese alike. In place of a simple black and white history punctuated by patriotic struggles and grand CCP congresses, we will see a riot of confusing and conflicting histories all demanding recognition. Some of this new history has already been written abroad, in for example a path-breaking study of a village in Hebei province that creates a history totally unfamiliar to those raised on the staples of CCP propaganda.[49] Inside China too, this rewriting of PRC history has begun, with histories of local struggles and identities that never made it onto the tablets of PRC propaganda.[50]

The new history will stretch back to earlier times too. The so-called "century of national humiliation" from the Opium War until 1949, long a staple of CCP propaganda, may be reimagined as a time of fabulous interchange, like the Tang dynasty, one that gave birth to modern Chinese liberalism, created the commercial hubs of Dalian, Shanghai and Hong Kong, and sent Chinese culture worldwide. The attention of historians will turn more to the indigenous rebellion and decay of the nineteenth-century China, away from the rag-worn "Western impact" historiography.[51]

As for the early twentieth century, issues like the collaboration of Chinese citizens with the Japanese occupation and the role of U.S. and KMT forces in driving Japan out of China will be brought to light.[52] Not least, the CCP's own rise to power on the back of opium sales from its Yanan redoubt and through the exploitation of localized nodes of protest against KMT rule will help to redress notions of a pure and popular grass-roots movement.[53]

The new history will also extend beyond China to encompass the PRC's misadventures in Asia—its support of communist insurgencies in Malaysia and Indonesia in the 1950s and 1960s, cheerleading of North Korea's ill-fated invasion of South Korea, backing for the genocidal Khmer Rouge regime in Cambodia in the late 1970s, invasion of the Vietnam border towns in 1979, and firing of missiles off Taiwan in 1995–96. This will be an important component of how China's relations with the rest of the world change as a result of a greater consciousness of its own past. The experiences of Russia's post-Soviet relations with the Baltic republics, or Japan's post-World War II relations in Asia, show that countries may not be willing to establish normal relations until that record is addressed.

Foreign governments should also be prepared for how this process may redound on them. The compromises and concessions made to China for the sake of "strategic" or business interests during the PRC era will come to light. Just as the secret visits to Beijing by top US officials after Tiananmen set off shockwaves, much more could erupt in the face of Western governments. Historical remembrance, notes one scholarly project, often "brings to light the price these societies paid for their nurturing of authoritarianism overseas."[54]

History, then, is a "ghost at the table" of democracy. It must be recognized and confronted, lest it haunt the future. China, despite its terrible suffering from misrule, had begun that process in the late PRC era. A full accounting awaits the coming of freedom.

10

A Changed International Role

Democratic Peace

The international implications of a democratic government in China will be far-reaching and profound. China's foreign policy will be turned upside down, as will the foreign policies of other nations toward China. No less important, the full compass of interactions between China and the world will be altered fundamentally. Two Western scholars do not exaggerate in predicting that democratization in China "would probably transform global politics at every level."[1]

At the most general level, the change to a democratic system internally should manifest itself in a "democratic foreign policy" externally. The China that previously used any and all means to advance its narrowly defined economic and strategic objectives would give way to one that defined both its means and ends in democratic terms, or at least tried to. The struggle to achieve a democratic foreign policy is part of the ongoing struggle to deepen democracy in every country, but consider its implications for China.

For one, a China pursuing a democratic foreign policy would be a salutary new force for global justice, peace, and development. As a democracy, China's external policies would become less aggressive and expansionist, in line with democratic peace theory. Kant's proposition has held elsewhere in Asia—helping to constrain wars within Asean, in East Asia and in South Asia—and there is no reason not to expect it will apply to China.

That will be a major change for a country whose late communist era was filled with talk of a "strong country dream," in which China would become the preeminent power in Asia, muscling aside U.S. forces and Asian rivals like Japan and India. While specific cases will be detailed below, the renunciation of this goal would bring a modulation of claims on Taiwan, border disputes with India and Russia, strident anti-Japanese rhetoric, lobbying to get U.S. forces out of Asia, territorial claims in the South China Sea, aggressive military occupation of Tibet and Xinjiang, and needless stationing of troops in Hong Kong and Macau.

Democratic peace also implies that the foreign policies of liberal democracies toward China would change. They would become less confrontational
and less alarmist. Suddenly, talk of a "China threat" would be so much nonsense. A China more attuned to the international political system would find
that its diplomacy is easier. The presumption that the Beijing government
was now a veritable representative of its people would win for it the same
tolerance and respect as is owed to other democratic governments. A common
ethical foundation would now exist for engaging Beijing as an equal. With its
domestic polity aligned with the normative principles of democracy, China's
ties to other nations would become less emotive and more technocratic. The
world community of policymakers, scholars, newspaper columnists, activists,
and guys-at-the-bar will be able to discuss China's very real developmental
challenges without having the conversation constantly cleft by the issue of its
dictatorship. As with India, foreigners will be able to engage China with less
ideological rancor. As China becomes "more political" domestically, the issue
of China will become less political globally.

This is not to say that ideological issues will disappear. But what will disappear, perhaps, is the "dialogue of the deaf" that beset China policy debates
in the past. Those outside China demanding that the world check its notions
of political right and wrong at the door when dealing with China will disappear once such notions become the subject of heated public debate in China
itself. The "realist" foreign policy analysts who urged the world to accommodate an essentialized Chinese sense of historical victimization that justified
its aggression toward Taiwan and Tibet would appear ridiculous once those
notions become the subject of contention and debate at home. In other words,
once the world is able to debate issues in China along with the Chinese, there
will be a common ground for reasonable debate. The results will not always
please the world. But for once, there will be a real dialogue.

China, as a newly responsible power, would now be trusted to share the
burden of Asian regional security, as Russia has begun to do in Europe and
the Middle East. It could join U.S. forces in joint exercises and might take a
new role in preventing piracy in the South China Sea. This would represent
a significant restructuring of influence in Asia and the world. China would
have new stature as the leader of an emerging regionalism in Asia. In short,
China would be a boon rather than a threat to international security.

Just as China's own democratization was influenced by democratic diplomacy and "border effects," it would now project those same effects abroad. It
would be expected to join in the condemnation of human rights abuses in
other countries, ending its much-touted though frequently violated policy of
"noninterference," in other countries. It might have a special role in moni-

toring human rights abuses and encouraging democratization in remaining dictatorships in Asia—North Korea, Burma, and Vietnam.

Even without a spirited democratic diplomacy, China's democratization would be a powerful incentive to people and elites in remaining dictatorships around the world. China's democratization would itself constitute an entire "fourth wave," but others may be brought along in the eddies. In Asia, it would almost certainly cause ruptures in North Korea, Burma, and Vietnam, whose dictatorships have benefited in varying ways from ongoing dictatorship in China. Singapore and Malaysia, which sit on the line between dictatorship and democracy, might be urged to move more firmly into the democratic camp.

Finally, a democratic China could prove a salutary force for a relaunch of a serious effort at global redistribution. The 14 percent of the world's people living in OECD countries continue to command an ever more disproportionate amount of world resources in the early twenty-first century, earning an income per capita six times that of the rest of the world and enjoying 89 percent of global health expenditures. Eleven million children—the entire population of Greece—and another 7 million adults die of poverty-related diseases every year. In the early 1950s, China was flush with a genuine esprit as a leader of a new global development drive, symbolized by Beijing's prominent role at the Bandung meeting of the the nonaligned movement in 1955. Once Mao's state went awry, however, that interest in global justice became an interest in fomenting revolution abroad and propping up corrupt dictatorships. In the reform era, Beijing became a rogue state of the right rather than left. Its state companies sold small arms to warlords in Africa, plundered the remaining tropical forests of Southeast Asia, and peddled missile technology to Pakistan and North Korea. This was not the global redistribution that the optimists of Bandung had in mind.

By joining other developing countries, China could easily emerge as the leader of a new "North-South movement," this time with the credibility that goes with being a democracy. It could take on perceived unfairness in the global regimes covering things like carbon emissions, intellectual property protection, agricultural policy, and multinational investment. It could challenge the selfishness of Western countries from the moral high ground that comes with being a democracy. China, in other words, could be a major force for creating a less unequal world.

While the ideological issue of democracy will disappear as a source of conflict between China and the world, this by no means implies that there will be no foreign policy conflicts. Just as fully-paid-up members of the democratic camp have frequent and strident foreign policy differences, so too differences would remain with China. Not only will China's interpretation of democracy at times conflict with those of others, but also its views on a whole range of policy issues like resources, immigration, environment, weapons proliferation, economic policy, cultural protection, nationalism, and terrorism will reflect its particular views and interests. China's foreign policy, like its democracy, will be very "Chinese," a trite statement perhaps but one worth keeping in mind.

The annual U.S. State Department report on human rights, for example, might continue to take issue with China's handling of certain rights issues, such as large-scale executions of prisoners, the banning of seditious or secessionist speech, or the destruction of ancestral halls for the sake of development. China would defend itself in a way consonant with international norms: not by deriding human rights universality, nor the problems of the United States itself, but by arguing that the alleged violations were mistakes, or were not so severe, or even that they were consonant with the ideals of democracy.

On technocratic issues, China's views might be even more at odds with the West. Its powerful claims to be excluded from carbon emission bans based on its low per-capita emissions and its early-development stage would continue. Its protests at Western protectionism would remain strong. It might still argue that Uighur separatists who took refuge in a foreign country were terrorists and should be extradited.

Beijing's foreign policy will also be more liable to change than in the past. The CCP's saving grace in diplomacy was that it was principled and consistent on most issues because it did not have to answer to domestic interests. This will change with democracy. As China's people change their views on international issues, foreign policy will change with it. In contrast to their dealings with the steely consistency of the old emperors of Beijing, foreign countries will now find themselves meeting with elected politicians who are trying to keep on top of public opinion. Capriciousness and volatility would be a new dimension of China's foreign policy.

While China's nationalism may not be an antidemocratic one, it would continue to affect foreign policy. Japan, South Korea, and the Philippines have had to deal with the sudden eruptions of anti-American protestors; so too China could easily find itself swept up in anti-U.S. protests over one slight or another. And in contrast to the past where the demonstrations were often orchestrated by Beijing, this time they may be aimed squarely at Beijing, forcing the government to respond with policy changes that might anger Washington.

Finally, foreign policy will almost certainly decline in importance in a democratic China. Just as leaders no longer sought legitimacy in global grandstanding, so too the exigencies of domestic governance would absorb more of their time. The experience of other post-communist countries like Russia and post-authoritarian countries like Indonesia shows how the domestic agenda dominates the early years of democracy, lowering the country's international profile. India is perhaps the best example of a country whose democracy demands most of the time of its leaders, who spend far less time on the road than those of the PRC.

As China's thirst for international power and recognition recedes, other democratic countries that have long punched far below their weight—Japan, India, Germany, Brazil—may rise in global importance, perhaps signified by an expansion of permanent seats on the UN Security Council. A China that no longer represents a competing ideological foe and that is increasingly devoted to solving its domestic problems will loom less large on the international stage.

Transitional Diplomacy

Like democracy itself, the pursuit of a democratic foreign policy is a process, a continued struggle to act democratically in foreign dealings that mirrors the struggle to act democratically at home. Even long-democratic countries see frequent eruptions of nondemocratic foreign policies, the United States being a tragic example.

For China, which has had a strictly realist foreign policy since Mao's death, the reorientation would be a slow one. The ups and downs of democratic consolidation would be mirrored by frequent departures from the norms of democratic foreign policy—reversions to chauvinistic nationalism, utilitarian justifications for injustice, and claims that sovereignty could not countenance foreign interference on human rights. The PRC's foreign policy—its great-power ambitions, its rejection of universal rights norms, its purely realist foreign policy, its claims on Taiwan—will not change overnight. As one Western scholar noted in light of Russia's first decade of democracy: "Even a smooth and peaceful exit from communism in China would require a good deal of foreign cooperation, patience, and delicate diplomacy if regional crises are to be avoided. . . . China's diplomatic and international role is likely to be as nerve-wracking as Russia's."[2]

As such, it will be important that the world community continue providing support and incentives to Beijing to stick to the democratic course and moderate its foreign policy. In the immediate period of collapse, as noted, there will be a threat of military aggression by the crumbling CCP regime. Yet this threat will continue to exist as the first government finds its feet. Taiwan is the most likely target for this aggression. Yet it could be loaded onto any neighbor, including rival claimants in the South China Sea or Japan's Senkaku (Diaoyutai) Islands. The threats of a strong anti-U.S. posture are also latent. The PLA was armed with 400 nuclear warheads and around 30 long-range nuclear missiles by the turn of the century, and the safe control of these weapons would be a critical task for the world community, just as it was in the USSR.

More generally, it has been common for newly democratic states to adopt strongly nationalist positions (Russia on Chechnya, Indonesia on East Timor) in the immediate wake of the fall of authoritarianism because new leaders do not want to be blamed for presiding over the end of their empires or the decline of their country's international prestige. In history, indeed, many democratic revolutions have been accompanied by international aggression — whether the American revolutionaries who invaded Canada or the French revolutionaries who marched on Europe under Napoleon.

In China, democracy movements have typically also been accompanied by an upsurge in nationalism. The May Fourth Movement was rabidly anti-Japanese while the 1989 Tiananmen students demanded to be recognized as "patriotic." A fledgling democratic government in China grappling with flaring nationalism could be a significant challenge for the world community.

Still, even if we assume that China's transition to a peace-loving and stabilizing democratic foreign policy may be delayed by a period of quite the opposite, there is reason to be optimistic about this period if properly handled for two reasons, one practical and one philosophical.

Practically speaking, there is a qualitative difference in reacting to an aggressive foreign policy driven by the transparent imperatives of democratic transition and one driven by the secret imperatives of authoritarianism — even if the results are the same, or worse. Knowing that a given action by Beijing results from popular pressures or unstable politics rather than any considered strategy of aggression will allow foreign countries to respond more effectively and intelligently. If a newly democratic China were to threaten a military expedition to remove Japanese lighthouses from the Senkaku Islands, for example, Western leaders could downplay the threat in public while engaging in close diplomacy in private. Likewise, if a national storm were whipped up about, say, steel dumping tariffs imposed in the United States, the very openness of the debate and protests would make it easier to formulate a response.

In addition, China will be in a period of rapid learning about democracy, not only at home, but also from abroad. Unlike the transition period, which is unique and unsettled in every country, the consolidation period is one where the models and patterns of other democracies are broadly applicable.

China's new leaders, even if they feel populist pressures to wage aggressive foreign policies, may also be informed by the knowledge of how damaging such actions can be to their international credibility, aid flows, and ultimately their own political positions.

At a more philosophical level, there is an argument that some degree of saber-rattling and nationalist aggression from China may simply be one of the prices the world has to pay to see the world's biggest country through the gateway to democracy. The CCP has long appealed to outside fears of strategic instability to attract support for the maintenance of its rule. The realist assumption underlying this argument, reflecting the CCP's own view of the world, is that the outside world does not care about the establishment of a just and moral polity for the people of China, only the material impact it might have on themselves. Therefore, the world community would seek to prevent a democratic transition if it carried costs.

Certainly, the frequent vacillation between realist and moral foreign policies by the world's established democracies means that the CCP propaganda strategy gains some adherents abroad, including in the West. But the generally stronger forces of democratic foreign policy imperatives ensure that the argument is not convincing. Like the domestic violence accompanying transition, an unstable Chinese foreign policy may be a price worth paying. As with fearmongering about social and economic collapse and its impact on the world, the dangers on the foreign policy front are probably overblown. Either way, the costs need to be put into the perspective of the larger gains for China and ultimately the world of the establishment of a democracy there.

It is that calculus that led the world's democratic majority to continue to urge political transition on the CCP in the late PRC era, despite the likely up-front costs. There might be doubts about that policy in the heat of the first foreign policy crisis involving a newly democratic China. But the ethical logic would hold.

Relations with the United States

China's relations with the United States may not loom so large after the fall of the PRC. A whole industry of China-watchers in government and the academy may be put out of business. Just as democratic Russia became less threatening and more cooperative in the wake of the fall of communism, so too China can be expected to diminish in immediate importance to the United States and the West in general. Like Japan, its influence in world affairs will be exerted more and more through its economic rather than its military or political muscle.

China's Leninist insistence on political control, its rejection of international norms of rights, and its realist foreign policy will all be removed as obstacles in Sino-U.S. relations. In their place will come less flammable issues of business, trade, environment, and cross-border crime and immigration. It is probably safe to say that Kant's "democratic peace" will work to improve Sino-U.S. relations.

Still, relations between Beijing and Washington will remain complex and far from trouble-free, as are Washington's ties to other democracies.

As above, China's ties to the United States should be separated into the transitional and the long-term perspectives. The transitional period, which could last a decade or more, will be the most difficult since all the promises of a democratic foreign policy may remain unfulfilled in this period. Some scholars believe that in this period, Sino-U.S. relations will remain tense on virtually all the same issues as before—human rights, Taiwan, rogue regime relations, and global peacekeeping—because China's foreign policy fundamentals will not be changed at first.[3]

For the United States, this will require the creation of a new foreign policy. Whereas under the CCP, the guiding U.S. policy was one of seeking to change the political system, it will now have to pursue truly "constructive" engagement, ties that aim to bolster the political system not dismantle it. If elements of the CCP are returned to power in the initial elections, the United States will have to treat them as respected officials. State Department reports on human rights in China will need to draw greater attention to achievements of China's new democracy such as growing civil society, political institutionalization, and of course participation.

Through the timely provision of financial assistance and the adjustment of strategic priorities in East Asia, the United States could ensure this process is a rapid and nondisruptive as possible. One shortcoming of post-Soviet U.S. assistance to Russia was the lack of funding—less than 2 percent of total aid in the period 1992 to 2002—which went toward supporting democracy.[4] This may have made the consolidation phase more difficult than it might have been. The same was true, with lamentable consequences, of aid for South Africa after its initial transition.

Thus a sensible policy for China would be the pursuit of a plan with a higher priority on spending to support democracy. As with the new democracies of Europe, that aid should be aimed at building the foundations of democracy through help to independent pro-reform media, policy think tanks, investigative arms of government, the judiciary and legal systems, and parliamentary powers and capabilities, all of it helping to create the internal momentum for reforms.[5]

The costs to the United States of aiding democracy in China should be compared to the billions spent maintaining 100,000 forward deployed forces in the region. In that light, the costs would be relatively small. All this needs to be carefully tailored to meet China's needs and phobias. The highly visible and condition-based support for democracy that the United States gave to Mongolia or Cambodia might be inappropriate for China, where fears of being manipulated by Western powers are longstanding.

Longer-term, China will be a major world power with which the United States needs to share global responsibilities. U.S.-led regional security structures in Asia should be expanded to include China, just as NATO expanded into Eastern Europe after the collapse of the Berlin Wall. China might be invited to join in the annual Cobra Gold exercises between the forces of the United States and Thailand or the annual Ulchi Focus Lens exercises between U.S. and South Korean forces. Ideally, China will emerge as a stable and responsible democracy that will make any U.S. forces in Asia unnecessary. After more than a half-century as the dominant power of Asia, the United States could finally go home.

Relations with Asia

The realization of the democratic peace will be no less important to China's relations with the rest of Asia. Asia would feel the fallout from an unstable transition or rocky consolidation of democracy in China most of all. China's role in regional security and across a range of technocratic issues—AIDS, drugs, crime, the environment, communications and transport, travel, and much else—already looms large in Asia. That alone gives Asian countries a big incentive to join with the West in making contingency plans to reduce and mitigate such impacts.

It is probable that some elements of the "strong country dream" will persist in Chinese minds vis-à-vis the rest of Asia. But they will come in a very different form. Most important, regional hegemony will no longer be official policy while the open political system will make any regional ambitions less threatening. Some liberal Chinese officials spoke in the late PRC era of being mainly a "cultural power" of Asia whose impact did not extent into the political arena.[6] All this portends a new gentleness in China's regional ambitions. A democratic China, predicts one liberal, would be more likely to pursue an "elephant strategy" (*daxiang zhanlue*), lumbering peaceably through the undergrowth of Asian politics munching on vegetation and trying not to step on anybody.[7]

China may be more able but less willing now to demand a larger role in

Asia's politics since the driving imperative behind that was one of seeking legitimacy at home. As India and Russia's leaders have found, pressing domestic concerns mean they get little traction out of engaging in high-minded diplomatic strategies abroad. One Chinese liberal has suggested that a democratic China should join the United States, Japan, and Taiwan in establishing an Asia Security Commission to keep the peace in the region.[8] Some such arrangement—although certainly also requiring India and Asean involvement—might be useful.

By removing a major undemocratic nation from the map of Asia, China's democratic change would be a major boost to regional security. Not only would the threat of aggression fall, but the developmental impact, assuming it is a positive one, would foster stronger economic and social links between China and the region that would further enhance security.

Strategically, India, Spratly Islands claimants, and Central Asian countries would need to ensure they do not provoke a flaring nationalism in China. Some countries might be willing to make unilateral concessions as a show of goodwill. India, for example, could agree to withdraw troops from the 90,000 sq. km of former Tibetan territory that is now inside the line of control it defends. Japan might declare a ban on its nationals landing on the Senkaku islands.

Preeminent among Beijing's ties are those with Japan. Asia's largest economy and its largest country need to get along better, both for their own sakes and for the future security of Asia. From many perspectives, the democratic process in China should help to moderate China's long-standing militant attitude toward Japan. A more moderate and less racist nationalism, a sense of the losses incurred under Mao compared to the Japanese Imperial Army, and a belief in a commonality of interests in promoting a peaceful and democratic Asia will all help reconciliation between Beijing and Tokyo, just as they have in Seoul's relations with Tokyo.

Democracy in China will also allow Tokyo to engage Beijing more in issues of human rights and democratic consolidation. If it took this step, Tokyo would help change Japan's image in China as a greedy economic power with a grisly historical record, both of which, in Chinese eyes, previously disqualified it from raising moral issues. Japan could be the leader of Asia's democracies in financially supporting China's consolidation. It is already the largest donor and now its aid could be grounded in clear moral aims.

Issues will remain at the social level, especially from World War II. No Chinese leader could be seen to toady to Japan, as South Korea's leaders have found. These issues still excite passions in open Hong Kong and Taiwan. But they will no longer dominate diplomatic ties. Beijing's new political openness will allow Tokyo to put on hold its cautious rearmament and engage in arms control talks with China. At a deeper level, the cultural jealousy with which China looks upon Japan—the country of "pirates and midgets" that took China's best culture, improved on it, and became a world leader—would moderate. As one Western scholar wrote: "Only a democratized China, made less nativistic by confronting its own repressed expansionist and inhuman activities and able to comprehend Japan as something other than inherently and cruelly militaristic, can realize the Tokyo-Beijing reconciliation required for prolonged peace and prosperity in the Pacific."[9]

Taiwan, Tibet and Xinjiang

How will a democratic China ultimately resolve the burdens of empire inherited from the Qing dynasty? As we have seen, Taiwan's autonomy could be tested at any point during China's transition to democracy—from a last-ditch effort by PRC politicians to maintain power to an early gambit by a newly elected politician to prove his or her patriotic credentials to a sudden policy decision in later years as China's democracy enters its troubled youth. Avoiding this will require all the wisdom and patience that Taiwan and its leadership have accumulated since the island began to democratize in the mid-1980s.

It will be important for Taiwan leaders not to take advantage of the situation in China to bolster their country's autonomy. Indeed, statements from Taiwan leaders to the effect that the transition makes prospects brighter for some form of political reconciliation would help the transition and further reduce incentives for an attack. The achievement of democracy in China will meet one crucial precondition for reunification long demanded by Taipei. If it is not to be seen as reneging on that stand, Taipei will need to at least pay lip service to the idea of closer political cooperation.

While the newly democratic China may have legally banned secession, Taiwan will not likely feel bound by this injunction given its de facto independence from China. Thus arguments against a formal declaration of independence by Taiwan will be not constitutional but political and strategic. Those arguments suggest that it should refrain from seeking independence— meaning shutting the door on any future political relationship with the mainland—in order not to sabotage the democratic project in China itself, which may be the best guarantee for Taiwan's future freedom. Russia's attacks on Chechnya, reflect the dangers of preemptive bids for independence when a former empire is going through democratization. Indonesia was a rare, if bloody and troubled, exception in begrudgingly allowing East Timor to secede. As with the difficult issue of secession, this provides a principled and just reason for foreign governments to urge Taiwan to constrain its justified desire for formal independence until such time as that independence can be guaranteed and will not undermine the quest for freedoms in China itself.

The "federal" arrangement long proposed by the CCP in which Taiwan would forfeit its de facto sovereignty and its de jure claims to international recognition was unacceptable because it would have been a backward step for Taiwan. A democratic China would be more likely to negotiate a pact acceptable to Taipei. Beijing could now conceive closer political ties with Taiwan as an issue of "contract" (freely entered into for mutual benefit) rather than "coercion" (necessary to accept in order to avoid punishment). Politicians in China who could show they had achieved progress on reunification would win electoral kudos.[10] Beijing may then be able to offer conditions that are attractive to Taiwan, such as some commonwealth-style arrangement.

Taiwan may be attracted since a democratic China's politicians will be more reliable given that hidden agendas are less feasible. The newly democratic ethos of China would appeal more to people in Taiwan too. Given the island's close economic integration with China, political cooperation could be widely welcomed beyond the tired old pro-China crowd in Taipei.

In some confederate arrangement, Taiwan and China would agree to a joint foreign policy and integration of their military commands. Something like the "Community of China" (zhonghua gongtongti), "New China" (xin zhonghua), or "Federation of China" (zhonghua liangbang) could be formed, with China, Hong Kong, Macau, and Taiwan as members. Taiwan's long insistence that China be democratic before any political coalition could be considered would thus emerge as more than just an ideological statement, although it had ideological roots in Sun Yat-sen's Three Principles of the People. Given that any confederation would require both sides to have independent judiciaries to mediate legal disputes and strong liberal institutions to manage them politically, a working democracy in China would be a very practical need.[11]

Still, such an arrangement could be torn asunder by strong independence sentiment in Taiwan and strong reunification sentiment in China. In Taiwan, as in East Timor, there will be a strong drive for independence no matter what China offers. China's flimsy assertion of sovereignty over Taiwan—it was first settled by Austronesian people, had tributary relations to Japan, and was ruled by the Spanish, Dutch, and Portuguese for longer than by China—makes even loose confederation seem illogical. A popular referendum, which Taiwan politicians were already proposing in 2002, might result in a landslide for independence once the threat of an invasion from China was removed.

In China, the response might be stern. It will take a long time before democracy cultivates a belief in the inherent right of self-determination of peoples. Canada only allowed Quebecois to hold the first of what would become periodic referendums on independence in 1980 after more than a decade of resistance to the idea. The UK took 80 years to accept the notion of self-determination for Northern Ireland. The experience of most countries, especially newly democratic ones, is that this belief appears only slowly. In China, long schooled to believe that Taiwan was an inalienable part of the mainland, coming to terms with the island's desire for independence will be a long-term process. At the very least, China might try to apply sanctions against Taiwan.

Even without bids for independence in Taiwan, the threat of irredentist claims from China will remain. Politicians in China may say that the loose political arrangements only provide the cover for Taiwan's quest for independence, just as the Commonwealth of Independent States provided cover for Russian politicians in asserting national unity while countries like the Ukraine and Georgia seceded.

The United States and its allies in Asia will play a crucial stabilizing role in making it clear to China's new leaders that the costs of attack on Taiwan would far outweigh potential benefits. They may also help to engender the belief in self-determination for Taiwan. Ultimately, the most that can be hoped for may be a formally independent Taiwan with perhaps some brotherly relationship to China as that between Britain and its former colonies in Canada and Australia who share consular resources and a monarch. This would be good for regional stability as it would remove the threat of war in key waterways. China would benefit politically as well as economically.

What of Tibet and Xinjiang? We left these regions under conditions of a ban on secession coupled with grants of real autonomy and the arrival of UN monitors to check on the condition of rights. We noted that even with fully implemented promises, the drive for autonomy in these regions will be strong, despite the best efforts of international leaders, their own elected governments, and of course Beijing itself. Such a drive in the period before democratic consolidation would threaten the democracy in China. It was an open-ended question about the results.

Now assume that democracy has consolidated in China, in spite of ongoing secessionist pressures in Tibet and Xinjiang. That is, suppose China is in a position like Spain, Canada, India, the Philippines, or Russia where a consolidated democracy confronts a secessionist land in its midst. How strong will secessionist strengths be in a truly democratic China? And what would be the results?

Suppose real freedom and autonomy have come to these places. Beijing may also have made many special concessions in terms of self-policing, cultural promotion and group rights policies, vetoes over constitutional changes, special fiscal transfers and control over natural resources, and much else, such as separate time zones that allow these regions to live in normal daylight hours. Democracy in China will allow many to argue that it is best for the regions to remain. In addition, proponents of union will be able to argue that on their own the regions might fall prey to theocratic political instability—highlighted by Nepal's royal family massacre in 2001—or international strategic posturing.

Tibet's government in exile has long stated that acceptable autonomy would be possible within a democratic China. Beijing could return to the liberal ideals of the 1980s under Hu Yaobang, which included a large-scale retirement of Chinese cadres in the region, the promotion of Tibetan culture, and the granting of real religious freedoms. Under an elected leadership and with the spiritual leadership of a returned Dalai Lama, Tibet could thrive, as have cultural fragments within larger states like Quebec and Tamil Nadu. The same goes for Xinjiang.

Still, there are likely to be splits within the Tibetan and Xinjiang ethnic communities on the issue of self-determination. Even with rights enhanced greatly, many people will not feel "liberated" by democracy but merely the subjects of a new colonial order. In the 1,000-member national parliament, the two Tibetan members and 14 Xinjiang representatives will be swamped. Both places will have groups arguing the merits of formal independence and statehood. Those in Tibet could argue that the region is a prime candidate for separation because, like East Timor, it has a strong national identity, a central leader, geographic unity, and global support. Whatever its modern-day softness, Chinese rule was imposed by force and kept in place by repression for decades and that alone justifies secession, they will argue. After a certain period, the ban on secession would come up and it is reasonable to assume that this would energize independence groups.

If, say, Tibet, did decide through a UN-sponsored referendum among Tibetan citizens of the PRC to become an independent states, it would be a complex affair. Negotiations with Beijing, probably sponsored by the UN, would need to resolve the boundaries of the new state, the status of Han populations there, and the ownership of extensive infrastructure and industry investments made by the PRC since 1949. The six-million odd Tibetans would also have to confront the sensitive issue of the democratizing their own nation by gently relieving the Dalai Lama of his political power.

How would China respond to such initiatives? To be sure, democracy would have lessened chauvinist attitudes toward Tibet and Xinjiang. The anti-

Western nationalism nurtured on a sense of victimization that saw any expression of Tibetan wishes as an externally generated Western conspiracy to split China would be weakened. The Marxist view, which sees ethnic identity as a result of economic deprivation, would also change. A new awareness of the financial and political costs of suppressing secession movements would also temper attitudes. As one Western scholar notes in a comment that could equally apply to Xinjiang: "China does not need Tibet, and if the Tibetans are lucky the Chinese will finally acknowledge that Tibet has become a huge and nonessential economic drain on China."[12]

But for the most part, people in China, even strong democrats, would most likely continue to feel opposed to the breakup of the country, just as nationalists in England long opposed any idea of self-determination for Northern Ireland, Scotland, and Wales. Even if this issue is not going to sink democracy in China, it would make politics more unstable. As two Chinese scholars write: "If it cannot be resolved it will be difficult for democracy to flourish."[13] The key "equation," in the political calculus of both places then will be the balance between two dynamic factors: the extent to which improved conditions and enlightened policies in the regions moderate demands for independence; and the extent to which democratic development in China moderates hard-line attitudes toward national political unity. The more this is the case, the greater will be the overlapping area which could form the basis of a permanent solution.

The possibility of such a solution, with Tibet and Xinjiang remaining in the Chinese fold, reminds us of the nonsense of an ineluctable "clash of civilizations" that promised to tear our world asunder along ethnic and cultural lines. That never has been the main line of contention in our world, which concerns economic deprivation and political repression, not constructed and manipulated "cultural differences."[14] Just as Huntington's prediction that the Ukraine would split into a Europeanized uniate west and a Russified orthodox east was proven wrong, so too the break-away of Tibet and parts of Xinjiang is by no means inevitable. A successful democracy in China could well embrace these regions as part of a liberal multiethnic state.

A China that exercises a just and legitimate sovereignty in Tibet will be a China that all the world can celebrate. As with Tibet, so too for the rest of the country. Democracy will not be a cure-all. But it will offer hope for a resolution of many problems that by the early twenty-first century had reached a deep impasse. China's democratic future will remind us that humanity, far from being the inert victim of history and structure, can be the agent of its own better destiny.

Conclusion

China's embrace of democracy will be one of the defining moments of modern political history, no less significant than the Russian Revolution of 1917 or the fall of the Berlin Wall in 1989. In myriad ways, it will force a rethinking of history itself and of the assumptions that we make about human societies and global politics. Like the French Revolution, China's democratic breakthrough may remain a work in progress for many decades, thus making immediate verdicts on its significance difficult. But it is worthwhile to anticipate some of the issues that will be under consideration.

From the commanding heights of modern Chinese history, democratization should be seen as the culmination of centuries of development. China's imperial tradition fell on a crisis of legitimacy beginning with the commercial revolution of the late Ming dynasty in the mid-sixteenth century. The rag-tag posse of Manchurian soldiers that overran the country a century later were no better disposed to resolve that crisis. End-of-dynasty afflictions—like corruption, eunuch power, and local rebellion—were apparent almost immediately in their Qing dynasty. The bureaucracy gradually took control of the country for lack of a more legitimate authority.

The Qing collapse, signified by the first Opium War in 1839 and formally declared in 1911, gave China's society its first chance to run the state. That attempt failed. Society remained too weak in the face of political elites styling themselves the heirs of imperial rule. Pro-democracy forces asserted themselves throughout the republican and PRC eras but were consistently repressed by political elites. The regressive tyranny of Mao showed how costly that weakness could be in the modern era. The restoration of autocracy exacted a heavy price—taking the lives of perhaps 55 million people, roughly the population of present-day Italy—even if it left in place strong state institutions.

Mao's death marked a resumption of society's largely successful attempts to win control of the state. Economic and social freedoms expanded quickly, while political power was constrained. In 1989, citizens reminded their leaders, and the world, that popular sovereignty was the ultimate goal. Democratization will mark the final triumph of society's ascendancy. From the perspective of the ground already covered, that triumph will be only a small leap.

And it will be a largely predictable event that is consistent with five centuries of national development. Democracy will be a fulfillment of history rather than a break with it.

China's tortuous path to democracy raises questions about what factors are critical to the defeat of dictatorship. This book has adopted a broad approach to that question, looking at both needs and resources, and at their generation in economic, social, international, and political spheres. But to hazard a guess, it is likely that deep underlying social shifts resulting from economic reforms will be the critical factor. While there was a great deal of international pressure to democratize, China was too large, sheltered, and sure of its uniqueness for this to be determinative. While the polity was troubled, there was enough confidence in the leaderships after Tiananmen to hold it together. But as society grew more diverse, organized, and powerful as a result of economic reforms, the wiggle room for dictators ineluctably narrowed.

I would hesitate to say that this conclusion differs from current thinking on democratization for the simple reason that no scholars, even if they highlight immediate issues of regime defections, reform elites, or economic crisis, fail also to place those contingent changes against a background of longer-term social (and economic) change. The short-term dynamics of democratic breakthrough provide only the final link needed to achieve democracy. In that sense my conclusions are at one with both traditional modernization theories and modern bargaining theories of democratization.

Likewise, China's democratic consolidation will raise broader questions about what makes democracies succeed and fail (or at least regress). Again, we may find that the expected success of China's democracy leads us to pinpoint the long-term or structural factors that underlie the feat: the market economy, the emergent media, the global democratic backstop, and much else. That said, the decisions of political elites will be critical in turning that potential into reality. As in Russia, a no less unlikely site of a working democracy, the emergence of a simple "belief" among elites in making democracy work may be the ultimate cause of a successful consolidation in China. This echoes the importance of new ideas in society that lead to the transition itself—the belief in justice, the reimagined liberal identity, the search for historical truth, and much else. If anything, it is this "revolution in values," the one Hegel noted always precedes revolutions, that proves to be the most useful indicator of democratic breakthrough and consolidation alike. In this respect, I find myself more closely aligned with political scientists who argue that public normative values, not narrow self-interests and payoffs, are the driving force in modern political development.

If China was indeed heading for democracy, might it not have been better had it embraced democracy as soon as the Maoist nightmare was over, just as Spain did when Franco died? A move toward democracy in the early 1980s could have culminated in full democratization by the turn of the century. It would have left a powerhouse economy and a global political giant. In the absence of this, China went the way of many a postcolonial order in Latin America and Africa, turning a worthy reform movement into an unholy scramble for individual gain. The lack of political reforms bred corruption, inequality, social malaise, and political cynicism.

Many have argued that "China got it right, Russia got it wrong," in comparing the paths from communism of the two countries. Russia moved toward political freedom quickly when the weight of totalitarian rule ended in 1985 after the deaths of Leonid Brezhnev and his two hoary successors. Without a doubt, as one scholar has argued, the "up front" transition costs toward democracy were higher in Russia, where the economy collapsed, political instability rose, and national conflict was rampant. By contrast, for more than 20 years after its totalitarian episode, China enjoyed widened freedoms and a growing economy as well as relative political stability.[1]

But the relevant metric of transition success is "total costs" rather than "upfront costs." These, of course, can be debated only after each country has attained a consolidated democracy. Russia certainly paid high up-front costs. Yet with a minimal, if still troubled, democratic polity and a growing economy by the early 2000s, it might well end up paying less heavily than China in overall terms. China is already paying a significant price for delaying political reform; the costs of its transition and consolidation processes have yet to be seen.

Indeed, it may be that China had the opportunity to pay far less than was even possible in Russia. China's economic and political systems suffered less complete and less enduring suffocation from totalitarianism. China's largely rural and agricultural entrepreneurs could embrace the market, while Russia's largely urban and industrial ones could only fear it. The figure to emerge from the totalitarian ordeal in China, Deng Xiaoping, also enjoyed greater legitimacy than Gorbachev, his counterpart in Russia. China, in other words, had a historic opportunity to make a quick and decisive leap to democracy that Russia was never afforded. To have paid as dearly as Russia appears needless. To have paid more, simply folly.

This question must remain an open one until China's democratic transition is complete. We can gauge the price that China is paying for delayed political reform now. But we cannot evaluate those costs until the country has constructed a democratic polity. If the transition and consolidation phases proceed with barely a hiccup, it might vindicate those who advocated the "politics last" model, at least for China. In a country with limited ethnic divisions, a readily marketizable economy, and a high degree of social and political consensus, it may be argued, a lengthy period of benevolent authoritarianism was the ideal pathway to democracy. If, on the other hand, those phases are turbulent and protracted, it will raise retrospective doubts about the late PRC era. Is China a thankfully averted Yugoslavia or a needlessly stifled Poland? Only time will tell. Suffice it to say for now that it is both premature and ahistorical to assert that China's path from communism was a success.

If it has not already been brought into serious question by the continued spread of democracy to every corner of the world, Samuel Huntington's thesis of a world dominated by a "clash of civilizations" rent between a liberal and progressive West and a conservative and benighted "other" should be given a final burial by China's embrace of democracy. It will confirm that the real clash in our world remains a clash of just versus unjust political conceptions, between dictatorship and democracy or minimal democracy and full democracy, not between some imagined, essentialized, and monoistic "cultures." The very terms "East" and "West" will finally be exposed as so bereft of any cultural or social meaning as to be virtually useless in our modern world except as geographic shorthand.

Still, if democracy is merely the most efficient and fair mechanism for organizing a polity—any polity—then its meaning will continue to change as each finds new ways to improve that mechanism. While "history" as defined by the monumental struggle between the notion of the political equality of individuals and rival conceptions appears to have ended, it will go on being spun out in competing conceptions of democracy. Debates about issues like compulsory voting, fair electoral systems, money in politics, judicial review, and the like will be the dominant "historical" issues of our time. As an ongoing experiment in best-practice politics, democracy is sure to be influenced by its practice in China, which will come to the game with a rich tradition of indigenous innovation and, arguably, deeper cultural roots in the essential principles of democracy such as tolerance, compromise, and egalitarianism. How will democracy change as a result?

There has been much recent discussion in the West of a "democratic malaise" where the associational and norms-oriented life of a democracy is breaking down. Many scholars see the democratic waves of the past as having ended and the old democracies in a state of slow regression. Some countries are thought to be stuck in minimal democracies of dispersed power but not true equality. To some, the value of political power is unequal, some freedoms more cared for than others, and economic justice unachieved. If modern-day social contractarians are right, a failure to achieve these things make a democracy's claim to goodness very thin indeed.

It is here that China's democratization may play a vital role. Most Chinese scholars harbor the hope that China will "surpass" traditional forms of democracy as practiced in the rest of the world—especially the imagined "Western model"—and introduce to the world a new system that will be "even better."[2] This is the so-called "surpass sentiment" (chaoyue qingxu) mentioned earlier. Of course, there is not a little bit of cultural chauvinism at work here, the desire for China to retake its rightful place as the dispenser of civilization to the world's benighted peoples, especially the stubbornly dynamic West. Even so, we should not rule out, nor rue, the possibility that China will pioneer a unique version of democracy. As one Western scholar notes: "It remains possible that some day the Asian, perhaps even the Chinese, vision of the best form of government will become the dominant vision."[3] If so, it would be a cause for celebration because everyone benefits when a more just system is available.

Many Chinese scholars conjure up a new form of political order that is both strongly democratic and strongly social-oriented. One talks of the emergence of a "creative ambiguity," in China which defies easy labels, in which a "mixed economy" with a state sector will exist alongside "mixed politics" with elements of both liberal democracy and social democracy.[4] Others seem to echo classical republican political theorists of the West with dreams of "deliberative democracy" (shangyi minzhu)[5] or "policy democracy" (zhengce minzhu) in which people's considered views on issues actually translate into outcomes.[6] Here, elections lose their pride of place as the hallmark of democracy, being replaced by other mechanisms for contesting state power and proposing interests and views of the good. One Chinese scholar anticipates a vast laboratory of democratic experimentation which, given the sheer size of the country, would create a whole new lexicon of democratic forms and theories: "There are actual opportunities for transcending historically known systems and they might be seized by a conscious people."[7]

There is much here that meshes with recent thinking on democracy in the West, which stresses issues like social capital, popular deliberation, equality of political opportunity, and more. In other words, the ongoing struggle to move from mere formal democracy to a substantive democracy of equal citizens will be helped by China. Its efforts at "real democracy" may inspire and push established democracies to "deepen" their own democratic experiences. One Indian author has said that "the future of Western political theory will be decided outside the West," noting, rightly, that India would loom large in that experience.[8] One could not but add China. Indeed, given that it was never imprinted with colonialism and given its long isolation from Western theory, China's impact may be much greater. Notes one scholar: "The final destination of the search remains veiled, but China's preoccupation with local innovation and adaptation certainly goes beyond mere rhetoric."[9]

Even without any major innovations in the practice of democracy emanating from China, the mere adoption of this long-evolving and never-perfected system by the largest country in the world and one of its most ancient will have a profound effect on deepening democracy. Just as the fall of the Berlin Wall reinstated some confidence in liberal regimes, and just as the collapse of authoritarian regimes in Asia has undermined advocates of soft authoritarianism there, so too China's democracy may shore up the loss of interest in the West about democracy.

To return to a quotation cited earlier, China's democratization will probably transform global politics at every level. It will mean that roughly three quarters of the world's population lives in democratic states, creating "an historic opportunity to bring a truly democratic world into being," notes one scholar.[10] Relations among the world's peoples could for the first time be governed according to the same norms that apply to their domestic polities. Much of this had already begun in the post-cold war era as new democracies in Africa, Asia, Eastern Europe, and Latin America forged alliances grounded in these norms. With China aligned with that global movement, the possibilities for positive change will be immense.

Afterword

One of the risks of writing a book about the future is being wrong. The other risk is being right too soon. Although I long ago accepted the former possibility, the latter also loomed several times during the five years that it took to research and write this book. Authoritarian regimes like the Chinese Communist Party are vulnerable to crisis and China has faced several in recent years. First the Asian financial crash, then the insurgency of the mystical Falun Gong religious sect, an international war against terror-sponsoring nations, a bumpy leadership succession, a plague-like virus known by its acronym SARS, and then a political crisis in Hong Kong—all these events at one time or another might have brought systematic political change to China.

Weak and illegitimate regimes are vulnerable to crisis, but the details of transition are always a surprise. End-of-regime watchers like myself are used to the unexpected. Contingency and oddity are the leitmotifs of political ruptures and China is sure to be no exception. All of these crises emerged in unexpected ways from unexpected quarters, quickly enveloped the political system, and led to often-daring acts of imagination by political and social elites struggling to resolve the centuries-old impasse between state and society in China.

Democracy has been the theme of this book, and each of these crises has provided an ideal tram in which to tour the theme park. From the windows, we saw all of the manifestations of dictatorship that make political liberalization so pressing in the minds of the Chinese today, as well as all the assorted means by which this change will be brought about. They powerfully highlight the forces that are moving China toward a democratic future.

The crisis over severe acute respiratory syndrome (SARS), which swept across the country in late 2002 and early 2003, was perhaps the best example. The crisis began because of bad government. A virulent strain of virus detected in southern China in late 2002 was allowed to spread unchecked because of censored information, unresponsive officials, an unaccountable public healthcare system, and elite political imperatives. Laws on disclosure passed a decade earlier to prevent just such a crisis proved ineffective in the absence of external constraints on power. One southern newspaper charged that inadequate decentralization and the repression of civil society groups had further delayed the political response.[1] Another commentator said that SARS could as well stand for a larger problem: "sclerotic authoritarian regime syndrome."[2]

The virus killed 350 people in China and sickened more than 5,000. At least a full percentage point was sliced off GDP growth for the year as hotels emptied and tourists stayed away. Villages erected feudal-like physical barriers at their gates. China's international reputation, under closer scrutiny as the 2008 Beijing Olympics neared, was sullied. If it needed any more reasons to be wary of union with China, Taiwan was given a clarion reminder. The official *China Youth Daily* warned that the crisis was "seriously affecting government credibility."[3] Others in China made dark predictions of the consequences: "Those who lie in order to run the country," wrote one commentator, "will ultimately face revenge."[4]

The means of revenge, if that is the best way to describe how an authoritarian regime is ousted for being unjust and incompetent, were in plain view as well. Despite official cover-ups, China's wealthier and better-connected urban citizens soon exposed the lie. Mobile phones and text message devices circumvented state controls on information. Media that have grown and diversified beyond measure since Mao's death in 1976 showed a capacity for autonomy that few could have guessed. Prominent business leaders with both the means and the needs to speak out in protection of a growing middle class called for democratic reforms. "China must adopt a more democratic administrative model that represents the interests of all people," said one trade lawyer.[5]

Within the wider public, open protests erupted over everything from official misinformation to the mismanagement of quarantines. Prominent social elites, from intellectuals to doctors, came forward to blow the whistle on government incompetence and demand liberalizing reforms. The same pressures came from the international community, whose demands for reforms are aligned closely with those of Chinese society. Within the CCP, a pluralism of views and a drive for change was also in evidence. Regime advisors who have remonstrated with the leadership to embrace political reforms found a new platform for their views. One senior Party policymaker called for a new system based on "an interactive relationship among government, citizens and the media."[6]

Similar vistas of the growing needs and means for democratization had been seen in previous crises, and of course on several occasions during the entire history of the People's Republic of China. As yet, there has been no democratic breakthrough. We know from comparative international experience, however, that such a breakthrough is a common result and how it usually unfolds. The SARS crisis provided several insights into its course in China.

I have argued in this book that China's democracy will be brought about by the CCP itself, or more specifically by an elite-led extrication sparked by reformists in its ranks. The role of a crisis in such transitions is to unlock the potential of regime reformers. It strengthens their hand over conservatives, allowing them to gain support for reforms that they believe offer the best hope for preserving the regime's power.

Evidence of this was seen when premier Wen Jiabao visited Qinghua University in Beijing on the anniversary of China's pro-democracy May 4 movement of 1919. In a secret speech later disseminated widely through liberal newspapers, internal Party documents, and the Internet, Wen said that "our first step should be to open the flow of information. Only then can we enable the public to supervise the government and prevent social instability."[7] This was precisely the tone of Gorbachev's appeal for *glasnost* in the wake of Chernobyl.

Meanwhile, the regime split that almost always foreshadows a breakthrough was suggested by the sacking of two senior government officials, the Minister of Health and the Mayor of Beijing, for their roles in the initial cover-up. In place of the former came Wu Yi, the lone woman in the Politburo and a person with exactly the type of moral authority and pragmatic vision to support systemic changes. In place of the latter came a similar figure, Wang Qishan, who in a remarkable echo of the revolutions in Eastern Europe and Russia shifted from the impersonal rhetoric of the communist state to the personal rhetoric of democratic leaders, frequently using the phrase "since I took office," in his reports on the crisis in the capital.

Of course for some observers, SARS proved that democracy was not in the offing, that the system was strong and change almost unthinkable. Through the levers of dictatorship, infected people were quickly identified and isolated without legal quibbles; propaganda organs mobilized people and prevented unnecessary panic; social movements were banned; and public political recriminations were kept to a minimum. Local governments used the crisis to reassert control over migrant populations, while Beijing used it to establish the omnipotent political authority of the new leadership. For some, the crisis showed that the CCP remains deeply entrenched, dominant over society, and remarkably agile in the face of threats.

Since most of this book has been a dialogue with these arguments, I will not repeat them here. In general, however, I have claimed two main bodies of evidence in support of the idea of a democratic future. One is that the argument in favor of democracy is the mainstream argument in China itself. Putting government into the hands of society is not a "Western" or "foreign" idea but one deeply resonant in today's China, as the bulk of commentary and opinion on SARS and on more mundane issues of governance demonstrate. Second, even without an overwhelming consensus for change, dictatorships like the CCP have proven to be unsustainable precisely because of their inability to respond to crises like SARS that arise on the back of accumulated misgovernance.

Many more crises will raise the specter of democracy over China in coming years. Democratic development in the rest of Asia—from Taiwan and Hong Kong to remaining dictatorships like Burma and North Korea—could provide an external impetus. At home, elite political struggles, surging urban unrest, or system-shaking economic shocks await the telling. Authoritarian regimes live from crisis to crisis and there will be many more to come in China.

There is simply no compelling argument that China will be a great exception to the nearly-worldwide movement of social emancipation from "sclerotic authoritarianism" that we now call democratization. The specific nature of the crisis through which it will be delivered to popular rule cannot be predicted or perhaps even imagined. The inevitability of such a transition, however, seems plain.

Notes

Notes to Chapter 1

1. Shen bao (Shanghai Shun Pao newspaper), February 11, 1913, p. 6.

2. Popular elections were also held in 1909 and 1954, but under undemocratic constitutional conditions of a dominant monarchy and communist party respectively.

3. According to the U.S.-based research institute Freedom House's 2001–2 annual survey of democracy and freedoms.

4. Bao Tong, "Jue bu xiang baoli ditou" (Never submit to violence), Kaifang (Open Magazine, Hong Kong), May 2002, p. 13.

5. Fukuyama, *The End of History*, p. xiii.

6. "Governance for sustainable human development," UNDP policy document, January 1997. See also the UNDP human development report for 2002 entitled "Democracy and Development."

7. Yi Feng, "Democracy, Political Stability and Economic Growth," in *British Journal of Political Science* 27, no. 3 (July 1997): 391–418.

8. UNDP, World Development Report, 2002, p. 3.

9. Edward Friedman, "Theorizing the Democratization of China's Leninist state," in Arif Dirlik and Maurice Meisner (eds), *Marxism and the Chinese Experience: Issues in Contemporary Chinese Socialism* (Armonk, NY: ME Sharpe, 1989), pp. 171–89, at p. 172.

10. Edward Friedman, "Immanuel Kant's Relevance to an Enduring Asia-Pacific Peace," in Friedman and McCormick (eds), pp. 224–55, at p. 244; see also his "Does China Have the Cultural Preconditions for Democracy?," in *Philosophy East and West* 49 (July 1999).

11. Pierre Elliot Trudeau, quoted in Seymour Martin Lipset, "The Social Requisites of Democracy Revisited," in *American Sociological Review* 59 (February 1994): 1–22, at p. 5.

12. Robert D. Kaplan, "Was Democracy Just a Moment?," in *Atlantic Monthly* (December 1997): 55–80.

13. Sunil Khilnani, *The Idea of India* (New Delhi: Penguin Books, revised edition 1999), p. 204.

14. See Roger V. Des Forges, "Democracy in Chinese History," in Des Forges et al. (eds).

15. Alexander Woodside, "Emperors and the Chinese Political System," in Kenneth Lieberthal et al. (eds); Perspectives on Modern China: Four Anniversaries; Armonk NY; M.E. Sharpe, 1991; ch. 1, pp. 5–30.

16. Amaratya Sen, "East and West: The Reach of Reason," in *The New York Review of Books* (July 20, 2000); also see: Hu Shaohua "Confucianism and Western Democracy," in Zhao Suisheng (ed) *China and Democracy* pp. 55–72; Thomas Metzger,

"Sources of Resistance," in *Journal of Democracy* (special issue): 18–25; He Baogang, Democratisation, p. 161.

17. Edward Friedman, *The Politics of Democratization: Generalizing East Asian Experiences* (Boulder: Westview Press, 1994) p. 27.

18. Xu Yingshi, "Yehuo shaobujin, chunfeng chui yousheng" (The wild fire never burns out, the spring wind gives it new life), in Jin Zhong (ed.), pp. 1–4, at p. 2; See also Huang Dechang et al., Zhongguo zhi ziyou jingshen (China's Liberal Spirit); Chengdu: Sichuan People's Press, 2000.

19. Ju Yanan, p. 71.

20. Zhang and Cheng, p. 276.

21. He and Guo, p. 205.

22. Friedman, *National Identity*, p. 340.

Notes to Chapter 2

1. See for example Mark Elvin's study of the Shanghai city council; "The Gentry Democracy in Chinese Shanghai: 1905–14," in Jack Gray (ed.) *Modern China's Search for a Political Form* (London: Oxford University Press, 1969) pp. 41–65.

2. Mao's "New Democratic Constitutional Government" speech on Feb 20, 1940 at the Yanan meeting of new Association for the Promotion of Constitutional Government.

3. Cited in Shih Chih-yu, p. 82.

4. Mao Yushi and Zhou Hongling, "Guanyu zhengzhi gaigede duihua" (A conversation on political reform), Sha and Zhang (eds), China Political Report 2000, pp. 191–99, at p. 193.

5. David Shambaugh, "After 50 Years of Communism," *The Independent* (London), October 1, 1999.

6. Barry Naughton, "The Pattern and Legacy of Economic Growth in the Mao Era," in Kenneth Lieberthal et al. (eds.) *Perspectives on Modern China* (Armonk, NY: M. E. Sharpe, 1991), pp. 226–54.

7. Tao and Chen, *Political Participation*, pp. 191, 197.

8. Rong Jingben et al., "Ruhe jianli minzhu hezuode xin tizhi" (How to build a new cooperative democratic system) in Dong and Shi (eds), pp. 314–51, at p. 350.

9. Martin King Whyte, "Prospects for Democratization in China," in *Problems of Communism* (May–June 1992): 58–70, at p. 70.

10. See Elise S. Brezis and Adi Schnytzer, "Communist Regime Collapse: Output and the Rate of Repression," *Eastern Economic Journal* (October 1998): 463–74.

11. Deng Xiaoping, Selected Works, Vol. 3, p. 219 (Beijing: Foreign Languages Press, 1994).

12. Ling and Ma, p. 422.

13. Cited in Craig Calhoun, *Neither Gods Nor Emperors: Students and the Struggle for Democracy in China* (Berkeley: University of California Press, 1994), p. 241.

14. Nathan and Link, pp. 107–8.

15. The former figure is from Zhang Liang quoted in Andrew J. Nathan; "The Tiananmen Papers: An Editor's Reflections," *China Quarterly*, no 167 (September 2001): 724–37, at p. 724; the latter is from James Tong; "The 1989 Democracy Movement: A Preliminary Spatial Analysis," Universities Service Centre, Chinese University

of Hong Kong Seminar Series No 9, 1994; Tong finds state media reports of demonstrations in only 132 cities.

16. The speaker is Li Ruihuan. Quoted in Nathan and Link eds., p. 134.

17. Ibid. p. 443.

18. Bao Tong, p. 148.

Notes to Chapter 3

1. See for example Guo Sujian, Post-Mao China.

2. The 2000 Polity IV rankings (on a scale of − 10 to + 10) give: North Korea − 9; China − 7; Singapore − 2; Malaysia + 3; Indonesia + 7; Philippines + 8; India + 9; Taiwan + 9; Japan + 10. In the Freedom House rankings for 2001, China rates as a 7 and 6 on political and civil freedoms on a scale ranging from 7 (least free) to 1 (most free). China also ranks in the bottom decile on "voice and accountability" in the indicators compiled by the World Bank. See "Governance Matters: Governance Indicators for 1996–2002," World Bank Institute.

3. Zhao Suisheng, "Three Scenarios," in *Journal of Democracy* (special issue, 1998): pp. 54–59, 56; This is a complete reversal of the 1950s when workers and peasants accounted for 80% of the membership, roughly the same as in China as a whole.

4. An example is Chen Jie et al.; "The Level And Sources of Popular Support for China's Current Political Regime," *Communist and Post-Communist Societies* 30, no. 1 (1997): 45–64.

5. Min Qi's 1987 survey, evaluation of party was 41% positive and 46% negative; Surveys in 1988 got 30% Yes, 62% No. Quoted in Zheng Yongnian; "Development and Democracy: Are They Compatible in China?," in *Political Science Quarterly*, 109, no. 2 (Summer 1994): 235–59, at table 3.

6. He Baogang, *Democratization*, p. 191.

7. This comment was made at a widely reported talk by Zhu Rongji to the State Council working group on honesty in government on March 24, 2002. See also the warning of party crisis in Zhonggong zhongyang zuzhibu ketizu, *China Survey Report*, ch. 1 pp. 62–120.

8. Zong Hairen, pp. 116–117.

9. See Bruce Gilley, "The Limits of Authoritarian Resilience," *Journal of Democracy* (special issue, January 2003).

10. The speaker is NPC delegate Li Baoqun. See Cindy Sui, "Snores, Platitudes and Anonymity: 10 Years In China's National Parliament," Agence-France Press, March 14, 2002.

11. Gill, pp. 13, 37.

12. Guo Dingping, pp. 120–26.

13. The case of Tan Caihuan was detailed in Zhongguo qingnian bao (China Youth Daily), May 23, 2001, p. 9; Lawyer Li Kuisheng's case is detailed in *South China Morning Post*, February 12, 2001, p. 17.

14. Li Shuguang "Zhengzhi tizhi gaigede fazhi quxiang" (The legal direction of political reforms) in Dong and Shi (eds), pp. 73–82, at p. 77.

15. Bao Tong, "Faking Reforms at the Communist Party Congress," *New York Times*, November 23, 2002.

16. Pei Minxin, "China's Governance Crisis," *Foreign Affairs* (September 2002–October 2002): 96 ff.

17. Ogden., p. 3.

18. Barrett McCormick in Friedman and McCormick (eds), p. 317.

19. In a 1988 survey, 75% agreed with the statement that "China needs democracy" quoted in Zheng Yongnian; "Development and Democracy: Are They Compatible in China?," in *Political Science Quarterly*, 109, no. 2 (Summer 1994): 235–259 at table 3; Political reform concern poll reported in Chinese Academy of Social Sciences (ed), 2000 nian: Zhongguo shehui xingshi fenxi yu yuce (China Social Situation Analysis and Forecast: 2000), Beijing: CASS Press, 2000, pp.112. The same survey in 2002 resulted in an even higher rating for political reform, which topped the list of issues concerning local cadres with 39% of the vote, more than twice the next leading issue. Qianshao (Frontline Magazine, Hong Kong), September 2002, p. 14. Quotation from CASS, cited above.

20. Deng Weizhi, Political Stability, p. 147.

21. Huang Weiping, On Political reform, p. 69.

22. The first is Qin Hui, "Dividing the big family assets," *New Left Review*, 20 (March–April 2003), pp. 83–110, at p. 107. The second is Wang Guixiu, "'Youxuan-zhilu': Zhengzhi tizhi gaige bixu yu jingji tizhi gaige xiang shiying" ('The Road of priority': political reforms must suit economic reforms) in Dong and Shi (eds.) pp. 293–313, at p. 313.

23. China's score from 0 (most corrupt) to 10 (least corrupt) in the 2002 survey by Transparency International was 3.5, compared to 5.6 in Taiwan and 8.2 in Hong Kong. It is also more corrupt than countries at the same income level in the World Bank Institute Governance Indicators.

24. Liu Ning and Tian Huiming (eds.) Zhongguozhi tong (China's Pain); Beijing: Culture and Arts Press, 2001.

25. He Qinglian, China's Plight, p. 384.

26. See Zhonggong zhongyang zuzhibu ketizu.

27. Zhang Jun, p. 2.

28. Deng Weizhi, p. 147.

29. Zhang Jun; Zhong Min, Huangyan wu zhongguo (China Covered in Lies): (Changchun: Shidai Wenyi Press, 1999).

30. Fang Jue, "China Needs a New Transformation: Program Proposals of the Democratic Faction," China Rights Forum (Human Rights in China), Spring 1998.

31. Gordon White, "Democratization and Economic Reform in China," in *Australian Journal of Chinese Affairs*, no. 31 (January 1994): 73–92, at pp. 82–83.

32. Hu Angang, quoted by Reuters, January 31, 2002.

33. Rong Jingben et al., "Ruhe jianli minzhu hezuode xin tizhi" (How to build a new cooperative democratic system) in Dong and Shi (eds.), pp. 314–51, at p. 342.

34. Sun Xiaoli, *State and Society*, p. 109.

35. Liu Junning "The Intellectual Turn: The Emergence of Liberalism in Contemporary China," in Carpenter and Dorn (eds.), pp. 49–61; The same idea of a liberal mainstream is catalogued in Ding Yijiang p. 43.

36. Li Liangdong, Stability, p. 168.

37. Huang Yasheng, Selling China: Foreign Direct Investment During the Reform Era (Cambridge University Press, 2003).

38. Chen Shaohua and Wang Yan. "China's Growth and Poverty Reduction: Recent Trends Between 1990 and 1999," World Bank Working Paper, July 2001.

39. Zhonggong zhongyang zuzhibu ketizu, p. 79. Another, citing a party survey in cities which found that 62% of people were unhappy with the income gaps, says: "Those who have been left behind are easily stirred up by others, having a destructive impact on social peace and political stability." Deng Weizhi, p. 158.

40. Zhang Jun, p. 62.

41. Qin Hui, "Chanquan gaige yu minzhu" (Property rights reform and democracy) in Dong and Shi (eds.), pp. 116–119, at p. 117.

42. Yu Depeng "Lixing yu zhengyide yaoqiu: chengxiang pingdenghua" (The demands of idealism and justice: urban-rural equality) in Zhonguo guoqing guoli, pp. 317–18.

43. Du Gangjian, "Huji zhidu bu si" (The residential control system will not die) from the now-banned liberal website Issues and Ideas (Wenti yu Zhuyi).

44. Deng Weizhi, p. 149.

45. Cao Jinqing, p. 463.

46. Zhang and Cheng, p. 267.

47. His words in Chinese were "yexu kualiao." Quoted in Renmin ribao (People's Daily), March 16, 2002, p. 5.

48. Huang Zhong, "Zhengzhi tizhi gaige bu neng zai wang hou tui: zhonggong zhongyang dangxiao jiaoshou wang guixiu dawenlu" (Political reform can never again go backwards: questions and answers with professor Wang Guixiu of the Central Party School) in Dong and Shi (eds.), pp. 288–92, at p. 289.

49. *South China Morning Post* April 2, 2002 quoting Xinhua News Agency.

50. Mao Yushi and Zhou Hongling, "Guanyu zhengzhi gaigede duihua" (A conversation about political reform) in Nanfeng Chuang (Southern Window) magazine June 1999, reprinted in Shang and Zhang (eds.), China Pol Report 2000, pp. 191–199, at p. 196.

51. Jeffrey D. Sachs, Wing Thye Woo and Xiaokai Yang, "Economic Reforms and Constitutional Transition," Harvard University Center for International Development, Working Paper no. 43, April 2000, p. 31.

52. Xie Qingkui, "Zhubu zouchu zhengzhi tizhi gaigede kunjing" (Gradually escape the plight of political reforms) in Dong and Shi (eds.), pp. 108–15, at p. 111.

53. Wang Jianqin, Strengthen Supervision, pp. 56–57.

54. The case of Wang Xiu was reported in South China Morning Post, June 13, 2000.

55. World Bank, News Release, August 9, 2001.

56. Ke Wenqi, "Zhongguo sijuan jijin bao heimu" (Exposing the black curtain over China's private funds), Guangjiaojing (Wide Angle Magazine, Hong Kong), February 16, 2002, pp. 84–87.

57. Feng Chongyi, "The Third Way: The Question of Equity as a Bone of Contention Between Intellectual Currents," unpublished paper.

58. Edward Friedman "A Comparative Politics of Democratization in China," Journal of Contemporary China, 12, no. 34 (2003): 103–123, at p. 107.

59. Xiao Shu, "Xue shang: qing yuanliang fuqinde shize: yougan yu tiananmen guangchang xueren beijin" (Laughing Silkworm, "Snow wound: Please forgive father's dereliction of duty: Feelings inspired by the ban on snowmen in Tiananmen

Square"), from an Internet posting in China, January 15, 2001, translated by David Cowhig.

60. UNDP, Human Development Report, 2002, p. 55.

61. Lei Yi, "Minzu, minsheng, minquan" (Nationality, livelihood and people's rights) in Dong and Shi (eds.), pp. 216–219, at p. 219.

62. He Qinglian, Plight, pp. 373, 378.

63. Zhou Yi; Zhongguo shehui jiaodian (China's Pressing Social Issues) Beijing: Dazhong Wenyi Press, 2000.

64. Gao Zhan, Washington Post, August 26, 2001.

65. Wang Xiaoying, "The Post-Communist Personality: The Spectre of China's Capitalist Market Reforms," in China Journal no. 47 (January 2002): 1–18, at p. 17.

66. Bao Tong, p. 140.

67. See UNDP annual report 2000, "Human rights and development."

68. Liu Junning, "Ziyou zhuyi" (Liberalism) in Nanfang zhoumou (Southern Weekend newspaper), May 29, 1998.

69. Quoted in Zheng Feng, "Beijing yulun zai yu zhenggai" (Beijing opinion again calls for political reform) in Qiaoshao (Frontline Magazine, Hong Kong), March 2001, pp. 9–12, at p. 12.

70. Tyrene White; "Domination, Resistance and Accommodation in China's One-child Campaign," in Perry/Selden, pp. 102–19, p. 116.

71. Cao Liqun and Dai Yisheng, "Inequality and Crime," pp. 73–85 in Liu Jianhong, Zhang Lening, and Steven F. Messner (eds.), Crime and Social Control in a Changing China (Westport, CT: Greenwood Press, 2001), p. 75; Feng Shuliang, "Crime in a changing China," in Ibid., pp. 123–130, at p. 124.

72. Liu Jianhong and Steven F. Messner, "Modernization and Crime Trends in China's Reform Era," pp 3–21, p. 7 in Ibid.

73. Zong Hairen, Disidai, p. 233; The proportion is based on the Amnesty International figures for worldwide total ex-China of 500 in 2001.

74. Zhang and Cheng, Transformation, p. 72.

75. He Baogang, Democratization, 47.

76. Deng Weizhi, p. 194.

77. Quoted in Washington Post, May 12, 2000.

78. Deng Weizhi, p. 260.

79. Michel Oksenberg, "Confronting a Classic Dilemma," in Journal of Democracy, special issue, January 1998, pp. 27–34.

80. Bates Gill, "Discussion of 'China: A Responsible Great Power'," in Journal of Contemporary China, 10, no. 26 (2001), 27–32, at p. 32.

81. Fang Jue, "China Needs a New Transformation: Program Proposals of the Democratic Faction of the CCP," issued November 20, 1997, in China Rights Forum, Spring 1998.

82. Li Shenzhi, "Ye yao tuidong zhengzhi gaige" (We should also push political reforms), in Dong and Shi (eds.), pp. 19–22, at p. 21.

83. Chris Patten, East and West (London: Pan Books, 1999), p. 311.

84. David Shambaugh, "The Dynamics of Elite Politics During the Jiang Era," in China Journal 45 (January 2001): 101–11, at p. 108;.

85. See the rare reports on Xinjiang independence activities in Xinjiang newspapers quoted in Qianshao (Frontline Magazine, Hong Kong) February 2002, pp. 21–23.

86. Swedish parliamentarian Per Gahrton writing in *South China Morning Post* August 25, 2001.

87. Nathan/Gilley, *China's New Rulers*, 218.

88. David Zweig; "China Rising: Regional Cooperation or Conflict" paper prepared for Northeast Asia Cooperation project, Institute of Asian Research, University of British Columbia, November 5, 2001.

89. Richard N. Haass, Director of Policy Planning Staff, U.S. State Department, "China and the Future of U.S.-China Relations," Remarks to the National Committee on U.S.-China Relations, New York, December 5, 2002.

90. Bao Tong, p. 115.

91. See Huang Jing, *Factionalism*.

92. They are premier Wen Jiabao and anti-corruption czar Wu Guanzheng. See Nathan and Gilley, *China's New Rulers*.

93. Rong Jingben et al., "Ruhe jianli minzhu hezuode xin tizhi" (How to build a new cooperative democratic system) in Dong and Shi (eds), pp. 314–51, at pp. 341–42. The article was based on study of Xinmi city in 1996.

94. Fewsmith, *Elite Politics*, p. 56.

95. Zong Hairen (pseud.), *Zhu Rongji zai 1999* (Zhu Rongji in 1999) (New York: Mirror Books, 2001), p. 139.

96. Chen Fang, *Tiannu* (English translation, *Heaven's Wrath*; Hong Kong: Edko Publishing, 2000), pp. 214–15.

97. See Julia Kwong, *The Political Economy of Corruption in China* (Armonk, NY: M.E. Sharpe, 1997); Lü Xiaobo; also Deng Weizhi quoted in Dong and Shi (eds.), pp. 37–38.

98. Zong Hairen, *Disidai*, pp. 116–17.

99. Bao Tong, p. 16.

100. Michael C. Davis, "The Case for Chinese Federalism," *Journal of Democracy* 10, no. 2 (April 1999): 124–38, at p. 125.

101. The case of Gao Xinrong was reported throughout China in 2000. See *South China Morning Post* July 17, 2000.

102. See the report on Zhang Erjiang, mayor of Danjiang and Tianmen in Xinwen zhoukan (News Weekly), April 6, 2002; also *South China Morning Post*, April 8, 2002.

103. Lin Shangli, Relations, p. 360.

Notes to Chapter 4

1. Zheng Yongnian "Development and Democracy: Are They Compatible in China?," in *Political Science Quarterly*, 109, no. 2 (Summer 1994): 235–59, at p. 259.

2. Elizabeth Perry and Mark Selden, "Introduction," in Perry/Selden (eds.), pp. 1–19, at p.16.

3. These terms are those used in the model of Dankwart Rustow "Transitions to Democracy: Toward a Dynamic Model," reprinted in Lisa Anderson (ed.), ch. 2.

4. Bruce Gilley, "People's Republic of Cheats," *Far Eastern Economic Review* 21 (June 2001): 59–60.

5. Geremie R. Barmé, "The Revolution of Resistance," in Selden/Perry (eds.), pp.198- 220, at p. 201.

6. Liu Junning, "Chanquan baohu yu youxian zhengfu" (Property rights and limited government) in Dong and Shi (eds.), pp. 40–48, p. 43; Also see Mao Yushi and

Zhou Hongling "Guanyu zhengzhi gaigede duihua" (A conversation on political reform) in Nanfeng Chuang (Southern Window magazine) June 1999, reprinted in Sha and Zhang (eds.), China Political Report 2000, pp. 191–99, at p. 196.

7. Liu Junning, "Shichang yu xianzheng" (Market and Constitution) in Dong and Shi (eds.), pp. 190–95, at p. 190.

8. Sun Xiaoli, pp. 113–14, 149.

9. See Ronald Inglehart, *Modernization and Postmodernization* (Princton: Princeton University Press, 1997).

10. The first is Samuel Huntington, *Third Wave*, pp. 61–62. His zone begins at $1,000 per capita GNP in 1976 dollars, which I have brought forward using CPI indices. When Huntington wrote in 1989 he said, China was "far from the political transition zone" [105]. The second is Dahl, *Polyarchy*, p. 68. The third is Alvarez et al. cited in UNDP Human Development Report 2002, figure 2.4 page 58. I have updated the 1985 dollar figure using CPI indices. The annual probabilities rise from 3 percent to 6 percent over this range, meaning a roughly one third chance in a ten-year period at the higher level. This follows closely the findings of Adam Przeworski and Fernando Limongi, "Modernization: Theories and Facts," *World Politics* 49, no. 2 (January 1997): 155–183 that the likelihood a dictatorship survives falls steeply between $1,675 and $8,375 (converted to 2002 dollars).

11. See Tatu Vanhanen, *Prospects of Democracy: A Study of 172 Countries* (London: Routledge, 1997), pp. 88–89.

12. Lu Xueyi, A Report, p. 54. This approach seems to accord with the considered views of most Chinese, who view their status mainly in terms of profession rather than income. See Xin bailing: dangdai qingnian remen zhiye fangtan shilu (The New White Collar Class: Interviews on the Popular Professions of Today's Youth): Beijing: China Archives Press, 2001. Calculations of the middle class come from Lu Xueyi (ed.), p. 44; Duan Silin, "Zhongguo shehui jieceng da fenhua" (The great split in China's social classes), in Guangjiaojing (Wide Angle magazine), Febuary 16, 2001, pp. 14–17; Xiao Qiu, "Zhongchan jieji jueqi dui dalu zhengzhide yingxiang" (The implications for mainland politics of the rise of the middle class) in Guangjiaojing (Wide Angle), March 16, 2002, pp. 14–17.

13. Xiao Qiu, ibid.

14. Larry Diamond, "Economic Development and Political Stability," unpublished paper, April 15, 2002.

15. There is a voluminous literature on this subject. Two good studies are Bruce J. Dickson, *Red Capitalists in China: The Party, Private Entrepreneurs, and Prospects for Political Change* (Cambridge: Cambridge University Press, 2003) and An Chen, "Capitalist Development, Entrepreneurial Class, and Democratization in China," *Political Science Quarterly*, 117, no. 3 (2002): 401–22.

16. Doug Guthrie, "The Declining Significance of Guanxi in China's Economic Transition," *China Quarterly* 154 (June 1998): 254–82; David Da-hua Yang, "To Get Rich is Glorious—and Good for Democracy," in *China Brief* (Jamestown Foundation), March 2002 pp. 9–12.

17. Sun Xiaoli, pp. 148–49.

18. Zhonggong zhongyang zuzhibu ketizu, p. 55; Jiang Zemin told a Japanese politician in early 2001 that the CCP needed to lift its ban on private entrepreneurs lest it be "stripped of cash"; talk with Takako Doi, leader of SDP, Kyodo, January 15,

2001; Pan Yue, an influential princeling and right-wing intellectual wrote of the need to coopt entrepreneurs in a submission to Jiang in 2001. Pan Yue, "Dui geming dang xiang zhizheng dang zhuanbiande sikao" (Thoughts on the transformation from a revolutionary party to a ruling party), reprinted in Kaifang (Open Magazine), Hong Kong, July 2001, pp. 28–38.

19. Lu Xueyi (ed.), pp. 199ff.

20. The Chinese sentence is "Ba zheng ge gongchandang lian guo duan." Ling and Ma, p. 195.

21. Wang and Hu, Chinese Economy, table 2.5, p. 55. Lin Shuanglin, "China's Government Debt: How Serious?" China: An International Journal 1, no. 1 (March 2003): 73–98. James Macdonald, A Free Nation Deep in Debt: The Financial Roots of Democracy (New York: Farrar, Straus and Giroux, 2003).

22. Cheng Xiaonong, "Breaking the Social Contract," in Andrew J. Nathan, Zhao-hui Hong and Steven R. Smith (eds.), Dilemmas of Reform in Jiang Zemin's China (Boulder, CO: Lynne Rienner 1999), pp. 107–25 at p. 123; Population growth alone distributes resources away from state as welfare demands grow—see Jack Goldstone "Population Growth and Revolutionary Crises," in Foran (ed.), pp. 102–23. Goldstone notes that "Even strong states—such as that of mainland China—are not immune from such pressures" (109) even though its population growth may be at or below his "danger zone" of 2 to 3%.

23. Guo Dingping, p. 252.

24. See Michael A. Santoro, Profits and Principles: Global Capitalism and Human Rights in China (Ithaca: Cornell University Press, 2000). Also his "Global Capitalism and the Road to Chinese Democracy," Current History 99, no. 638 (September 2000): 263–68.

25. Cao Siyuan, talk at Chinese University of Hong Kong, April 11, 2002.

26. Wang Yongqiang, China Political Report 2001, pp. 19–20; see also Joseph Fewsmith. "The Political and Social Implications of China's Accession to the WTO," in China Quarterly, 167 (September 2001): 573–91.

27. Dagong bao (Ta Kung Pao newspaper, Hong Kong), January 20, 1996, p. A2.

28. This 1993 survey is reported in Shi Tianjian, "Cultural Values and Democracy in the PRC," in China Quarterly (June 2000): 540–59; a 1990 survey is reported in Nathan, China's Transition, ch. 11.

29. See Chu Yun-han and Chang Yu-tzung, "Culture Shift and Regime Legiti-macy," in Hua Shiping (ed.), pp. 320–48; at table 12.2, p. 332; The comparison with Taiwan in the late 1980s is derived from the work of Shyu Huoyan of National Taiwan University reported in Diamond, Developing Democracy, table 5.7, p. 189. See also Kuan Hsin-chi and Lau Siu-kai, "Traditional Orientations and Political Participation in Three Chinese Societies" Journal of Contemporary China 11, no. 31 (2002): 297–318.

30. World Values Survey results quoted in Ronald Inglehart and Christian Welzel, "Democratic Institutions and Political Culture," Figure 2, available at www.world valuessurvey.org.

31. See Ding Yijiang ch. 6.

32. See Xia Xueluan; Zhuanxingqide zhongguoren (China's people in a time of transition); Tianjin: Tianjin People's Press, 2001, table 12, p. 92; also Daniel Dowd, Allen Carlson and Mingming Shen, "The Prospects For Democratization in China:

Evidence from the 1995 Beijing Area Study," in Zhao Suisheng (ed.), pp. 189–206.

33. See Ralph Crozier, "The Avant-garde and the Democracy Movement: Reflections on Late Communism in the USSR and China," in *Europe-Asia Studies* (May 1999): 483 ff.

34. See Jin Zhong (ed.).

35. Qin Xiaopeng, "Zhongguo minzhu xingzheng lilunde fazhan yu shixian" (The development and practice of the theory of democratic administration in China) in Huang Weiping (ed.), *Report on Politics*, pp. 87–109, at p. 105.

36. Tang Wenfang, "Party Intellectuals' Demands for Reform in Contemporary China," Stanford University, *Hoover Institution Essays in Public Policy*, April 2002.

37. As one party book put it: "Nationalism (*minzu zhuyi*) is a natural political resource. In the face of foreign pressures, state leaders can appeal to nationalism to the glorious history, culture, bravery and intelligence of the nation and by setting off nationalist emotions can win greater recognition from the people of the legitimacy and legality of the political authority." Guo Dingping, p. 258.

38. John Rawls, *The Law of Peoples* (Cambridge: Harvard University Press, 1999), p. 35.

39. John Fitzgerald, "China and the Quest for Dignity," in *National Interest* (April 1999): 47 ff.

40. See the sustained treatment by Friedman.

41. He Baogang, pp. 168–69.

42. Survey of Internet Usage and Impact, Center for Social Development, Chinese Academy of Social Sciences, 2001.

43. Berkman Center for Internet and Society, Harvard University Law School, "Empirical Analysis of Internet Filtering in China," December 2002.

44. Liu Junning "The Intellectual Turn: The Emergence of Liberalism in Contemporary China," in Carpenter and Dorn (eds.), pp. 49–61, at p. 54.

45. Nailene Chou Wiest; "Financial Journalism and Market Reforms in China," unpublished paper.

46. According to the New York-based Committee to Protect Journalists.

47. O'Donnell and Schmitter, p. 50.

48. For example Wang Ming et al; Zhongguo shetuan gaige: cong zhengfu xuanze dao shehui xuanze (The Reform of China's Civic Organizations: From Government Selection to Society Selection) (Beijing: Social Sciences Documentation Press, 2001), p. 237; see also Zhongguo qingshaonian fazhan jijinhui (China Youth Development Fund); Chuyu shizi lukoude zhongguo shetuan (China's Civic Organizations at the Crossroads) (Tianjin: Tianjin People's Press), 2001.

49. Gao Bingzhong "The Rise of Associations in China and the Question of Their Legitimacy," in *Social Sciences in China* no 1 (2001): 73–87; Tony Saich "Negotiating the State: The Development of Social Organizations in China" China Quarterly (Mar 2000); Rebecca R. Moore; "China's Civil Society: A Force for Democratization," in *World Policy Journal* (April 2001): 56–66.

50. Figures are rounded, from Zhongguo minzheng tongji nianjian (China Civil Affairs Annual Report), 2000, 2001 editions (Beijing: China Statistics Press). Quotation is from 2001 edition, p. 3.

51. Guo Dingping, pp. 147–48.

52. Wang Ming et al; Zhongguo shetuan gaige (op. cit, note 48), p. 237.

53. Huang Weiping, On Political Reform, p. 45.

54. On local courts actually acting in interests of law more and more see Wang Yongqiang (ed.), China Political Report 2001 172 ff.

55. See Fang Jiangshan. See also Yu Jianrong, "Organized Peasant Struggle and its Political Risks—A Survey of a County in Hunan Province," in Chinese, Zhanlue yu guanli (Strategy and Management Magazine), June 2003 (3): 1–16.

56. It is thoroughly documented in the banned book Ying Xing; Dahe yimin shang- fangde gushi (The story of the protests by Dahe migrants); Beijing: Sanlian (Joint) Publishing, 2001.

57. See Valerie M. Hudson and Andrea Den Boer, "A Surplus of Men, A Deficit of Peace," International Security 26. no. 4 (March 2002): 34–39. They conclude that because of the skewed sex ratio "The prognosis for developing a full democracy in China is poor."

58. Li Fan passim pp 331, 338, 363.

59. See the article by Jin Xide of the Institute of Japanese Studies under CASS entitled "China Must Adopt A Great-Power Mentality and Make Psychological Change Part of its Modernization," in Huanqiu Shibao (Global Times) Sept 12, 2002, p. 4.

60. Mikhail Gorbachev, Memoirs (London: Bantam Books, 1997), p. 517.

61. Premier Zhu commented that he "greatly enjoyed" the speech. South China Morning Post, April 13, 2002.

62. Rosemary Foot, "Chinese Power and the Idea of a Responsible State," in China Journal, no. 45 (January 2001): 1–19, at p. 19.

63. See Elizabeth Economy, "The Impact of International Regimes on Chinese Foreign Policy-Making," in David Lampton (ed.), The Making of Chinese Foreign and Security Policy in the Era of Reform 1978–2000 (Stanford University Press, 2001), pp. 230–253.

64. Feng Lin (ed.); Zhongguo gongmin renquan duben (The textbook of human rights for Chinese citizens) (Beijing: Economic Daily Press), 1998.

65. Samuel Kim, "Human Rights in China's International Relations," in Friedman and McCormick (eds.), pp. 129–62.

66. Testimony by Bates Gill of Brookings Institution remarks to U.S.-China Security Review Commission, August 3, 2001.

67. Su Shaozhi and Michael J. Sullivan, "Aggressive Engagement, not Contain- ment," in Friedman and McCormick (eds.), pp. 284–304, at p. 302.

68. Peng Ming, pp. 49–51.

69. Arthur Waldron, "A Free and Democratic China?," in Commentary (November 2000).

70. Author's interview with UNDP chief administrator Mark Malloch Brown, Jan- uary 2001.

71. Henry Hyde, Chairman of U.S. House of Representatives International Rela- tions Committee, speaking in Taipei, quoted in South China Morning Post August 25, 2001.

72. Li Liangdong, "'Disan bo' yu dangdai zhongguode minzhu" (The Third Wave and contemporary China's democracy) in China Political Report, 2001, pp. 153–56, at p. 154.

73. Liu Junning "The Intellectual Turn: The Emergence of Liberalism in Contemporary China," in Carpenter and Dorn (eds.), pp. 49–61, at p. 54.

74. He Qinglian, Plight, p. 387.

75. Steve Tsang; "Transforming a Party State Into a Democracy," in Tsang/Tien (eds.), pp. 1–22, at p. 16.

76. Sunil Khilnani, *The Idea of India* (New Delhi: Penguin Books, rev. ed., 1999), p. 207.

77. See Joydeep Mukherji, "View from the Silk Road: Comparing Reform in China and India," *Standard and Poor's Credit Week* (February 6, 2002): 32–46.

78. Li Changping, Talk at Chinese University of Hong Kong, January 25, 2002.

79. Tsang Yok-sing, *South China Morning Post* March 1, 2002, p. 14.

80. Adrian Karatnycky, "Nations in Transit: Emerging Dynamics of Change"; Freedom House, www.freedomhouse.org, 2001.

81. On the views of former vice premier Tian Jiyun see Ling Zhijun and Ma Licheng. Hu Han, pp. 173–74. The CASS book is Xu Xin et al; Chaoji daguode bengkui: sulian jieti yuanyin shenxi (The collapse of a superpower: Analysis of the reasons for USSR breakup) (Beijing: Social Sciences Documentation Press; 2001), pp. 357–65. The quotation is from Huang Zhong, "Zhengzhi tizhi gaige bu neng zai wang hou tui: zhonggong zhongyang dangxiao jiaoshou wang guixiu dawenlu" (Political reform can never again go backwards: questions and answers with professor Wang Guixiu of the Central Party School) in Dong and Shi (eds.), pp. 288–92.

82. Zong Hairen, Disidai, p. 223; Nathan and Gilley, p. 190.

83. Qin Xiaopeng, "Zhongguo minzhu xingzheng lilunde fazhan yu shixian" (The development and practice of the theory of democratic administration in China) in Huang Weiping (ed.), *Report on Politics*, pp. 87–109, at p. 105.

84. Ren Zhongyi, Zai tan jianchi si xiang jiben yuanze (On uphoding the four cardinal principles), in Nanfang zhoumou (Southern Weekend), April 29, 2000, p. 4; it is reprinted in Zhang Yueqi and Li Ciyan (eds.); Ren Zhongyi luncong (Ren Zhongyi's expositions), 3 vols (Guangzhou: Guangdong People's Press, 2000), 3: 126–33.

85. Li Rui "Guanyu zhengzhi tizhi gaigede yijian" (Suggestions on political reform), Kaifang (*Open* Magazine, Hong Kong), December 2002, pp. 8–10. A speech he gave based on the article to some delegates to the November 2002 party congress meeting was published in the mainland's history journal Yanhuang Chunqiu (China Chronicle) in January 2003.

86. Andrew Walder "The Quiet Revolution from Within: Economic Reform as a Source of Political Decline," in Walder (ed.), *The Waning*, pp. 1–24.

87. Liu Ji quoted in Dagong bao (Ta Kung Pao newspaper, Hong Kong) March 12, 2001.

88. Fang Jue, "China Needs a New Transformation: Program Proposals of the Democratic Faction," *China Rights Forum* (Human Rights in China), Spring 1998; See also the appeal by Jiang Zemin's former student colleague Zhong Peizhang; "Yu Jiang Zemin yixitan—Yige lao gongchandangrende shijie sisuo" (A Talk With Jiang Zemin: Thoughts of a Long-Time Communist Party Member), (Hong Kong: Gaowen Press, 2002).

89. Talk to Guangdong delegates at NPC; March 16, 1995, Wenhuibao (Wen Wei Po newspaper Hong Kong).

90. Zong Hairen, pp. 112–17.

91. In an early 2003 survey of 1,500 senior cadres by the Chinese Academy of Social Sciences, 36% chose political reform as the biggest reform concern, the top answer. When asked about their top priority for political reforms, the cadres mostly chose internal party democracy (33%) and changing government functions (24%) while expanding legislative powers (6%) and strengthening media supervision (2%) came at the bottom. See Qing Lianbin, "Zhenggai cheng gaoguan xinsheng" (New voices on political reform from senior officials), Qianshao (Frontline Magazine, Hong Kong) March 2003, p. 18.

92. Yang Jianping, "Fazhi minzhu: Houfa guojiade zhengzhi xuanze" (Legal democracy: the choice for late developing countries," in Zhanlue yu guanli (Strategy and Management) (June 2001): 86–92. Similar proposals come from the leading neo-conservative Pan Wei. See his "Toward a Consultative Rule of Law Regime in China," *Journal of Contemporary China* 12, no. 34 (2003): 3–43.

93. See Pan Yue, "Dui geming dang xiang zhizheng dang zhuanbiande sikao" (Thoughts on the transformation of a revolutionary party into a ruling party), in Kaifang (Open Magazine), July 2001, pp. 28–38.

94. Michel Oksenberg "Confronting a Classic Dilemna," in *Journal of Democracy* special issue pp 27–34, at p. 29.

95. See Richard D. Anderson, Jr., "The Discursive Origins of Russian Democratic Politics," in Anderson et al (eds.), *Postcommunism*, pp. 96–125.

96. See Zhen Xiaoying and Li Qinghua, "Yi dangnei mingzhu tuijin renmin minzhu" (Advancing people's democracy through inner-party democracy", Qiushi (Seeking Truth Magazine), 16 June 2003.

97. Linz and Stepan, p. 72.

98. Peng Ming, p. 54.

99. Zhu Huaxin, "Caogen minzhu" (Grassroots democracy) in Dong and Shi (eds.), pp. 352–67, at pp. 353, 364–66.

100. A celebrated example was Yao Lifa, a teacher in Hubei province who won a seat on his city's people's congress in 1998 after being thwarted by local cadres three times. *South China Morning Post* August 24, 2001 and Nanfeng Chuang (Southern Window magazine), July 2001. Similar cases are now covered extensively by the Carter Center's special Chinese-language site for elections: www.chinaelections.org.

101. Deng Weizhi, p. 151.

102. Cao Siyuan: "Zhengzhi gaige guanjian zaiyu dang zishende gaige" (The key to political reforms is reform of the party itself) in Zhongguo guoqing guoli zazhi (China's National Strength and Conditions Magazine), no. 101 (May 2001): 43–45, at p. 44. Cao has also published two books on political reform: Zhongguo zhenggai fanglue (A Strategy for Political Reform in China), Hong Kong: Xiafeier Press, 1999; and Zhengzhi wenming ABC—Zhongguo zhengzhi gaige gangyao (ABC's of Political Civilization—A Program for Chinese Political Reform), New York: Cozy House Press, 2003.

103. He Baogang, p. 3.

Notes to Chapter 5

1. Fan Weibin p. 205; Peng Ming; W.J.F. Jenner, The Tyranny of History: The Roots of China's Crisis (London: Penguin Books, 1992), p. 235; Jack A. Goldstone, "The

Coming Chinese Collapse," in *Foreign Policy* (June 1995): 35ff; Joel Starr, "Prospects for a Democratic China Within 10 years," in *Washington Journal of Modern China* (Spring 2001): 65–74; Gordon Chang, *The Coming Collapse of China* (New York: Random House, 2001).

2. Hu Shaohua Footnote 48 p. 160; Henry Rowan, "The Short march: China's Road to Democracy (China as a democratic state in 2015)," in *The National Interest* (Sept 22, 1996): 61ff; Xu Xing, "Zhongguo yi zai yanbianzhong" (China is already evolving), Kaifang (Open Magazine, Hong Kong), special, May 2002, pp. 24–27.

3. Shih Chih-yu, p. 321; Robert Scalapino "Current Trends and Future Prospects," in *Journal of Democracy*, special issue (January 1998): 35–40, p. 35; Edwin A. Winckler, "Describing Leninist Transitions," in Winckler (ed.), pp. 3–48.

4. Edward Friedman, p. 42.

5. Domestic proposals for gradual transition include Wang Lixiong, Dissolving Power; Fang Jue, "China Needs a New Transformation: Program Proposals of the Democratic Faction, reprinted in *China Rights Forum* (Human Rights in China) Spring 1998; Cao Siyuan, A Strategy for Political Reform; Huang Weiping, On Political Reform. Overseas proposals include, Zhuge Muqun, Constitutional China; Wang Juntao, "A 'Gray' Transformation," in *Journal of Democracy*, special issue (January 1998): 48–53, 51; Zhao Suisheng, "Three Scenarios," in ibid, pp. 54–59; Pei Minxin, "Creeping Democratization in China," in *Journal of Democracy* 6, no. 4 (October 1995): 65–79; Larry Diamond, Foreword in Zhao Suisheng (ed.), pp. ix–xv, p. xiv; He Baogang, p. 225.

6. Zhao Suisheng, "Political Liberalization without Democratization: Pan Wei's Proposal for Political Reform," *Journal of Contemporary China* (2003), 12(35), 333–55, at 355.

7. O'Donnell/Schmitter, p. 16.

8. Deng Xiaoping, *Collected Works*, Vol. 3; Beijing: Foreign Languages Press, 1992, p. 219.

9. The speech was reprinted in Wen Wei Po newspaper (Hong Kong), March 17, 1995; On his being rebuked by Jiang Zemin for "disorderly speeches" see Gao Xin, "Shunle mindai nile hexin" (Taking the people's place, opposing the core), in Zhongguo shibao zhoukan (China Times Magazine, Taipei) May 14–20, 1995, pp. 48–49.

10. Pei Minxin, "Will China become another Indonesia?" *Foreign Policy* (October 1999): 94ff.

11. Barrett McCormick "China's Leninist Parliament and Public Sphere: A Comparative Analysis," in McCormick and Unger (eds.), pp. 29–54, at 37.

12. Bruce J. Dickson. "China's Democratization and the Taiwan Experience," in *Asian Survey* (April 1998): 349ff.

13. This point is made by Joel E. Starr, "Prospects for a Democratic China Within Ten Years," *Washington Journal of Modern China* (Spring 2001): 65–74.

14. Chalmers A. Johnson, *Revolutionary Change* (Boston, Little, Brown, 1966).

15. Shambaugh (ed), *Is China Unstable?* pp. ix–x.

16. See Gill, pp. 10–13; Haggard and Kaufman find that in 21 of 27 transitions in 1970s and 1980s there was falling growth or rising inflation in the years before transition, table 1.1, pp. 34–5; Foran says economic crisis is virtually required in all cases

for an opening for revolution; John Foran, "The Comparative-Historical Sociology of Third World Social Revolutions," in Foran, pp. 227–67, at p. 229.

17. Charles Wolf, Jr., "Uncertain Times for Foreign Investment in China," *Financial Times*, June 24, 2002.

18. Peng Ming, p. 26.

19. Nicholas Lardy quoted in James Kynge, "Creaking Economy Needs Stronger Foundations" *Financial Times*, October 29, 2002.

20. "Is China Heading for a Banking Crisis?," Citibank, Greater China Insights research note, September 17, 2002; Steven H. Solnick has a model of how a bank run can spur breakdown of a Leninist regime. See his "The Breakdown of Hierarchies in the Soviet Union and China," *World Politics* 48 (1995–96): 209–38.

21. Cheng Xiaonong, "Breaking the Social Contract" in Andrew J. Nathan, Zhaohui Hong and Steven R. Smith (eds.), *Dilemmas of Reform in Jiang Zemin's China* (Boulder, CO: Lynne Rienner 1999), pp. 107–25, at p. 123.

22. Xiao Gongqin, "Jiandude quewei" (the lack of supervision) in Zhongguo guoqing guoli, pp. 6–8.

23. Gerardo L. Munck and Carol Skalnik Leff, "Modes of Transition and Democratization: South America and Eastern Europe in Comparative Perspective," in Lisa Anderson (ed.), pp. 193–216.

24. Alexis de Tocqueville, *The Old Regime and the French Revolution*, Stuart Gilbert trans. (New York: Doubleday 1955), p. 177.

25. Andrew Nathan, "Even Our Caution Must Be Hedged," in Journal of Democracy, (special issue, 1998), pp. 60–64, at p. 64.

26. Jane S. Jaquette and Sharon L. Wolchik, "A Comparative Introduction," in Jaquette and Wolchik (eds); *Women and Democracy: Latin America and Central and Eastern Europe* (Baltimore, MD: Johns Hopkins University Press, 1998), pp. 1–28, at pp. 12–13. Also see Jill M. Bystydzienski and Joti Sekhon (eds); *Democratization and Women's Grassroots Movements* (Bloomington: Indiana University Press, 1999).

27. Dang Guoying, "Qingnian nongmin shi dangjin zhongguo zuida de zhengzhi" (Young peasants are the most important political issue in China today) in Zhongguo guoqing guoli zazhi (*China National Conditions and Strength Magazine*), no. 101 (May 2001): 4–6.

28. Li Liangdong, pp. 159, 181.

29. Bermeo notes: "When the known costs of governance rise, the projected costs of democracy will seem relatively low if pivotal elites predict that nonextremist forces will take control of the new democratic regime." Nancy Bermeo, "Myths of Moderation: Confrontation and Conflict During Democratic Transitions," in Lisa Anderson (ed.), pp. 120–40, at p. 133.

30. He Baogang, p. 222.

31. Wei Jingsheng, "China's Road to a Democratic Society" ch 5, in Timothy B. Weston and Lionel M. Jensen (eds.), *China Beyond the Headlines* (Lanham, MD: Rowman & Littlefield, 2000), pp. 113–20, at p. 119.

32. Wang Zhen, quoted in Nathan/Link (eds.), Tiananmen Papers, p. 357.

33. Christopher Tuck, "Is the Party Over? Political Instability in Post-Deng China," *Contemporary Review* (May 1995): 244 ff.

34. Ibid.

35. Edwin A. Winckler, "Military Dimensions of Regime Transition," in Winckler (ed.), pp. 81–109, at p. 82.

36. In Chinese, "gongheguohua, guojiahua, feidanghua, feizhengzhihua." See Weng et al., pp. 248–49; *PLA Daily*, June 6, 2001; Nathan and Gilley, "China's New Rulers," p. 225.

37. Jiao Jian; Gonggong quanli yunxing wuqu: quanli cuowei (The Abuse of Power: Misconceptions About the Use of Public Power) (Tianjin: People's Press, 2001).

38. for example Ren Yuzhong and Chen Bin "Minzhu yu fazhi: xiangpu er xiangcheng: yu Pan Wei xiansheng shangque" (Democracy and Rule of Law: Complementary and Coexistent: A discussion with Pan Wei) in Zhanlue yu guanli (Strategy and Management Magazine) no 2 (2001): 116–20.

39. Edward Friedman, "Theorizing the democratization of China's Leninist state," in Arif Dirlik and Maurice Meisner (eds.), *Marxism and the Chinese Experience: Issues in Contemporary Chinese Socialism* (Armonk, NY: M. E. Sharpe, 1989), pp. 171–89.

40. See Susan V. Lawrence, "To Rebel Is Justified: Police Worry That Mass Protests Could Happen Again," *Far Eastern Economic Review* (May 27, 1999): 12; The Politburo Standing Committee voted only 4 to 3 to declare the group an evil cult. See Zong Hairen (pseud), Zhu Rongji zai 1999; English trans.: *Zhu Rongji in 1999* (New York: Mirror Books, 2000), p. 59.

41. Edwin A. Winckler, "Military Dimensions of Regime Transition," in Winckler (ed.), pp. 81–109, at 82.

42. Arthur Waldron, "A Free and Democratic China?," in *Commentary* (November 2000): 27–32.

43. Linz and Stephan, p. 68.

44. Pan Wei "Democracy or Rule of Law? China's Political Future," paper given at University of Hong Kong conference on China's intellectuals and the 21st century, December 15–16, 2000.

45. Cited in Dalpino, p. 25.

46. Wang Hui, "Tongyi zhongguode junshi zhunbei kebu ronghuan" (We cannot delay making military preparations to unify China), Guangjiaojing (Wide Angle magazine, Hong Kong), April 16, 2002, pp. 34–37, at p. 37.

47. Peng Ming, p. 32.

48. This was contained in the draft book *Inside China's Nuclear Weapons Program* by Danny Stillman, retired chief intelligence officer at Los Alamos National Laboratory. As of 2003 the book remained unpublished because of litigation with the U.S. federal government over security issues. See Steve Coll, "The Man Inside China's Bomb Labs; U.S. Blocks Memoir of Scientist Who Gathered Trove of Information," *Washington Post* May 16, 2001, p. 1.

49. Linz and Stepan.

50. Deng Xiaoping, *Collected Works*, vol. 3 (Beijing: Foreign Languages Press, 1992), p. 344.

51. Ogden 7.

52. Dalpino 16.

53. Kenneth Lieberthal, "U.S. Policy Toward China," Brookings Institute Papers, No. 72, March 2001.

Notes to Chapter 6

1. Huntington used the word "transplacement" for what we refer to here as extrication, *Third Wave*, p. 114, Table 3.1, p. 113. The 29 of 41 figure is my own calculation which includes 8 of 10 in the USSR and Eastern Europe, 19 of 27 in the rest of the pre-1992 period of the Third Wave, and 2 of 4 since then (namely Indonesia and Tanzania but not Serbia and Cambodia).

2. Liu Xiaobo; "That Holy Word, 'Revolution'," in Wasserstrom and Perry, pp. 309–325, at p. 309.

3. Yan Jiaqi, "Lun yong heping fangshi jieshu zhongguo zhuanzhi zhidu" (On using peaceful means to end dictatorship in China), in Qianshao (Frontline Magazine, Hong Kong), (November 2002): 43–45.

4. Li Fan, pp. 341, 354, 363.

5. He Xin, pp. 445–46.

6. Andrew Nathan, "China's Path from Communism," in *Journal of Democracy* 4, no. 2 (April 1993): 30–42, at p. 41.

7. David Shambaugh, in Shambaugh (ed.), *Is China Unstable?*, p. 37.

8. The phrase was coined by the German intellectual and writer Hans Magnus Enzensberger.

9. Peng Ming 40.

10. Xiao Gongqin, "Jiandude quewei" (The lack of supervision) in Zhongguo guoqing guoli, pp. 7–8.

11. Elizabeth Perry and Mark Selden, Introduction in Perry/Selden (eds.), pp. 1–19, at p. 13.

12. See his open appeal for democratic reforms in 2002 "Guanyu zhengzhi tizhi gaigede yijian" (Suggestions on political reform), Kaifang (Open Magazine, Hong Kong), December 2002, pp. 8–10.

13. Nathan and Gilley, pp. 200–201.

14. Friedman pp. 85, 339.

15. Arthur Waldron, "The End of Communism, in *Journal of Democracy* special issue, (1998): 41–47, at p. 43.

16. Jeff Goodwin, "State-Centered Approaches to Social Revolutions," in Foran, pp. 11–37, at p. 20.

17. Pei Minxin 206.

18. "Aquino Wins Ovation from Business Leaders," Associated Press, January 6, 1986.

19. Richard Anderson, et al., *Postcommunism.*

20. Zbigniew Brzezinski, "Disruption Without Disintegration," in *Journal of Democracy* special issue (1998): 4–5, at p. 5.

21. This is Gill's main thesis. See also Richard Lachmann, "Agents of Revolution: Elite Conflicts and Mass Mobilization from the Medici to Yeltsin," in Foran (ed.), pp. 73–101, at p. 73; Stephan Haggard and Robert R. Kaufman; "The Political Economy of Democratic Transitions," in Lisa Anderson (ed.), pp. 72–96; also Anderson's, Introduction, p. 6.

22. Fan Shuo, *Ye Jianying zai 1976* (Ye Jianying in 1976), revised edition (Beijing: Central Party School Press, 1995), pp. 132–33.

23. Arthur Waldron, "The End of Communism," in *Journal of Democracy* special issue, (1998): 41–47, at 47.

24. This section follows Philip G. Roeder, "The Rejection of Authoritarianism," in Richard Anderson et al. (eds.), pp. 11–53. I have renamed his "exclusive republic" as aristocracy.

25. Roeder, ibid., p. 40.

26. See Alan Wachman, *Taiwan : National Identity and Democratization* (Armonk, N.Y.: M.E. Sharpe, 1994).

27. John Waterbury, "Fortuitous Byproducts," in Lisa Anderson (ed.), pp. 261–89.

28. Edward Friedman, "Implications for Democracy," speech at conference on China's WTO entry at Vail Colorado, May 25, 2001.

29. Dankwart Rustow "Transitions to Democracy: Toward a Dynamic Model," reprinted in Lisa Anderson (ed.), p. 31.

30. Gill, ch. 4.

31. Zheng Yongnian, p. 145.

32. Ling and Ma; Jiaofeng, p. 425.

33. Bao Tong, "Call to the Leadership," in *China Rights Forum* (Summer 1999); Bao Tong, pp. 149, 151.

34. Wang Lixiong, "Yi 'zhu ceng di xuan' shixian zhongguode pingxun zhuang-xing" (Realizing China's smooth transition through indirect upper level elections), online essay, January 2002, www.dijin-democracy.net. Also his book *Dissolving Power*.

35. Joel E. Starr, "Prospects for a Democratic China Within Ten Years," *Washington Journal of Modern China* (Spring 2001): 65–74.

36. Michael Kennedy makes this point about the 1989 Polish revolution in "Contingencies and the Alternatives of 1989: Toward a Theory and Practice of Negotiating Revolution," in *East European Politics and Societies* (March 22, 1999): 293 ff.

37. Edward Friedman 289, 291.

38. Richard Lachmann, "Agents of Revolution: Elite Conflicts and Mass Mobilization from the Medici to Yeltsin," in Foran (ed.), pp. 73–101, at p. 95.

39. Mark Selden, "The Social Origins and Limits of the Democratic Movement," in Des Forges et al. (eds.), pp. 107–129, at p. 128.

40. Valerie Bunce; "Lessons of the First Postsocialist Decade," *East European Politics and Societies* (March 22, 1999): 236 ff.

Notes to Chapter 7

1. Yossi Shain and Juan Linz; *Between States: Interim Governments and Democratic Transitions* (Cambridge University Press, 1995) p. 14.

2. Deng Xiaoping; *Selected Works*, vol. 3, 1982–1992 (Beijing: Foreign Languages Press, 1994), p. 347.

3. Zhou Xincheng et al; Ping rendaode minzhu shehui zhuyi (A critique of humanist democratic socialism), (Beijing: People's University Press, 1998).

4. He Xin, pp. 456–57.

5. Yan Jiaqi, Zhongguode weiji he 'jianshen zhi dao' (China's danger and its "road to fitness"), Kaifang (Open Magazine, Hong Kong), April 2002, pp. 41–42, at p. 42.

6. Zong Hairen, "Li Ruihuan tuixiu neiqing" (The inside story of Li Ruihuan's fall) in Xinbao (*Hong Kong Economic Journal*), December 17–20 2002, December 20 quoting internal figures.

7. Peng Ming, p. 53.

8. Robert Scalapino "Current Trends and Future Prospects," in *Journal of Democracy*, special issue (1998): 35–40.

9. Peng Ming, p. 58.

10. Pei Minxin, p. 23.

11. See Anthony Kuhn, "Corrupt Officials' 'Escape Routes' Alarm China," *Los Angeles Times*, April 22, 2001, p. A-4. See also the testimony on official corruption of He Qinglian and Cheng Xiaonong to the U.S.-China Economic and Security Review Commission, December 11, 2002, available at www.uscc.gov.

12. *Houston Chronicle*, August 20, 1991, p. 8.

13. There is evidence of change however. In February 2003, all U.S. government agencies with an interest in China—military, security, diplomatic, aid, development, and information—attended a seminar in Washington on "Prospects for Democratic Reform," in China. The seminar was sponsored by the Central Intelligence Agency.

Notes to Chapter 8

1. Adrian Karatnycky; "Nations in Transit: Emerging Dynamics of Change," Freedom House, 2001.

2. Yan Jiaqi, p. 228.

3. Edward Friedman, p. 256.

4. Arthur Waldron, "China's Coming Constitutional Challenges," in *Orbis* (January 1995): 19ff.

5. Edwin A. Winckler, "Describing Leninist Transitions," in Winckler (ed.), pp. 3–48, at 13.

6. Adam Przeworski et al "What Makes Democracies Endure?" *Journal of Democracy* 7, no. 1 (1996): 50–51. Also Adam Przeworski and Fernando Limongi, "Modernization: Theories and Facts," *World Politics*, 49, no. 2 (January 1997): 155–83. They report $6,000 in 1985 prices, which I have converted to 2002 dollars.

7. Alvarez et al 2002 cited in UNDP Human Development Report 2002, figure 2.4 p. 58. I recalculated the 1985 prices using U.S. CPI indices.

8. Samuel P. Huntington, "Reforming Civil-Military Relations," *Journal of Democracy* 6, no. 4 (1995): 15. His figure of $3,000 in 1985 dollars would be roughly $5,000 in 2003 dollars. The upper limit set by Dahl is also around $5,100 in 2002 dollars, Dahl, *Polyarchy*, p. 68.

9. The Freedom House ratings for political and civic liberties in 2002 were Bulgaria (1 and 3), Albania (3 and 4), and Romania (2 and 2), where 7 is totally unfree and 1 is totally free. All were (7 and 7) under communism, similar to China's (7 and 6) in 2002.

10. See for example Andrew Arato, *Civil Society, Constitution, and Legitimacy* (Lanham, MD: Rowman & Littlefield, 2000), pp. 229–30.

11. Wolfgang Merkel, "The consolidation of post-autocratic regimes: a multilevel model," in Chung-in Moon and Jongryn Mo (eds), *Democratization and Globalization in Korea* (Seoul: Yonsei University Press, 1999), pp. 25–68, pp. 37–43.

12. Peng Ming, p. 135.

13. Arato, cited above, note 10, pp. 250–55.

14. He Baogang, p. 130.

15. George Santayana, *The Life of Reason* (New York: Prometheus Books, 1998), p. 218.

16. Yan Jiaqi, "Jianli yange xianrende 'zongtong—neigezhi' gouxiang" (An idea to set up a 'presidential—cabinet' system with strict term limits), in Qianshao (Frontline Magazine, Hong Kong), November 2002, pp. 43–45.

17. Grame Gill, p. 236; Adrian Karatnycky; "Nations in Transit: Emerging Dynamics of Change"; Freedom House, 2001; Linz/Stepan pp. 181–83; Friedman, p. 259; also M. Steven Fish, "The Dynamics of Democratic Erosion," in Richard Anderson et al., *Postcommunism*, pp. 54–95.

18. Eg., Peng Ming, pp. 109–110.

19. Peng Ming 110. In the immediate post-Mao period, party reformer Liao Gailong suggested an NPC of 1,000 members representing 300 geographic and 700 functional constituencies. See his "Historical experience of our road of development," part 3, *Issues and Studies*, vol.17, no.12 (1981): 79–104 at 86–87.

20. Democrat Yan Jiaqi and neoauthoritarian Pan Wei have both endorsed an examination system for the civil service, See He Baogang, p. 68.

21. Ezra Suleiman, "Bureaucracy and Democratic Consolidation: Lessons from Eastern Europe," in Lisa Anderson (ed.), pp. 141–67.

22. Peng Ming, p. 137.

23. Lin Shangli, p. 346.

24. Eg., Hu Shaohua, p. 154; Maria Hsia Chang, "China's Future: Regionalism, Federation or Disintegration," in *Studies in Comparative Communism* 25, no 3 (September 1992): 211–27. Michael C. Davis, "The Case for Chinese Federalism" *Journal of Democracy* 10, no. 2 (April 1999): 124–38.

25. Diamond, *Democracy*, p. 120.

26. See Lin Shangli, pp. 358–69, at 368.

27. Bo Guili; Jiquan fenquan yu guojia xingshuai (Concentrated versus devolved power and national wellbeing), (Beijing: Economics and Science Press, 2001), pp. 243–44, at p. 221.

28. In the 4,000 years of recorded history, the country was roughly 40% unified, 40% federation and 20% disunified according to an estimate by Maria Hsia Chang; cited in Edward Friedman, p. 58.

29. Joydeep Mukherji, "View from the Silk Road: Comparing Reform in China and India," in Standard and Poor's *Credit Week*, February 6, 2002, pp. 32–43, at p. 40.

30. This is proposed by Bo Guili, cited above, n. 27, p. 257.

31. See Alan P.L. Liu; "Provincial Identities and Political Cultures," in Hua Shiping (ed.), pp. 246–75, at p. 268.

32. Peng Ming, table 1, pp. 98–106. His plan also includes a seventh self-governing province covering the Spratly Archipelago, but it is on paper only until the disputes can be resolved under the new democracy.

33. The lack of time zones was beginning to arouse some debate by the early 2000s. See Sun Yuan, "Ruoda zhongguo zhiyou yige shijian" (Such a large China has only one time) in Kaifang (Open Magazine), August 2002, pp. 52–55. See also Bruce Gilley, "Time for Zones in China," *Asian Wall Street Journal*, August 29, 2002, p. A7.

34. He and Guo, p. 128.

35. Donald L. Horowitz, quoted in Diamond, p. 156.

36. See He Baogang, pp. 88–95; He and Guo, p. 203; Dawa Norbu, *China's Tibet Policy* (Richmond, Surrey: Curzon Press, 2001), pp. 352–54; Wang Lixiong, "Tibet: The Soft Rib of China in the 21st Century" from *Zhanlue yu Guanli* (Strategy and Management), January 1999, pp. 21–33. Also his Reflections on Tibet," *New Left Review* 14 (March–April 2002): 79–111. A general statement of the normative and practical benefits of a secession clause is given in Daniel Weinstock, "Towards a normative theory of federalism," *International Social Science Journal* 53, no. 167 (March 2001): 75–83.

37. See Jack L. Snyder, *From Voting to Violence : Democratization and Nationalist Conflict* (New York: Norton, 2000).

38. Paul G. Lewis, "Conclusion: Party Development and Democratization in Eastern Europe," in Paul G. Lewis (ed.), *Party Development and Democratic Change in Post-Communist Europe: The First Decade* (London: Frank Cass, 2001), pp. 199–211, at p. 206.

39. Yan Jiaqi, p. 224.

40. This point is made in Fan Wenbin, p. 205.

41. Andrew Nathan "Chinese Democracy: The Lessons of Failure," in Zhao Suisheng (ed.), pp. 21–32, at p. 29.

42. David Bachman, "China's Democratization: What Difference Would It Make for US-China Relations?," in Friedman and McCormick (eds.), pp. 195–223.

43. Thomas Friedman, *New York Times*, October 3, 2000.

44. Ju Yanan, pp. 73–74.

45. Yan Jiaqi, p. 224.

46. Tina Rosenberg, "The Unfinished Revolution of 1989," in *Foreign Policy* (July 1999), pp. 90 ff.

47. Gerardo L. Munck and Carol Skalnik Leff, "Modes of Transition and Democratization: South America and Eastern Europe in Comparative Perspective," in Lisa Anderson (ed.), pp. 193–216, at pp. 209, 210.

48. Stephan Haggard and Robert R. Kaufman; "The Political Economy of Democratic Transitions," in Lisa Anderson (ed.), pp. 72–96.

49. A positive scenario like this is mentioned by Larry Diamond, Foreword, in Zhao Suisheng (ed.), pp. ix–xv, at p. x.

50. Stephan Haggard and Robert R. Kaufman; "The Political Economy of Democratic Transitions," in Lisa Anderson (ed.), pp. 72–96, at 92.

51. Yan Jiaqi, p. 226.

52. See Catharin Dalpino, "Democracy Gains a Foothold in Cambodia," in *Japan Times* March 23, 2002.

53. Huntington, *Third Wave*, p. 262.

54. Peng Ming, p. 58.

55. Gordon White, "Democratization and Economic Reform in China," in *Australian Journal of Chinese Affairs*, no. 31 (January 1994): 73–92, at p. 91.

56. Point made by Shi Tianjian, *Political Participation*, p. 281; Also see He Baogang, p. 38; Zhang Baohui, "Corporatism, Totalitarianism and Transitions to Democracy," in *Comparative Political Studies* 27, no. 1 (1994): 108–36, at p. 127.

57. Francis Fukuyama, p. 256.

58. Liu Zuoxiang, "Siquanli: Yige zhide zhongshide fazhilingyu (Private rights: an area of law worthy of attention), in Dong Yuyu and Shi Binhai (eds.), pp. 267–77, at pp. 276–77.

59. On democracy-compatible nationalism see Yael Tamir, *Liberal Nationalism* (Princeton University Press, 1993).

60. Edward Friedman, p. x.

61. One 1995 survey of 5,000 citizens found that less than 1% believed the death penalty should be abolished, while more than 22% believed that there were too few death sentences.

62. The best example is Hu Yunteng of the Chinese Academy of Social Sciences who has spoken against the widespread use of the death penalty in China. See Michael Laris, "Chinese Scholars Speak Out on Rights Issues," *Washington Post*, September 8, 1998, p. A18.

63. Diamond, p. 219.

64. See Stephen E. Hanson, "Defining Democratic Consolidation," in R. Anderson et al, Postcommunism, pp. 126–51.

65. See John Ferejohn, Jack N. Rakove, and Jonathan Riley (eds.), *Constitutional Culture and Democratic Rule* (Cambridge University Press, 2001). This distinction between private and public "doctrines" mirrors the theory of political liberalism of John Rawls. Rawls, *Political Liberalism* (New York: Columbia University Press, 1993) 1996 reprint.

66. Li Fan, et al., p. 337.

67. Rawls, *Political Liberalism*, p. lxi.

68. Richard D. Anderson, Jr. et al, "Conclusion: Postcommunism and the Theory of Democracy," in Anderson et al. (eds.), pp. 152–68, at p. 158. Also, Nancy Bermeo, "Democracy and the Lessons of Dictatorship," *Comparative Politics* 24, no 3 (April 1992): 273–91.

69. See He Baogang, "New Moral Foundations of Chinese Democratic Institutional Design," in Zhao Suisheng (ed.), pp. 89–107.

70. Yu Keping, "Quanli zhengzhi, haishi gongyi zhengzhi" (Rights politics or public interest politics) in Dong and Shi (eds), pp. 281–87.

71. Barrett McCormick, "US-PRC Relations and the Democratic Peace," in Friedman/McCormick (eds.), p. 317.

72. See for example Fareed Zakaria, *The Future of Freedom: Illiberal Democracy at Home and Abroad*, New York: W.W. Norton, 2003.

73. Diamond, *Developing Democracy*, p. 192.

74. Ibid., p. 62.

75. Yan Jiaqi, p. 224.

76. Wolfgang Merkel, "The Consolidation of Post-Autocratic Regimes: A Multilevel Model," in Chung-in Moon and Jongryn Mo (eds.), *Democratization and Globalization in Korea* (Seoul: Yonsei University Press, 1999), pp. 25–68.

77. Diamond, p. 68.

78. Shih Chih-yu, p. 329.

79. Ogden, p. 358; this is also Shi Chih-yu's thesis.

80. Stephan Haggard and Robert R. Kaufman; "The Political Economy of Democratic Transitions," in Lisa Anderson (ed.), pp. 72–96.

81. Guo Dingping, p. 285.

82. Guo Xuezhi, "Dimensions of Guanxi in Chinese Elite Politics," in *China Journal* 46, (July 2001): 69–90.

83. He Baogang, "New Moral Foundations of Chinese Democratic Institutional Design," in Zhao Suisheng (ed.), pp. 89–107; Rawls, *Political Liberalism*.

84. See Peter Moody, "The Antipolitical Tendency in Contemporary Chinese Political Thinking," in Hua Shiping (ed.), pp. 161–87.

85. See Jane S. Jaquette and Sharon L. Wolchik (eds.), *Women and Democracy: Latin America and Central and Eastern Europe* (Baltimore: Johns Hopkins University Press, 1998). Also see Jill M. Bystydzienski and Joti Sekhon (eds); *Democratization and Women's Grassroots Movements* (Bloomington,: Indiana University Press, 1999).

86. Arthur Waldron, "The End of Communism," in *Journal of Democracy*, special issue, (1998): 41–47, p. 46.

87. Alan P.L. Liu; "Provincial Identities and Political Cultures," in Hua Shiping (ed.), pp. 246–75.

88. Deng Xiaoping. *Collected Works* (Beijing: Foreign Languages Press, 1992), 3: 217.

Notes to Chapter 9

1. Zong Hairen, The Fourth Generation, p. 560.

2. Wang Lixiong, "Shexiang zhongguo shixing xifang minzhuzhi" (Imagine if China implemented a Western democratic system), online essay, www.dijin-democracy.net, September 2002.

3. Kenneth Lieberthal, "U.S. Policy Toward China," Brookings Papers, no 72, March 2001.

4. Yan Jiaqi, p. 224. Qin Hui, "Dividing the big family assets," New Left Review (March–April 2003), 20, 83–110, at p. 108.

5. M. Steven Fish shows that "economic performance does not appear to be related" to whether a new democracy succeeded or failed in the case of former communist states in Europe and Central Asia. See his "The Dynamics of Democratic Erosion," in Anderson et al. (eds.), Postcommunism, pp. 54–95, at. p. 64; also Diamond, *Developing Democracy*, ch. 3.

6. The speaker is Bo Xilai. See Zong Hairen, The Fourth Generation, pp. 505–6.

7. See Sorensen, pp. 64–92; Haggard and Kaufman, p. 152; UNDP Human Development Report 2002, pp. 56–59; and Daniel Kaufmann and Aart Kraay, "Governance and Growth: Causality Which Way?" World Bank Institute 2003.

8. See Bruce Bueno de Mesquita et al., "Political Competition and Economic Growth" *Journal of Democracy* 12, no. 1 (January 2001).

9. Wing Thye Woo, "China: Confronting Restructuring and Stability," unpublished paper given at University of Washington conference on China and the WTO, Hong Kong, March 1999.

10. Peng Ming, p. 141.

11. Vaclav Smil, "The Dimensions of China's Environmental Challenge," in Timothy B. Weston and Lionel M. Jensen (eds.), *China Beyond the Headlines* (Lanham, MD: Rowman and Littlefield, 2000), pp. 195–215 at p. 197.

12. Quoted in Zong Hairen, The Fourth Generation, pp. 163–64.

13. Charles Wolf, Jr., "Uncertain Times for Foreign Investment in China," *Financial Times*, June 24, 2002.

14. Terry Lynn Karl, "Economic Inequality and Democratic Instability," in *Journal of Democracy* 11, no 1 (2000): 149–56.

15. Liu Guokai, p. 4.

16. Zhang Xuebin et al., p. 374.

17. Peng Ming, p. 138.

18. Peng Ming, p. 139.

19. See Jonathan Unger and Anita Chan, "Corporatism in China," in McCormick/Unger (eds.), pp. 95–129.

20. See Edward X. Gu, "State Corporatism and Civil Society," in Wang/Zheng (eds.), pp. 71–102.

21. Feng Chongyi, "The Third Way: The Question of Equity as a Bone of Contention Between Intellectual Currents," unpublished paper.

22. Yang Fan and Lu Zhoulai; Yi min wei ben, guanzhu minsheng: Zhongguo xin shijide qiantu yu xuanze (Putting People First, Paying Attention to People's Livelihood: China's Future and Choices in the New Century) (Beijing: Petroleum Industry Press, 2001).

23. UNDP Annual Report 2002, p. 3.

24. Peng Ming, pp. 140.

25. Andrew Nathan "Chinese Democracy: The Lessons of Failure," in Zhao Suisheng (ed.) pp. 21–32, at p. 29.

26. A 1995 to 2010 Pearl River Delta development plan called for $250 billion in new infrastructure investments in the delta region. See Bruce Gilley, "Get a Grip," *Far Eastern Economic Review*, Feb 22, 1996, p. 47. About three quarters of the $60 billion in spending on key projects in the province's five year plan from 2000 to 2005 was concentrated in the Pearl River Delta region.

27. Wang Furen, "Yingxiang 21 shiji zhongguo wenhuade ji ge xianshi yinsu" (A few practical factors affecting China's 21st century culture) in Zhanlue yu Guanli (Strategy and Management), no. 2 (1997): 87–96, at p. 87.

28. See the sustained treatment in Edward Friedman, esp. pp. 71–79.

29. See Ma Shuo, Henan ren ruo sheile? (Who's So Angry at the Henan People?) Haikou: Hainan Press, 2002.

30. See Rubie S. Watson, "Memory, History and Opposition Under State Socialism: An Introduction," in Rubie S. Watson (ed.); *Memory, History and Opposition Under State Socialism* (Santa Fe: School of American Research Press, 1994), pp. 1–20; Also see Alexandra Barahona De Brito (ed.), *The Politics of Memory and Democratization: Transitional Justice in Democratizing Societies* (2001) and Kenneth Christie and Robert Cribb (eds.), *Historical Injustice and Democratic Transition in Eastern Asia and Northern Europe: Ghosts at the Table of Democracy* (New York : RoutledgeCurzon, 2002).

31. O'Donnell/Schmitter, p. 30.

32. "Overview," Legacies of Authoritarianism Project, University of Wisconsin-Madison, http://wiscinfo.doit.wisc.edu/globalstudies/LOA.

33. The German word *vergangenheitsbewältigung* literally means coming to terms with the past. In its usage, heavily affected by post-Nazi era, it connotes a social process of honestly admitting and vigorously interpreting the past such that one "masters" its hold over the future.

34. Adrian Karatnycky; "Nations in Transit: Emerging Dynamics of Change"; online essay, Freedom House, 2001.

35. See Louis Bickford, "Human Rights Archives and Research on Historical Memory: Argentina, Chile and Uruguay," *Latin American Research Review* (January 2000): 160–82.

36. Vera Schwarcz; "Memory and Commemoration: The Chinese Search for a Livable Past," in Wasserstrom/Perry (eds.). *Popular Protest*, ch. 8 pp. 170–83.

37. Typical will be works like those about the 1989 Tiananmen protests, such as Liu Binyan, *Tell the World: What Happened in China and Why*, with Ruan Ming and Xu Gang (New York: Pantheon, 1989).

38. See the self-criticism letters of the poet Guo Xiaochuan, who died in a re-education camp in 1976 after 17 years of persecution, published in 2001. Guo Xiaohui (ed.); Jiantaoshu: Shiren Guo Xiaochuan zai zhengzhi yundong zhongde linglei wenzi (Self-criticism report: Another kind of writing by poet Guo Xiaochuan in the midst of political campaigns) (Beijing: China Workers Press, 2001).

39. Yang Xianhui, *Jiabiangou jishi* (A memoir of Jiabiangou), (Tianjin: Tianjin Ancient Books Press, 2002).

40. "Basically speaking, the difficulties were primarily a result of leftist guiding ideology. In those years of building communes, communist zeal, exaggeration, and misdirected leadership were widespread," said a standard text for university students published in 1997. He Qin, p. 221.

41. For example, the online memorial sites at *China News Digest* (www.cnd.org) and www.chinese-memorial.org which do not include memorials for the Great Leap Famine.

42. Beijing artist Shao Yinong "There's even a prostitute in our family. But that's just it, we're a very average family in China," Shao has commented. *South China Morning Post*, Feburary 4, 2002. On the horrors in Inner Mongolia see Wu Di, "The Aftermath of the Cultural Revolution in Inner Mongolia," in Kenneth Christie and Robert Cribb (eds.), *Historical Injustice and Democratic Transition in Eastern Asia and Northern Europe* (London: Routledge, 2002), pp. 24–37.

43. The site is: www.chinese-memorial.org.

44. Qian Gang, Tangshan da dizhen (Tangshan's Great Earthquake) (Beijing: Liberation Army Literature and Art Press, 1986. English translation, Beijing: Foreign Languages Press, 1989). p. 237.

45. On the comparisons of Mao to others see Ian Buruma, "Divine Killer," *New York Review of Books* (Feburary 4, 2000): 20–25.

46. Edward Friedman, p. 288.

47. "Overview," Legacies of Authoritarianism Project, University of Wisconsin-Madison, http://wiscinfo.doit.wisc.edu/globalstudies/LOA.

48. Brandon Hamber and Richard Wilson, "Symbolic Closure through Memory, Reparation, and Revenge in Post-Conflict Societies," *Journal of Human Rights*, Volume 1, no. 1 (March 2002).

49. Edward Friedman, Paul G. Pickowicz, Mark Selden, with Kay Ann Johnson, *Chinese Village, Socialist State* (New Haven : Yale University Press, 1993); and *Revolution, Resistance and Reform in Village China* (New Haven: Yale University Press, 2004).

50. See the story of mass protests in the 1980s and 1990s over the Three Gorges dam by Ying Xing; Dahe yimin shangfangde gushi (The story of the protests by Dahe migrants) (Beijing: Sanlian [Joint] Publishing, 2001).

51. The standard work on this new history is Paul A. Cohen; *Discovering History in China: American Historical Writings on the Recent Chinese Past* (New York: Columbia University Press, 1984).

52. David Barrett and Larry Shyu (eds.), *Chinese Collaboration with Japan 1932–1945: The Limits of Accommodation* (Stanford: Stanford University Press, 2001).

53. On opium sales see Chen Yung-fa, "Blooming Poppy under the Red Sun: The Yan'an Way and the Opium Trade," in Tony Saich and Hans J. van de Ven (eds.), *New Perspectives on the Chinese Communist Revolution* (Armonk, NY: M. E. Sharpe, 1995), 263–98; on local protest against KMT rule as basis of CCP power see Ralph A. Thaxton Jr.; *Salt of the Earth: The Political Origins of Peasant Protest and Communist Revolution in China* (Berkeley: University of California Press), 1997.

54. "Overview," Legacies of Authoritarianism Project, University of Wisconsin-Madison, website, http://wiscinfo.doit.wisc.edu/globalstudies/LOA.

Notes to Chapter 10

1. Larry Diamond and Ramon Myers, "Elections and Democracy in Greater China," *China Quarterly* (June 2000): 365–86, at p. 371.

2. Arthur Waldron, "China's Coming Constitutional Challenges," in Orbis (January 1995): 19ff.

3. David Bachman, "China's Democratization: What Difference Would It Make for US-China Relations?," in Friedman/Mccormick (eds.), pp. 195–223. Barrett McCormick, "US-PRC Relations and the Democratic Peace," in McCormick/Friedman (eds.), pp. 309–26.

4. See Sarah E. Mendelson, "Democracy Assistance and Political Transition in Russia: Between Success and Failure," *International Security* 25, no. 4 (Spring 2001): 68–106.

5. For similar policy advice for Europe's new democracies see Adrian Karatnycky; "Nations in Transit: Emerging Dynamics of Change"; Freedom House, online report, 2001.

6. Fu Ying, a foreign ministry official and former Chinese ambassador to the Philippines, in a talk to a group of Asian editors in Beijing in May 2001 said: "We have always been a cultural power rather than a colonial power" and that Beijing would expand its role in Asia only when "everyone is comfortable." Asia News Network, www.asianewsnet.net, June 7, 2001.

7. Peng Ming, p. 137.

8. Peng Ming, p. 137.

9. Edward Friedman, "Preventing War Between China and Japan," in Friedman / McCormick (eds.), pp. 99–128, at p. 114.

10. He and Guo make these points, pp. 147–52.

11. See Larry Diamond's Foreword to Zhao Suisheng (ed.), pp. ix–xv.

12. Lee Feigon, *Demystifying Tibet: Unlocking the Secrets of the Land of the Snows* (London: Profile Books, 1999), p. 214.

13. He/Guo, p. 30.

14. Huntington, *Clash of Civilizations*, pp. 165–68. The theory has also proved to

be false in large-n studies. See Jonathan Fox, "Ethnic Minorities and the Clash of Civilizations: A Quantitative Analysis of Huntington's Thesis," *British Journal of Political Science* 32, no. 3 (July 2002): 415 ff.

Notes to Conclusion

1. Pei Minxin, p. 209.

2. Feng Chongyi, "The Third Way: The Question of Equity as a Bone of Contention Between Intellectual Currents," unpublished paper.

3. Ogden, p. 16.

4. Feng, "The Third Way," see note 2.

5. Xu Jilin, "Zai hefa yu zhengyi zhijian: guanyu liang zhong minzhude fansi" (Between legality and justice: reflections on two types of democracy) in *Strategy and Management* (June 2001): 113–20.

6. Yi Yangsheng, "Cong 'gaige kaifang' dao 'kaifang gaige' — 2002 nian zhongguo zhengzhi fazhan dongxiang" (From "reform and opening" to "opening and reform" — trends in China's political development in 2002), Guangjiaojing (Wide Angle Magazine, Hong Kong) (February 16, 2002): 6–10.

7. Lin Chun, "Situating China," in *Social Justice* (March 22, 1996): 262 ff.

8. Sunil Khilnani, *The Idea of India* (New Delhi: Penguin Books, rev. ed., 1999), p. 198.

9. Chung Jae Ho, "China's Reforms at Twenty-five: Challenges for the New Leadership," China: An International Journal 1, no.1 (March 2003): 119–132, at p. 130.

10. Diamond, *Developing Democracy*, p. 273.

Notes to Afterword

1. "Peiyu gongmin yishi, tuidong zhili zhuanxing" (Nurture civic consciousness, promote a transformation of governance) 21 shiji jingji baodao (21st Century Economic Herald), May 15, 2003, p. 1.

2. Pei Minxin, "Don't hold your breath for openness in China," *Financial Times*, May 7, 2003, p. 15.

3. Ai Wenbo, "SARS tests the government's credibility," Zhongguo qingnian bao (China Youth Daily), reprinted in *China Daily*, April 28, 2003.

4. Zhou Jiu, chief editor of *Koushu zazhi* (Oral Accounts Magazine), "Huangyan zhiguo bi zao baofu" (Those who lie to run the country will be avenged), in *Kaifang* (Open Magazine, Hong Kong), June 2003, pp. 32–34.

5. Guan Anping, quoted in *South China Morning Post*, May 13, 2003.

6. Xue Baosheng, "Valuable lesson for government to learn," *China Daily*, June 6, 2003.

7. Zuo Sifang, "Ke 'minzhu' yu 'kexue' yu xinzhong" (Taking "democracy" and "science" to heart), Nanfang zhoumou (Southern Weekend newspaper), May 8, 2003.

References

Anderson, Lisa (ed.). *Transitions to Democracy*. New York: Columbia University Press, 1999.

Anderson, Richard D., Jr. et al. *Postcommunism and the Theory of Democracy*. Princeton: Princeton University Press, 2001.

Bao Tong. *Zhongguode yousi* (Pondering China). Hong Kong: Pacific Century Press, 2000.

Cao Jinqing. *Huanghebiande Zhongguo: Yi ge xuezhe dui xiangcun shehuide guancha yu sikao* (China Along the Yellow River: A Scholar's Observations and Thoughts on Rural Society). Shanghai: Shanghai Arts Press, 2000.

Cao Siyuan. *Zhongguo zhenggai fanglue* (A Strategy for Political Reform in China). Hong Kong: Xiafeier Press, 1999.

Carpenter, Ted Galen and James A. Dorn (eds.). *China's Future: Constructive Partner or Emerging Threat?*: Washington, D.C.: Cato Institute, 2000.

Dahl, Robert A. *On Democracy*. New Haven: Yale University Press, 1998.

Dahl, Robert A. *Polyarchy, Participation and Opposition*. New Haven: Yale University Press, 1971.

Dalpino, Catharin. *Deferring Democracy: Promoting Openness in Authoritarian Regimes*. Washington D.C.: Brookings Institution Press, 2000.

Deng Weizhi (ed). *Biange shehui zhongde zhengzhi wending* (Political Stability Amidst a Changing Society). Shanghai: Shanghai People's Press, 1997.

Des Forges, Roger V., Luo Ning, and Wu Yen-bo (eds.) *Chinese Democracy and the Crisis of 1989: Chinese and American Reflections*. Albany: State University of New York Press, 1993.

Diamond, Larry. *Developing Democracy: Toward Consolidation*. Baltimore: Johns Hopkins University Press, 1999.

Ding Yijiang. *Chinese Democracy After Tiananmen*. Vancouver: University of British Columbia Press, 2001.

Dong Yuyu and Shi Binhai (eds.). *Zhengzhi zhongguo: Mianxiang xin tizhi xuanzede shidai* (Political China: Facing the Era of Choosing a New Structure). Beijing Today's China Press, 1998.

Fan Wenbin. *Zhonggongde xiaowang ji qi shijian biao* (The End of the Chinese Communist Party and Its Timetable): Hong Kong: Pacific International Press, 1999.

Fang Jiangshan. *Fei zhidu zhengzhi canyu: Yi zhuanxingqi zhongguo nongmin wei duixiang fenxi* (Non-Institutional Political Participation: An Analysis of Chinese Peasants in the Transitional Period). Beijing: People's Press, 2000.

Fewsmith, Joseph. *China Since Tiananmen: The Politics of Transition*. Cambridge: Cambridge University Press, 2001.

Fewsmith, Joseph. *Elite Politics in Contemporary China*. Armonk, NY.: M. E. Sharpe, 2001.

281

Foran, John (ed.). *Theorizing Revolutions*. London: Routledge, 1997.

Friedman, Edward and Barrett L. McCormick (eds.). *What If China Doesn't Democratize: Implications for War and Peace*. Armonk, NY: M. E. Sharpe, 2000.

Friedman, Edward. *National Identity and Democratic Prospects in Socialist China*. Armonk, NY: M. E. Sharpe, 1995.

Fu Zhengyuan. *Autocratic Tradition and Chinese Politics*. Cambridge: Cambridge University Press, 1993.

Fukuyama, Francis. *The End of History and the Last Man*. London: Penguin, 1992.

Fung, Edmund S.K. *In Search of Chinese Democracy: Civil Opposition in Nationalist China, 1929–1949*. Cambridge: Cambridge University Press, 2000.

Gill, Graeme. *The Dynamics of Democratization: Elites, Civil Society, and the Transition Process*. New York: St. Martin's Press, 2000.

Gilley, Bruce. *Tiger on the Brink: Jiang Zemin and China's New Elite*. Berkeley: University of California Press, 1998.

Guo Dingping. *Zhengdang yu zhengfu* (The Ruling Party and Government). Hangzhou: Zhejiang People's Press, 1998.

Guo Sujian. *Post-Mao China: From Totalitarianism to Authoritarianism?* Westport, CT: Praeger, 2000.

Haggard, Stephen and Robert R. Kaufman. *The Political Economy of Democratic Transitions*. Princeton, N.J.: Princeton University Press, 1995.

He Baogang and Guo Yingjie. *Nationalism, National Identity and Democratization in China*. Brookfield, VT: Ashgate Publishing, 2000.

He Baogang. *The Democratization of China*. London: Routledge, 1996.

He Qin (ed.). *Zhonghua renmin gongheguo shi* (A History of the PRC). Beijing: Tertiary Education Press, 1997.

He Qinglian. *Zhongguode xianjing* (China's Plight). Mississauga, Ont.: Mirror Books, 1997.

He Xin. *Zhongguo fuxing yu shijie weilai* (China's Renaissance and the Future of the World). 2 vols. Chengdu: Sichuan People's Press, 1996.

Hou Shaowen. *Yifa zhiguo yu dangde lingdao* (Rule By Law and Party Leadership). Hangzhou: Zhejiang People's Press, 1998.

Hu Angang. *Zhongguo fazhan qianjing* (China's Development Prospects). Hangzhou: Zhejiang People's Press, 1999.

Hu Shaohua. *Explaining Chinese Democratization*. Westport, CT: Praeger, 2000.

Hua Shiping (ed.). *Chinese Political Culture: 1989–2000*. Armonk, NY: M.E. Sharpe, 2001.

Huang Jing. *Factionalism in Chinese Communist Politics*. Cambridge: Cambridge University Press, 2000.

Huang Weiping (ed.). *Dangdai zhongguo zhengzhi yanjiu baogao: I* (Report on Politics Research in Contemporary China: I). Beijing: Social Sciences Documentation Publishing House, 2002.

Huang Weiping. *Zhongguo zhengzhi tizhi gaige zonghengtan* (On Political Reform in China). Beijing: Central Compilation and Translation Press, 1998.

Huntington, Samuel P. *The Clash of Civilizations and the Remaking of World Order*. New York: Simon and Schuster, 1996.

Huntington, Samuel P. *The Third Wave: Democratization in the Late 20th Century*. Norman: University of Oklahoma Press, 1993.

Jin Zhong (ed.). *Qiliang: zhongguo sandai ziyou zhishifenzi pingzhuan* (Backbone: Essays and Biographies of Three Generations of Chinese Liberal Intellectuals). Hong Kong: Open Magazine Press, 2001.

Johannen, Uwe and James Gomez (eds.). *Democratic Transitions in Asia.* Singapore: Select Publishing, 2001.

Journal of Democracy, "China" (special issue) 14 no. 1 (January 2003).

Journal of Democracy, "Will China Democratize?" (special issue) 9, no. 1 (January 1998).

Ju Yanan. *Understanding China: Center Stage of the Fourth Power.* Albany: SUNY Press,1996.

Kaifang (Open Magazine). "Zhonggong zhengquan changshou mijue" (The secret of the CCP's long life). special section, May 2002, pp. 23–47, various articles as cited.

Li Fan et al. *Chuangxin yu fazhan: Xiangzhen zhang xuanju zhidu gaige* (Innovation and Development: Reform of the Election System for Township Heads): Beijing: Eastern Press, 2000.

Li Fan. *Jing qiaoqiaode geming: Zhongguo dangdai shimin shehui* (The Silent Revolution: Contemporary Civil Society in China). Mississauga, Ontario: Mirror Books, 1998.

Li Liangdong et. al. *Wending: Yadao yiqiede daju* (Stability: The Most Important Overall Situation). Beijing: Central Party School Press, 1999.

Lieberthal, Kenneth. *Governing China: From Revolution Through Reform.* New York: Norton, 1995.

Lin Shangli. *Guonei zhengfu zhijian guanxi* (Relations between government levels). Hangzhou: Zhejiang People's Press, 1998.

Ling Zhijun and Ma Licheng. *Hu Han: Dangjin zhongguode wu zhong shengyin* (Calling: Five Voices in Present-Day China). Guangzhou: Guangzhou Press, 1999.

Ling Zhijun and Ma Licheng. *Jiaofeng: Dangdai Zhongguo san ci sixiang jiefang shilu* (Crossed Swords: The Story of Three Thought Liberations in Contemporary China): Beijing: Today's China Press, 1998.

Linz, Juan J. and Alfred Stepan. *Problems of Democratic Transition and Consolidation: Southern Europe, South America and Post-Communist Europe.* Baltimore: Johns Hopkins University Press, 1996.

Liu Guokai. *Lishi chaoliu: shehui minzhu zhuyi* (The Historical Tide: Social Democracy). New York: Mirror Books, 2000.

Lü Xiaobo. *Cadres and Corruption: The Organizational Involution of the Chinese Communist Party.* Stanford: Stanford University Press, 2000.

Lu Xueyi (ed.). *Dangdai zhongguo shehui jieceng yanjiu baogao* (A report on social classes in contemporary China). Beijing: Social Sciences Documentation Press, 2002.

Lum, Thomas. *Problems of Democratization in China.* New York: Garland Publishing, 2000.

McCormick, Barrett and Jonathan Unger (eds.). *China After Socialism: In the Footsteps of Eastern Europe or East Asia?* New York: M. E. Sharpe, 1996.

Nathan, Andrew J. and Bruce Gilley. *China's New Rulers: The Secret Files.* New York: New York Review Books, 2002.

Nathan, Andrew J. and Perry Link (eds.). *The Tiananmen Papers.* New York: Public Affairs, 2001.

Nathan, Andrew J. *China's Transition*: New York, Columbia University Press, 1997.

Nathan, Andrew J. *Chinese Democracy*. New York: Alfred A. Knopf, 1985.

O'Donnell, Guillermo and Phliippe C. Schmitter. *Transitions from Authoritarian Rule: Tentative Conclusions About Uncertain Democracies*. Baltimore: Johns Hopkins University Press, 1986.

Ogden, Suzanne. *Inklings of Democracy in China*. Cambridge: Harvard University Asia Center, 2002.

Pei Minxin. *From Reform to Revolution: The Demise of Communism in China and the Soviet Union*. Cambridge: Harvard University Press, 1994.

Peng Ming. *Minzhu gongcheng* (The Democracy Project). San Francisco: China Federation Development Committee, 2002.

Perry, Elizabeth J. and Mark Selden (eds.). *Chinese Society: Change, Conflict and Resistance*. New York: Routledge, 2000.

Perry, Elizabeth J. *Challenging the Mandate of Heaven: Social Protest and State Power in China*. Armonk, NY: M. E. Sharpe, 2002.

Pu Xingfu (ed.). *Dangdai Zhongguo zhengzhi zhidu* (Contemporary China's Political System). Shanghai: Fudan University Press, 1999.

Rosenbaum, Arthur Lewis (ed.). *State and Society in China: The Consequences of Reform*. Boulder, CO: Westview Press, 1992.

Ru Xin, Lu Xueyi and Dan Tianlun (eds.). *2001 Nian: Zhongguo shehui xingshi fenxi yu yuce* (Analysis and Forecast of China's Social Situation: 2001). Beijing: Social Sciences Documentation Press, 2001.

Run Yun et al. (eds.). *Jiang Zemin tongzhi lilun lunshu dashi jiyao* (A Summary of the Major Theoretical Expositions of Comrade Jiang Zemin). 2 vols. Beijing: Central Party School Press, 1998.

Saich, Tony. *Governance and Politics of China*. New York: Palgrave, 2001.

Sha Jiansun and Gong Shuze (eds.). *Zou shenme lu: Guanyu zhongguo jinxiandai lishishangde ruogan zhongda shifei wenti* (Choosing the Road to Take: On Some Important Questions of Right and Wrong in Contemporary and Modern China's History). Jinan: Shandong People's Press, 1997.

Sha Yongzhong and Zhang Xinping (eds.). *Dongfang linian: Zhongguo zhengzhi nianbao: 2000 nian ban* (Oriental Ideals: China Political Report 2000). Lanzhou: Lanzhou University Press, 2000.

Shambaugh, David (ed.). *Is China Unstable?* Armonk, NY: M. E. Sharpe, 2000.

Shambaugh, David (ed.). *The Modern Chinese State*. Cambridge: Cambridge University Press, 2000.

Shi Tianjian. *Political Participation in Beijing*. Cambridge: Harvard University Press, 1997.

Shih Chih-yu. *Collective Democracy: Political and Legal Reform in China*. Hong Kong: Chinese University Press, 1999.

Sørensen, Georg. *Democracy and Democratization: Processes and Prospects in a Changing World*. 2nd edition. Boulder, CO: Westview Press, 1998.

Sun Xiaoli. *Zhongguo xiandaihua jinchengzhongde guojia yu shehui* (State and Society in China's Modernization). Beijing: China Social Sciences Press, 2001.

Tao Dongming and Chen Mingming. *Dangdai zhongguo zhengzhi canyu* (Political Participation in Contemporary China). Hangzhou: Zhejiang People's Press, 1998.

Tsang, Steve and Tien Hung-mao. *Democratization in Taiwan: Implications for China.* New York: St. Martin's Press, 1999.

Walder, Andrew (ed.). *The Waning of the Communist State: Economic Origins of Political Decline in China and Hungary.* Berkeley: University of California Press, 1995.

Wang Gungwu and Zheng Yongnian (eds.). *Reform, Legitimacy, and Dilemmas: China's Politics and Society.* Singapore: Singapore University Press, 2000.

Wang Jianqin. *Qianghua jiandu, zhiyue quanli: Zhongguo fan fubaide lixing sikao* (Strengthen Supervision, Restrain Power: Thoughts on Anti-Corruption Work in China). Beijing: China Fangzheng Press, 1997.

Wang Lixiong. *Rongjie quanli: Zhuceng dixuanzhi* (Dissolving Power: A level-by-level gradual elections system). Mississauga, Ont.: Mirror Books, 1998.

Wang Shaoguang and Hu Angang. *The Chinese Economy in Crisis: State Capacity and Tax Reform.* Armonk, NY: M. E. Sharpe, 2001.

Wang Yongqiang (ed). *Zhengdao: Zhongguo zhengzhi nianbao, 2001 nian ban* (The Just Path: China Political Report, 2001). Lanzhou: Lanzhou University Press, 2001.

Wasserstrom, Jeffrey N. and Elizabeth J. Perry (eds.). *Popular Protest and Political Culture in Modern China.* Boulder, CO: Westview Press, 1992.

Weng Jieming et al (eds.). *Yu zongshuji tanxin* (Heart-to-Heart Talks with the General Secretary). Beijing: China Social Sciences Press, 1996.

Weston, Timothy and Lionel Jensen (eds.). *China Beyond the Headlines.* Lanham, MD: Rowman & Littlefield, 2000.

Winckler, Edwin A. (ed.). *Transition from Communism in China: Institutional and Comparative Analyses.* Boulder, CO: Lynne Rienner Publishers, 1999.

Wu Daying and Yang Haijiao (eds.). *You zhongguo tesede shehui zhuyi minzhu zhengzhi* (The Politics of Socialist Democracy With Chinese Characteristics). Beijing: Social Sciences Documents Press, 1999.

Yan Jiaqi. *Minzhu zenyang cai neng laidao zhongguo* (How Democracy Can Come to China). Taipei: Yuanliu Press, 1996.

Yang Qingtao et al. *Shehui zhuanxingqi renmin neibu maodun wenti yanjiu* (Studies in Conflicts Among the People During the Period of Social Transition). Beijing: China Youth Press, 2000.

Zhang Jianhua (ed.). *Zhongguo mianlinde jinyao wenti* (The Key Issues Facing China). Beijing: Economic Daily News Press, 1998.

Zhang Jun. *Zouchu heidong: Zhongguo dangdai shehui shifan xianxiang pipan* (Escaping the Black Hole: A Critical Look at the Phenomenon of Irregularity in Contemporary China). Beijing: China Economics Press, 2000.

Zhang Lei and Cheng Linsheng. *Zhuanxing yu wending* (Transformation and Stability). Shanghai: Xuelin Press, 1999.

Zhang Xuebin et al. *Gaigede weixian qi* (The Dangerous Period of Reforms). Beijing: China Industrial and Commercial United Press, 1999.

Zhao Suisheng (ed.). *China and Democracy: Reconsidering the Prospects for a Democratic China.* New York: Routledge, 2000.

Zheng Yongnian. *Jiang Zeminde yichan zai shoucheng he gaige zhijian* (Jiang Zemin's Legacy: Between Preservation and Reform). River Edge, N.J.: Global Publishing, 2002.

Zhonggong zhongyang zuzhibu ketizu (Study Group of the Organization Department of the CCP Central Committee). 2000–1: *Zhongguo diaocha baogao: xin xingshixia renmin neibu maodun yanjiu* (China Survey Report 2000–1: Research on Social Frictions under New Conditions). Beijing: Central Compilation and Translation Press, 2001.

Zhongguo guoqing guoli zazhishe (China's National Conditions and Strength Magazine) (ed.). *Zhongguo redian* (China's Hot Issues). Beijing: China Statistics Press, 1999.

Zhuge Muqun. *Xianzheng Zhongguo* (Constitutional China): Mississauga, Ont.: Mirror Books, 1998.

Zong Hairen. *Disidai* (The Fourth Generation). Flushing, NY: Mirror Books, 2002.

Index